A GREAT ADVENTURE STORY

In his introduction to Homer's *Odyssey* (which appears in a companion Mentor volume), W. H. D. Rouse explained his method of translation: "Homer speaks naturally, and we must do the same. This is what I have tried to do in this book, and I ask that it may be judged simply as a story." He has applied the same method to his translation of *The Iliad*: "a translation into plain English of the plain story of Homer."

And what a fascinating story it is! Again to use Dr. Rouse's own words: "Homer is full of merriment, full of open fun and delicate comedy, even farce—as when Arês, wounded, bursts up to Olympus like a bomb. And the divine family! What a delightful natural party—human beings raised a degree or two but all the same funnier than that. They are the comic background for the tragedy below—for the story of Achilles is a tragedy —the fiery conflict of a man divided against himself, who in a few short days drops to the lowest hell of savagery, then rises to self-mastery and inward peace."

Of this translation Gilbert Highet wrote in the *New York Times Book Review*: "A great poem cannot be fully translated unless by a poet almost as great as its original author . . . W. H. D. Rouse . . . retells the story in fast, modern, colloquial prose. It is the first version I have ever seen which drives on as rapidly as the original and therefore it makes an excellent introduction to Homer. This is the translation to read first, if you have never read the *Iliad* . . ."

THIS BOOK IS A REPRINT OF THE ORIGINAL HARDCOVER EDITION PUBLISHED BY THOMAS NELSON AND SONS, LTD.

ἔπεα πτερόεντα προσαυδῶ

*If I abhore from the sense that others
wrest, and racke out of him, let my best
detractor examine how the Greeke word
warrants me.*

GEORGE CHAPMAN,
The Preface to the Reader.

HOMER
THE ILIAD

The Story of Achillês

TRANSLATED BY
W.H.D. ROUSE

A MENTOR BOOK

Published by THE NEW AMERICAN LIBRARY

Published as a MENTOR BOOK
by arrangement with Thomas Nelson and Sons, Ltd.,
who have authorized this softcover edition.
*A handsome clothbound edition is available from Thomas
Nelson and Sons, Ltd.*

First published by Thomas Nelson and Sons, Ltd.,
April, 1938.

FIRST AMERICAN PRINTING, JANUARY, 1950
NINETEENTH PRINTING, SEPTEMBER, 1964

MENTOR TRADEMARK REG. U.S. PAT. OFF. AND FOREIGN COUNTRIES
REGISTERED TRADEMARK——MARCA REGISTRADA
HECHO EN CHICAGO, U.S.A.

MENTOR BOOKS are published *in the United States* by
The New American Library of World Literature, Inc.,
501 Madison Avenue, New York, New York 10022,
in Canada by The New American Library of Canada Limited,
156 Front Street West, Toronto 1, Ontario,
in the United Kingdom by The New English Library Limited,
Barnard's Inn, Holborn, London, E.C. 1, England

PRINTED IN THE UNITED STATES OF AMERICA

PREFACE

THIS book, like *The Story of Odysseus*, is a translation into plain English of the plain story of Homer, omitting the embellishments which were meant only to please the ear—stock epithets and ecurring phrases where the meaning is of no account. Any who wish to know more of this matter will find it in the Appendix to *The Story of Odysseus*. Readers who are surprised by the simple and familiar words of this translation will be still more surprised when they find how often Homer's words are the same; where the phrases are different, that is because the idioms of Greek and English are different, but the tone is the same. Most of Homer is a story naturally told; and the lovely bits of poetry which come here and there can be expressed with equal beauty in our own beautiful language, without the help of artificial expressions, such as twain for two. So also the most moving scenes move us not less, but more, when they are described without trying to make them more intense by high-flown expressions. The great critic Longinus, who has preserved for us many lovely pieces of Greek poetry, quotes only one sentence from foreign literature as an example of the Grand Style: "God said, Let there be light: and there was light."

Such grand and lovely passages come in the midst of common things, just as they do in life: even in the grim work of the battlefield they are found, and there is nothing more terrible in literature than the simple words of Achillês to Lycaon, which send a shiver down my spine whenever I read them. I noticed in the happy days when we used to read Homer together in Greek, without translating at all, that the general mood of the company was the schoolboy's high spirits, with continual banter and jest, but whenever one of these great things came in, a sudden silence fell. They never failed to feel them, although a schoolboy cannot understand them as a man of wider experience can. Then just like Homer's own childlike men, they slid back into their normal high spirits and welcomed his touches of merriment. For Homer is full of merriment, full of open fun and delicate comedy, even farce—as when Arês, wounded, bursts up to Olympus like a bomb. And the divine family! What a delightful natural party—human beings raised a degree or two, but all the funnier for that. They are the comic background to the tragedy below—for the story of Achillês is a tragedy—the fiery conflict of a man divided against himself, who in a few short days drops to the lowest hell of savagery, then rises to self-mastery and inward peace. The last ineffable scene between him and Priam seems to me Homer's reading of the riddle of human life—purification by suffering; and without one direct word, he discloses his faith that this is not the end. Life has done all it was meant to do for those two souls, one so young and one so old. They must die now and they know it, but their future lies in the hand of that awful and supreme power which Homer calls Fate, who dwells in the clouds and darkness above Zeus and his court. And if Homer had put into words what he thought, that might have been the same as the Hebrew patriarch said, "Shall not the Judge of all the earth do right?"

CONTENTS

CONTENTS

There thou shalt hear and learn the secret power.
Of harmony, in tones and numbers hit
By voice or hand, and various-measured verse,
Aeolian charms and Dorian lyric odes,
And his who gave them breath, but higher sung,
Blind Melesigenes, thence Homer called,
Whose poem Phoebus challenged for his own.

MILTON, Paradise Regained, IV. 245.

BOOK I

*How Achillês and Agamemnon quarrelled over Briseïs,
and how Thetis persuaded Zeus to support her son*

A N ANGRY MAN—THERE IS MY STORY: THE BITTER RAN-
cour of Achillês, prince of the house of Peleus, which
brought a thousand troubles upon the Achaian host. Many
a strong soul it sent down to Hadês, and left the heroes themselves a prey to dogs and carrion birds, while the will of God
moved on to fulfilment.

It began first of all with a quarrel between my Lord King
Agamemnon of Atreus' line and the Prince Achillês.

What god, then, made the feud between them? Apollo, son
of Leto and Zeus. The King had offended him: so he sent a
dire pestilence on the camp and the people perished. Agamemnon had affronted his priest Chrysês, when the priest
came to the Achaian fleet, bringing a rich treasure to ransom
his daughter. He held in his hand a golden staff, twined about
with the sacred wreaths of Apollo Shootafar, and made his
petition to the Achaian people in general but chiefly to the
two royal princes of Atreus' line:

"My lords, and you their subjects, for you I pray that the
gods who dwell in Olympos may grant you to sack Priam's
city, and to have a happy return home! but my dear daughter—set her free, I beseech you, and accept this ransom, and
respect Apollo Shootafar the son of Zeus!"

Then all the people said good words, and bade them respect the priest and accept the ransom; but my lord King
Agamemnon was not well pleased. He told the priest to be off,
and in harsh words too:

"Don't let me find you here any more, you; don't stay now
and don't come again, or else your staff and sacred wreaths
may not protect you. The woman I will not release! She shall
live to old age in our house, far away in Argos, working the
loom and lying in my bed. Begone now! don't provoke me,
or it will be the worse for you."

The old man was afraid, and did as he was told. Silent he

passed along the shore of the murmuring sea; and when he came home, he prayed earnestly to Apollo:

"Hear me, Silverbow! thou who dost bestride Chrysê and holy Cilla, thou who art the mighty lord of Tenedos, O Smintheus! If I have ever built a temple to thy pleasure, if I have ever burnt for thee fat slices of bulls or of goats, bestow on me this boon: may the Danaäns pay for my tears under thy shafts!"

Phoibos Apollo heard his prayer. Down from Olympos he strode, angry at heart, carrying bow and quiver: the arrows rattled upon his shoulders as the angry god moved on, looking black as night. He sank upon his heel not far from the ships, and let fly a shaft; terrible was the twang of the silver bow. First he attacked the mules and dogs, then he shot his keen arrows at the men, and each hit the mark: pyres of the dead began to burn up everywhere and never ceased.

Nine days the god's arrows fell on the camp; on the tenth day Achillês summoned all to a conference. The goddess Hera put this in his mind, for she was distressed to see the Danaäns dying. And when they were all gathered together, Achillês rose up and spoke.

"My lord King," he said, "I think we shall seem just foiled adventurers when we get home—if indeed we get off with our lives, now you see war and pestilence allied to beat us. Come then, let us inquire of some prophet or priest, or even a diviner of dreams—for God, it seems, doth send our dreams—and let him tell us what has made Phoibos Apollo so angry. Does he find fault with us for prayer or for sacrifice? Does he desire the savour of sheep or goats without blemish, that he may spare us this pestilence?"

He said his say, and sat down. Then up rose Calchas o' Thestor, most excellent diviner of dreams, who knew what is and what will be, and what has been in ancient days; he had guided the fleet to Ilios by the divination which Phoibos Apollo had taught him. He spoke to them from an honest heart, and said:

"Prince Achillês, whom Zeus delights to honour! you bid me explain the wrath of Lord Apollo Shootafar: therefore I will speak. Mark what I say, and swear me an oath that you will defend me with all your might in word and deed. For I think I shall provoke a man who rules all our people, one whom all the people obey. A king when angry always can be stronger than a common man; even if he smothers his anger for the day, yet indeed he keeps a grudge long in his heart until he can pay it off. Consider then if you will hold me safe."

Achillês answered:

"Fear nothing, but speak the word of God which you know. For I swear by Apollo, whom Zeus delights to honour, to whom you pray, Calchas, when you declare God's word to the nation:

no man while I live and see the light shall lay heavy hands on you in this fleet, none of all the nation, not even if you name Agamemnon, who now claims to be first and best of us all."

Then the seer took courage and spoke out:

"He finds no fault with us then, for prayer or sacrifice, but for his priest, whom Agamemnon affronted, when he would not accept a ransom and set his daughter free. For his sake Shootafar has sent us trouble, and will send. Nor will he stay the noisome pestilence among our people, until the King gives back to the father his lovely girl, unbought, unransomed, and sends a solemn sacrifice to Chrysê: then we may trust that the god will be appeased."

No sooner had he sat down, than up rose my lord King Agamemnon in his majesty. He was displeased, the dark places in his heart were full of resentment, his eyes were like flashing fire; and he began by rating Calchas:

"Prophet of evil, you have never had a decent word for me! It is always your delight to prophesy evil, but good you have never said and never done! And now you get up and harangue the people with your oracles. So *that* is the reason why Shootafar sends trouble! because of that girl Chryseïs! because I would not accept the ransom—but I want to keep her myself, and take her home! Why, I like her better than my own wife Clytaimnestra, she is just as good in face or figure, brains or fingers. Never mind, I will give her back if that is better. I would rather have the people alive than dead. Only get a prize ready for me at once, or else I shall be the only man in the army without a prize. That is not right! Just look here, all of you, my prize is going away somewhere else!"

Then Achillês answered:

"Your Majesty, gettings are keepings with you, there's no doubt about that. Pray how will our brave men give you a prize? I do not know of any common store anywhere. What we got from the towns we have taken, has been divided, and you cannot expect people to collect it all again in a heap. For the present, then, give the girl up to the god; and we will pay you threefold or fourfold, if Zeus ever allows us to sack the proud city of Troy."

King Agamemnon answered:

"None of that; you may be a great man, Achillês, you may be more than a man, but do not try cheating—you will neither cajole me nor persuade me. Do you want to keep your own prize, and tell me to give up mine and just sit forlorn without any? If our brave men will give me a prize, and satisfy me that I get as much as I give, well and good; but if they will not give, then I will take—I'll come to you, or to Aias, for a prize, or Odysseus, and away I'll go with my gettings! Then it will be his turn to be angry. But we will see about that later. For the time being, let us launch a good ship and find a special crew and put Chryseïs on board; and let one of the princes from our council be in charge, Aias or Idomeneus or Prince Odysseus, or yourself, my young friend, you terror of the world, *you* shall pacify Shootafar by making sacrifice."

Achillês scowled at him, and said:

"Ha! greedyheart, shamelessness in royal dress! How could any man be willing to obey you, whether on some errand or in the battlefield? I cared nothing about the Trojans when I came here to fight; they had done nothing to me, never lifted my cattle, or horses either, never destroyed my fruit or my harvest in Phthia—too many hills and forests between us, and roaring seas. No, it was you I came for, shameless man! to give you pleasure, to revenge Menelaos, and you too, dogface! for the Trojans' wrong. You don't trouble about that, you care nothing for that! And now you threaten to rob me of my prize, which I worked hard to get, which the army gave me. I never get a prize equal to yours if our men capture some town; but most of the hard fighting is done by my hands. Only when sharing-time comes, you get most of the good things, and I have a scrap to comfort me—not much, but all I can get!—as I come back tired out with fighting. Now I will just go home to Phthia, since it is much better to take ship and go, and I don't think I shall fill my hold with riches if I stay here despised."

King Agamemnon answered:

"Do go, if that's what you want, go by all means—I do not sink on my knees and beg you to stay for my sake. I have others in plenty who will honour me, first and foremost Zeus Allwise. I hate you more than any prince on earth, for you are always quarrelling and fighting. If you are such a mighty man, God gave you that, I suppose. Go home with your ships and your men and lord it over your Myrmidons, but I care nothing for you. I don't mind if you *are* in a rage. Now I give you fair warning: since Apollo robs me of Chryseïs, I will send her home with my own ship and crew; but I will take your beautiful Briseïs, and I will come for her myself to your quarters— for your prize! to show you how much stronger I am than you are. Then others will take care not to stand up to me and say they are as good as I am!"

This pierced Achillês to the heart; and he was of two minds, whether he should draw sword from thigh, to push through the crowd and strike down King Agamemnon, or whether he should calm his temper and keep himself in check. As these thoughts went through his mind, and he began to draw the great sword from the sheath, Athena came down from heaven: Queen Hera sent her, loving and anxious at once. She stood behind him, and held him back by his long red hair. No other man saw her, but Achillês alone. Achillês turned round startled —at once he knew Pallas Athenaia. His eyes flashed wildly and he spoke words that winged like arrows to the mark:

"Why have you come again, daughter of Zeus Invincible? To see the insult of my lord King Agamemnon? I'll tell you what, and I will do it too: his own highhandedness one day may be his death!"

Athena replied, with her bright eyes glinting:

"I came to check your passion, if you will listen; and I was sent from heaven by Queen Hera, loving and anxious at once. Come, come, drop the quarrel, don't pull out that sword. Just give him a sound rating and tell him what to expect. For I declare to you that this is what will happen: a time will come when you shall have a magnificent offer, with three times as much offered to make up for this insult. Hold back now, and do what I say."

Achillês answered:

"I must observe the bidding of you both, goddess, angry though I am indeed. It is better so. What the gods command you, do, then the gods will listen to *you*."

So he stayed his heavy hand on the silver hilt, and drove back the sword into the sheath, in obedience to Athena; and she returned to Olympos, where Zeus Invincible dwells with the company of heaven.

But Achillês was angry still. Once more he addressed the King in violent words:

"You drunkard, with eyes like a bitch and heart like a fawn! You never arm yourself with your men for battle, you never go out on a raid with the fighting men—no pluck in you for that! You think that certain death! It is much better, isn't it, to stay in camp and rob any one who tells the truth to your face! The king feeds on his people, for they are a worthless lot—or else, my lord, this would be your last outrage. But one thing I will tell you, and take my solemn oath: as truly as this staff will never grow again, never again will put forth leaves and twigs, after it has been cut from the stump in the mountain forest, and the axe has scraped off leaves and bark, but now it is held in men's hands, men of judgment who guard the statutes of Zeus —hear my solemn oath to you: so truly a time shall come when Achillês will be missed by the nation one and all; then you shall not be able to help them for all your grief, while many are falling and dying before bloodthirsty Hector. Then you shall tear your temper to tatters that you would not respect the best man of all."

As he spoke, Achillês dashed down on the ground the gold-studded staff, and took his seat again; while King Agamemnon opposite fumed with rage. But Nestor rose: a famous orator he was, gracious in speech, whose voice ran off his tongue sweeter than honey. He had seen already in Pylos two generations of men grow up before him and pass away, and he was king still over the third. He now spoke with an honest heart and said:

"For shame, sirs! Here is a great trouble for the Achaian land! How glad Priam would be, and Priam's sons, how all Troy would be in jubilation, if they could only hear you two quarrelling—you, the leaders in wisdom and leaders in war! Now listen to me. You are both younger than I am. Nay more, I have met even better men than you, and they never disregarded me. For never have I seen, and never shall I see, such men as Peirithoös, and that great ruler Dryas, Caineus and Exadios and the noble Prince Polyphemos.[1] I tell you, those were the mightiest men ever born upon earth, mightiest I say and fought against mightiest foes, the monsters of the mountains,[2] whom they horribly destroyed. Yes, those men I knew well; I travelled all the way from distant Pylos to visit them at their own request. And I fought by their side as a volunteer. Those were men whom no mortal now living on earth could fight! And they heard my advice and took it too. Listen to me then, you also, and take my advice, and you will find it better. You, sir, do not rob this man of the girl, although you are strong; leave her alone, as the army gave her to him at first for his especial prize. And you, Achillês, do not provoke your king, force against force; for greater honour belongs to a sceptred king, when Zeus has given him dignity. If you *are* a mighty man, if your mother *is* divine, yet he is above you for his dominion is greater. Your Grace, forget your bitterness: and I beseech Achillês to let his anger pass, for he is the strong tower of our nation against the horrors of war."

King Agamemnon answered:

"Indeed, sir, all that you say is fair and right. But this man wishes to be above all, to rule every one, to be King over every one, to order every one about—and there is some one who will not obey, I think! If the gods everlasting have set him up as a warrior, does it follow that they have set him on to call ugly names?"

Achillês interposed, and said:

"Yes, for I should be called coward and outcast, if I yield to you in everything you choose to say. Lay your commands on others, don't order me about, for I do not think I shall obey you any more. I tell you one thing, and you will do well to remember it. I will never use my hands to fight for a girl, either with you or with any one—those who gave, may take away; but you shall never carry off anything else of what I have

[1] Not the cannibal monster of the Odyssey.   [2] Centaurs.

against my will. Just try and see, that these also may know: very soon there will be red blood on the spear-point!"

They finished their bout of hard words, and dismissed the assembly. Achillês with Patroclos and his friends returned to his quarters. Agamemnon launched a good ship, and put on board twenty men with the sacrifice, and brought Chryseïs; Odysseus took charge, and they set sail. Then Agamemnon ordered the people to purify themselves; they cast their peace-offerings into the sea, and slew bulls and goats on the shore to make full sacrifice to Apollo, and the savour went up to heaven through the wreathing smoke.

While all this business was going on, Agamemnon did not forget his quarrel with Achillês and the threats he had made. He called his two trusty servants, the heralds, Talthybios and Eurybatês, and gave them his orders:

"Go to the quarters of Prince Achillês, take Briseïs by the hand and bring her here. If he will not give her up, I will come with a larger party and take her myself, which will be more unpleasant for him."

So he sent his envoys with strict orders. They did not like their errand, but they went along the shore to the place where the Myrmidons had their ships. They found Achillês sitting before his hut, and he was not pleased to see them. They indeed were both afraid and ashamed before the young prince. They only stood, and said nothing to him, and asked nothing; but he understood what they wanted, and spoke:

"Heralds, I greet you, for the envoy is held sacred by gods and men. Come near, I find no fault in you, but in Agamemnon, who has sent you for the girl Briseïs. Here, Patroclos my friend, bring out the girl and let them take her away. Let them both be witnesses before the blessed gods and mortal men, and before this hard-hearted king, if ever the people shall need me to stand between them and dire destruction! Indeed, he is mad with fury and cannot look both before and behind, so that his army may live to fight before our camp."

Patroclos heard him, and brought out the beautiful Briseïs, and handed her over to the envoys. Then they returned to their ships, and the woman followed them unwillingly. But Achillês burst into tears, and went apart from his friends; he threw himself down by the grey salt sea, and gazing over the waters stretched out his hands, calling loudly to his mother:

"O my mother! I was born to die young, it is true, but honour I was to have from Zeus Olympian, Thunderer on high! And now he has not given me one little bit! Yes, my lord King Agamemnon has insulted me! He has taken my prize and keeps it, he has robbed me himself!"

His divine mother heard his sorrowful cry, as she sat in the

depths of the sea beside her ancient father. Quickly she shot
up like a mist out of the grey sea, and sat down beside her
weeping son; she stroked him with her hand, and said:

"My child, why do you weep? What is your trouble? Tell
me, don't hide it, then we shall both know."

Achillês answered with a deep groan:

"You know! Why should I talk when you know everything?
We attacked Thebê, Eëtion's famous city; we sacked the place
and carried off everything. The spoil was divided, and they
chose for Agamemnon a beautiful girl, Chryseïs. Chrysês the
priest of Apollo Shootafar came to our camp with a heap of
treasure, to ransom his daughter; he carried a golden staff
twined about with the sacred wreaths of Apollo Shootafar, and
made his prayer to the whole people, but especially to the two
royal princes. All the people spoke good words, and told them
to respect the priest and accept the ransom; but my Lord
Agamemnon did not like it. He told him to be off, and rudely
too.

"The old man went away very angry, and prayed to Apollo.
The god heard him, for he loved the man dearly; he shot us—
the deadly shafts fell all over our camp, the people died in
heaps. Our prophet knew what it meant, and told us Shootafar's mind. I stood up at once and advised them to pacify the
god; but the king fell in a rage and threatened me, and now he
has made good his threat. They are sending a ship to Chrysê,
with offerings for the god, and the heralds have just gone from
my hut and taken away the girl Briseïs whom the people had
given to me.

"Do help your son, if you can! Go to Olympos, pray to Zeus,
if you have ever pleased him and served him by word or deed!
How often have I heard you boasting to father at home, telling
how you saved Cronion Thundercloud from violence and ruin,
all by yourself, when there was a conspiracy in heaven! The
other Olympians wanted to tie him up, Hera and Poseidon and
Pallas Athena; but you came and saved him from that, by
summoning old Hundredhand, whom the gods call Briareos,
but all men call Aigaion—he is stronger than his own father! [3]
Hundredhand came in and sat down beside Zeus, triumphant
—the blessed gods were frightened, and did not tie him up.
Remind him of that, mother, fall down and clasp his knees—
see if he will help the Trojans and drive the Achaians back to
their ships with slaughter! Let them enjoy their king! Let his
gracious Majesty King Agamemnon know his own delusion,
when he would not respect the best man of all!"

Then Thetis answered, as the tears ran down her cheeks:

"O my poor child, why did I ever bring you up for such a

[3] Poseidon.

dreadful fate? Why could you not have stayed behind? Why could you not have been spared tears and tribulation, since your life is but a minute, no long day indeed! But now you have both a speedy doom and sorrow beyond all men! Indeed it was a cruel fate you were born for.

"Very well, I will tell your story to Zeus Thunderer—I will go myself to snowy Olympos and see if I can persuade him. Be sure now to stay beside your ships, and be as angry as you like but keep clear of battle altogether. For Zeus went yesterday to the Ocean stream on a visit to the pious Ethiopians, for a feast, and all the other gods with him; but he will be back in twelve days, and then I will go at once to the brazen halls, and make my prayer. I think I can persuade him."

And there she left him, brooding over the loss of his beautiful Briseïs, whom they had torn from him against his will.

But Odysseus came safely to Chrysê with his holy offerings. They entered the deep harbour and furled the sails, and stowed them below; quickly they lowered the mast into the crutch, and rowed the ship to her moorings, where they dropt the anchor stones and made fast the hawsers. Then they landed, and carried out the offerings for Apollo Shootafar. Chryseïs landed also, and Odysseus led her to the altar and gave her into her father's arms with these words:

"Chrysês, my lord Agamemnon has sent me to bring your daughter back, with a holy offering for Phoibos on behalf of the Danaäns; that we may propitiate the Lord who has lately sent mourning and trouble upon the people."

He gave her into her father's arms, and he received his daughter with joy. The men quickly set the holy offerings around the altar, then washed their hands and took up the barley-grains. Chrysês lifted up his hands, and prayed aloud:

"Hear me, Silverbow! thou who dost bestride Chrysê and holy Cilla, thou who art the mighty Lord of Tenedos! Verily thou hast heard my prayer, and done me honour, and smitten hard the Achaian people: grant me now again this boon, even now save the Danaäns from this dire pestilence!"

So he prayed, and Phoibos Apollo heard his prayer. And when they all had prayed and cast the barley-grains, they first drew back the heads, and killed, and flayed, carved out the thigh-slices and rolled them between pieces of fat, and laid more raw flesh upon them: then the old priest burnt them upon sticks of wood, and poured sparkling wine over, while the young men held their five-pronged forks ready by his side. After the thigh-pieces were burnt and the inner parts were divided, they chopt up the rest and ran splits through the meat, roasted all properly and drew it off. This work done, they prepared their meal and enjoyed it, and no one lacked a fair share.

When they had all had enough, the lads filled the bowls to the brim, and served the wine to all after spilling the sacred drops.[4]

So all day long the young men of Achaia appeased the god with sweet music, singing the Healer's chant, a hymn to the Farworker; and his heart was glad to hear.

When the sun set and darkness came they lay down to rest beside their moorings; but as soon as Dawn showed her rosy fingers through the mist, at once they rose and sailed for their own camp. Apollo Farworker sent them a following breeze. They lifted the mast, and spread the white sails; the wind filled the great sail, the purple wave swished and poppled against the stem, the ship ran free on her way over the waters. At last they arrived at their camp, and drew the ship ashore high on the sands, and set up the long line of dogshores: then all scattered among the huts and the ships.

But Achillês brooded still over his anger, and did not move from his vessels. He never went to the meeting-place, never to the battlefield, but wore out his heart where he was, although he longed for war and battle.

When the twelfth day dawned, the gods returned to Olympos in a body, led by Zeus.

Thetis did not forget her son's request; but she came out of the sea, and early in the morning she climbed to Olympos in the highest heavens. She found Allseeing Cronidês sitting apart from the rest on the topmost peak of craggy Olympos. There she knelt before him, and threw her left arm about his knees, catching his chin with the right hand as she made her prayer:

"O Father Zeus! If ever I have served you by word or deed, grant me this boon: give honour to my son! He of all others is to die an early death, but now see how my Lord Agamemnon has insulted him. He has taken his prize and keeps it, he has robbed my son himself! Satisfy my son, Zeus Olympian most wise! Let the Trojans prevail, until the Achaian nation shall satisfy my son and magnify him with honour!"

Zeus Cloudgatherer did not answer, but long sat silent; and Thetis—how she clasped his knees, how she clung fast to him and cried out once more:

"Say yes now, and promise me faithfully! Or else say no— for you have nothing to fear! Show me that you care less for me than for any god in heaven!"

Zeus answered in great vexation:

"Bother it all! You'll set me curry-worrying with Hera and make her scold me again! She is always at me as it is before them all, and says I help the Trojans to win. You just go away

---

[4] The server poured a few drops into each man's goblet, which he then spilled on the ground with a prayer; then the server filled the goblet, and passed on.

again now, and don't let Hera see: I will manage to do what you want. Look here, I will bow my head to you that you may believe me. That is my sure and certain sign here among us; when I bow my head, my word can never be recalled, and never deceive, and never fail."

As he spoke, Cronion bowed his black brows; the Lord's ambrosial locks swung forward from his immortal head, and high Olympos quaked.

So they had their talk and parted; Thetis dived from radiant Olympos into the deep sea, and Zeus entered his own hall. All the gods rose up from their seats to receive their father: not one of them dared to sit still, but all rose up to greet him. So he took his seat upon his throne.

But Hera had seen; she knew there had been a confabulation, and a visit from Silverfoot Thetis, the daughter of the Old Man of the Sea. She lost no time in scolding at Zeus Cronion.

"Who is it this time?" she began, "who has been confabulating with you now, you deceiver? You always like to go behind my back and make secret plans, and lay down the law! You never would tell me a word of your notions if you could help it!"

The Father of men and gods made answer:

"My dear Hera, do not expect to know everything I say. You must not expect as much as that, although you are my wife. Whatever is proper for you to hear, you shall be the first to hear before any in heaven or earth; but when I choose to consider things by myself, do not be inquisitive and ask questions about everything."

Queen Hera said at once, opening her fine eyes:

"O you dreadful creature, what a thing to say! I inquisitive? I ask you questions? I never did such a thing in my life! I just leave you alone, and you decide whatever you choose. But I am dreadfully afraid this time. I can't put it out of my mind that you may be cajoled by Silverfoot Thetis, that daughter of the Old Man of the Sea! Early this morning she was kneeling and clasping your knees. I suppose you bowed your head and promised faithfully to honour Achillês and kill crowds on the battlefield."

Zeus Cloudgatherer answered:

"You are a strange creature: always supposing, always watching me. But you shall gain nothing by it. You will only make me dislike you more, and that will only be more unpleasant for you. If this is as you say, it must be my pleasure. Silence please, and sit down, and do what I tell you. All the gods in Olympos will not help you if I come near and lay my heavy hands upon you."

This frightened the Queen; she sat down in silence and took

herself in hand. But the other gods were disturbed, and Hephaistos the master-craftsman was the first to speak. He took
his mother's side, and said:

"Bother it all! It is really too bad, if you two quarrel like
this about mortals, and make a brawl among the gods. What's
the pleasure in good fare with bad manners everywhere? My
advice to my mother is this, and she knows it is good; give
way to dear Father Zeus, and don't let father scold any more
and spoil our breakfast. What if Olympian Flashlightning
choose to knock us out of our seats? He is much stronger than
we are. Come now, speak him fair and gentle, Olympian will
be kind in one minute."

Then he jumped up, and put the double cup in her hand,
saying:

"Be patient, mother dear, bear it patiently although it hurts!
I love you, and I don't want to see you beaten before my eyes.
I shall not be able to help you then, however sorry I am, for
Olympian is hard to tackle. Once before I tried to help you,
and he caught me by the leg and threw me from the threshold
of heaven. All day long I fell, and at sunset down I came in
Lemnos, with very little breath left in my body; there I fell,
and the Sintians looked after me."

Queen Hera smiled at this, and smiling received the cup
from her son's hand. Then he drew sweet nectar from the bowl,
and carried it to all the gods, moving round rightways.[5] Laughter unquenchable rose among the blessed gods when they saw
Hephaistos butler puffing about the hall.

So they feasted all day until sunset, and there was no lack;
plenty to eat and drink, a splendid harp with Apollo to play it,
and the Muses singing turn by turn in their lovely voices. But
when the bright light of the sun sank down they went each to
his room for sleep; for the famous Crookshank Hephaistos had
built them each a chamber by his clever skill. And Zeus Olympian Flashlightning went to his own bed, where he used to
sleep sound when slumber came upon him; into that bed he
climbed and slept, with Queen Hera by his side.

[5] As the sun goes, as the clock goes, "through the buttonhole": keeping the company on the right hand.

complete Ch I

BOOK II

How a Dream came with a message from Zeus, and how the Achaians debated in their camp. The names and numbers of the two hosts.

ALL OTHERS, BOTH GODS AND MEN, SLEPT THE WHOLE NIGHT long; but Zeus could not sleep. For he was pondering how he could destroy crowds of men on the battlefield and cover Achillês with glory. It seemed to be the best plan to send a bad dream to King Agamemnon. So he called one, and spoke plainly and to the point:

"Away, Bad Dream! Go to the Achaian camp; enter the hut of King Agamemnon, and tell him exactly what I say. Bid him arm the Achaians with all haste; for now he may take the city of Troy. The Olympians are no longer divided; Hera has now bent them all by her entreaties, and troubles hang over the Trojans."

Away went the Dream; quickly he flew to the camp, and made his way to King Agamemnon's hut, where he found the King deep in blissful sleep. The Dream leaned over his head in the shape of Nestor Neleïdês, whom Agamemnon respected most of all the elders, and spoke in these words:

"You are asleep, O son of Atreus, the lord of many horses! No master mind ought to sleep the whole night long, when his cares are so many and nations are in his charge. Now hear me quickly. I am a messenger from Zeus, who far away cares for you and pities you. He bids you arm the Achaians with all haste, for now you may take the city of Troy. The Olympians are no longer divided, since Hera has bent them all by her prayers and troubles hang over the Trojans from Zeus. Be sure to keep this in your memory, and forget not when honey-hearted sleep shall leave you."

Then the Dream departed, and left him there, believing what was destined not to be done; for he thought he would take Priam's town on that day, foolish man, and he knew not what Zeus meant to do. For Zeus was yet to bring more sorrow and groaning upon Trojans and Danaäns both before the war should end.

The King awoke with the divine voice echoing about him.

He sat upright, and slipt into his fine soft tunic, and threw a wide cloak about him; next he laced his boots and slung the silver-studded sword over his shoulders. Then he took up the sceptre of his fathers which had been handed down from generation to generation, and holding this he made his way among the ships.

By this time Dawn had come to high Olympos, proclaiming to Zeus and the gods that it was light; and the King commanded his heralds to use their good lungs and summon the people to meeting. They cried their summons and the people came quickly. But first the King held a council of the elders beside the ship of Nestor; and when these were gathered he proposed a clever plan.

"Listen, friends," he said. "A Dream from heaven appeared to me last night. He was exactly like Nestor in looks and voice, and he stood by my head and said: 'You are asleep, son of Atreus, the lord of many horses! No master mind ought to sleep the whole night long, when he has so many cares and nations are in his charge. Now hear me quickly. I am a messenger from Zeus, who far away cares for you and pities you. He bids you arm the Achaians with all haste, for now you may take the city of Troy. The Olympians are no longer divided, since Hera has bent them all by her entreaties, and troubles hang over the Trojans from Zeus. Be sure to keep this in your memory.' This said he flew away, and I awoke. Well then, see if we can get the men under arms. But first I will try their temper as usual. I will tell them to ship and go home; you must post yourselves here and there, and urge them not to go."

Then King Nestor rose and said frankly:

"My friends, my lords and princes of our nation, if any other had told of this vision, we might think it false and take no notice: but now he has seen it who claims the highest place among us. Come then, and see if we can get the men under arms."

He led the way out, and the princes followed obedient. Meanwhile the people came crowding on. They were like a great swarm of buzzing bees, which come on and on out of a cave and hover in clusters over the flowers of spring: here they fly, and there they fly, no end to them. So the men swarmed out of their huts and ships over the deep sand and marched in throngs to the place of meeting. Among them God's messenger Rumour blazed abroad and quickened their steps. The place was all confusion, the earth groaned under them as they sat down and there was a great din. Nine ushers tried to keep order with loud shouts, to stop their noise and make them listen to their princes.

At last they were seated and arranged in rows, and the uproar ceased. Then King Agamemnon rose, holding the sceptre which Hephaistos had made and given to Zeus Cronion, who gave it to Hermês king's messenger; my lord Hermês gave it to Pelops, and Pelops to King Atreus; then Atreus dying left it to Thyestês, and Thyestês left it to Agamemnon, the sign of his rule over the whole of Argos and many islands of the sea. On this sceptre Agamemnon was leaning as he addressed the assembly.

"My friends, my Danaän heroes, servants of Arês! Zeus Cronidês has wholly deluded me, cruel god! First he bowed his head, and promised that I should sack the walled castle of Ilion and return safe; but as it seems now, his will was to ruin and deceive—he bids me return inglorious to Argos, after losing thousands of men. Such I suppose is the pleasure of Zeus high and mighty, who has overturned many towering cities and yet will overturn; for his power is greatest of all. What a disgrace for coming generations to hear! how this great host of Achaians fought so long for nothing, and failed like this, no end to be seen yet—and against fewer men, too. For just consider: suppose we should make a truce and both Achaians and Trojans have a count; pick out all the householders of the city, and sort ourselves in tens, and each ten choose one Trojan to pour our wine; many tens would be without a man to pour! So many more are we, I tell you, than the Trojans of the city; but they have allies from many other places, good soldiers, who baffle me and keep me from taking the city as I want to do. Nine years gone, as you see, thanks to Zeus, our ships' timbers are rotten, as you see, and rigging loose, our wives and our children I suppose are sitting at home and waiting for us, and here is the work we came to do undone like this! Well, I will tell you what we must do now. Let us go on board and sail home again. For Troy we shall never take."

These words excited the great multitude who had not been present at the council. The assembly was stirred like the long billows of the Icarian Sea, when a sudden squall from east or south has burst out of the clouds of heaven. Then as a strong west wind stirs a deep cornfield, rustling the ears and bending them low, so all that gathering was stirred; with loud clamour they rushed towards their ships, the dust rose under their feet and hung over them in clouds, they shouted to one another to get hold of the ships and draw them down into the sea, they cleared out the running-ways, and knocked away the dog-shores—their noise went up to the heavens, as the multitude pressed for home.

And they would have gone, fate or no fate, if Hera had not observed it. She called Athena and said:

"Bless us all, Atrytone, look there, you daughter of Zeus

Almighty! Is this to be the end? Are they to go like this, sailing over the sea for home, and leave the boast to Priam and his people? Leave their own Argive Helen, after losing so many lives in this foreign land to get her back? Go now to the camp, speak to each man in your kindly way, hold them back, and keep them from launching their ships!"

Athena lost no time. She shot down from the peaks of Olympos, and found Odysseus standing not far from the ships; but he did not lend a hand to launch them, because his heart was full of regret and sorrow. Athena came up to him and said with her bright eyes glinting:

"Odysseus Laërtiadês, can you do nothing now, my prince? Is this to be the end? Will they tumble aboard and go sailing home? Will they leave their boast to Priam and his people? Will they leave their own Argive Helen, after so many men have died in a foreign land to get her back? Don't stand idle here! go among your men, speak to each fellow in your kindly way and keep them from launching the ships!"

Odysseus knew the voice of the goddess: he threw off his cloak and ran. His marshal Eurybatês, who had come with him from Ithaca, attended him. He found Agamemnon, and received from him the sceptre of his fathers which had been handed down from generation to generation, and holding this he passed along.

Whenever he met a prince or a man of note, he stayed by his side and tried to check him with kindly words:

"How is this, my dear sir? I would not think of threats, as if you were a coward, but do sit down and make the others do the same. You do not know yet exactly what is in our King's mind. He is only trying them now—soon he will come down on the fellows. Did we not all hear in council what he said? I should not be surprised if he flew in a temper and let them have it. A royal prince has a high temper! His honour is from Zeus, and Zeus Allwise cares for him."

If he found a man of the people shouting and making a noise, he would bring down the sceptre across his back and say:

"What's this? Sit still and listen to your betters, you battle-shy skulker! Muscle or tongue *you* count for nothing! We can't all be kings. Too many kings spoil a nation! One king's enough for me, and why? He gets the right from God on high!"

So he went about, giving them all a lead; and the men were herded back from the ships and huts to their meeting-place once more, with a murmuring noise like waves of the sea when the deep roars and the breakers thunder upon the shore.

Now they sat orderly in long rows, but one man was blustering and railing still. This was Thersitês, a man with an inexhaustible flood of words, always ready to talk, with no manners and no sense, anything to annoy the princes, anything to raise a laugh: and he was the ugliest man ever seen before Ilion. He was bandy-legged and lame of one foot, a hump-back, with his two shoulders crushed together into his chest; on the top he had a sugar-loaf head with a few tufts of fluff. Achillês hated him heartily and so did Odysseus, for he was always badgering them; but this time he chose Agamemnon to revile with his piercing outcry. All the men were horribly angry with him and thought him a disgrace. But he shouted aloud his insults against Agamemnon:

"Your Majesty! what's wrong now, what do you want now? Plenty of treasure in your quarters, plenty of women in your quarters, the best of them, chosen by us to give you whenever we take a place! Or is it more gold you want, which some gentleman will bring you out of Ilios to ransom his son, when *I* caught him, or some other fellow did, and brought him in fast bound? Or do you want a young woman to love and keep for yourself? It's not the proper thing for the master to drive his men into trouble.—You fellows are all softies, disgraces, a lot of women, not men at all! Let us make sail for home, and leave this man in the place to digest his gorge of prizes. Let him see whether we are any help to him or not. Look how he has insulted Achillês, a much better fellow than he is: took his prize and keeps her, robbed the man himself. But there's not an angry thought in Achillês, he is a gentle one; or else, your Majesty, this would be your last outrage!"

There was a fine ranting speech against Agamemnon King of men! Odysseus was by the man's side in a moment, and frowned as he mercilessly told him off:

"You are a great orator, Thersitês, we know, ready to say anything—but hold your tongue now, you had better not defy princes in a minority of one! I declare you are the vilest man of all those whom our royal captains brought to Ilios. Then you should be the last man to take a king's name in your mouth, and pour out insults on him, and think of going home! We do not know yet clearly how things will turn out, whether good or evil will go with our homeward voyage. And so you sit here and revile my lord King Agamemnon because the fighting men give him a handsome share of the spoil: a regular jeering speech! Listen to me, and don't make any mistake about it. If I find you playing the fool again like this, may the head of Odysseus no longer sit on his shoulders, may I no longer be called the father of Telemachos, if I don't strip the clothes from your body, strip off the cloak and shirt that cover your nakedness, and send you off to the ships roaring with pain after a good sound drubbing!"

With this he brought down the sceptre with a whack between the man's shoulders. He shrank down, and great tears fell from his eyes as a blood-red weal showed up across his back. He sat down terrified, and wiped his eyes with a helpless look, in great pain. Then all forgot their troubles, and burst into merry laughter, and you might hear one say to another:

"Ha, ha! Odysseus has done us many a good turn—good lead in the council, good lead in the field, but he never did us a better turn than this; now he has stopped this damned word-slinger from his speechifying. I don't think he will pluck up courage to rail at kings again with his foul tongue!"

Such was the common talk when Odysseus rose holding the royal staff; and by his side Athena in the likeness of a herald called for silence, that all might hear from front to back and understand what he said. Then Odysseus gave them some good advice:

"My lord King," he said, "these men, as you see, wish to make you the most contemptible of mankind; and they will not keep the promise which they made when they set out from Argos, that you should destroy Ilios before you returned. They are like so many little children or widow women, weeping and wailing together that they want to go home. Indeed there is hardship enough here to make one go home disgusted. If a man has to stay one month from his wife he is impatient, when his ship cannot get out for the winter storms and the raging sea; but here we have the ninth year at the turn, and still we stay. So I cannot find fault with the men if they are impatient.

"But all the same, it is disgraceful to stay long and then to return empty. Bear it, my friends! Stay a little while, and let us learn whether Calchas tells the truth or not. One thing we know well, and you are all witnesses, all whom fate has not carried away. Only the other day, when the Achaian fleet was gathering in Aulis, bringing terror for Priam and his people, we were sitting round a spring near a holy altar and did solemn sacrifice to the immortals, under a fine plane-tree with the clear water flowing from its roots. Then a great sign was seen. A serpent with dappled back, a frightful creature which the Olympian himself had sent into the light, shot from under the altar and leapt upon the tree. In that tree were a sparrow's chicks, quite young, huddled under the leaves on the topmost branch; there were eight chicks, that made nine with the mother. Then the serpent swallowed the chicks, chirping piteously; the mother fluttered about, wailing for her young ones. He quivered round, and caught her by the wing, screaming. As soon as he had swallowed the chicks and the mother, God made him disappear, as he had made him appear—turned him into stone: we all stood amazed at this miracle.

"When this strange portent had come into our sacrifice, Calchas at once told us the meaning. He said, 'Why stand ye silent, men of Achaia? We have seen a great miracle of Zeus Allwise, late shown, late to be fulfilled, which will be told for ever and ever. As this serpent swallowed the sparrow and her chicks, eight chicks, nine with the mother, so for nine years we shall make war there, but in the tenth we shall take the great city.' That is what he told us, and now all shall come to pass. Come now, men of Achaia, stay here one and all in this place until we take the strong fortress of Priam.'"

The whole assembly cheered loudly at these words, and the echo of their cries resounded among the ships. They were well pleased with the speech of Odysseus, but Gerenian Nestor had something to say too.

"Upon my word," said he, "you are like a lot of boys playing at debate! Much you care about real fighting! What will become of our compacts and our oaths? Into the fire with all the plans and schemes of men, into the fire with our libations and our hand-claspings on which we put our trust! There is no use in fighting with words; we can do no good with words, however long we stay here. You, my lord King, as before, lead your men with unshakable will to the battlefield; and let these cowards dwindle away, the one or two with their independent parliaments! *They* will never do anything. What is *their* plan? 'Don't wait, but back to Argos!' Don't wait for God Almighty, to see whether his promise is a lie or not! For I tell you the Lord did bow down his proud head, on that day when Argos set sail in those ships, laden with death and destruction for Troy! On that day lightning flashed on the right hand, and showed omens of good.

"Then let no man think now of flight, now before he has taken some Trojan's wife to bed, before he has avenged our struggles and groanings for Helen's sake! But if any one is so horribly in love with flight, let him lay hands on his own ship, that he may perish and die before the rest of us.

"And you, my lord, it is yours to decide, but listen to good advice. My own advice is not to be thrown away. Sort out the men by tribes and clans, Agamemnon; let clan support clan, and tribe support tribe. If you make them do this, you will know at once which of your captains and which of your men is good or bad; for they will be fighting among their own people. You shall also know whether it is God's will that you fail to take the city, or the cowardice of the men and their folly in the field."

Agamemnon answered:

"I declare, Sir, once more you show yourself best in debate out of all the nation. O Father Zeus, Athenaia, Apollo! If I only had ten such counsellors in the nation! Soon that city of King Priam would bow her head, stormed and sacked by our hands! But trouble and sorrow is my lot; Zeus Cronidês Almighty has thrown me into fruitless quarrels and bickerings! Here am I and Achillês fighting about a girl, railing at each other, and I began it. If we can only make it up, there will be no delay, not one moment—Troy will be done for!

"Now then, men, dismiss for your meal, and let us make ready for battle. Sharpen your spears each man, look to your shields, give the horses a good feed, see that the chariots are all right—let war be the word! This whole day is for hard fighting; for there shall be no truce, not one moment! until night shall come and part the furious hosts. Sweat shall run over many a chest under the strap of his covering shield, many a hand shall tire in grasping the spear! sweat shall bathe the horse's flanks as he pulls the tight car! And if I see any one shirking the fight, and dallying beside the ships, he shall have no hope to escape the carrion dogs and vultures!"

At this speech a loud cheer arose from the multitude, like the roar of the waves against a headland on some rock-bound shore, when the south wind drives them against a cliff that has no peace from the waters in all the winds that blow. They rose and hurried scattering among the ships; they lit their smoking fires, and made their meal; and they offered sacrifice to the everlasting gods, each man to his own, praying to be spared death in the maul of war. My lord King Agamemnon sacrificed to awful Cronion a fat bull of five years. Then he summoned the elders and chief men, Nestor first and lord Idomeneus, Aias the great and Aias the lesser, and Diomedês, and sixth Odysseus, his counsellor wise as Zeus himself. Menelaos, that stout champion, needed no summons; for he knew himself what his brother was about. These all stood round the bull, and picked up the barley-grains, while my lord Agamemnon uttered the prayer:

"Zeus most glorious and most great, Thundercloud, throned in the heavens! Let not the sun go down and the darkness come, until I cast down headlong the citadel of Priam in flames, and burn his gates with blazing fire, and tear to rags the shirt upon Hector's breast! May many of his men fall about him prone in the dust and bite the earth!"

But Cronion would not yet grant his prayer. He accepted the sacrifice, but gave him toil and trouble yet more.

When they had finished the prayer and cast the barley-grains, they first drew up the head and cut the throat and flayed, then carved out the thigh-slices and wrapped them between two layers of fat, and laid raw meat upon them: these they burnt upon dry leafless billets, and spitted the inner parts to roast over the fire. After the pieces were burnt and the inner parts were eaten, they carved up the rest and broiled the slices upon the spits until all was properly cooked. Then they drew off the portions and laid their repast, they had their meal and there was plenty for all. When they had finished, Nestor began:

"May it please your Majesty, we have been here long enough; let us not delay any longer the work which God puts into our hands. Make haste, let the criers assemble the men, and then we will all soon get on the battlefield together."

Agamemnon made no delay; he sent out the criers at once to sound the call for battle, and the army was soon assembled. He and his staff of princes were everywhere, arranging the men in their sections. With them went Athena, holding her goatskin-tippet, precious, unfading, incorruptible, with a hundred dangling tassels of solid gold, neatly braided, worth each a hundred oxen. Through the host she passed, dazzling them with the vision, and filling each heart with courage to wage war implacable and unceasing. In a moment war became sweeter to them than to sail back safely to their own native land.

As a ravening fire blazes over a vast forest on the mountains, and its light is seen afar, so while they marched the sheen from their forest of bronze went up dazzling into high heaven.

As flocks of wildfowl on the wing, geese or cranes or long-necked swans, fly this way and that way over the Asian meadows and about the stream of Caÿstrios, proud of the power of their wings, and they settle on and on honking as they go until they fill the meadow with sound: so flocks of men poured out of their camp onwards over the Scamandrian plain, and the ground thundered terribly under the tramp of horses and of men. There they stood on the flowery meadow of Scamandros in tens of thousands, as many as the leaves and flowers that bloom in the season of the year.

Like swarms of quivering flies, which flit about the herdsman's shippen in springtime, when the milk drowns the pails, so many were the Achaians on that plain, facing the men of Troy and eager to tear them in pieces.

And as goat-keepers easily sort out the solid flocks of goats, when they are mixt together at pasture, so their leaders arrayed the men in this place and in that place, ready for battle. Among them was my Lord Agamemnon, eyes and head like Thundering Zeus, his girdle like Arês, his breast like Poseidon. As one amid the herd stands out from the rest, the great bull, high above the gathering cattle, so Zeus made the great king appear on that day, tall amid many, standing out from the other heroes.

O ye Muses who have your home in Olympos! You also are

divine, you are present among us, and you know all things; but we hear only a rumour and know nothing at all! Tell me then, I pray, who were the leaders and lords of the Danaäns: for the common men I could never tell and never name, not if I had ten tongues and ten mouths, a voice that could not tire, lung of brass in my bosom, unless the Olympian Muses, whose father is Zeus Almighty, should call to mind all those who came to Ilios.

Well, I will name the captains of the fleet and number all their ships.

The Bœotians were led by Peneleos and Leïtos, Arcesilaos, and Prothoënor, and Clonios. These came from Hyria and rocky Aulis, from Schoinos and Scolos, from hilly Eteonos, from Thespeia, Graia, and widespread Mycalessos; from the districts round Harma, Eilesion, and Erythrai; from Eleon, Hylaê, and Peteon, Ocalea, and the well-built fortress of Medeon; from Copai and Eutresis and Thisbê with its flocks of doves; from Coroneia and grassy Haliartos, from Plataia and Glisas; from the well-built fortress of Hypothebai, and from sacred Onchestos, the glorious grove of Poseidon; from grape-clustered Arne and Midea, from Nisa the divine and Anthedon lying upon the coast. From these came fifty ships, and in each a hundred and twenty Bœotian lads.

There were those who dwelt in Aspledon and Minyeian Orchomenos, led by Ascalaphos and Ialmenos, son of Arês. Their mother was Astyochê, a maiden of high rank; their father was mighty Arês, who lay with her in secret. She bore her sons in her upper chamber in the house of Actor Azeïdês. Thirty ships were their squadron.

The Phocians were there, led by Schedios and Epistrophos, the sons of a proud man, Iphitos Naubolidês. These came from Cyparissos and rocky Python, Crisa the divine and Daulis and Panopeus; others came from Anemoreia and Hyampolis, or lived along the noble river Cephisos, or at Lilaia beside the noble springs of Cephisos. Forty black ships were in this command; their captains kept their lines of battle close on the Bœotian left.

The Locrians were led by runner Aias, King Oïleus' son, the lesser Aias, not so big as the Telamonian, far smaller indeed. He was quite small, and wore a linen corselet, but with spear he excelled all the Hellenes and Achaians. These men came from Cynos and Opoeis and Calliaros, from Bessa and Scarphê and lovely Augeiai, from Tarphê and Thronion beside the streams of Boagrios. Their captain had forty black ships of the Locrians who are settled opposite sacred Euboia.

There were the Abantês, breathing fury, from Euboia, who held Calchis and Eretria and grape-clustered Histiaia, Cerinthos by the sea and the steep castle of Dios, with those of Carystos and Styra, all led by Elephenor Calchodontiadês, a true sprig of Arês, chief of the proud Abantês. His men followed him, quick men, with hair grown long behind, spearmen ready and eager to push their ashen pikes and tear the tunics off their enemies' breasts. He had forty black ships with him.

There were the men of Athens, that well-built citadel, the people of greatheart Erechtheus. In ancient times he was born out of mother earth, and Athena the daughter of Zeus nursed him and set him up in Athens, in her own rich temple; there the Athenian lads seek his favour with bulls and goats as the years roll on. These Athenians were led by Menestheus Peteos' son. No mortal man upon this earth was ever his equal in marshalling horses and spearmen: Nestor alone could challenge him, for he was the elder. He commanded fifty black ships.

Aias from Salamis brought twelve ships, which he ranged beside the Athenian lines.

There were the men from Argos and Tiryns with the massive walls; from Hermionê and Asinê, which hold the deep gulf; from Troizen and Eïonai and vine-clad Epidauros; Achaian lads from Aigina and Masês. These were led by Diomedês the stout champion, and Sthenelos, the son of famous Capaneus; third with them was Euryalos, noble as a god, the son of Mecisteus Talaïonidês, but Diomedês was their commander-in-chief. They had eighty black ships in their squadron.

There were the men from Mycenai, that well-built citadel, from rich Corinth and comely Cleonai, from Orneai and Araithyrea the beautiful, and Sicyon, where Adrastos was king at first; from Hyperesia and steep Gonoessa, from Pellenê and Aigion, from all Aigialos and wide Helicê. These were led by King Agamemnon Atreidês, one hundred ships. His men were the most and the best of all; and he was among them himself in bronze armour, proud and conspicuous because he was the best and his people the most.

There were the men from Lacedaimon, with its wide valley and long ravines; from Pharis and Sparta and dove-haunted Messê; from Bryseiai and beautiful Augeiai; from Amyclai and Helos, the castle by the sea; from Laäs and from Oitylos. They were led by his brother, the stout champion Menelaos, sixty ships: they had their station apart. There he moved among them, confident in his own ardour, inspiring them for war. His dearest wish was to avenge his passion and groanings for Helen's sake.

There were the men from Pylos and lovely Arenê, and Thryon the ford of Alpheios, and well-built Aipy, from Cyparissëeis and Amphigeneia; from Pteleos and Helos and Dorion, where the Muses met Thracian Thamyris and made an end of his singing, on his way from the house of Eurytos at Oichalia. For he avowed with boasts that he would beat the very daughters of Zeus Almighty if they would sing for him; then they were angry and maimed him, took away his inspired song and made him forget his harping. These men were led by Gerenian Nestor, who loved horses so well. Ninety ships followed him.

There were the men from Arcadia and Cyllenê's lofty hill, beside the tomb of Aipytos, where men fight hand to hand; from Pheneos and Orchomenos with all those flocks of sheep; from Rhipê and Stratia and windy Enispê; from Tegea and lovely Mantinea; from Stymphelos and Parrhasia. These men were led by prince Agapenor, Ancaios' son, sixty ships: in each were embarked many Arcadian men, well acquainted with fighting. Their ships were the gift of my lord King Agamemnon himself, well-built and fit to traverse the purple sea; for seafaring was not their business.

There were the men from Buprasion and sunny Elis, all that stretch enclosed by Hyrmina and Myrsinos on the coast, by the Olenian rock and Alision. These had four captains, each with ten swift ships, and large crews of Epeians. Two captains were Amphimachos and Thalpios, both of Actor's line, sons of Cteatos and of Eurytos; one was the mighty Diorês Amarynceus' son; the fourth was the noble Polyxeinos, the son of my lord Agasthenês Augeas' son.

There were the men from Dulichion and sacred Echinai, two islands which lie opposite Elis across the sea. These were led by Meges Phyleïdes, like a new god of war. Phyleus his father, the famous horsemaster whom Zeus loved, had passed over to Dulichion when he quarrelled with his father. Meges had forty black ships.

But Odysseus led the proud Cephallenians, who were settled in Ithaca and Neriton with its quivering trees, in Crocyleia and rugged Aigilips, in Zacynthos and in Samos all about, and they held the mainland opposite these islands. These were all under Odysseus, a man wise with the wisdom of Zeus himself. Twelve ships he had, all with vermilion cheeks.

The Aitolians were led by Thoas Andraimon's son, those who came from Pleuron and Olenos and Pylenê, from Calchis by the seashore and rocky Calydon. For the sons of proud Oineus were no more, nor he himself, and red-headed Meleagros was dead, whose lot had been to rule over the Aitolians. Thoas had forty black ships.

The Cretans were led by Idomeneus the famous spearman. They came from Cnossos and Gortys, the walled city; from Lyctos and Miletos and chalk-white Lycastos; from Phaistos and Rhytion, flourishing cities both, and others from the hundred cities of Crete. These were led by Idomeneus the spearman and Mionês, one like death-dealing Enyalios in person. They had eighty black ships under them.

Tlepolemos, a great handsome man, and a son of Heraclês, brought out of Rhodes nine ships of sturdy Rhodians, who came from the three districts of Rhodes, Lindos, Ialysos, and chalk-white Cameira. Their leader Tlepolemos was a famous spearman; his mother was Astyocheia, whom Heraclês brought out of Ephyra from the river Sellëeis, after he had sacked many cities of lusty young fighting men. But as soon as Tlepolemos grew up, he killed his father's uncle, Licymnios the sprig of Arês, who was then growing old.[1] At once he built ships and gathered a great company, and took flight over the sea; for he had been threatened by the other son and the grandson of his puissant father. He suffered much on his travels, but came at last to Rhodes. There his people settled in three tribal divisions; they were dear to Zeus, the lord of both gods and men, and he poured out infinite wealth upon them.

Nireus again from Symê brought three ships, Nireus, the son of radiant Aglaïa and gracious Charopos, Nireus the handsomest man of all the host before Troy next to the admirable Achillês. But he was feeble, and few followed him.

There were the men from Nisyros and Crapathos and Casos, from Cos the city of Eurypylos, and the Calydnian islands: these again were led by Pheidippos and Antiphos, two sons of King Thessalos whose father was Heraclês. They had a squadron of thirty ships.

Now again there were those from Pelasgian Argos, from Alos and Alopê and Trechis, from Phthia and Hellas the land of lovely women—these were named Myrmidons and Hellenes and Achaians. There were fifty ships of these, led by Achillês. But these had no mind for the din of battle, when there was no one to lead them to their place. For Prince Achillês lay idle beside the ships, angry for the loss of beautiful Briseïs, whom he had chosen out of Lyrnessos after a hard fight; when he had destroyed Lyrnessos and the walls of Thebê, and cut down Mynês and Epistrophos, the two warlike sons of King Euenos Selepiadês. That is why he lay idle in sorrow, but he was soon to rise up again.

There were the men from Phylacê and flowery Pyrasos, the precinct of Demeter; from Iton, mother of sheep; from Antron by the seashore and Pteleos in the grassy meadows. These again had been led by Protesilaos the warrior while he yet lived; but by that time he was deep in the black earth. His

[1] Half-brother of Alcmenê, the mother of Heraclês.

wife was left in Phylacê, tearing her two cheeks for woe, with the house only half-finished [2]: he was killed by a Dardanian as he leapt ashore first of all the Achaians. Yet the men were not leaderless, though they missed their leader; but they were taken in charge by Podarcês a true sprig of Arês, son of Iphicos Phylacidês the master of many flocks, own brother to proud Protesilaos but younger. Protesilaos was older and a better man of war; but the men did not want a leader, although they missed the good man they had lost. He had forty black ships in his squadron.

There were the men from Pherai beside the Boibeïan Lake, from Boibê and Glaphyrai and well-built Iaolcos; these in eleven ships were led by Eumelos the beloved son of Ademetos, whose mother was the noble Alcestis, most lovely of Pelias' daughters.

There were the men from Methonê and Thaumacia, from Meliboia and rugged Olizon, led by the master-bowman Philoctetês in seven ships; fifty oarsmen were in each ship, all expert with the bow. But Philoctetês lay in an island suffering dreadful pain, in sacred Lemnos, where they had left him behind tormented by a horrible wound from a poisonous serpent. There he lay in suffering; but the Argives were soon to remember my lord Philoctetês. Nor were his men leaderless, though they missed their leader; but they were taken in charge by Medon, the bastard son of Oïleus and Rhenê.

There were the men from Tricca and Ithomê amid the hills, and from Oichalia, the city of Eurytos. These were led by the two sons of Asclepios, Podaleirios and Machaon, good physicians both. Their squadron was thirty ships.

There were the men from Ormenios, and from the fountain Hypereia, and from Asterion, and the white crags of Titanos, led by Eurypylos the fine son of Euaimon: forty black ships were his.

There were the men of Argissa and Gyrtonê, from Orthê and Elonê and white Oloösson; these were led by Polypoitês that trusty fighter, the son of Peirithoös whose father was Zeus immortal. His mother Hippodameia conceived him on that very day when Perithoös punished the shaggy monsters,[3] when he drove them out of Pelion away to the Aithicês. He was not alone: with him was Leonteus, that true sprig of Arês, the son of proud Coronos Caineïdês, and they had forty black ships.

Guneus from Cyphos had forty black ships. He led the Erienês and the trusty Peraiboi, who came from cold stormy Dodona, and from the farms beside the delightful Titaresios which pours his flood of water into Peneios; the water does not

[2] He had no son, whose birth would have completed the "house."
[3] The Centaurs.

mix with the silver eddies of Peneios, but runs above it like olive oil, for it is a rivulet of Styx, that awful oath.[4]

The Magnesians were led by Prothoös the runner, son of Teuthredon—those from the banks of Peneios and from leaf-shaking Pelion. Forty black ships were with him.

These were the leaders and lords of the Danaäns. But which was the best of these, best among horses and best among men, in all the Achaian host?

Horses the best by far were those of Pheretiadês,[5] which Eumelos drove, swift on the foot as birds, of one coat and one age, level as a builder's rule across their backs. Apollo Silverbow bred them in Pereia, mares both, bringing with them the terror of war. Of men the best by far was Telamonian Aias, while Achillês was angry; for Achillês was first of all, and so were the horses which drew the admirable Achillês. But he lay idle beside the ships enraged against my lord King Agamemnon, and his people on the seashore amused themselves with quoits and javelins and arrows; their horses stood each near his own car, champing clover and marshgrown parsley, while the cars were in the huts of their masters well wrapt up, and the masters wandered about the camp, longing for their leader, out of the fight.

So all this host went sweeping over the earth like a conflagration. The ground groaned under their tramp, as when Zeus Thunderer in wrath lashes the ground round about Typhoeus where he lies in Arima. So under their trampling feet the ground loudly groaned, and quickly they passed over the plain.

But a messenger came to the Trojans, stormfoot Iris, with a lamentable message from Zeus Almighty. They were in conclave by the city gates, all assembled together, both young and old. Iris came near and spoke to Priam with the voice of his son Politês, who was the Trojan scout. He used to post himself on the barrow of old Aisyetês, to watch when the enemy was coming out, and then ran back at full speed. Iris made her voice like his, and said to Priam:

"Sir, you go on talking for ever, as if we were still at peace! But here is war upon us, overwhelming war! Indeed I have been in many battles already, but such a host, and so many men I never did see! Like the leaves of the forest, or the sands of the seashore, they are coming over the plain to attack our city. Hector, you are the man I want, and this is what you must do. We have many allies about the walls, from all parts of the country, and each has his own language. Let each man take charge of his countrymen, and tell them where to go."

[4] The oath of the immortal gods was taken in the name of Styx.
[5] Admetos.

Hector at once dismissed the assembly, and they hurried to arms. All the gates were opened, the men poured out, horse and foot; there was a great uproar.

Now there is a steep hillock away in the plain, with a clear space all round, which men call Batieia, but the immortals call it "dancing Myrinê's barrow." There the Trojans and allies mustered their ranks.

Hector Priamidês commanded the Trojans. He had under his own hand much the larger division of armed spearmen, and the best men.

The Dardanians were led by Aineias son of Anchisês. His mother was the divine Aphroditê, who lay with Anchisês on the foothills of Mount Ida, goddess with mortal man. With Aineias were the two sons of Antenor, Archelochos and Acamas, complete warriors both.

Those who came from Zeleia under the lowest foot of Ida, and drank the water of the Aisepos, wealthy men and Trojans, were led by Lycaon's son Pandaros, who received his bow from Apollo himself.

Those who came from Adresteia and the land of Apaisos, from Pityeia and the steep hill of Tereia, were led by Adrestos, and Amphios in his linen corselet, two sons of Percosian Merops. He understood divination beyond all others, and he forbade his sons to go to the war; but they disobeyed him, since the fate of black death drove them on.

Those who came from Percotê and Praction, from Sestos and Abydos and sunny Arisbê, were led by Asios Hyrtacos' son. He came from Arisbê besides the river Sellëeis driving great chestnut horses.

Hippothoös led the bands of Pelasgian spearmen, those who are settled on the rich soil of Larisa: Hippothoös and Pylaios, that true sprig of Arês, the two sons of the Pelasgian Lethos Teutamos' son.

The Thracians were led by Acamas and Peiroös, all those enclosed by the strong-flowing Hellespont.

Euphemos was the leader of the Ciconian spearmen. He was a son of Prince Troizenos Ceadês.

Pyraichmês led the Paeonians with curving bows. He brought them a long way, out of Amydon from the broad river Axios, from Axios, the finest water that runs over the earth.

The Paphlagonians were led by hairy Pylaimenês from the Enetai, where the wild she-mules[6] are found. They were settled at Cytoros and Sesamos about the river Parthenios, át Cromna and Aigialos and lofty Erythinoi.

The Alizonês were led by Odios and Epistrophos, from Alybê far away, where silver has its birth.

[6] The wild ass or onager.

The Mysians were led by Chromis, and Eunomos the diviner of birds; but his birds did not save him from black death, for he was brought low by the hand of Achillês at the river, when Achillês despoiled other Trojans too.

Phorcys led the Phrygians, and noble Ascanios, from distant Ascania: they were eager to join in the fray.

The Meionians were led by Mesthlês and Antiphos, two sons of Talaimenês born beside the Gygaian lake; they brought the Meionians from their birthplace under Tmolos.

Nastês again led the Carians, men of barbarous speech, who came from Miletos, and the leafy mountain of Phthira, from the streams of Maiandros and the high peaks of Mycalê. Amphimachos and Nastês were their leaders, Nastês and Amphimachos the fine sons of Nomion. One came to the war all over gold, like a girl. Poor fool! it did not save him from cruel death; but he was brought low by the hands of Achillês at the river, and prudent Achillês carried off the gold.

Sarpedon and the admirable Glaucos led the Lycians, out of far-off Lycia, from the eddying Xanthos.

BOOK III

How Menelaos and Alexandros fought a duel together, and what came of it

AND NOW THE TWO ARMIES ADVANCED, EACH UNDER ITS OWN leaders.

The Trojans raised a loud din and clamour, like a huge flock of birds. So you may hear cranes honking out of the sky before a storm of rain, as they fly with a great noise towards the Ocean stream, bringing death and destruction to the Pygmy men; and in the early morning they open their fight. But the Achaians marched in silence, breathing fury, shoulder to shoulder, with grim determination. The dust rose in clouds under their feet as they marched apace over the plain, as thick as the mist which a south wind spreads over the mountains. Shepherds hate it, the robber likes it better than night; a man can see a stone's throw and no farther.

No sooner had the two armies come near than a champion stept out of the Trojan ranks, the noble prince Alexandros.[1] A

[1] That was the name of Paris, who had carried off Helen.

leopard-skin hung over his shoulders with bow and sword; he shook his two sharp spears, and challenged all comers to fight him man to man. So he strode out with long steps. Menelaos saw him with joy, as a lion spies a victim, when he is hungry and finds a horned stag or a wild goat: greedily he devours his prey, even if dogs and lusty lads set upon him. So Menelaos was glad when he set eyes on Alexandros, for he thought he was sure to punish the traitor; at once he leapt down from his chariot in his armour.

But as soon as Alexandros saw him come out in front, his heart sank and he slunk back into the ranks to save himself. He might have been some one walking through the woods who suddenly sees a snake, and jumps back all of a tremble pale with fear. So Alexandros jumped back, and so he slunk into safety.

Then Hector rated him with scorn:

"Damn you, Paris, you handsome woman-hunter, you seducer! I wish you had never been born, I wish you had died unwedded! Yes, I wish that! and it would have been much better than to be a public pest, a thing of contempt. What guffaws there must be over there! They thought you a prime champion because you are good-looking. But there's no pluck in you, no fight!

"Were you like this when you got your fine company and set sail over the sea, and travelled in foreign lands, and brought home a handsome woman? She was to marry into a warlike nation, she was to be the ruin of your father and all his people, a joy to your enemies, a disgrace to yourself! So you would not stand up to Menelaos? You ought to find out what sort of fellow he is whose wife you are keeping. There would be little use then for your harp and the gifts of Aphroditê, your fine hair and good looks, when you lie in the dust. Well, the Trojans are all cowards, or you would have had a coat of stone long ago for the evil you have done!" [2]

Alexandros replied:

"That is true enough, Hector, that is true enough. Your heart is always as hard as steel. Like a shipwright's axe, when he slices off a spar from a tree with all the strength of a man! A hard heart indeed! Don't taunt me with Aphroditê's adorable gifts. You can't throw away a god's gifts, offered unasked, which none could win by wishing.

"Very well now, if you want me to fight, make both armies sit down on the ground, and put me between them with Menelaos to fight for Helen and all her wealth. Whichever proves the better man, let him take both wealth and woman home with him. Then let both sides swear friendship and peace:

[2] Stoned to death.

you to stay in Troy, they to go back to Argos, where there are plenty of fine women!"

Hector was very well satisfied with this. He went out between the ranks, holding his spear by the middle, and waved back his men. The Trojans sat down in order; but the Achaians at first went on shooting at him and throwing javelins and stones, until King Agamemnon shouted in a loud voice:

"Stop it, men, don't shoot, men! Hector wants to say something."

They stopt at once, and fell silent; and then Hector spoke out between the armies.

"Hear me, Trojans, and you men of Achaia, while I give you a message from Alexandros, who was the cause of our war. He asks that both Trojans and Achaians lay down their arms on the ground, and let Menelaos and himself fight a duel for Helen and all her wealth. Whichever proves the better man shall take both wealth and woman home with him: then let both sides swear friendship and peace."

All heard this in silence; then Menelaos cried out:

"Hear me also! This touches me most nearly, but my mind is, that Achaians and Trojans should now be reconciled. You have suffered enough for this quarrel of mine which Alexandros began. Whichever of us is fated to die, let him die, and let the others make friends forthwith. You bring two lambs—a white ram and a black ewe, for Earth and Sun, and we will bring another ram for Zeus. Call his Grace King Priam that he may take the oath himself, for his sons are overbearing and faithless, and we do not wish anything done to violate the solemn oath. Young men's minds are always a-flutter; but when an old man is there, he looks both before and behind, to see that the best is done for both sides."

Achaians and Trojans were all glad that there was some hope to end that lamentable war. They arranged their chariots in order; the men got out and put off their armour, laying it all upon the ground close together, and leaving a small space between the armies. Hector sent two heralds into the city to fetch the animals and to call Priam; King Agamemnon sent Talthybios to the camp with orders to bring the ram.

Meanwhile Iris had her own errand to Helen. She took the likeness of her goodsister,[3] Laodicê, the most beautiful of Priam's daughters, the wife of Helicaon Antenor's son. Iris found Helen in her room. She was weaving a great web of purple stuff, double size; and embroidering in it pictures of the battles of that war which two armies were waging for her sake. Iris came up to Helen, and said:

[3] The traditional English names for the group of relations-in-law are goodfather, goodbrother, etc.

"Come along, my love, and see a wonderful sight! They were all fighting in the plain like fury, and now all of a sudden they are sitting down, not a sound to be heard, no more battle, all leaning upon their shields, and their spears stuck in the ground! But Alexandros and Menelaos are going to fight for you! and you are to be the wife of the winner!"

These words pierced Helen to the heart. She longed for her husband of the old days, for home and family. At once she threw a white veil over her, and left the house quickly with tears running down her cheeks. Two maids were in attendance, Aithra and Clymenê with her great eyes. They made their way to the Scaian Gate.

Priam was sitting over the gatehouse in a group of the city elders, Panthoös and Thymoites, Lampos and Clytios, Hicetaon once well known in the field, and two men of tried wisdom, Ucalegon[4] and Antenor. These were old men long past their fighting days, but excellent speakers. There they all sat on the tower, chirruping in their thin old voices like so many crickets on a tree. As they saw Helen coming up, they whispered to one another in plain words:

"No wonder Achaians and Trojans have been fighting all these years for such a woman! I do declare she is like some divine creature come down from heaven. Well, all the same, I wish she would sail away, and not stay here to be the ruin of us and our children."

But Priam called Helen to his side:

"Come here, my dear child, and sit by me, to see your husband that was, and your family and friends. I don't blame you, my dear, I blame only the gods, for sending that host of enemies to bring tears to our eyes. Tell me the name of that prodigious man yonder? Who is he, that big handsome man? Others there are a head taller, that is true, but so fine a man I never did see, or so royal. He is every inch a king."

Helen answered: "You do me honour, my dear goodfather! How I wish I had died before I followed your son here, and left my bridal chamber and my family, my beloved daughter and all my young friends! But that was not to be; and so I pine away in sorrow. But I must answer your question. That is the great King Agamemnon of the house of Atreus, a good king and a strong spearman, both. He was my own goodbrother, to my shame, as sure as ever he was born."

The old man gazed at him with admiration, and said: "Atreidês, you are blessed indeed, a son of fortune happy in

---

[4] This name means Careless; and Virgil plays upon it neatly in describing the sack of Troy (*Aeneid*, ii. 312), "proximus ardet Ucalegon," Careless is on fire next door.

your lot! A great nation indeed is under your sway! I have travelled as far as vine-clad Phrygia, and there I saw hosts of Phrygian men with their dapple nags, the people of Otreus and splendid Mygdon, who were there campaigning on the banks of Sangarios; for I was among them as a volunteer on the day when the Amazons came, those women as good as men. But all those hosts were not so many as the Achaians here."

Next the old man asked about Odysseus.

"Tell me again, dear child, who is that—a head shorter than my lord King Agamemnon but broader in shoulders and chest? His arms lie on the ground, and he is patrolling the ranks of men like a tame wether; indeed, he looks very like a thick-fleeced ram marching through a flock of white ewes."

Helen answered, "That is Odysseus Laertês' son, the man who is never at a loss. He was bred in Ithaca, a rugged rocky land: there is no device or invention which he does not know."

At this Antenor broke in.

"Yes, my lady," he said, "you have spoken nothing but the truth. Odysseus has been here already: he came with Menelaos on a mission concerning yourself. I entertained them both in my house, and I got to know their looks and their many inventions. When they came before our assembly, standing Menelaos was head and shoulders above him; while they both sat, Odysseus was more dignified. But when they put the patterns of their minds and inventions into words before us all, Menelaos ran smoothly on, said not much, but very clearly, for he was not one of many words or one to miss the right word; yet he was the younger man. Then Odysseus rose, this man who is never at a loss: he would stand with his eyes fixt on the ground, didn't move the staff backwards or forwards, but held it stiff, like a dull fellow: you would call him surly and stupid both. But as soon as he let out his great voice from his chest, and a shower of words falling thick and soft like snowflakes in winter time, no other man alive could come near Odysseus. But then we did not think him so very much to look at."

Then the old man saw Aias, and asked again:

"Who is that other big handsome man among the Achaians, standing head and broad shoulders above the rest?"

Helen answered: "That giant of a man is Aias, a real tower of strength. And opposite him is Idomeneus, standing among his Cretan captains like a god. Menelaos often entertained him in our house, when he used to come over from Crete. And now I can see all the others that I know, and I can tell you their names; but two I cannot see, two young princes, Castor, who can tame any horse, and Polydeuces the boxer—my own two brothers, my own mother's sons! I wonder if they never left

Lacedaimon? or perhaps they did come, and now they will not show themselves in the field because I have brought all that shame upon them!"

But it was not as she said; already mother earth held them fast, far away in Lacedaimon, their own native land.

By this time the heralds in the city were bringing the lambs for the sacrifice, and the generous wine in a goatskin. Idaios holding a large bowl and golden cups, came up to the old King, and said:

"Rise up, Laomedontiadês! You are summoned by the chief captains of the embattled hosts of Ilios and Achaia, to come down into the plain and to make a sworn league of friendship. Alexandros and Menelaos will fight with long spears for the woman. The victor shall hold both woman and wealth; but we shall all make a sworn league of friendship, that we may hold our own rich land, and they may return to their country of noble horses and fair women!"

The old man shivered; but he ordered his men to harness the horses, and they set to with a will. Priam entered the car and picked up the reins. Antenor took his place beside him, and they drove the team swiftly through the Scaian Gate.

When they reached the plain, they dismounted between the two armies. Then Agamemnon rose up, and Odysseus; the heralds solemnly brought the offerings together, and mixed wine in the bowl, and poured water over the two kings' hands. Agamemnon drew the knife which hung by the sheath of his great sword, and cut hairs from the lambs' heads; the heralds gave some to the chief men on each side. Then Agamemnon lifted up his hands and prayed in a loud voice:

"O Father Zeus, almighty and most glorious, lord of Ida! O Sun, who seest all things and hearest all things! O Rivers and Earth, and ye two who in the world below punish after death men who swear a false oath![5] Be you witnesses, keep this oath sacred! If Alexandros shall kill Menelaos, then let him keep Helen and all her wealth, and we will return home with our fleet. But if Menelaos shall kill Alexandros, the Trojans shall give up Helen and all her wealth, and they shall pay to the Argives such compensation as is proper, such as may be noised abroad in generations to come. And if the compensation shall not be paid by Priam and Priam's sons when Alexandros falls, then I will fight for satisfaction, and here I will stay until I shall end the war."

Then he cut the throats of the lambs and laid them upon the ground, struggling and gasping for breath when the knife had taken their strength away. The wine was drawn from the bowl

[5] Zeus of the underworld (Hadês) and Persephone, p. 111.

and poured into the cups, and they offered prayer to the death-less gods. This was the prayer of Trojans and Achaians alike:

"O Zeus, almighty and most glorious, and all ye immortal gods! If either of our nations hurt the other against this oath, may their brains run out on the ground like this wine, theirs and their children's, and may their wives be servants to others!" But Zeus Cronion did not bring that yet to fufilment.

Now Priam Dardanidês spoke:

"Hear me, Trojans and Achaian men of war! I am going back to the city since I cannot endure to see my dear son fighting with Menelaos. Zeus knows, the gods know, which of the two is destined to die!"

He took the lambs with him, and entered the chariot and picked up the reins; Antenor took his place beside him, and they drove away.

But Hector and Odysseus first measured out a space, then put lots in a helmet and shook them for the first spearcast. The men of each side lifted up their hands and prayed:

"O Father Zeus, almighty and most glorious, lord of Ida! Whichever of these two brought the troubles upon both our nations, grant that he may perish and go down to the house of Hadês, and grant that we may have friendship and keep this oath!"

Then Hector shook the helmet, looking behind him; in a moment the lot of Paris leapt out. The others all sat down in ranks beside their horses and armour; while Alexandros armed himself. First he put on his fine greaves with silver anklets. Next a corselet across his chest, his brother Lycaon's which fitted him. Over his shoulders he slung the sword with silver knobs, then a strong broad shield, and upon his head a fine helmet with horsehair plume that shook fit to frighten a man! Last he caught up a spear that suited his grip. Menelaos also armed himself in the same way.

Now the two strode out into the middle, with grim looks that struck awe into all beholders. They came to a stand in the measured space, shaking their spears at each other in defiance. Alexandros first cast his spear; Menelaos caught it neatly upon the shield. The spear did not break through the metal, but the point was bent.

Menelaos had the second shot, and before he cast he made his prayer to Father Zeus:

"O Lord Zeus, grant vengeance upon Alexandros, who has wronged me unprovoked! Bring him low by my hand, that many a man may shudder in long generations to come, at the thought of wronging a friend who shows him hospitality!"

He balanced the spear, and cast it, and struck the shield of

Alexandros. Right through the shield ran the stout spear, tore right through his corselet, and cut through the tunic along his side; but he swerved away from his death. Then Atreidês drew his sword, and stretching over struck the horn of the helmet; but the blade broke upon it in three or four splinters and fell from his hand. Atreidês groaned, and looked up to heaven crying:

"O Father Zeus, such an unkind god as you there never was! You do spoil everything! I did think I had paid out that scoundrel, and here is my sword broken in my hand, and my spear missed and never touched him!"

He made one leap and caught hold of the horsehair plume, turned and dragged Alexandros towards his own ranks; the helmet-strap choked him, pulled tight under his chin. And Menelaos almost got him—a glorious victory it would have been! But Aphroditê saw it and broke the strap, so all he got was the empty helmet. He threw it over with a swing to his friends, and leapt back to kill his enemy with the spear; but Aphroditê carried him off in a thick mist, as a god can easily do, and put him down in Helen's sweet-scented chamber.

Now she took the shape of an old woman who used to comb wool for Helen in her old home before she left Lacedaimon, one whom she dearly loved. In this shape she went in search of Helen. She found her on the battlements with a crowd of women, and plucked her by the skirt. "Come here!" she said, "thi man wants tha at home. He is in thi room, on the bed, all finery and shinery! That'st never think he's fresh from fighten a man! More like just come from a dance, or just goen maybe!"

These words stirred Helen's temper. Now she knew the goddess by her beautiful throat and lovely breast and shining eyes! She was amazed, and cried out:

"This is strange indeed! Why do you wish to befool me? Will you carry me away somewhere still farther off, to some city of Phrygia or Meionia, where you have another friend among the sons of men! I suppose Menelaos has killed him, and wants to take me home, the woman whom he hates. I suppose that's why you are here with more of your tricks and schemes. Go and sit by him yourself. Forget the way to Olympos, and never let your feet feel it again! Fuss about the man, take good care of him, and perhaps he will make you his wife one day, or his slave at least. To that place I will not go—it would be a shame. I will not make his bed! What will the Trojan women say? and I have troubles enough already."

The goddess flew into a rage and said:

"Don't try me too far, hard-hearted woman! or I may be angry and leave you, and hate you as much as I love you desperately now! I may make Trojans and Danaäns hate each other like death, so that you will have a cruel fate between them!"

Helen was terrified, and followed her in silence, wrapping her robe close about her; the other women saw nothing. When they reached the house, her attendants turned to their work and she went up to her room. Aphroditê all smiles, put a chair for her in front of Alexandros; and there Helen sat down. But she turned her eyes away, and said with contempt:

"You have come back from the battle. I wish you had died there, and a strong man had killed you—he that was my husband before you! It was your boast once that you were the better man in fair fight. Then go and challenge Menelaos to fight again!—But no, I advise you not to try. Fight no duel with Menelaos; leave him alone, don't be a fool, or perhaps you may go down before his spear."

Paris answered:

"You need not scold me, my dear. This time Menelaos has won because Athena helped him. Next time it will be my turn; for I have my gods too. Let us love and be happy! I was never so much in love before, not even when I carried you off in my ship from Lacedaimon, and we shared our first love in that island. I am more in love with you now than ever, and I want you more!"

So saying, he lay down on the bed, and she came to him.

While they lay there together, Menelaos was striding up and down like a wild beast, looking everywhere for Alexandros. But no one could show him a glimpse of Alexandros among the Trojans or their allies. Not for love! They were not going to hide him if they did see him; for they all hated him like black death. At last my lord Agamemnon said before them all:

"Take notice, Trojans and Dardanians and allied nations! Victory lies with Menelaos, as you see. Your duty is then to hand over Helen and all her wealth, and pay whatever compensation is right and proper, such as may be noised abroad in generations to come."

And all the Achaians raised a cheer.

BOOK IV

The first battle between Trojans and Achaians

T HE GODS WERE ALL IN THEIR PLACES ON THE GOLDEN FLOOR, sitting with Zeus in conclave. Hebê went round with the nectar, and they pledged one another with their golden goblets, while they watched what was going on before Troy. Suddenly Zeus thought he would tease Hera a little, and he said in a mocking tone, to draw her:

"Two of our august company are allies of Menelaos, I mean Hera, who backs Argos of course, and our Boiotian guardian Athena.[1] But here they are both, keeping out of the way and watching the show with great enjoyment. And there is the enemy, there is Aphroditê always beside him, all smiles, keeping off the shots! Look there now—she has just saved him, when he thought he was a dead man. But there's no doubt victory goes to Menelaos. Let us consider what is to be done. Shall we make them begin the war again and fight it out? Or shall we make them friends? If that is good and pleasing in the sight of all, the city of Priam may still remain inhabited, and Menelaos can take his Helen back to Argos."

Athena and Hera were close together, plotting trouble for Troy. When he said this, they were both furious, and grunted something. Athena held her tongue, but Hera could not find room for all that fury inside her, and she cried out:

"O you dreadful creature, what a thing to say! How can you wish me to waste all my trouble for nothing! How I sweated and sweated! All my drudgery thrown away, the horses tired out with collecting the people, to destroy Priam and his sons! Go on, do as you like, but let me tell you, we do not *all* agree!"

Zeus Cloudgatherer was angry himself now. He said:

"O you amazing creature! What harm has Priam or Priam's sons done to you, that you never cease trying to make a wilderness of the noble city! Go through the gates, go into the fortress, munch up Priam raw with Priam's sons and all his people, and then perhaps you could cure that fury of yours!

---

[1] He calls Hera the Argive because she had a very ancient shrine in Argos. Athena is called Alalcomaneïs in allusion to a little shrine in Boeotia, but the word means guardian.

"Very well, do as you please. I have my fears that this quarrel may leave a bitter grudge between us. But one thing I tell you, and don't forget it. If I ever want to destroy some city where you have friends of yours, do not try to thwart my vengeance but leave me alone. I will not be the only one to say yes when I wanted to say no. For of all the cities of mortal men which are built under the stars of heaven, I have always loved best sacred Ilios, and King Priam, and the people of that fine old soldier king! My altar there never lacked public feast, or the savour of burnt-offering and drink-offering which is our solemn right."

His Queen opened her great eyes wide, and said:

"I tell you, there are three cities which I love best, Argos, and Sparta, and the broad streets of Mycenai: sack them all, whenever you take a dislike to them! I tell you, I do not defend them or care about them! For even if I grudge it and ask you to spare them, what is the use of my grudging? You are much stronger than I am. Still I have my rights too, my trouble ought not to go for nothing; since I am a god too—of the same birth as yourself, eldest daughter of Crookmind Cronos, eldest and most honourable, both by birth and because I am called your wife, and you are lord of the immortals. Come then, let us give way to each other, I to you, and you to me; then all the others will go with us. But now be quick and send down Athena to the battlefield; let her contrive somehow to get the Trojans to break the oath, and attack those overproud Achaians before the others can!"

Zeus did not refuse. He told Athena in plain words what he wanted: "Look sharp, go right into the battle, and contrive somehow or other to get these Trojans to break their oath and attack before the others can!"

Athena was only too glad to do it, and shot down from the peaks of Olympos. Like a blazing star which the lord of heaven shoots forth, bright and scattering sparks all around, to be a portent for sailors or for some great army of men, so Pallas Athena shot down to earth and leapt into the throng, to the amazement of Trojans and Achaians both. You might have heard one man say to another, "This means more battles and hard fighting!"—or else, "Here is friendship set up between us by Zeus the dispenser of war!"

Athena now took the form of a Trojan, the doughty warrior Laodocos Antenor's son, and went about searching for Pandaros. She found him standing among the ranks of targeteers who had marched with him from Aisepos river, and she spoke to him plainly:

"Will you take my advice, and show your good skill? Then dare to have a quick shot at Menelaos! This will give you great credit, and all the Trojans will thank you, most of all Prince Alexandros. He will be the first to heap rewards upon you, if he sees that mighty man of war, King Menelaos, brought down by your arrow and laid out on a funeral pyre. Come along, have a shot at Menelaos! And offer your vow to Apollo Lycegenês Prince of Archers, that you will make a solemn sacrifice of firstling lambs when you return home to the sacred city of Zeleia."

He let himself be persuaded, poor fool! and at once he stript his bow. This was a bow made of the polished horns of a wild ibex, which he had once caught while out hunting; he had shot it through the chest as it came from behind a rock, and knocked it back upon the rock. The two horns measured sixteen hands from the head. A skilful horner had worked it and fitted the pieces together, polished them up, and put a gold hook on the top.

Pandaros steadied the end on the ground and strung the bow, then laid it down carefully, while his friends held their shields before him, for fear that the Achaians might get up to their feet before Menelaos was hit. Then he stript off the quiverlid, and chose a feathered arrow which had never been shot, a carrier of black pains indeed! Without delay he fitted the arrow to the string, and made his vow to Apollo Lycegenês Prince of Archers, that he would offer a solemn sacrifice of firstling lambs when he returned home to the sacred city of Zeleia. He took fast hold of the string and the notches together,[2] and drew back the string to his breast, the iron point to the bow. So he drew it into a great round: clang went the bow, jing went the string, out leapt the arrow, and flew sharp and fast, fierce to strike.

But the immortal gods did not forget you, Menelaos! And Athena first and foremost stood before you and saved you from the arrow's point. She just swept it away from the flesh as a mother sweeps away a fly from her sleeping child; and she made it go straight where the golden buckles of the belt were joined and the corselet was folded over. The arrow struck right on the buckle; through the belt it drove, through the corselet, and the loin-piece which he wore to protect his flesh from a thrust, his last and chief defence—it went through that also. And the arrow pierced his skin, so that red blood ran down from the wound over his thighs and shins and ankles.

The red blood on his fine white skin was like vermilion on ivory, when some clever craftswoman, Carian or Meonian, makes a cheekpiece for horses. See it stored in a treasure-chamber! Many a horseman would love to use it, but the treasure lies waiting for a king, to make the horse fine and the driver proud.

[2] He put his fingers along the notches which hold the feathers, and fitted the head of the arrow to the string. Thus he held arrow and string in his right hand.

My lord King Agamemnon shuddered when he saw the red blood running out of the wound; Menelaos himself shuddered, but when he noticed that barbs and binding were outside, he recovered his spirits again. Agamemnon groaned deep as he caught his brother by the hand, and the men groaned; then he said:

"Dear brother, it was death for you when I swore that oath and put you in front of the fight as our champion! For the enemy have shot you and trampled their oath underfoot. But an oath is not an empty form, nor is the blood of lambs, and drink-offerings, and hands clasped, in which we put our trust. For even if the Olympian does not act at once, he will act at last, and a heavy price men have to pay—their own heads, their own wives and their children. I know full well in my heart of hearts that a day shall come when sacred Troy shall perish, and the people of Priam the mighty king; when Zeus Cronidês, enthroned on high in the heavens, himself will shake his black mantlet over them in wrath for this deceit. This indeed shall be, and shall not fail; but you will bring dreadful pain upon me, Menelaos, if you die now and fill up your count of days! In deep disgrace I should return to Argos; for our people would at once remember their native land, and we should leave to Priam and his Trojans their boast, our Argive Helen! But your bones would lie in the enemy's land and rot there, with your work undone; the Trojan's would stamp in triumph on the tomb of Menelaos and cry aloud, 'I wish Agamemnon the same good luck against his other enemies as he has had here with his contemptible army! Just look now! he has sailed away with empty ships, and left brave Menelaos behind!' But if that should ever come true, may the earth open and swallow me up!"

Menelaos made light of it, and said:

"Take courage, and don't alarm the men. It is not a mortal wound. The belt saved me first, and then my kilt underneath and the good armourer's work of the loin-piece."

Agamemnon answered:

"God grant it, my dear man. But we must see to this wound. The surgeon shall feel it, and put some stuff in to ease the pain." Then he called out, "Talthybios! Bring Machaon here as quick as you can. You know the fellow, Asclepios' son, the surgeon, and a good one too. Let him see to King Menelaos. Some one has shot him with an arrow. Some Trojan, or some Lycian it will be, they are good archers. And it was a fine shot, I must say! but bad luck for us."

Talthybios went off at once, looking everywhere in the lines for Machaon. At last he found him standing among his own targeteers, the men from Trica. Talthybios came up and told him plainly what had happened. "Quick, Asclepiadês, King

Agamemnon wants you, to have a look at our commander
Menelaos. Some one has shot him with an arrow, a Trojan or
some good Lycian archer. He says it was a fine shot, but bad
luck for us!"

Machaon was alarmed, and together they made their way
through the lines. Soon they reached the place where the
wounded man stood with a crowd of nobles round him. Machaon pulled out the arrow, and the barbs broke in the belt as
he pulled it back. Then he loosened the belt and the kilt and
loin-piece underneath. He found the wound, and sucked out the
blood, and put on a plaster of soothing drugs; these were drugs
which dear old Cheiron[3] had given to his father, and he knew
them well.

While they were attending to Menelaos, the Trojans began
to come on under arms, and so the Achaians armed themselves
and prepared for battle. Then you would not see Agamemnon
napping, or shirking, or unready to fight! No, he was all eagerness for battle and glory! He left car and snorting horses in
charge of his man Eurymedon, and ordered him strictly to keep
them at hand until he should want a rest from his labours. Then
he marched through the ranks on foot to give his orders. If he
found the men brisk and lively, he encouraged them with a few
words:

"Stick to it, men, to it with all your might! Liars will not
have Father Zeus to help them! Those who began it, those who
broke their solemn oath, shall be a dainty meal for the vultures!
And we will take their city and carry off their wives and children in shiploads!"

But if he found any slack, and cursing the war, he rated them
roughly:

"Call yourselves fighting men? Long distance champions with
the bow is what I call you![4] A disgrace to the army! Have you
no shame? Why do you stand there like a herd of deer, tired
with running about all over the place, dazed and helpless? Yes,
you stand there dazed and afraid to fight! Perhaps you are waiting till the enemy come as far as your ships. Fine ships, aren't
they, all along the shore! You want to see whether God will
spread his hand over you!"

So he went through the army, giving his orders to all. By-
and-by he came to the Cretans, who were arming under their
captain, Idomeneus. He was in the front rank, furious as a wild
boar; Meriones was speeding up the rear. This was a pleasant
sight to the King, and he said in a friendly tone:

---

[3] Cherion the Centaur, who knew all the secrets of herbs and the
arts of healing.

[4] The archer was thought a coward as compared with the fighting
man.

"Idomeneus, you are the man for me! first at a feast, and first in the field! Here you are, hard at work, and what when the big men have a banquet, and bring out the best company wine to fill the flowing bowl? The others drink what is given them, but you always have a full bumper by your side as I do, and as much as you like to drink. Now then, hey for battle, and keep up your reputation!"

Idomeneus answered:

"Sir, I will not fail you; I am your loyal servant, as I promised and gave my pledge to be. But you should speed up the others and let us get to fighting as soon as we can. For the Trojans have broken their oath. Death and disaster shall be their lot, because they began it by breaking that oath!"

Agamemnon left him well satisfied; and next he came upon the great Aias and his little namesake, who were arming themselves amid a cloud of footmen. Thick black clumps of sturdy younkers moved towards the battle, bristling with spears and shields, like some heavy cloud blown over the deep by the west wind; the goat-herd sees it afar from his watching-place, blacker than pitch over the deep as the whirlwind drives, and he shudders and guides his herd into a cave. My lord Agamemnon was glad to see this sight, and he told them what he thought in plain words:

"You need no pressing from me, you doughty pair of captains. That you do for yourselves, and on your people go. O Father Zeus, Apollo, Athenaia! I wish all the others had the same temper! Then King Priam's castle would soon bow down its head, and we should sack it and lay it waste with our hands!"

He passed on to Nestor, and found him amongst his Pylians, giving orders in that sonorous voice, placing his men and sending them out under his captains—Pelagon and Alastor, Chromios and Haimon and Prince Bias. In front he put the cars with horses and drivers, behind them the footmen in formidable array, like a wall, with the cowards in the middle so that they would have to fight whether they liked it or not. He was giving his orders first to the men in the chariots, to keep their horses in hand and not to go rattling about in the mellay. "Don't try to show off your driving and your courage. No one is to dash out in front and fight by himself, no one is to move to the rear: keep your line, or you'll only be the weaker. But if any one comes within reach of an enemy car, try a spear-thrust, that's the way to fight.[5] Many a strong city has been taken by those tactics."

The old man had seen war before, and he knew all about it. Agamemnon was glad, and he told him plainly how he felt:

"You may be old, sir, but I only wish your knees were as

[5] Do not get out, and do not throw the spear.

nimble and your strength as firm as the temper in that heart of yours! Ah, well, such is life. Old age is old age. I only wish others were old and you were young!"

The old hero loved a good horse; and he answered:

"Ah, your Grace! I do wish indeed I were now as young as I was when I killed Ereuthalion! Well, well, the gods do not give us everything at the same time. If I was young then, I am old now. Never mind, I will be with the horses and tell these people what to do. Words are the privilege of an old man. Spearing with spears is the young men's work; they have more youth and more strength than I have."

Agamemnon passed on in great contentment. He found Menestheus standing amongst his warlike Athenians. Not far off was Odysseus and the Cephallenian division. These were no weaklings, but they had not heard the call to arms, for the opposing armies had only just begun to move; and they stood waiting until some other battalion should come up and give them a lead. But Agamemnon rated them soundly, and left no mistake as to his feelings:

"You, Menestheus! What would your royal father say to see you here?—And you, the master of mischievous tricks, what cunning scheme is hidden in your mind? Why do you both skulk in the rear, and wait for a lead? You ought to be standing right in front and facing the fire! You are always first to hear my invitation whenever we give a dinner to the great men. Then you are pleased to eat your roast beef and to drink your nice wine at your ease: now you would be pleased to see a dozen battalions go out before you to the fight!"

Odysseus frowned, and replied:

"What a thing to say, Prince! Bite it back, and let it stay behind your teeth. Do you say we are slack when our people go out to battle? You shall see for yourself if you like, and if such matters interest you, you shall see the father of Telemachos fighting in the enemy's front line. What you say is so much wind."

Agamemnon smiled when he saw him angry, and took back his words:

"No, no, Odysseus Laërtiadês. I know the master of stratagems! You do not want my scolding or ordering. I know the loyalty of your heart, for we are of one mind, you and I. Come along, we will make it all right by and by if any harm has been said; let us forget it, for God's sake."

He passed on, and the next he found was Tydeus' son, proud Diomedês, standing amongst his chariots and horses with Sthenelos Capaneus' son beside him. Agamemnon rated him too in plain language:

"What pity to find you skulking here, goggling your eyes

at the battlefield! What would your noble father have said!
It was not your father's way to skulk. He used to be first at the
enemy by a long way, as they say who saw him about the business. I never met him myself, never saw him, but they say he
had no equal. Once indeed he came to Mycenê, not in war—he
came as a guest with Prince Polyneicês to enlist men; for they
were besieging the sacred walls of Thebes. They begged hard
for volunteers, and the people were ready to go, but Zeus
changed their minds by showing unfavourable signs. So the
envoys went away and got as far as the river Asopos. There
they waited in the reeds and grass while Tydeus went on a
parley to Thebes. He found a party of the Cadmeians feasting
in the house of Eteoclês. There was Tydeus alone among a
host of Cadmeians, a stranger; but he feared nothing, he challenged them to trials of strength and beat them all easily by
the help of Athena. Then the Cadmeians were enraged, and
laid an ambush for him on his way home, forty lads with two
leaders, Maion Haimon's son and Polyphontês the son of
Autophonos. Tydeus made an end of these also; he killed them
all but one, whom he sent back. Maion was the man, and he let
him go in obedience to omens from heaven. Such a man was
Aitolian Tydeus; but his son is not so good on the battlefield,
although he is a better talker."

Diomedês made no answer, for he respected the King's re-
proof: but Sthenelos spoke out:

"My lord, do not say what is false when you know the truth.
We are better men than our fathers, and we are proud of it!
We took the fortress of sevengate Thebes, although we had a
weaker force against a stronger wall, because we trusted in the
help of Zeus and omens from the gods above: but our fathers
perished through their own reckless folly. So please don't put
them equal to *us*!"

But Diomedês frowned at him and said:

"Hold your tongue, old boy, and listen to me. I do not take
it ill that his Grace would urge the men to fight. He is our
commander and we are his men. He will have the glory if his
men destroy the sacred city of Ilios; he will have the grief if
his men are defeated. Come along, and let us join the battle!"

As he said the words, he leapt out of his car, and his armour
clanged loudly upon him. It was enough to strike fear into a
brave heart.

Then the Danaän battalions moved on to battle line after
line, as the long billows roll to the shore line after line when
the west wind drives: the swell gathers head far out on the
sea, then bursts on the land in thunder, rearing and curving its
crest about the headlands and spitting out the salt spray. So the
army moved, each mass with its own leaders; their words of

command were heard, and the rest marched in silence, so that you might think that all that mighty host were dumb men clad in shining armour.

But loud clamorous cries resounded throughout the Trojan host; for they had not one speech and one language, but a confusion of tongues, since they were called from many lands. They were like a huge flock of ewes innumerable standing in a wide farmyard to be milked, which bleat without ceasing as they hear the cries of their lambs. Arês marshalled the Trojans; Athena Brighteyes the others, along with Terror, and Rout, and Discord ever restless, sister and comrade of bloodthirsty Arês: she is little at first, then her crest rises, and she thrusts her head against the heavens while she strides upon the earth. So then Discord cast direful war among them, marching through the throng and multiplying troubles for mankind.

Now the two armies met, dashing shield against shield and spear against spear, fury meeting fury in the mailed ranks; the embossed bucklers clashing made a dreadful din. Here was groaning, there shouts of triumph, as men slew and men were slain, and the earth ran with blood. The uproar and the turmoil was like two great rivers in flood, pouring down a mass of water from the mountains into a deep ravine where two valleys meet, and the sound is heard far away by shepherds upon the hills.

First blood to Archilochos, who killed a Trojan champion in the front rank, Echepolos Thalysiadês. He struck the man on his horse-hair plume, and the spearpoint pierced his forehead running into the bone; darkness covered his eyes, and he fell flat like a tower in the mellay. When he fell Elephenor caught him by the feet, Elephenor Chalcodontiadês captain of the Abantians, and tried to drag him out under the spears, for he wanted to strip him of his armour; but the struggle was soon over, for while he was dragging the body with his own side uncovered as he stooped, Agenor saw him and ran him through with his spear. So Elephenor fell and died, and over his body there was sharp work between Trojans and Achaians, who leapt upon one another like wolves and knocked each other about.

Then Telemonian Aias struck down Anthemion's boy, the lusty lad Simoeisios. They called him Simoeisios because he was born beside the river Simoeis, while his mother was on the way from Ida with her parents to visit their flocks. He never repaid the son's debt to his parents, for he died young by the spear of Aias. As he stept out in front Aias struck him on the right breast by the nipple; the spear ran right through his shoulder, and he fell. There he lay like a poplar tree which has grown up in the hollow of a great marsh, a smooth stem with branches growing at the top; some cartwright has cut it down with his axe to bend into the felloe of a fine car, and there it lies drying on the river-bank. So lay Simoeisios, when Aias struck him down. Then Antiphos, one of the sons of Priam, cast a spear at Aias; he missed Aias, but hit Leucos, a good comrade of Odysseus, in the groin, as he was dragging the man away, so that he fell flat over the body and let go. Odysseus was enraged to see his friend fall. He strode forward to the place, looking round watchfully; and the Trojans shrank back as he cast his spear, and struck down a bastard son of Priam, Democoön, who had come at his father's summons from the mares at Abydos. That was the counterstroke for his friend's death. The spear pierced the man's temple, and darkness came over his eyes; he fell with a thud amid his crashing armour. Then the first ranks gave ground, and Hector with them; the Achaians cheering dragged away the slain and moved a long way forward.

But Apollo looked down out of Pergamos in anger, and called aloud:

"On Trojans, on! do not give way to Achaians! Their flesh is not stone or iron—volley away, and your points will cut their skins! And now there's no Achillês to fight for them—he is away by the ships, nursing his grievance in a bitter heart!"

The awful voice of the god resounded from the city walls, but Athena was in the field; up and down went most glorious Tritogeneia when she saw any giving way.

Then fate caught hold of Diorês Amarynceïdês. He was struck by a jagged stone on the right shin near the ankle: a Thracian captain threw it, Peiros Imbrasidês who came from Ainos. The cruel stone smashed the bones and both sinews, and the man fell backwards in the dust, holding out both hands to his friends as he breathed his last—for Peiros ran up and thrust him through by the midnipple; his bowels gushed out, and darkness came over his eyes. But as Peiros sprang back, Aetolian Thoas cast a spear at his breast and pierced the lung. Thoas ran up and pulled out the spear, then drew his sword and struck him right in the belly, which was his death. But he did not strip off the armour, for there were other Thracians round him, with the topknots on their heads and the long spears in their hands, who drove him back staggering, for all his size and strength. So these two lay in the dust together, Thracian captain beside the Epeian; and many others fell round about.

No one could make light of that battle, if any indeed were left untouched and unwounded, if Pallas Athena took him by the hand and led him through the midst, if she kept him free of hurt. For many Trojans and many Achaians fell on that day and lay prone in the dust side by side.

BOOK V

*How Diomedês did great deeds of valour, and wounded
Aphroditê and Arês himself*

NOW COMES THE TURN OF DIOMEDÊS TYDEUS' SON; FOR PAL-
las Athena gave him courage and boldness, to make him
come to the front and cover himself with glory. She kindled a
flame that blazed steadily from his helmet and shield, like the
star that shines brightest of all in late summer after his bath
in the Ocean. Such was the fire that blazed from the head and
shoulders of Diomedês, when she drove him through the midst
where the fighting was thickest.

There was one Darês among the Trojans, a man of substance
and worth, a priest of Hephaistos. He had two sons, Phegeus
and Idaios, both fine soldiers. These two came out to meet
Diomedês; they in their car, he on foot. When they came
within range, Phegeus began by casting a spear at Diomedês.
The spear passed over his left shoulder without touching him;
Diomedês countered with a cast which did not miss—it struck
the other full in the breast, and rolled him out of the car. Then
Idaios leapt out, but he durst not bestride his brother's body;
and he would never have escaped himself, but Hephaistos hid
him in darkness and saved him, that his old father might not
be wholly bereaved. Diomedês drove off the team, and gave it
in charge to his friends.

The Trojans were all dismayed at the fate of these two, one
dead beside his car, and one gone. Then Athena caught Arês
by the hand and said:

"Arês, Arês, you mensbane! you bloodthirsty fort-stormer!
Why can't we leave Trojans and Achaians to fight, and see
which of them Father Zeus will favour? Do let us two retire
and keep clear of the anger of Zeus!"

So she led Arês away, and found him a seat on the lofty
bank of Scamandros. Now the Danaäns drove back their
enemy; and each of the captains brought down his man. First
King Agamemnon: Odios the Halizonian chief was the first
to turn, and Agamemnon drove his spear between the shoulders
and out at the chest. He fell with a crash in his rattling armour.

Next Idomeneus brought down Phaistos, the son of Meion-
ian Boros from Tarnê. Idomeneus pierced his right shoulder as
he was mounting his car; he fell out of the car, and darkness
took him. While the grooms were stripping off his armour,
King Menelaos killed Strophios' son Scamandrios. A great
hunter he was, a mighty hunter; for Artemis herself taught him
to kill all the wild beasts which the mountain forest breeds.
But no help was there for him then from Artemis Archeress,
nor the long shots for which he was famous; Menelaos caught
him as he fled, and ran him through the back between the
shoulders. The spear came out through his chest, and he fell
on his face under his rattling armour.

Merionês again killed Phereclos. This was the son of Tecton
Harmonidês, an artist who knew how to make all sorts of
lovely and precious things with his own hands; for Pallas
Athena loved him well. It was he that built those fine ships for
Alexandros, the beginning of all the troubles, which were the
ruin of himself and all the people of Troy; for he knew nothing
of what God had ordained. Merionês chased him and caught
him and struck him in the right groin; the point ran through the
bladder under the bone. He fell groaning upon his knees, and
death covered him up.

Then Megês slew Pedaios. He was a bastard son of Antenor,
but the lady Theano brought him up as lovingly as her own
children to please her husband. Megês struck him on the sinew
behind the head, and the blade cut his tongue at the root and
went through the teeth. He fell in the dust, biting hard on the
cold metal.

Eurypylos Euaimon's son killed Hypsenor the son of Dolo-
pion. He was priest of Scamandros, honoured among the people as if he were himself a god. Eurypylos gave chase, and
with a sweep of his sword cut off the man's arm at the shoulder as they ran. The arm fell bleeding on the ground, and dark
death took his eyes, a cruel fate.

So the hard business of the fight went on. As for Diomedês,
you could not tell which side he belonged to, Trojan or Achaian.
For he stormed all over the plain, and the dense battalions of
the enemy rolled away in confusion before him; that great
company would not stand. It was like some winter torrent in
flood which thrusts away all dikes: no dike can hold it, no
walls of the fruitful orchards, when it comes with a sudden
burst swollen by the pouring rain, and beats down in ruin the
noble works of strong men.

When Pandaros saw Diomedês storming over the plain and
rolling the battalions before him, he aimed an arrow quickly at
him, and hit him on the right shoulder on the plate of the

corselet as he came rushing on. The sharp point ran right through, and the blood ran over the corselet. Then Pandaros shouted:

"On, Trojans, on my brave horsemen! I have shot the best of the Achaians! I do not think he will last long after that shot, if Lord Apollo really did send me here from Lycia!"

There was a boast for you! But the shot did not bring the man down. He drew back and stood in front of his horses, and said to Sthenelos:

"Wake up, old fellow, look sharp and get down from that car, and pull out this arrow from my shoulder."

Sthenelos was down with one leap at his side, and he pulled the arrow right through the shoulder. The blood shot out in a spirt through the tunic. Then bold Diomedês prayed aloud to his goddess:

"Hear me, O daughter of Zeus Almighty, Atrytonê! If thou didst ever stand by my father's side in friendship on the battle-field, now again show thy love to me, Athena! Grant me to come within spear-cast of that man, and to slay that man, who shot me unawares, and now declares boasting that I shall not long see the light of the sun!"

Pallas Athena heard his prayer. She made his limbs nimble, the feet and hands on him, and spoke in words that winged like arrows to the mark:

"Courage now, Diomedês, and fight away. For I have put your father's courage in your breast, the fearless courage of that shield-shaking master of horses! And I have taken away the mist which was upon your eyes, that you may know man from god. Then if some god comes here to try you, never fight against any god except Aphroditê. But if she comes into the field, you may wound her with your spear."

With these words Athena left him, and he returned to the front of the battle. If he had been eager to fight before, now he was three times as wild. He was like a lion when he has leapt into the sheepfold after the woolly flocks, and the shepherd has wounded but not killed him. But this only makes the lion more furious, and the shepherd defends the sheep no more, but slinks into the hut and leaves them helpless in panic: they huddle in heaps, and the maddened beast leaps out of the fold. So Diomedês maddened fell upon the Trojans.

Then he slew Astynoös and Hypeiron, one with a thrust through the breast, one with a sword-stroke on the collar-bone near the shoulder that shaved the shoulder clean off. These he left, and chased Abas and Polyeidos, the two sons of Eury-damas the old diviner of dreams. They never came back for the old man to read their dreams for them; but strong Diomedês killed them. Then he went after Xanthos and Thoön, the two sons of Phainops, whom their father loved well; but his old age was passed in sorrow, and he got no other son for his possessions. They were killed both and stript, and they left mourning and lamentation for their father; they lived not to be welcomed home from the war, and their kinsmen divided the goods.

Then he took two sons of Priam Dardanidês, Echemmon and Chromios, in the same chariot. As a lion leaps among cattle grazing under the trees and breaks the neck of a cow or heifer, so this unwelcome visitor smashed them out of their car, and stript them of their armour. The team he gave to his men to drive away.

When Aineias saw him running riot in the field, he went searching amid the mellay to see if he could find Pandaros anywhere. He found that formidable man, and said to him:

"Where is your bow now, Pandaros? where are your winged arrows? Where is that fame, in which you have here no rival and none in Lycia? Come now, lift up your hands to Zeus, and then have a shot at this man, who is master of the field. Look what damage he has done already, how many good men he has brought down. I wonder if he is some god who has a grievance against our people and wants a sacrifice: heavy is the wrath of God upon men!"

Pandaros answered:

"There speaks Aineias, the wise counsellor! Indeed yon man is exactly like Diomedês, if I may judge by the shield and the vizard, and I can see his horses. But I am not sure he is not really a god. If he is only a man, the clever son of Tydeus does not run mad like this without a god to back him. There must be some god beside him invisible, and he turned the shot aside even as it hit the man. For I have tried already, and I hit the right shoulder through the corselet-plate. I thought I should send him to Hadês, but yet I did not bring him down. It must be some angry god.

"And I have no horses here, and no car for my use. Yet my father has eleven fine chariots covered up carefully somewhere in his place, new-built, new-finished, with a pair of horses for each champing rye and barley in the stable. How often the old warrior advised me when I was coming here, to mount my car and drive my team, and take the lead in the battle! But I would not listen—I only wish I had! The truth is I wanted to spare the horses; I thought they might lack fodder in all this crowd of men, when they were used to plenty.

"So I left them behind and came as a footman, with only my bow and arrows. And they were to do no good, as it seems.

For I have already shot two of the champions, Tydeidês and Atreidês, and hit them fair and drew blood from both, but it only made them more lively.

"So it was bad luck when I took my bow from peg, on the day when I led my men to this beautiful city to please prince Hector. Well, when I get home again, and set my eyes on my native land and my wife and my tall house, if I don't break up these useless sticks with my own hands and chuck them into the fire, I will let a perfect stranger come in and chop off my head."

Aineias answered:

"No, no, don't say that. We shall do no good until you and I drive against the man and see what spears can do. Up with you into my car, and I'll show you what the horses of Tros are like.[1] They know how to put on the pace, into the battle or out of the battle! They will carry us safe to the city, if Zeus lets Diomedês win. Here, take whip and reins, and I will get out and do the fighting; or tackle him yourself and I will drive."

Pandaros answered:

"You take the reins, Aineias; the horses are yours, they will go better with a hand they know, if we have to run for it after all. They may take fright and run wild and refuse to carry us out of the battle, if they miss your voice, and then the man will leap on us and kill us both and drive off the horses himself. No, you must drive your own team, and I will face him with my spear."

So they got in and went off at a gallop. Sthenelos saw them coming and called out clearly:

"Diomedês, my dear old friend! Here are two strong men hot upon you! A pair of invincibles, Pandaros the crack bowman—you know, Lycaon's son, and Aineias, whose father is Anchises, and his mother is Aphroditê herself! Here's the car —let us be off, and don't go storming about in front like this or you may lose your life!"

Diomedês said with a frown:

"Don't talk of running away, for I will not listen to you. Shirking and lurking is not in my blood; I am not a coward yet. I don't care to use a car, I will stay as I am and face them: Pallas Athena forbids me to fear. As for these two, their horses shall not save them both, if one does get away.—And look here a minute, there is something else. If Athena vouchsafe to me out of the riches of her grace to kill them both, you leave our horses here and just hitch the rein over the handrail; then be sure to make a dash for those horses of Aineias and drive them safely away. You know that they come of that stock which

[1] Tros, the grandson of Dardanos, gave his son Ganymedês to Zeus in return for a gift of divine horses, which began a famous breed.

Zeus Allseeing gave Tros as the price of his son Ganymedês, because they were the best of all horses under the sun; and my lord Anchisês stole a spat of that breed, when he put his mares to them without asking leave of Laomedon. They brought him six colts in the stable. Four of them he kept and fed at the stall, two he gave to Aineias, and they *can* go! If we could get those two, it would be grand!"

As they talked together the others came galloping near, and Pandaros called out:

"You are a hardy one, you are a clever one, a worthy son of Tydeus! Sure enough my shot did not bring you down—my sharp arrow! Now then I will see whether my spear will have better luck!"

With these words he cast his spear and hit Diomedês on the shield: right through it the point went and struck the corselet. Then Pandaros shouted:

"A hit! right through the side! and I don't think you will last long now. Victory for me!"

Diomedês answered undismayed:

"A miss, not a hit! But I think you two will never give over till one of you at least shall fall, and give a surfeit of blood to the strong-shielded God of War!"

Then he threw. Athena guided the point upon the man's nose beside the eye; it ran through his white teeth and cut off the root of the tongue, and the blade came out under his chin. He tumbled out of the car in his rattling armour, gleaming and flashing in the sun. The horses shied, and there his life and courage vanished away.

Now Aineias leapt out with shield and spear, to save the body from the spoilers. He bestrode his friend like a strong lion, spear and shield well in front, ready to kill any one who should face him and shouting defiance. But Diomedês lifted a large stone, such as two men could not lift as men are now, but he handled it easily by himself. This he crashed down upon the hip of Aineias, where the thigh turns in the socket, what they call the cup; the jagged stone smashed the cup and burst both the sinews, and tore away the skin. The hero fell forward on his knees and leaned with one hand upon the ground: then black night covered his eyes.

And that would have been the death of my lord Aineias; but his mother Aphroditê saw what had happened to her son. She threw her white arms about him and covered him with a fold of her shining robe, to shelter him from the blows of any who might wish to kill him.

But Sthenelos had not forgotten what Diomedês had told him to do. He left his own horses out of danger, hitching the reins over the handrail; then he dashed at Aineias's horses and drove them away to his own people. These he sent back to the camp in charge of Deïpylos, his familiar friend and the nearest to his heart, then quickly got into his own car, and galloped after Diomedês. But Diomedês was following Aphroditê, spear in hand. He knew she was a timid goddess, not one of those who lord it in men's battles, not Athena, or city-sacking Enyo. At last after a long chase he caught her, leapt on her and thrust, and wounded the skin of her soft hand. The spear tore through that incorruptible robe which the Graces themselves had made for her, and pierced the flesh just above the palm of her hand. The blood ran out, that immortal blood of the gods, the ichor which runs in those blessed veins; for they eat no bread and drink no wine, therefore they are bloodless and never die. She shrieked aloud, and dropt her son; but Phoibos Apollo picked him up and saved him in a black cloud, so that no enemy could strike him and take his life.

Then Diomedês shouted to the goddess:

"Away from the battle, you daughter of Zeus! Isn't it enough that you beguile weak women? But if you *will* visit the battle-field, I think after this a battle will make you shiver if you hear only its echoes in the distance!"

She hastened away raving in her agony. Iris took her out of the throng as swift as the wind; she was in great pain, the pretty flesh was stained. Soon she found Arês sitting on the left of the battle near a cloud, with spear and horses. She fell on her knees begging and praying her brother for the loan of his horses— "Brother dear, do help me and lend me your team! I want to go home to Olympos! This hurts me too much—this wound! A mortal man did it, Tydeidês—and he's quite ready now to fight Father Zeus himself!"

Arês let her have the horses, and she climbed into the car much distressed; Iris followed and took the reins, and touched up the horses, and they flew with a will. They soon reached the heights of Olympos, safe at home. Then Iris loosed the horses and gave them their ambrosial fodder.

But Aphroditê threw herself on her mother's lap. Dionê took her daughter in her arms, and stroked her with her hand, and said:

"My dear child! which of the sons of heaven has treated you like this, you poor innocent, as if you had been caught doing something naughty?"

Aphroditê answered—and where are her smiles now?—

"O my wound! Diomedês hit me! that bully! because I was trying to save my own son Aineias, my darling favourite! This war of Trojans and Achaians has become a war of Achaians against gods!"

Dionê said:

"Make the best of it, my love, be patient even if it hurts. Many of us Olympians have had to make the best of what men do, and we have brought much trouble upon one another. Arês made the best of it, when Otos and Ephialtês made him their prisoner—they shut him up in a brazen jar for thirteen months. Indeed, that would have been the end of Arês the greedy fighter, if their stepmother Eëriboia had not brought the news to Hermês; and Hermês stole him away, when he was already in great distress from his cruel prison.

"Hera made the best of it, when mighty Heraclês shot her in the right breast with a three-barbed arrow; and she had to bear pain intolerable.

"Hadês the tremendous made the best of it, when that very same man—the son of Zeus Almighty, you know—shot him in Pylos among the dead men, and the sharp arrow hurt him sorely. He went up to Olympos in his trouble, pierced with cruel pains, for the arrow had run through his shoulder and distressed him. Paiëon put on a plaster of soothing simples and made it well, for Hadês could not die.

"O that hard violent man! that worker of evil! who distressed the Olympian gods with his arrows! And now you—but Athena set the man on you. Silly fool, he has not sense enough to know that he who fights with the immortals has not long to live; he will never come home from the war, his children will not climb on his knees and daddy him. Then let this Diomedês take care; he may be very powerful, but a stronger foe than you may meet him. One day his loving wife may waken the household with lamentations when she misses her wedded husband, the best man of the Achaian host. So much for the queenly Aigialeia, so much for Diomedês, who knows so well how to manage a horse!"

While she spoke she was wiping away the ichor from the wounded wrist with both her hands. The arm grew whole, the throbbing pains were assuaged.

Athena and Hera were looking on, and now they began to tease Zeus Cronidês with their raillery. Athena led off:

"Father Zeus, will you be angry if I say something? I feel sure Cypris has been tempting some Achaian woman to join the Trojans whom she loves now so desperately. She must have been fondling one of their pretty frocks, and scratched her little hand on a golden brooch!"

He smiled at that, the great Father of gods and men, and calling Aphroditê to him, he said, "My dear child, war is not your department. Leave all that to Arês and Athena, and busy yourself with marriage and love."

While they were talking like this together, the bold Diomedês had leapt upon Aineias, although he perceived that Apollo was holding his arms above the man. He did not trouble about the great god, but wanted only to kill Aineias and strip off his armour. Three times he leapt at the man to kill him, three times Apollo beat back his shield; but when he came on the fourth time like a devil, Apollo shouted at him with a loud cry:

"Beware, Diomedês! Forbear, Diomedês! Do not try to put yourself on a level with the gods; that is too high for a man's ambition. The immortal gods are one race, men that walk upon the earth are another."

Tydeidês moved back a step when he heard these words, fearing the wrath of Apollo Shootafar. And Apollo took Aineias away from the crowd, and set him down in Pergamos within his own temple. Then Leto and Artemis healed him and made much of him in the great sanctuary; while Apollo Silver-bow created a phantom like Aineias in armour like his, and let Achaians and Trojans batter one another upon their leathern shields and fringe-fluttering bucklers.

Then Phoibos Apollo called out to Arês:

"O Arês, Arês! you mensbane! you blood-thirsty fort-stormer! Go in now, will you, and drag out this man from the battle, this Diomedês, who is ready to fight against Father Zeus himself! First he tackled Cypris and wounded her wrist, then he made a leap at me like a devil!"

He stepped back, and took his seat on the citadel; and dreadful Arês went into the Trojan ranks, rallying them to the fight. He took the form of Acamas the Thracian captain, and called loudly to the sons of Priam:

"Now my young princes! how long will you let the Achaians kill and kill? Will you wait till they assault the city gates? There lies a man whom we honoured as high as Hector himself, Aineias Anchises' son. Come on, let us bring our good comrade out of the turmoil!"

Then Sarpedon cried out in reproach:

"Where is your old courage, Hector? I think you said you could hold the city without a crowd of allies, alone with your brothers and the rest of your family; but I don't see any of them now. I don't notice them here! No, they are like a pack of dogs shrinking away from a lion.

"*We* have to do the fighting; we your allies! I am one of your allies, and I came from far away. Yes, Lycia is far away, beside the eddying Xanthos; there I have left my own wife and little boy; there I have left all the goods I have, which all the have-nots covet. All the same I lead my Lycians, I am ready to fight any man, though there is nothing of mine here for Achaians to harry and lift. And there you stand, you don't even tell your people to defend their wives! A fine haul your enemies will have to play with, like fish caught in the meshes of a net! They will soon sack that noble city of yours. It should be your care night and day to make yourself pleasant to your allies. Go down on your knees and beg them to hold their ground firmly, and then you would have no reproach."

That stung Hector. He jumped out of his car, and went everywhere shaking his two spears, rallying all to the fight. Now they turned their faces toward the enemy, The Achaians stood firm, and battle was joined again. The chariots ran wheeling about, the horses' hooves beat up the dust, which drove in a great cloud to the brazen sky and covered the Achaians with white. The whole place was like some great threshing-floor, when the farm-hands are winnowing and throwing up their shovelfuls into the wind: Golden Demeter divides corn and chaff, and the chaff is blown away into white heaps. So they fought with might and main; and Arês covered the battle with darkness to help the Trojans. He was here and there and everywhere, doing his best for the Trojans, as Apollo had told him to do when he saw that Athena was gone; for she had been helping the Danaäns.

Apollo himself brought Aineias out of the sanctuary, and made him well and strong again. Then Aineias joined his friends; very glad they were to see him alive and hearty with all his limbs; but they asked no questions. They had quite enough to do with Silverbow and blood-thirsty Arês, and Discord, who gave them no peace.

The Danaäns were kept hard at it by Aias big and Aias little, by Odysseus and Diomedês. But they needed no driving; Trojans might storm, and Trojans might strike, they knew no fear. They stood immovable, like the clouds which Cronion masses upon the mountain-tops in fine weather, while all the blustering winds are asleep—Boreas and the other winds which scatter the dark clouds with their whistling blasts. There stood the Danaäns, and faced the enemy immovable, and Atreidês was among them with cheering words:

"Show yourselves men, my friends, and keep a stout heart! Think of your honour, with all men's eyes upon you! It is a shame to be a coward. He that fights and will not run may live to see another sun; he that runs and will not fight is bound to die—and serves him right!"

He cast a spear quickly, and hit the front man, Deïcoön Pergasidês, by the side of Aineias. The Trojans honoured him equally with Priam's own sons, because he was always quick to push to the front. The spear went through his shield and ran through the belt into the belly. The man fell with a thud under his rattling armour.

Then Aineias struck down the two sons of Dioclês, Crethon and Orsilochos, strong men both. Their father lived in Phera, a man of wealth, and sprung for Alpheios, the river-god. This river flows through the Pylian country. The god begat Orsilochos, who was king over a great people; Orsilochos begat Dioclês, a stout warrior himself, and so were his twin sons. These two when they grew up to manhood sailed for Ilios with the fleet, to avenge the wrong of Agamemnon and Menelaos: and there they found their deaths. So one might see a couple of young lions bred in the mountain forests, which ravage the folds and carry off cattle and sheep, until they are killed at last by the hand of man. And here the hands of Aineias brought them low, and they lay like two fallen fir-trees.

Menelaos saw them fall; he was sorry for the lads, and strode through the press shaking his spear. Arês himself had made him angry, because he wished Aineias to kill him. But Nestor's son Antilochos caught sight of the King; he was anxious that nothing should happen to him and so they might waste all their labours, and he came up just as the two were face to face ready to begin, and stood beside him. When Aineias saw two instead of one, he did not wait, although he was no mean warrior. The two dragged away the dead bodies and handed the poor devils over to their people, and then returned to the fight.

There they killed Pylaimenês, the Paphlagonian captain. Menelaos struck him standing with a spear-thrust through the collar-bone; Antilochos cast a stone at his driver, Mydon Atymniadês, as he was managing the horses in his chariot, and struck his elbow. He dropt the reins, and Antilochos, leaping upon him, drove his sword through the man's temple. He rolled out gasping, and tumbled half-over with head and shoulder dangling in the dust. There he stuck a long time—for the dust was deep—until the struggling horses kicked him out into the dust. Then Antilochos whipped them up and drove them to the rear.

Hector spied them across the ranks, and made for them with shouts, while a strong body of his men followed. Arês and Enyo were in front, she carrying the merciless din of war, Arês wielding a monstrous spear, and showing himself now before Hector, now behind.

Diomedês shuddered when he saw Arês. As a man after a long march stops helpless when he sees a furious river foaming and flowing along, and leaps back, so Diomedês leapt back, and cried out to his people:

"How could we admire Hector, my friends, and call him hero and champion! There is always some god beside him to keep him safe. See there is Arês now, in the shape of a mortal man. Keep your faces to the foe and move to the rear. We must not think of pitched battle against gods."

As he spoke the Trojans closed up. Then Hector killed two

good fighting men in one chariot, Menesthês and Anchialos. But big Aias saw them fall; he could not leave them there, so he made a stand beside them, and with his spear he struck down Amphios Selagos' son. This was a man rich in cattle and rich in corn, whose home was at Paisos; but fate had brought him to fight for Priam and his sons. Aias struck him in the lower belly through the belt. When he fell, Aias ran up to seize his arms, but he was met with a shower of spears, most of them falling on his shield. He set one foot on the body, and pulled out his own spear, but he could not strip off the body-armour in that shower of spears. He was afraid he might be surrounded by such a crowd of enemies strongly armed. They pushed him away from them, strong though he was, and he retired staggering.

So the turmoil of the battle went on. One fine strong man, Tlepolemos Heraclês' son, was driven by hard fate against prince Sarpedon. There the two men stood face to face, son and grandson of Zeus Cloudgatherer; and Tlepolemos said the first words:

"Sarpedon, you are a high councillor among your own people, but why must you be skulking here, an unwarlike fellow like you? They lie who say you are a son of Zeus, for you are far behind those who were sons of Zeus in former times. How different was the great Heraclês, my father, all-daring, lion-heart! He came to this place about Laomedon's horses with only six ships and a few men, and sacked the city of Ilios and made her streets a desert! But you are a coward heart, and your people are dwindling away. I don't think you will be much help to the Trojans after your journey from Lycia, even if you are very strong; but you shall be vanquished by me and go to the gates of Hadês."

Sarpedon answered:

"Tlepolemos, that great man destroyed Ilios because of the folly of Laomedon, who mocked him after honest service, and refused to give the horses which he had travelled so far to earn. As for you, I declare death and destruction shall be yours in this place; you shall be vanquished by my spear, you shall give glory to me and your soul to Hadês!"

As he spoke, Tlepolemos lifted his ashen spear, and both let fly at the same moment. Sarpedon struck his man in the neck; the cruel point ran right through, and dark night covered his eyes. The other spear eagerly pierced the left thigh of Sarpedon, grazing the bone, but his father still kept his life safe.

Sarpedon was carried out of the battle by his friends. The spear dragging along gave him great pain, but no one noticed it or thought of drawing it out to let him stand on his feet; they were in great haste, and had too much to do in looking after him. On the other side, Tlepolemos was carried away by the Achaians.

Odysseus was furious to see this, though he was a patient man. He was in two minds, whether he should go on in pursuit of Sarpedon, or kill more Lycians instead. But it was not ordained that Odysseus should slay the son of Zeus Thunderer, and Athena turned his mind to the Lycian crowd. There he killed Coiranos, Alastor, Chromios, Alcandros, Halios, Noëmon, Prytanis, and more he would have killed; but Hector saw him, and hastened to the spot, bringing terror with him. Sarpedon was glad indeed when he came near, and called out piteously:

"Priamidês, my friend, don't let them get hold of me! Help me, and then let me die in your city, since it seems I was never to return to my native land, or to make my wife happy and my little boy!"

But Hector passed by without a word; he was mad to drive the enemy back, and to kill many. So Sarpedon was carried on and laid under a noble oak tree; and there his friend Pelagon pushed out the spear from his thigh. Sarpedon fainted dead away, but he came to again, as the north wind breathed upon him and brought life back to his fainting spirit.

The Argives before Arês and Hector neither turned about, nor could they hold their ground, but they moved backwards facing the foe when they found Arês to be with their enemies.

And who was first slain, and who last, by Hector and brazen Arês? Teuthras, and then Orestês, Aitolian Trechos and Oinomaos, Helenos Oinopidês, and Oresbios in his flashing kilt, who used to live in Hylê, near the Cephisian lake, husbanding his wealth, near neighbour to the other Boiotians in their land of plenty.

But now Hera saw the Argives getting the worst of the battle; and she called out to Athena in plain words:

"Bless us all, Atrytonê! Aren't you the daughter of all-triumphant Zeus? and is our word to go for nothing? We promised Menelaos that he should destroy Ilios, and are we going to let Arês ruin everything in this mad way? Let us see if our help can mend matters."

Athena was willing enough. Then Hera ran about harnessing the horses, and putting on their golden frontlets—Hera herself the Queen of heaven, daughter of mighty Cronos! Hebê fitted the wheels to the car, brazen wheels with eight spokes, at each end of an iron axle-tree. Each had a felloe of gold incorruptible, with a brazen tire fitted all round, wonderful things. Each had a nave of silver turning about the end of the axle-tree. The body was of gold and silver bands braided tightly, and there was a handrail curving round on each side. The pole in front was of silver; on the end of this Hebê fastened the golden yoke and hung the golden neck-straps. Lastly Hera led the horses under the yoke, hot for the battle.

Then Athena slipped off her soft linen robe, which she had made and embroidered with her own hands; it fell on her father's floor, and she put on the tunic of Zeus Cloudgatherer, and arrayed herself for the weeping work of war. Over her shoulders she cast the tasselled goatskin cape—an awful thing! for Panic is wreathed about it; Discord is there, Valour is there, blood-curdling Shock is there, and there is the Gorgon's head, that awful prodigy, awful and horrible, the sign and wonder of Zeus Almighty. Upon her head she put a helmet with two horns and four bosses, all of gold, and decorated with the champions of a hundred cities. She set her foot in the fiery car, grasping the spear, so heavy, huge, and strong, with which when she is angry she vanquishes battalions of fighting men, a true daughter of her mighty sire. Hera quickly touched up the horses. The celestial gates opened of themselves, groaning upon their hinges, those gates which the Seasons used to guard; for they have a charge of Olympos and high heaven, to close or unclose the solid cloud. There through the gates they drove the obedient horses.

They found Cronion sitting alone upon the topmost peak of Olympos. Then Hera drew up and said to him:

"Father Zeus, have you nothing to say to these violent doings of Arês? What a mort of men he's been killing, wiping out the whole Achaian nation, slap dash, most improper I declare, Cypris and Apollo Silverbow just enjoying themselves, quite at their ease, after setting on this idiot who won't keep the rules! Father Zeus, will you be angry with me if I beat him well and chase him out of the field?"

Zeus Cloudgatherer answered:

"Go along do, send Athena on the hunt, she knows how to make him smart."

Hera lost no time, but whipt up the horses, and away they flew with a will between earth and the starry sky. One leap of those whinnying thoroughbreds takes them as far as a watcher on the mountains can see into the dim distance over the waves. On the plain of Troy, where the two rivers Simoeis and Scamandros join their streams, Hera pulled up, and loosed the horses, and left them unseen in a thick cloud. Simoeis made a crop of ambrosia grow up for them to graze upon. Then the two goddesses scuttled along like a pair of pigeons, to the rescue of their friends, the Argives.

They found Diomedês in the midst of a throng of the best fighting men, who pressed close about him, furious as roaring lions or wild boars in all their strength. There Hera stood still, and taking the shape of Stentor, that greatheart with a trumpet-voice, who could shout as loud as any fifty men, she cried out:

"Shame on you, Argives, you are a disgrace to your good looks! Handsome is that handsome does! When Achillês showed himself in the field, not a Trojan would come outside the gates. They were too much afraid of that man's mighty spear! And now they have left Troy far behind, and here they assault you beside your own ships!" So she kindled a fiery temper in each one.

But Athena leapt to the place where Diomedês was among the chariots, cooling the wound of the arrow. He was holding up the broad strap of his shield, and wiping away the blood and sweat from his weary arm, for he was in great distress. The goddess took hold of his horses' yoke, and said:

"Ah, you are not much like your father Tydeus. He was a small man, but a fighter. I told him myself not to fight, and not to show off, that time when he was sent alone into Thebes to parley with the Cadmeians—I told him to feast away and sit quiet! But he had a spirit, then and always, and he challenged the young men and beat them all. But you! I stand by you and take care of you, and bid you to fight with all my heart; but perhaps you are tired out with your impetuous assaults? or can it be you are afraid? Then you are no son of Tydeus Oineidês!"

Diomedês answered:

"I know you, divine daughter of Zeus Almighty! So I will tell you the truth with all my heart. I am not afraid, I shrink from nothing, but I still remember your commands. I was not to fight with any of the blessed gods at all, except Aphroditê; but if she came into the battle, I was to give her a wound. That is why I now retreat, and why I have gathered all these men here: for I know Arês master of the battlefield."

Athena said:

"Diomedês, you are a man after my own heart. Don't be afraid of Arês or any other immortal! You shall see, I will be with you. Drive straight for Arês! Hit him hard; don't bow down to Arês, that mad furious creature, that graven image of wickedness, Mr. Facing-all-ways! Yesterday he stood up in front of Hera and me and vowed he would fight the Trojans and help the Argives, and now he is on the Trojan side and forgets all about that!"

So saying she pulled back Sthenelos and pushed him out of the car—out he jumped in a jiffy, and she got in beside Diomedês in great excitement. How the axle-tree groaned under the weight! for it carried an awful goddess and a mighty man. Athena grasped whip and reins, and away went the horses straight for Arês. At that moment he was stripping the armour from Periphas, covered with blood—Periphas Ochesios' son, a huge man, the first champion of the Aitolians; but Athena put on the hiding-cap of Hadês, for she did not want Arês to see her.

But Arês did see Diomedês; and as soon as he saw him, he left the dead man lying where he fell and went straight for Diomedês. He came up on the offside and let fly with his spear over yoke and reins; but Athena caught it as it flew past, and sent it harmless over the car. Diomedês followed up with a thrust at Arês, and Athena drove the spear straight into his belly where the kilt was girded: the point ran in and tore the flesh, and Diomedês pulled the spear back. Then Arês roared like a trumpet, as loud as nine thousand men could shout, aye, ten thousand men in the turmoil of battle! Trojans and Achaians alike trembled to hear the roar of the insatiate God of War!

What was this Diomedês now beheld? Sometimes after sultry heat a furious whirlwind arises, and you may see a great black mass blowing up from the clouds: that is what Diomedês beheld now—and it was Arês, blowing up through the clouds into high heaven. Instantly he was in Olympos where the gods do dwell! Down he sat by the side of Zeus in a miserable state, and showed him the immortal blood running from his wound, and said in a dismal tone without mincing words:

"Father Zeus, have you nothing to say to these violent doings? We gods have to put up with the most terrible things from one another, if we do a good turn to a man. And we're all against you, for you begat that crazy girl, curse her, who has always some mischief in hand. All the rest of our family obey you, we submit every one of us; but that girl—you don't care what she says or what she does, indeed you set her on, for she is your own child, confound her. Now see what she has done—put up this young bully Diomedês to run amuck against the immortal gods! First he wounds Cypris on the wrist, then he is on me like a devil. But I got away, thanks to my quick heels. I don't know how long I might have been there most uncomfortable among the damned corpses—or if I lived, I should be a cripple from those spear-prods!"

Zeus Cloudgatherer frowned at him, and said:

"Don't sit there whimpering, you Facing-all-ways, I won't have it. I hate you more than any other god alive. All you care for is discord and battle and fighting. You are just like your mother with that stubborn insufferable temper; it's all I can do to control her without using my hands. It is some plan of hers, I am sure, which brought you into all this. However, I will not let you suffer any longer, for you are my son after all. But if any other god had begotten such a nuisance, you should have been down below the heavenly host long ago."

Then he sent for Paiëon, the Healer; Paiëon put on a plaster of soothing simples and made him well, for he was not mortal. The wound healed over at once, just as you might drop fig-juice into a bowl of milk and it curdles as you stir. Hebê bathed him and dressed him up smart; and he took his seat beside Zeus Cronion quite happy and cheerful.

Soon Hera and Athena returned home, Hera the friend of Argos, and Athena, an ever present help in time of trouble, as soon as they had put an end to the murderous exploits of Arês the enemy of mankind.

BOOK VI

How Paris was brought back into battle, and how Hector parted from Andromachê

SO THE GREAT CONFLICT WAS LEFT TO THE TROJANS AND Achaians. This way and that way the battle moved over the plain between Simoeis and the estuary, as the two armies fought and struggled together.

Telamonian Aias was the first to show a gleam of hope for his side, when he broke into a Trojan battalion by striking down Acamas. This was a great strong man, Acamas Eussoros' son, the best man of the Thracians. Aias pierced through the helmet into the bone of his forehead, and darkness covered his eyes.

Next Diomedês killed Axylos Teuthranidês, whose home was in Arisbê. He was one wealthy and loved by all; for he lived near the highroad and entertained all who came. But none of all those was there that day to stand before him and shield him from death; no, they were both killed, he and his man Calesios who drove his car, both passed below the earth.

Euryalos brought down Dresos and Opheltios; then he went after Aisepos and Pedasos, both sons of Bucolion by the Naiad nymph Abarbareë. Bucolion was the son of Laomedon, his eldest son, but it was a secret love; he also lay with his nymph while tending the sheep, and she bore him the twin sons who were slain and despoiled by Euryalos Mecisteiadês.

Astyalos was killed by Polypoitês, Odysseus killed Pidytês, and Teucros Aretaon. Nestor's son Antilochos brought down Ableros, and King Agamemnon killed Elatos, whose home was on the banks of broad Satnioeis, in Pedasos on the hill. Leïtos caught Phylacos in flight, and Eurypylos stript Melanthios.

Then Menelaos took Adrestos alive; for his horses in head-long flight ran against a tamarisk branch and broke off the end of their pole. The horses galloped towards the city among the crowd of runaways; the master was rolled out over the wheel and fell on his face in the dust. Menelaos was beside him, spear in hand, and Adrestos clasped his knees and prayed for his life:

"Mercy, my lord king, and you shall have a good ransom! There is plenty of treasure in my father's house, bronze and gold and wrought iron. My father would gladly give a rich ransom to hear that I am alive in your camp!"

Menelaos was willing to agree; and he was just going to send him back when Agamemnon came running up, and called out loudly:

"Don't be so soft, Menelaos! What do you care for the man? Have you been so well treated by the Trojans? Then let no one escape death at our hands—not the boy in his mother's womb, spare not even him, but let all perish together out of Ilios, unlamented and unnoted!"

Thus he changed his brother's mind, as was right and proper. Menelaos pushed the man away, and Agamemnon thrust him through the side. He fell backwards, and the King set his foot on him and drew out the spear.

Then Nestor called out in a loud voice:

"Friends and Danaäns! you are the servants of Arês, and no one must linger and throw himself on spoils. Our business is not to go back to the camp laden, but to kill. Then you can strip the bodies lying dead, and get all that afterwards at your leisure."

So they fought on with fury, and the Trojans would have returned to their Ilios cowed and defeated but for Helenos Priamidês the great prophet of birds. He said to Aineias and Hector:

"The chief burden lies on you two, Hector and Aineias; Tro-jans and Lycians look to you, because you are the best men for every enterprise, in council or in the field, to fight or to provide. Then make a stand here. Go up and down and keep the men away from the gates, or they will run for it and throw themselves into the women's arms and leave the victory to our enemies. Once you have got the ranks in order, we will stand our ground and fight, weary as we are; for we cannot help it. Then you, Hector, go into the city, and tell our mother to collect the older women into Athena's temple upon the citadel; let her open the doors of the holy house, and lay on Athena's knees the finest and largest robe she has in her stores, the one she prizes most of all, and let her promise to offer

in the temple twelve yearling heifers that have never felt the
goad: only let the goddess pity our town and the wives and little
children of Troy, let her hold back Tydeus' son from sacred
Ilios—that wild warrior, that strong contriver of defeat, whom I
declare to be the mightiest champion of the enemy! Not even
Achillês was so terrible, although he is the son of a goddess as
they say. This man is all madness, and no one can match him."

Hector leapt out of the car at his brother's call. Shaking his
spears he went up and down, cheering and encouraging his
men, and rallying them to the fight. They turned at last and
faced their adversaries; then the Achaians gave way and ceased
their killing. Some god must have come down from heaven,
they thought, to help the Trojans, when they saw them rally.
And Hector cried in a loud voice:

"Brave men of Troy! noble allies and friends! Be men! and
hold your own stoutly, while I make my way into the city,
and tell our elders and counsellors, and our wives, to offer
prayer to the powers above and vow a solemn sacrifice."

With these words he left them, and as he marched the black
shield slung behind him struck its rim upon his ankles and
his neck.

Into the space between the armies came out Glaucos the
son of Hippolochos and Diomedês Tydeus' son, hot for a fight.
But as soon as they were close enough, Diomedês spoke first:

"Who are you, noble sir, of all men in the world? I have never
seen you before in the battlefield, but now here you are in front
of the whole host, bold enough to face my long spear! Unhappy
are they whose sons will face my anger. But if you are some god
come down from heaven, I had rather not fight against the gods
of heaven. Even Dryas' son, that strong man Lycurgos, did not
last long after he challenged the gods of heaven. He once drove
the nurses of mad Dionysos over the sacred Nyseian mount.
They all threw away their holy wands, when Lycurgos beat
them with an ox-goad; and Dionysos ran away and dived into
the sea, where Thetis received him in her arms all terrified, for
the man had frightened him out of his wits. Then the gods were
made angry in their life of peace, and Cronion struck the man
blind. He did not live long, after he had made himself an enemy
of the immortal gods; and I had rather not fight against the
gods, blessed be their name! But if you are a mortal and one of
those who eat the fruits of the field, come here, and you shall
soon be caught in the bonds of destruction!"

Glaucos answered undismayed:

"Proud son of Tydeus, why do you ask my name and generation? The generations of men are like the leaves of the forest. Leaves fall when the breezes blow, in the springtime others

grow; as they go and come agen so upon the earth do men. But if it is your pleasure to learn such a thing as that, and to know the generations of our house, which indeed many men know—there is a city Ephyra, in a nook of Argos the land of horses; and there lived Sisyphos the cleverest man ever born, Sisyphos Aiolidês. He had a son Glaucos, and Glaucos was father of the incomparable Bellerophontês. The gifts of the gods to him were handsome looks and noble manhood. But Proitos plotted mischief against him, and drove him from the land of Argos; for he was the stronger and Zeus had subdued the land under his sceptre.

"Now the wife of Proitos, the lady Anteia, was mad after him and wanted his love in secret, but she could not persuade Bellerophontês, being as he was a chaste man with an honourable heart. So she came to Proitos with a lying tale. 'Proitos,' she said, 'kill Bellerophontês, or die yourself! He tried to take me by violence!' The King was angry to hear this tale. Kill the man he would not, for he thought that an impious thing; but he sent him to Lycia with a dangerous token. He gave him a folded tablet with a message scratched on it in deadly signs, and bade him show it to his goodfather, that he might be put to death.[1]

"He travelled to Lycia, then, with the gods to guide him; and in Lycia, by Xanthos river, the king of that broad realm entertained him generously for nine days and killed nine oxen. Not until the tenth day dawned did he question him and ask to see any token that he brought from Proitos.

"When he received the fatal token, first he asked Bellerophontês to kill the ravening Chimaira. This creature came of divine stock, with nothing of man—lion in front, serpent behind, she-goat in the middle, and her breath was blazing fire. Bellerophontês slew her, encouraged by signs and omens from heaven. In the second place, he fought against the redoubtable Solymans; that was the hardest fight he ever fought against men, so he said. Thirdly, he destroyed those manlike women the Amazons. But when he was on his way back, the King wove another cunning plot. He chose the best fellows out of all the country and set them in ambush. But not one of them ever returned home, for Bellerophontês killed them all.

"So the King saw at last that he was a true son of the godhead. Accordingly he kept him there, and gave him his own daughter, and half of all his royal honour. The Lycian people allotted him the finest estate in the land, orchards and farms for his use. His wife bore him three children, Isandros and Hippolochos and Laodameia. Zeus lay with Laodameia, and she bore a son

[1] This is the only allusion in Homer to writing. But Shakespeare never once mentions printing.

Sarpedon, the warrior prince. But when at the end Bellerophontês gave offence to the gods,[2] he became a lonely wanderer on the Aleian plain, eating out his heart and shunning the paths of men. His son Isandros was killed by Arês when fighting against the Solymans; his daughter was killed by Artemis in anger; Hippolochos was my father, and I am his son. He sent me to Troy, and commanded me strictly always to be first and foremost in the field, and not to disgrace my fathers who were first and best, both in Ephyra and in broad Lycia. There you have my lineage, and the blood which is my boast."

Diomedês was delighted with this speech. He planted his spear in the ground, and said in a friendly tone:

"I declare you are my family friend from a long way back! Oineus once entertained the incomparable Bellerophontês in his house, and kept him there for twenty days. When they parted, they exchanged gifts of friendship; Oineus gave a girdle bright with crimson, Bellerophontês a double cup of gold—it was there in my house when I came away! But Tydeus I do not remember, for I was only a little tot when he left me, at the time when the Achaian army perished before Thebes. So I am your friend and host in Argos, and you are mine when I go to Lycia! Let us avoid each other if we happen to meet. There are plenty of Trojans and Trojan allies for me to kill, if God grants me to catch them, and plenty of Achaians for you to spoil if you can. Let us exchange armour, and show the world that we are family friends!"

They both dismounted and clasped hands, and swore friendship. Then Zeus Cronidês sent Glaucos clean out of his wits; for he gave his armour in exchange to Diomedês Tydeidês, golden for brazen, the price of a hundred oxen for nine.

When Hector got to the oak tree at the Scaian Gate, the women ran crowding round, asking news of husbands and brothers, sons and friends. He exhorted them each and all to make their prayer to heaven; but sorrows hung over many.

Then Hector went to Priam's noble palace with its portals and galleries of polished stone. There were fifty chambers built of stone standing side by side, where the sons of Priam slept beside their wives; his daughters and their husbands had twelve roofed chambers of stone, standing in a row on the opposite side of the courtyard. Here his gracious mother met him, leading Laodicê the most beautiful of her daughters. She clasped his hand, and said:

"Why have you left the battle, my boy?—They must be pressing you hard, those accursed invaders, and you thought you might lift up your hands in prayer to Zeus from our citadel. Just wait a bit and let me bring you some wine. Pour

[2] He tried to fly to heaven on the winged horse Pegasus.

a libation to Father Zeus and All Gods, and then it will do you good to have a drink yourself. You're tired out with defending your friends, poor dear. When a man is tired out, a drop of wine will make him stout!"

Hector answered:

"No wine for me, my dear mother; you will cripple me, and make me forget that I must fight. And I dare not pour a libation to Zeus with unwashen hands. It is quite impossible to offer prayers to Cronion Thundercloud bespattered like this in blood and mud. You must approach Athena yourself. Gather all the older women, and go to her temple with your burnt offering; take the finest and largest robe you have in your store, the one you prize most, and lay it upon Athena's knees; promise to sacrifice twelve yearling heifers that have never felt the goad, if only she will have compassion upon the wives and children of Troy, if only she will hold off the son of Tydeus from our sacred city, that wild warrior, that strong contriver of defeat!

"I leave you then to visit Athena's temple. Now I must find Paris, and see if he will listen to me. If only the earth would swallow him up! A great trouble the Olympian bred in him, for Troy and for proud Priam, and the sons of Priam! If I could once see that man go down into Hadês, I would say that my heart had forgotten how to grieve."

The Queen called to her servants, and sent them through the city summoning the older women. She herself went down into her vaulted storeroom, where she kept robes embroidered by the women of Sidon, which Alexandros had brought from Sidon when he went on that voyage across the sea and came back with royal Helen as his bride. She chose one of these for Athena, a great spread of the finest needlework, shining like a star, which lay under the rest.

Bearing this she led the great company of women to Athena's temple upon the citadel. The gates were opened by the priestess, Cisseus' daughter and Antenor's wife, the handsome Theano. All cried aloud the women's alleluia, lifting up their hands. Theano took the robe and laid it on the knees of the goddess, and then she offered her prayer and vow:

"Queen Athena, goddess divine, saviour of our city! Do thou break the spear of Diomedês, and strike him to the ground before the Scaian gates! Then we will sacrifice to thee in this temple twelve yearling heifers that never felt the goad, if only thou wilt have compassion upon our town and the wives and little children of Troy!"

So the priestess prayed, but Athena refused her prayer. Meanwhile Hector had made his way to the mansion of Alexandros, a fine place built by the best workmen in the land— hall and women's room and courtyard; it stood on the citadel next door to Priam and Hector. He entered, holding his great spear eleven cubits long, with a bright blade of bronze made fast with a golden ferrule. He found Alexandros in his wife's room, handling his shield and corselet and fingering his bow. Helen was sitting there with her women and seeing about their work. Hector said to him reproachfully:

"My good man, you should not be sulking here. Men are falling in the fight outside our walls, war and battle is blazing round the city for your sake! You would be the first to attack any one else you might see shirking his part. Up, man! or soon fire will warm up the place!"

Paris answered:

"You are right to reproach me, Hector, quite right indeed! But let me tell you this: I give you my word that I was not sulking. It is not bad temper keeps me here, but simply a bitter heart. Just now my wife has been trying to persuade me with gentle words, and driving me back to the battle. I think it will be better so myself. Victory chops and changes. Just wait a bit, and I will put on my armour.—Or go on, and I will follow; I think I shall catch you up."

Hector answered nothing, but Helen said warmly:

"Brother dear, I am ashamed; I shudder at myself! I can do nothing but evil! I wish a whirlwind had carried me off to the mountains on the day that I was born, or thrown me into the roaring sea—I wish the waves had swept me away before all this was done! But since the gods ordained it so, I wish I had been mated with a better man, one who could feel the contempt and indignation of the world! But this man is unstable, and ever shall be; some day I think this fault will find him out. But do come in now, brother, come in and sit down; I know your heart is most heavy with this world of trouble about us—all for my shame and his infatuation. Indeed, Zeus has laid a cruel fate upon us, to be a byword for generations to come!"

Hector answered:

"Don't ask me to sit, Helen: I thank you all the same, my dear, but I must not stay. They miss me outside, and I must go and do my part. Just keep this man up to the mark; let him make haste himself and catch me up before I go out of the gates, for I am going home first for one look at my wife and my little boy. I don't know if I shall ever see them again. It may be God's will to lay me low by the enemy's hand."

So he took his leave and went on to his own house. But he did not find Andromachê there, for she was already upon the battlements with her boy and a servant, weeping in her sorrow. Hector, when he found she was not within, stood at the door, and said to the maids:

"Be so good as to tell me where your mistress has gone.

To one of my sisters or to my goodsisters, or to Athena's temple where the women are making supplication?"

The housekeeper said:

"No, sir, not to any of the family, nor to Athena's where the women are all gone to offer their supplication. To tell the truth, she has gone up on the walls, because she heard that our people were in danger and the enemy were getting the best of it. She has just gone off in a great hurry like one distracted, and the nurse carrying the boy."

So Hector went back by the same way along the streets till he reached the Scaian gates, by which he meant to go out into the plain; and there his precious wife came running to meet him. Andromachê was the daughter of Eëtion, the Cilician King, and her home was in Thebê, below the forest of Placos. She came to meet him, and the nurse followed with the boy in her bosom: quite a little child, cheerful and merry—their little Hector, the tiny champion of Troy, like a shining star, whom they dearly loved. Hector called him Scamandrios, but to others he was Astyanax, "his Gracious Majesty"; for Hector was the sole saving help of the city.[3]

The father smiled quietly as he looked at his boy. But Andromachê stood by his side with tears running down her cheeks, and caught his hand fast while she said:

"My dearest, how can you do it? Your courage will be your death! Have you no pity for your baby boy, or your unhappy wife, who will soon be your widow? Soon they will all rush upon you and kill you! And I—if I lose you, it would be better for me to go down into my grave. There will be no more comfort for me if you are taken, but only sorrow.

"I have no father and no mother now. My father was slain by Achillês; he laid waste my home, Thebê with its lofty towers; he killed Eëtion, although he did not despoil him, for he thought that a wicked thing—he burnt him with his armour and raised a barrow upon him, and the divine Oreads of the mountains planted elm-trees round about. My seven brothers all went down to Hadês in one day, for that terrible Achillês killed them all amid their cattle and sheep. My mother who was queen in that place he brought away a prisoner, with the other spoil; he set her free for a heavy ransom, but Artemis Archeress shot her in her father's house.

"So you are my father and my mother, Hector, you are my brother, you are my loving husband! Then pity me and stay here behind the walls; do not make your boy an orphan and your wife a widow! But post your men by the fig-tree, where the wall may be scaled most easily, where the wall is open to assault—three attacks there have been already in great strength

3 "Hector" means the same as ἄναξ, lord and king.

—Aias and the other Aias, then Indomeneus, then the two
kings with Diomedês, whether it be some diviner gave them
a hint or it may have been their own thought."

Hector answered:

"I have not forgotten all that, my wife, but I could not
show my face before the men or the women of Troy if I skulk
like a coward out of the way. And I will not do it, for I have
learnt how to bear myself bravely in the front of the battle,
and to win credit for my father and myself. One thing I know
indeed in my heart and soul: a day shall come when sacred
Troy shall perish, and Priam and the people of Priam; but
my sorrow is not so much for what will happen to the people,
or Queen Hecabê herself, or King Priam or my brothers,
when all those good men and true shall fall in the dust before
their enemies—as for you, when some armed man shall drive
you away weeping, and take from you the day of freedom.
To think that you should live in a foreign land, and ply the loom
at the orders of another woman; that you should carry water
from strange fountains, crushed under stern necessity—a hateful task! that some one should see you shedding tears, and say,
'There is Hector's wife, and he was the first and best of the brave
Trojans when there was that war about Troy'—and he will make
your pain ever fresh, while there is no such man to save you
from the day of slavery. May I be dead and buried deep in the
earth before I hear your cries and see you dragged away!"

As he spoke, Hector held out his arms for his boy, but the
boy shrank back into the nurse's bosom, crying, and scared at
the sight of his father; for he was afraid of the gleaming metal
and the horsehair crest, when he saw that dreadful thing nodding from the top of the helmet. Father and mother
laughed aloud, and Hector took off the helmet and set it down
on the ground shining and flashing. Then he kissed his son and
dandled him in his hands, and prayed aloud to heaven:

"O Zeus and all ye heavenly gods! Grant that this my son
may be as notable among our people as I am, and let him be
as strong, and let him rule Ilios in his strength! When he goes
to war let them say, This man is much better than his father!
May he kill his enemy and bring home the blood-stained
spoils, and give joy to his mother's heart!"

Then he gave his boy back into the mother's arms, and she
pressed him to her sweet-scented breast, laughing through the
tears. Her husband was moved with pity as he saw this; he
stroked her with his hand, and said:

"My dearest, do not grieve too much. No man will send me
to my grave unless it be so ordained. But destiny is a thing
which no man can escape, neither coward nor brave man,
from the day he is born. Go home now, and see to your own

household work, the loom and the distaff, and keep your servants to their tasks. War shall be men's business, and mine especially of all those who are in Ilios."

Then Hector took up the helmet with its nodding crest; but his wife went on her way home, turning again and again to look, as the tears flowed thick and fast. And when she got to her own house, all the women fell a-weeping too; they mourned for Hector in his own house while he still lived, for they never thought he would escape his enemies and return from the battle again.

Paris made no delay either. As soon as his armour was on, he hurried through the city at the top of his speed. He was like a stallion after a good feed at the manger, who breaks his halter and runs whinnying over the plain to his usual bath in the river; he bears himself proudly, arches his neck, the mane shakes over his shoulders, he knows his own fine looks as he gallops along to the place where the mares graze. Such was Paris Priamidês, as he marched down from Pergamon in armour shining like the sun, chuckling with glee as his quick feet ran.

He caught up his brother just as he was leaving the place where the two loving hearts had spoken. Paris at once said:

"Well, your worship, you see what a drag I am on you when you are in a hurry; I'm late, and I did not come along fair and square as you told me!"

Hector said:

"My good fellow, no fair-minded man could despise your work in battle, for you fight well. But you do not really want to fight, and you are glad to hang back. What I regret is that I hear people speak ill of you, when all their hardships are borne for your sake. But let us go on. We will satisfy them by and by, if Zeus ever grant us to set up a bowl of deliverance in our hall, in gratitude to the deathless gods of heaven, when we have driven the enemy host away from Troy."

BOOK VII

How Aias and Hector fought in single combat, and how the Trojans sent a herald to propose peace

HECTOR NOW SALLIED FORTH FROM THE GATES, AND HIS brother Alexandros with him, both full of ardour for the battle. The sight of them was as welcome to the Trojan host as a fair wind, when God is pleased to send it for sailors who are weary and worn out with rowing over the sea.

Then Alexandros killed Menesthios, whose father was Areï-thoös the Bludgeon-man, and his mother Phylomedusa, his home in Arnê; Hector struck Eïoneus on the neck under the helmet, and brought him down. Glaucos the Lycian ran his spear through the shoulder of Iphinoös Dexiadês, as he was mounting his chariot; he fell to the ground and moved no more.

But when Athena saw her friends falling thus, she shot down from Olympos; Apollo saw her come, and issued out of the citadel to help his Trojans. The two met by the oak tree, and Apollo called out:

"Why are you here again, you daughter of Zeus, in all this excitement? Why has your hot temper brought you from Olympos? Do you want to turn the battle and give the victory to your Danaäns? You have no pity when Trojans fall. But listen to me, and I will tell you what is best to do. Let us put a stop to fighting for this day. Afterwards they shall fight again until they make an end of Ilios, for I see you goddesses mean to destroy this city."

Athena replied:

"So be it, Shootafar: that was just what I had in mind myself in coming here. Very well, how do you think to stop it?"

Apollo said:

"Let us move Hector to challenge all comers to single combat. Then the Achaians will be put on their mettle and send some one to fight Hector."

Athena consented; and at once their compact became plain to the mind of Helenos Priam's son, the diviner. So he said to Hector:

"My dear Prince, you know a good notion as well as Zeus

could himself. Would you listen to me for a moment—I am
your brother, you know. Go out yourself and challenge all
comers to single combat, and let both armies sit down and look
on. For it is not your fate to die now; the voice of the immortal gods has told me so."

Hector was delighted when he heard these words. He marched
between the armies holding his spear by the middle of the shaft,
and kept back his own battalions; they all sat down, and then
Agamemnon made his men do the like. Apollo and Athena in
the form of two vultures perched upon the tall oak tree, and
looked on with great enjoyment. The ranks were set close, and
bristled with shields and helmets and spears, as the waves of
the sea ripple and crinkle when the west wind blows it black.
Then Hector addressed them all:

"Hear me speak, Trojans and Achaians both, and let me tell
you what is in my mind. Cronidês throned on high would not let
us keep our sworn treaty; but he ordains a hard struggle for us
all, until either you shall take the castle of Troy, or you shall be
vanquished yourselves beside your own ships. Here among you
are the greatest men of all the Achaian peoples. Now then, if
any one of you has a mind to fight with me, let him come forth,
and be your champion against Hector.

"Here is what I propose, and let Zeus be witness on both
parts: if that man shall strike me down, let him strip me and
take my armour for his spoil; but my body he shall give back to
be carried home, that my people may give me dead my portion
of fire. But if Apollo grant me success, and I strike him down, I
will strip off his armour and take it into sacred Troy, and hang
it before the temple of Apollo Shootafar; but the body I will
give back, that his friends may carry it to their camp, to give
him funeral and build him a barrow beside the broad Hellespont. Then men will say in far distant generations to come, as
they sail along the shore, 'Yonder is the barrow of a man dead
long ago, a champion whom famous Hector slew.' So my fame
will never be forgotten."

Silence fell upon all. They were ashamed to refuse, and they
feared to accept; but at last Menelaos rose to his feet, and cried
out loudly in anger and contempt:

"O you boasters! you women—I cannot call you men! Here
is a stain upon us, a terrible terror of a stain, if not a man will
go out to meet Hector! May you all rot into mud and water
where you sit, weak and inglorious! I will arm me against
this man myself; but the cords of victory are held above by
the immortal gods."

Then he put on his armour; and then, Menelaos, the end of
your life would have come, for Hector was far stronger, had not
the Achaian princes sprung up and laid hold of you!—King

Agamemnon himself caught his brother by the right hand, and cried:

"You are mad, Menelaos, and what is the use of madness like that? Hold back, however hard it is, and don't fight a better man than yourself just for a challenge! Every one dreads Hector Priamidês. Even Achillês shudders to meet this man in battle, and he is a much better man than you. Just sit down among your friends, and they will put up another champion for this man. Even if he is fearless and a glutton for a fight, I vow he will be glad to rest his knees if he gets clear out of this battle!"

He succeeded in changing his brother's mind, for what he said was true; and the servants took off his armour. Then Nestor rose and spoke:

"Look there now, what tribulation has come upon our country and our people! It would make Peleus groan aloud, poor old man. Ah, what a wise man he was, what a good king! I remember well how he enjoyed asking me all about the great men of our people, who were their fathers and who were their sons. If he could hear about them now all trembling before Hector, how he would lift up his hands to heaven and pray that his soul might leave his body and go down to Hadês!

"O Father Zeus! Athenaia! Apollo! If I were young and strong now as I was, when Pylians and Arcadians gathered and fought beside the swift river of Celadon, before the walls of Pheia, about the stream of Iardanos! On the other side stood their champion, Ereuthalion. A grand fellow he was, and he wore the armour of King Areïthoös, the glorious Areïthoös, a name of note among men and women—they called him the Bludgeon-man, because he fought not with bow or spear, but with an iron bludgeon, which broke up the battalions!

"Lycurgos killed him; he trusted to skill, not to force, and killed him in a narrow lane where his bludgeon could not save his life. Lycurgos got in first and ran him through the middle with his spear, and down he came on his back. The victor took his arms, which were the gift of Arês. After that, Lycurgos wore them himself in battle; but when he grew old, he gave them to Ereuthalion his faithful squire; and Ereuthalion wearing these challenged all the best.

"They were all trembling and affrighted, not a man would dare; but my daring mind in its boldness set me on to fight him, although I was youngest of them all. And fight him I did, and Athena gave me the victory. That was the biggest and strongest man I ever killed; he covered a great space sprawling all abroad. If I were only young now as I was then, if my old strength were still in me! Then Hector would soon have a fight. But as for you, the best of all the Achaians, not one of you is ready to face Hector cheerfully."

At the taunting words, nine men rose up. First my lord King Agamemnon strode forward; Diomedês followed, then big Aias and little Aias, after them Idomeneus and his comrade Merionês, Eurypylos Euaimon's son, Thoas Andraimon's son, Prince Odysseus himself. All these were ready to fight Hector. To these Nestor said:

"Cast lots now all of you, and that shall be the choice. That man will be a blessing to the Achaians, and he shall have a blessing upon his own spirit if he comes out safe from the dangerous contest."

Then each man put a mark on his lot, and all the lots were thrown into King Agamemnon's helmet. And all the host lifted up their hands to heaven, and prayed, "O Father Zeus! let Aias win the lot, or Diomedês, or the great King of Mycenê himself!"

Gerenian Nestor shook the helmet, and out jumped the lot which they had prayed for, the lot of Aias. A herald carried it round from left to right, and displayed it to the champions. Each took a look at it and shook his head; last of all it came to Aias, who held out his hand, and when the lot was dropt in his hand, he knew the mark he had scratched upon it. Great was his joy! he threw the lot down by his foot, and called out loudly:

"My friends, this is my lot! I am glad indeed, for I think I shall conquer Prince Hector! Come along and let me put on my armour. Then pray all of you to Lord Zeus Cronion, quietly by yourselves, that the enemy may not hear,—or indeed openly, why not? We fear no man. No one is strong enough to make me run unless I want to run, and no one is clever enough. Greenhorns like that are not born and bred in Salamis!"

So they all made their prayer to Zeus Cronion:

"O Father Zeus, throned upon Ida, most glorious and most great! Grant victory to Aias and high renown! Or if thou lovest Hector and carest for him, grant equal power and equal glory to both!"

Now Aias armed himself and made ready. Then he marched out prodigious, like the God of war, when he goes forth to battle among men whom Cronion has pitted against each other in mortal combat. So terrible was that prodigious man, the safeguard of the nation, as he marched with long strides and a smile on his grim face, shaking his long spear. This was a joyful sight for his countrymen, but the Trojans felt their limbs tremble, and Hector's own heart beat fast: but he could not now retreat or disappear among the crowd, since he was the challenger. Aias came near, holding that great shield like a tower, seven oxhides with a coating of bronze, which had been made for him by Tychios of Hylê the master armourer: seven layers of oxhide, I say, the hide of prime bulls, with an eighth of bronze.

That shield Telamonian Aias held before his breast as he stood within reach of Hector, and said in threatening tones:

"Now, Hector, you shall know man to man, you alone and I alone what champions remain among the Danaäns even without Achillês lion-heart, manbreaker! He stays away nursing his grudge against Agamemnon; but we are left to meet you, and not a few. You begin, sir, and strike first!"

Hector answered:

"Telamonian Aias, my very good lord! Do not tease me as if I were a feeble boy, or a woman, who knows nothing of the works of war. I tell you that I know well how to fight and how to kill. Round to the right of me, round to the left of me, I know well to handle the buckler, trusty shield of seasoned hide! I know how to charge my chariot into the mellay of galloping mares! I know well to tread the war-dance when it comes to a stand-up fight!—But I don't care to use a sly furtive shot at a man such as you are. Let the world see if I can hit you!"

With these words, he poised the spear and cast. It struck the great shield full upon the outer bronze, the eighth coat; through six coats the point ran, but held at the seventh. Then Aias cast his own long spear, and struck Hector's round buckler: right through it went, and through corselet also. The blade cut the tunic on Hector's side, but he swerved, and saved his life. Then both pulled out their spears, and leapt at each other like a couple of lions or wild boars. Hector struck the middle of the great shield, but he did not pierce the metal, and the point was bent. Then Aias with a leap pierced the round buckler; the blade went through and cut the neck, so that the red blood bubbled up and Hector staggered back. But Hector was not finished yet. He moved back a pace or two and picked up a stone lying on the ground, black, big, and ragged; this he threw and struck the great shield on the boss till the metal rang again. Aias followed up with a still larger stone, swung it round his head and cast it with all his might. This great millstone smashed the round buckler inwards, and brought the man down; he fell on his back huddled under the buckler, but Apollo set him on his feet again.

And now they would have been hard at it, cut and thrust with swords, but suddenly the two heralds came forward, Talthybios from the Trojan side, Idaios from the Argives, who knew well their duty as spokesmen in the name of men and gods. They held their staves between the fighters, and Idaios spoke in solemn words:

"Enough, dear sons, fight no more. For Zeus Cloudgatherer loves you both, and you are warriors both: that indeed we all know. Night is now upon us; it is good to give way to Madam Night."

Telamonian Aias answered and said:

"Then bid Hector give the word; it was he who challenged all comers. Let him speak first; I am ready to do whatever he may say."

Hector said:

"Aias, indeed God has given you stature and strength and skill, and you are the greatest spearman of your nation. Then for this time let us break off, for this one day; later we will fight again, until fate shall decide between us and give the victory to one or the other. Now night is upon us, and it is good to give way to Madam Night. Then you shall comfort all your people, especially your friends and comrades; and I will return to my city to comfort the men and the women of Troy, who will enter the congregation of the gods with thanksgiving for my sake. But let us each bestow a gift upon the other, that all the world may say—These two fought indeed in bitter combat for a match, but they parted again in friendship."

Then Hector brought forward and gave his sword with silver knobs, and with it the sheath and well-cut shoulderstrap; Aias offered his girdle brilliant with crimson dye.

Thus they parted, and went each to his own friends. Glad indeed the Trojans were to see their man returning whole in life and limb, safe from the invincible hands of fiery Aias; glad were the Achaians on their part, when they led back Aias to Agamemnon in the pride of victory.

King Agamemnon made a feast in his quarters. He killed a bull of five years at the altar of Zeus Cronion. They flayed him, and cut him up, carved the meat deftly and put it on the spits, grilled all with care and laid it out on the board. Then there was a fine feast, enough for all; but Aias had the honours of the chine-piece, which King Agamemnon gave him with his own hands.

When the guests had eaten and drunken well, then came Nestor's turn: Nestor, the grand old man whose counsel was always the best. He rose first, and spoke with words of good advice:

"Your Majesty, and you my good lords and gallant gentlemen, many of our people lie dead upon the field: Arês has poured out their blood on the banks of Scamandros, their souls have gone down into the house of death. To-morrow then let us make no battle. Let us assemble with oxen and mules and bring in our dead. Then we will burn their bodies a little beyond where the ships lie, that we may take home the bones for their sons when we return to our native land. Let us gather them in from the battlefield, and raise one great barrow for all without distinction; and joined to the barrow let us make walls and towers to protect our ships and our camp. We will build proper gateways by which horses and chariots can pass; and outside we will dig a moat near the walls, to keep off horses and men on the other side in case the Trojans press us too hard." This was approved by all.

The Trojans also held an assembly, alarming and riotous, on the citadel before Priam's doors. Antenor spoke first:

"My countrymen, and our good allies and helpers! I have something to propose to you. Come with me, and let us hand over Argive Helen and her wealth to the princes of Argos. We have broken our oath by this late fighting, and that can bring us no good."

Then Prince Alexandros arose, Helen's husband, and said plainly:

"Antenor, I don't like what you say there; you can find a better proposal than that. If you really mean what you say, the gods have surely taken away your wits. Now I will speak to the brave men of Troy: I tell you straight, I will not give up my wife; but all the wealth which I brought with her from Argos I will give gladly, and add more of my own."

When he ended, Priam Dardanidês himself arose, and gave them prudent advice:

"My countrymen, and our good allies, let me speak and tell you what I think. Take your meal as usual, set guards and let all keep watch. Then in the morning let Idaios go on parley to the princes of Argos, Agamemnon and Menelaos. Let him tell them the proposal of Alexandros for whom all this quarrel came about; and let him add another if they approve, that we keep truce until we shall burn our dead. After that we will fight again, until fate shall decide between us and give victory to one or the other side."

They did accordingly: and next morning Idaios went to the enemy camp. The herald found the Danaäns in assembly beside Agamemnon's vessel; and there standing in their midst he gave his message in a loud voice:

"Princes of Argos, and my good lords of all Achaia! Priam and the men of Troy have commanded me to tell you, if it be your good will and pleasure, a proposal of Alexandros for whom all this quarrel came about. The wealth which Alexandros brought to this place—would that he had died first!—all this he will gladly give, and add thereto more of his own; but the lawful wife of King Menelaos he says he will not yield, although the people demand that he should do it. They told me also to propose to you, if it please you, that we should keep truce until we can burn our dead. After that we will fight again, until fate shall decide between us and give the victory to one or the other side."

They heard this in deep silence. After a while Diomedês spoke:

"Let no man now accept this offer from Alexandros, neither the treasure nor Helen herself. Even a plain fool knows that the bonds of destruction already are fast about the people of Troy!"

All cheered loudly at this, and approved what Diomedês had said; and then King Agamemnon answered the herald:

"You hear what the Achaians say to your message, Idaios, you have their answer; and this is my pleasure too. For the dead, I do not demur; for no one can begrudge the bodies of the dead their consolation of fire. To our oaths let Zeus be witness, the loud-thundering lord of Hera!"

With these words, he lifted up his sceptre to All Gods, and Idaios returned to Ilios. There Trojans and Dardanians sat all together in assembly, awaiting the herald. He came and delivered his message standing in their midst. Then they made ready to fetch wood and to bring in the dead. The Argives on their part went out to bring back their dead, and to fetch their wood.

The sun had now risen from the deep stream of Ocean gently flowing, to begin his upward path, and he was just striking the fields, when the two peoples met. It was hard to tell man from man; but they washed off the blood and lifted them into the carts, weeping bitterly. Priam ordered them not to make loud lamentation; so in silent sorrow they piled the bodies upon the pyre, and burnt them with fire before they returned to the city. So on the other part, the Achaians piled the bodies upon their pyre in sorrow, and burnt them, and returned to their ships.

Next day before it was quite dawn, while the night was between light and dark, men chosen from the Achaian army gathered about the pyre, where the bodies lay as they had been brought from the plain: and they made one barrow for all in common. Then joined to the barrow they built walls and ramparts to protect the ships and the camp, with proper gateways large enough for horses to pass. Outside they dug a deep wide moat, and fixed stakes along the edge.

While the Achaians were busy on this work, the gods were watching the great enterprise in the presence of Zeus Flashlightning, and Poseidon Earthshaker addressed the company:

"Father Zeus, is there any mortal man left upon the earth who will tell the immortals what he means to do? Do you see now again how the Achaians have built a wall round their ships, and run a great moat about it, without any sacrifice to the gods? The fame of this will spread wherever the morning shines, and they will forget that wall which I and Phoibos Apollo built with such hard labour for Laomedon!"

Zeus Cloudgatherer was angry at this, and said:

"Good gracious, Earthshaker, what a thing to say! Another god might have been startled at this notion, but not a strong and mighty god like you. Your fame spreads as far as the morning shines. Why look here—when the Achaians go back to their native land, you can break down their wall and smother it in the sea, and cover the beach with sand, and there will be an end of the great wall of the Achaians!"

So the sun set, and the work was done, and they all slaughtered oxen and took their meal in the camp. And a fleet of ships came in from Lemnos with plenty of wine, sent by Euneos Iasonidês, Hypsipylê's son: he sent a special cargo of wine for the princes, a thousand gallons. From this fleet the Achaians got their wine, and paid in bronze or iron, or some in hides, or oxen on the hoof, or slaves. They made a grand feast, and enjoyed themselves all night long, and so did the Trojans in their own city. And all night long Zeus Allwise thundered awfully, and meditated trouble for them. They were green with fear, and they spilt their wine upon the ground, and no man would drink until he made his libation to Zeus Cronion. Then they lay down and took the boon of sleep.

BOOK VIII

The battle wavers to and fro

DAWN WAS SPREADING HER SAFFRON ROBE OVER THE WORLD, when Thunderbolt Zeus called an assembly of the gods on high Olympos. He addressed them in these words:

"Listen to me, gods and goddesses all, and let me tell you what is in my mind. Not one of you, either male or female, shall try to chop and change my words; you must assent, one and all, that I may lose no time in bringing my will to pass.

"If I see any god going to help either Trojans or Danaäns on his own account, he shall get a thunderstroke and go home very uncomfortable. Or I'll catch him and throw him down into Tartaros! A black hole that! A long way down! A bottomless pit under the earth! Iron gates and brazen threshold! As far below Hadês as heaven is above the earth! He shall discover how much stronger I am than all the rest of you.

"Come on now, have a try, my good gods, the whole lot of you, and I'll show you! Hang a gold chain from heaven, gods all and goddesses all, a long pull and a strong pull and a pull all together! You will not pull down most high Zeus to the ground, pull as hard as you like. But if I give one real good pull, up you will come with the earth and sea besides. Then I will tie the chain round a peak of Olympos, and there in the air you will dangle! Gods or men, I am stronger than them all!"

They heard him in deep silence, struck dumb by his loud voice and threatening words; but at last Athena found courage to speak, and she said:

"Cronidês our father, King of kings and Lord of lords! We know well that your strength is unassailable; but still we do pity the brave Danaäns, when they perish and find such a cruel fate. Certainly we will take no part in the battle; we will obey your commands, but we will offer them useful advice at least, that they may not all be destroyed by your anger."

Zeus Cloudgatherer smiled at his daughter, and said:

"Cheer up, my dear child, my Tritogeneia! I didn't mean it really, I always have a soft heart for you."

Then he had the horses harnessed to his chariot, that swift brazen-foot pair with flowing manes of gold. He clad himself in gold, and took his golden whip, and mounted the car. Then he touched them up, and they flew with a will between earth and sky, until they reached Ida with her mountain springs, Ida the mother of wild beasts; where stood an altar of his in a holy precinct. There he loosed the horses and hid them in a cloud. He sat on the hilltop by himself in great contentment, watching the city and the Achaian ships.

Now the Achaians were arming themselves after a hasty meal in camp. The Trojans also were making ready in their city, fewer in number, but no less eager to fight: for fight they must, to defend their wives and children. Then all the gates were opened, and the men poured out, horse and foot, with a great noise and turmoil.

When at last the two armies met, shield clashed with shield, spear against spear, bossy buckler beat on buckler, and there was noise and turmoil indeed! Groans and cries of triumph resounded, as men slew and men were slain, and the earth ran with blood.

While it was morning and the day was growing, the blows came thick and the people fell; but when the sun stood in the middle of the sky, the Father laid out his golden scales. In them he placed two fates of dolorous death, one for Trojans and one for Achaians; he took the balance by the middle, and lifted it up: down sank the day of death for the Achaians, and the lot of the Trojans rose high. Then Zeus thundered loud from Ida and cast a blazing light among the Achaians. They saw it with amazement, and grew pale with fear.

Now neither Idomeneus dared to stand, nor Agamemnon, nor Aias big and Aias little, brave men though they were. Only

Gerenian Nestor stood fast, and he could not help it, for his trace-horse was badly hurt by an arrow. Paris had shot it on the top of the skull where the first hairs grow on a horse's head, a fatal spot. The arrow pierced the brain; the horse leapt high in agony writhing about the barb, and threw horses and all into confusion.[1] While the old man was cutting the traces with his sword, Hector's car came galloping up in pursuit with bold Hector driving. Then and there the old man would have lost his life, if Diomedês had not seen it and shouted out:

"Prince Laërtiadês! Odysseus, you're the man to help! Where are you going with your back turned like a coward in this throng? Some one may run you through between the shoulders. Stay, and let us keep this savage man from Nestor!"

Odysseus did not hear, and went on; but Diomedês pushed to the front by himself, and stood before Nestor's horses, calling out loud and plain:

"You are old, sir, your force is worn out, and strong young men are attacking you. Old age is heavy upon you, your groom is a weakling, your horses are slow. Come into my car, and see what the horses of Tros are like! They know how to gallop and go with the wind, up and down, into the battle or out of the battle! They are the ones I took from Aineias, fine ones to go. Let your men look after yours, and we two will go straight for the Trojans. We will show Hector if my spear is not as mad as his!"

Nestor left the horses to his men, Sthenelos and Eurymedon, and got in with Diomedês. Then he took the reins, and drove up to Hector. Diomedês cast his spear; he missed Hector, but hit the driver Eniopeus in the breast. The driver tumbled out, and there was the end of life and courage for him. The horses shied at the body; Hector was furious and distressed at his friend's fate, but he had to leave him and seek another driver for his masterless team. He soon found Archeptolemos Iphitos' son, who got in and took the reins from Hector.

Then there had been havoc, and no help for the Trojans. They would soon have been penned in Ilios like a flock of sheep: but the Father of gods and men saw it all. With an awful thunderclap he shot a blazing bolt which fell in front of Diomedês' horses; there was a flare of burning sulphur, and the terrified horses crouched under the car. Nestor dropt the reins affrighted, and said:

"Here, Tydeidês, turn them and let us save ourselves. Don't you see that God has no victory for you? Yon man wins to-day by the will of Zeus Cronidês; another time we shall win, if it be

[1] There were two pole-horses and an extra trace-horse. A car usually had only the two.

his pleasure. Man's might is nothing against God on high, for he is stronger far than you or I."

Diomedês answered:

"That is quite right and proper, sir, but I am tormented to death all the same. Think how Hector will boast in his next public speech—'I made Tydeidês run, and away he went to his camp!' When he can say that, I hope the earth may swallow me up!"

Nestor said:

"My dear man, that's a fine thing for your father's son to say! Even if Hector does call you coward and weakling, no one will believe him, not Trojans, not Dardanians, nor the wives of those brave men you have brought down in the dust."

So he turned the horses and drove away through the battle, while Hector and the Trojans cheered and shouted, with showers of spears. Hector called out after him in a loud voice:

"Tydeidês! You have always had the honours of the feast— a front seat, and lots of meat; some one up to fill your cup! But no more honours for you now. After all, you're no better than a woman. Get out, you base puppet! I will never give way and let you scale our walls or carry off our women! Before that, I will deal you destiny!"

Then Tydeidês was in two minds, whether to turn the horses and fight him or not. Thrice he hesitated—and thrice did Zeus Allwise thunder from the Idaian heights; his sign to the Trojans that they should turn the battle and prevail. And Hector shouted in a loud voice:

"Trojans! Lycians! Dardans! Prove yourselves men, my friends, fight and win! I know that Cronion of his grace has granted me victory and glory, and disaster for our foes. Fools! look at the wretched wall they have contrived, not worth a scrap! That will not help them against me. Why, the horses will just jump over their ditch! And when I get near the ships, don't let us forget a little fire—I will burn the ships, and kill the men!"

Then he called to his horses:

"Bonny Bay and Whitefoot, Sorrel and Shinycoat, pay me now for your feed! Think of all the honey-hearted wheat which your lady Andromachê used to put in your manger, all the wine she poured in your buckets when you wanted it, horses first, husband second! Yes, her own loving husband second! Come up, gallop along! We'll soon have Nestor's buckler, all solid gold, belly and rods and all, famous from earth to heaven! we'll strip Diomedês and take from his shoulders the glorious corselet which Hephaistos made himself! Once we have those two, I would hope this very night to make the Achaians get aboard their ships!"

At this boast, Queen Hera was indignant. She shook upon her throne, and made high Olympos quake, and cried out to Poseidon:

"For shame, Earthshaker! Even you for all your strength care nothing for the perishing Danaäns! And what offerings they bring you at Helicê and Aigai, heaps of them, magnificent things, and once you wished them victory! If only we who help the Danaäns could make up our minds to push back the Trojans and to keep Zeus away, he might sit by himself and sulk on his mountain!"

My lord Earthshaker said in high dudgeon:

"You Rattlechatterbox, don't talk nonsense. I could never make up my mind that we should fight Zeus Cronion, because he is far stronger than us all."

Meanwhile all the space between the ships and the moat round the wall had been filled with a crowd of men and horses: Hector had driven them in, now Zeus had made him master of the field. And he would have burnt the ships then and there, but for Queen Hera. She put a thought into Agamemnon's mind that he must bestir himself and encourage his men; so he passed along the camp and the ships, carrying a great purple robe, until he reached the towering hull of Odysseus' vessel, which was in the middle. There he could be heard on both sides; and he shouted loud and strong:

"Shame on you, Argives! A fine-looking lot of men, but a disgrace to your looks! Where are your boasts now, those empty boasts in Lemnos, when we said we were such grand fellows? You could eat your plates of beef, and drink your tubs of wine, and boast away that one of you would stand up to a hundred Trojans or two hundred, and now we are all together not worth one—Hector! who will soon burn our ships in one great blaze! O Father Zeus! Was there ever another proud king whom thou didst blind with madness like to mine, to take his glory from him! I declare and avow that I did not pass one altar of thine on this accursed voyage, but I burnt fat and rump slices on every one, in my passion to sack the castle of Troy. But now, O Zeus, grant me this one boon: let us escape with our lives, and spare the Achaians such a defeat at the hands of Trojans!"

The tears ran down his cheeks as he prayed; our Father was sorry for him, and vouchsafed to spare the people's lives. At once he sent the most trusty omen of all the birds that fly, an eagle, holding a young fawn in his talons; the eagle dropt the fawn beside the altar of Zeus, where sacrifice used to be made to Zeus of All the Voices. When the men saw that Zeus had sent this bird, they took heart and leapt on the Trojans with fresh vigour.

Then out of all that great army not one could boast that he

was in front of Diomedês, as they fought to drive the enemy out of their moat. He was the first to kill an enemy, Agelaos Phradmon's son, who had turned his horses in retreat; but Diomedês ran him through the back from behind, and he rolled out of his car in his rattling armour.

Next to him came the princes Agamemnon and Menelaos; then Aias the great and Aias the little, full of warlike fury: then Idomeneus with his comrade Merionês, a very god of battle; then Eurypylos Euaimonidês; and Teucros the ninth, who stretched his bow and crouched under the great shield of Aias Telamoniadês. Aias would let him out from under the shield; Teucros would spy his man, and shoot, and if the shot hit him down he would come, and Teucros dived back to Aias like a boy hiding behind his mother. Aias kept him covered with the great shield.

And who was the first man Teucros hit? Orsilochos first, and then Ormenos, and Ophelestês, Daitor and Chromios and Lycophontês, Amopaon Polyaimon's son and Melanippos! My lord King Agamemnon was highly delighted to see whole battalions falling before the bow of Teucros, and he came and told him so:

"Teucros, darling of my heart! You prince among men! Shoot away like that, and you will be the hope of the Danaäns, the hope of your father Telamon! He brought you up in his own house, although you were a little love-child—now you can make him famous a thousand miles away. I'll tell you what I will do. If Zeus Almighty and Athena grant me to sack the city of Troy, you shall have the first gift of honour after myself—a tripod, or a pair of horses with chariot complete, or a woman to put in your bed!"

Teucros answered:

"Your gracious majesty! I am as keen as you are, so why prick me on? I do my best all the time. Ever since we turned them back I have been watching to pick the men off. Eight shots I have made already, and all have stuck in the flesh of some lusty lad. But this mad mongrel I cannot hit."

As he spoke he let fly another straight at Hector. He missed him—not for want of will—but hit in the breast one of the sons of Priam, a brave man, Gorgythion; his mother was the beautiful Castianeira from Aisymê, a woman divinely beautiful. The man's head in the heavy helmet drooped upon his shoulder, as a poppyhead droops in the garden, heavy with seed and the raindrops of spring.

Once more Teucros sent an arrow straight at Hector, determined to kill him. This also missed Hector, for Apollo made it swerve past him; but it hit the charioteer Archeptolemos on the nipple. He rolled out of the car, and the horses shied, but he was left dead on the spot. It was a cruel blow for Hector; but he left the body there for the time, though he grieved deeply for his friend. He called his own brother Cebrionês, who was near, to take the reins, which he did. Then Hector jumped out with a terrible shout, picked up a stone and made straight for Teucros, to knock him down. Teucros had just chosen a sharp arrow and put it on the bowstring, and when Hector came up he was drawing and aiming at him; but Hector threw, and the jagged stone struck on the collar-bone between neck and breast, a very deadly place, and also snapt the bowstring—wrist and hand were benumbed, he sank on his knees and the bow fell from his hand. Aias was watching his brother, and when he saw him fall, he ran up in time to bestride him and cover him with his great shield; Mecisteus Echios' son and Alastor, two of his comrades, picked him up and carried him away groaning to the ships.

Once more the Olympian put courage into the Trojans, and they drove the Achaians back to their moat, Hector triumphant at their head. He hung on to the Achaians, ever striking down the rearmost. He was like a coursing hound which bites at a wild boar or a lion from behind, flank and buttock, watching his twists and dodges. At last the fugitives got over the moat and stakes, many falling by the way, and halted hemmed in beside the ships. How they prayed aloud to all the gods in heaven, and called to one another holding up their hands! And Hector wheeled his horses round and about, glaring like Gorgon or the bloodthirsty god of war.

Queen Hera saw this lamentable sight, and protested to Athena:

"For shame, you daughter of Zeus Almighty! Shall we let our Danaäns perish without an effort, our very last chance? Just look—they will be utterly destroyed by the rush of one man! Intolerable! There he goes like a madman, that Hector Priamidês; and he has done damage enough already!"

To her Athena said:

"I only wish he were dead and done for! I wish they would kill the madman on his native soil! But my own father is as mad as he is, full of mischief, stubborn, always thwarting my plans. He never thinks how often I saved his son Heraclês, when he was tormented by Eurystheus and his tasks. Yes, the man would often appeal to heaven, and Zeus sent me from heaven to help him out. If I had only known all this when Eurystheus sent him to Hadês the Warder, and told him to bring up the watchdog of Hadês out of Erebos, he never should have come back across the waters of Styx.

"But now my Father hates me and listens to Thetis: this is *her* scheme, when she kissed his knees and fingered his chin and prayed him to satisfy Achillês! Never mind, a time shall come when he will call me again his bright-eyed darling.

"Well then, you had better harness the horses. I will go indoors and put on my armour, and see if Hector Priamidês in his gleaming helmet will be pleased to see us two appear on the battlefield. I declare a good few of the Trojans will fall before those ships, and feed dogs and vultures with their fat and their flesh!"

So Queen Hera harnessed the horses; and Athena slipt off the robe she had made for herself, and put on the tunic of Zeus Cloudgatherer for the battle. She took the huge heavy spear which the awful goddess uses to vanquish the battalions of men, when she is angry, and mounted the chariot; Hera touched up the obedient horses, and the celestial gates opened of themselves to let them through: those gates which the Seasons held in charge, to open the solid cloud and to close it.

But Zeus saw it all from Ida, and mightily angry he was. He called Iris Goldenwing, and sent her with these orders:

"Off with you, Iris, my quick one, and turn them back. Do not let them come before my face; there will be trouble if we meet! I tell you plainly, and I will make it good: I will maim their horses under the car; I will smash the car to pieces and throw them out; not in ten revolving years will they heal the wounds of my thunderbolt. Then Brighteyes will know what it is to fight with her father! I am not so angry with Hera, for I am used to her ways. She always chips up everything I say."

Then away went Iris on her errand swift as the storm; down she came from Ida and up to high Olympos. She met them and checked them at the very gates with her message from Zeus:

"Whither away in this haste? What madness is in your minds? Cronidês commands that you give no help to the Argives. Hear the threat of the Lord God, which he will make good: He will maim your horses under the car, he will smash the car to pieces and throw you out; not in ten revolving years will you heal the wounds of his thunderbolt. Then you shall know, Brighteyes, what it is to fight with your father. Hera he is not so angry with, for he is used to her ways; she always chips up everything he says. But you are a terrible one, shameless and fearless, if you will really dare to lift your monstrous pike against Zeus!"

So Iris gave her message, and she was gone. Then Hera said:

"Bless us all, daughter of Zeus Almighty! I think now we had better not fight against Zeus for the sake of mortal men. As for them, let one die and another live, just as it may happen. As for him—let him keep his own counsel and judge between Trojans and Danaäns, for that is right and proper."

Then she turned back the horses. The Seasons unharnessed

them and tied them up at their ambrosial mangers, and leaned the chariot against the wall: then the two returned to their golden couches among the other gods, very unhappy indeed.

But now Father Zeus drove from Ida to the assembly of the gods. The Earthshaker took out the horses, and set the car on the stands, and covered it over. Zeus took his seat on his golden throne: under his feet great Olympos did quake. Athena and Hera were sitting by themselves, and they did not speak to him or ask a question. But Zeus understood quite well, and he said to them:

"Why are you so unhappy, Athena and Hera? I don't suppose you are tired out with killing those Trojans, whom you hate so terribly. Whatever happens, with my strong will and my invincible hands, not all the gods in Olympos could turn me. Look at yourselves: your powerful muscles went all on a tremble before you came in sight of the ugly works of war. I tell you this, and I would have done it too: you would have had no chariot to drive back to our Olympian home, when once the thunderbolt struck you!"

Athena and Hera grunted at this: they were sitting close together, thinking what they could do to hurt the Trojans. Athena held her tongue, although she was full of resentment and anger against Father Zeus: but Hera burst out—her feelings were too much for her:

"O Cronidês, you dreadful creature, what have you said! We know quite well that your strength is unassailable. But after all we are sorry for the brave Danaäns, with such a hard road to travel! They are likely to be destroyed altogether."

Zeus Cloudgatherer answered:

"To-morrow at dawn, if you like, you shall see something more of Cronion in his fury, my stately Queen, you shall see him with those lovely eyes slaying yet more of the Argive host. For Hector shall not cease from battle until Peleion shall rise up beside the ships, on that day when they shall fight upon the decks in dire extremity for the body of fallen Patroclos. That is fate's decree, and for your anger I care nothing; not if you travel to the farthest ends of earth and sea, where Iapetos and Cronos abide for ever, deep in the pit of Tartaros, without the rays of Helios Hyperion or the breezes of the air to give them comfort. Even if you travel as far as that, I care nothing for your resentment, for you are the most shameless of all creatures." [2]

Queen Hera made no answer to her lord. Then the sun's bright light fell in the Ocean, drawing black night over the

---

[2] He hints that they may try to rally the Titans to rebel against him.

fruitful earth. Unwilling indeed the Trojans were to see the light go; but for the Achaians welcome, thrice prayed-for, came the darkness of night.

Now Hector withdrew his men to an open space near the river, where the ground was clear of the dead; and there he called an assembly. All dismounted from their chariots, and came to hear his speech. Hector held the pole of his spear, eighteen feet in length, with its gleaming blade of bronze held by a golden ring; and leaning upon this, he spoke:

"Trojans, Dardanians, allies! I thought but now to destroy those ships and all the Achaians with them, before we returned to Ilios. But darkness came on first, and this chiefly has saved them and their ships upon the seashore. So then we must yield now to the night. We will take some food, and unloose the horses and give them a feed. Bring out oxen and sheep, and wine to comfort us, and bread from the stores, and collect plenty of firewood. We must keep the fires alight everywhere blazing high all night long until daylight comes again, or the enemy may try to get away during the night.

"Now then, you must not let them embark at their pleasure without a blow. Take care that some of them have a shot to digest when they get home—an arrow, or a spear-prod, as he jumps aboard. That may teach other people not to bring war to this country! Send criers through the city to cry, 'All young lads and greyheads man the walls!' Every woman is to keep a big fire alight in the house. Keep strict watch that no enemy troop shall get in while the men are away.

"Those are my orders for the night, my brave boys, and see they are carried out; to-morrow I shall have wholesome orders for the day. Full of hope, I pray to Zeus and all the gods of heaven to drive out from this place in rout these mongrels whom the fates are now driving upon their ships!

"This night then we will guard ourselves well; to-morrow at dawn we will arm and assault the enemy ships. I will see whether Diomedês Tydeidês will be strong enough to throw me back upon our walls, or if I shall strike him down and carry off his blood-stained spoils! To-morrow he shall find out what he is worth, if he stands to face my spear. But I think he will fall among the first before me, and many of his companions around him, as the sun rises upon the morrow. I wish I were as surely an immortal God and worshipt like Athenaia and Apollo, as the coming day will surely bring ruin for the Argives!"

Hector's speech was loudly applauded. Then they loosed the sweating horses from the yoke, and tethered each by its car. They brought out from the city cattle and sheep in haste, and wine to comfort their hearts, and bread from the stores, and gathered plenty of firewood: the wind carried the savour of meat up to heaven.

Proud and hearty they spent that night on the battlefield, with watch-fires burning all round: fires as many between the ships and the river Scamandros, as the stars in heaven that shine conspicuous round the shining moon, when no wind blows, and all the peaks and headlands and mountain glades are clear to view; a strip is peeled away down through the mists of the infinite heaven, and all stars are seen, so that the shepherd is glad at heart. So ten thousand fires burnt upon the plain, and beside each sat fifty men in the light of the blazing fire. The horses stood by their cars, champing white barley and gram, and waiting for Dawn upon her glorious throne.

BOOK IX

How Agamemnon repented of his violence and sent envoys to Achillēs

So THE TROJANS KEPT THEIR WATCH; BUT THE ACHAIANS were possessed by Panic, the freezing handmaid of Rout, and their strongest were pierced with grief intolerable. Their spirit was torn in pieces, like the sea lashed by those two fierce winds from Thrace, Boreas from the north parts and Zephyros from the west, when they come in a sudden gale, and roll up the dark water into crests, and sweep the seaweed in heaps along the shore.

Atreidēs went about crushed with this heavy pain at heart, bidding his heralds summon all to assembly one by one, but not to cry aloud; and he himself did his share with the foremost. They took their seats despondent. Then Agamemnon rose with tears running down his cheeks, as a clear spring trickles over a rock; and groaning deep, he addressed the assembly:

"My friends, my lords and princes, Zeus Cronidēs has shackled me in the chains of blind madness. Hard god! Once he promised me that I should sack the fenced city of Ilios before I should return; but now he has contrived a cruel deceit, and he bids me go back to Argos dishonoured, after losing so many lives. Such must be the pleasure of Almighty God, who has brought low the heads of many cities, and will yet bring many low, for his power is greatest of all. Ah well, let us make up our minds to it, and escape with our ships to our native land: for now we never shall take the city of Troy."

They heard him in dead silence. Long they sat silent in their sorrow, until at last Diomedês broke the silence and said:

"My lord King, I must answer you to begin with, where such a thing is lawful, Sir, in public assembly; and I say your advice is foolish: pray do not be angry with me. You attacked me first before the whole nation, and blamed my courage, and said I was unwarlike, a weakling; how that may be every one knows, both young and old. But you, Sir—Cronidês has enriched you by halves. He has given you the sceptre with honour above all others, but courage he has not given you, and that is the true supreme power. Good heavens, do you really think our people are such unwarlike weaklings, as you say? If your own mind is set on retreat, go. There is the road, there are the ships beside the sea, all the great fleet which came with you from Mycenê. But others will yet remain until we utterly destroy that city! Indeed, let them go too, and sail away for happy home! Two of us will go on fighting, Sthenelos and I, until we make our goal! for God has sent us here."

All cheered bold Diomedês in admiration, and Nestor rose to speak:

"Tydeidês, you are first in the hard-fought field, and in counsel you are best of all men of your years. Not one true man of all our nation will find fault with what you say, or gainsay it; but there is something to seek in your words.[1] The truth is, you are young; you might be my own son, my youngest; yet what you say is right and proper, good advice for our princes. Well, let me speak, and I will put all in proper order, for I am older than you are. No one will disregard what I say, not even my lord King Agamemnon.

"Clanless, lawless, homeless is he who is in love with civil war, that brutal ferocious thing.—But we must think of the present. We must give way to the night. Let us have a good meal; then let bodies of guards be posted outside between wall and moat. This is for the young men; after that, you take command, Atreidês, for you are the paramount king. Call the elder men to dine; that is right and proper for you. There is plenty of wine in your stores, which comes every day in our ships over the sea from Thrace; all entertainment is yours, and your subjects are many. There will be many to help with advice, and you will accept the best advice that is offered. That is the great need for all our nation, good sound

[1] You have no policy to propose.

advice; for the enemy are near our ships—look at their count-less watch-fires! Who could be pleased at that! This night will either break our army to pieces, or save us alive."

All listened attentively to this and they wasted no time. Guards were sent out fully armed. One picket was under the command of Thrasymedês Nestor's son; one under Ascala-phos and Ialmenos, both tried warriors; others under Meri-onês and Aphareus and Deipyros, and under Creion's son Lycomedês. Thus there were seven pickets, with a hundred lads under each commander, all armed with long spears. They took post between moat and wall; each picket kindled a fire and made their meal.

But Atreidês led all the elder men to his quarters, and gave them a good repast. When they had finished, Nestor was the first to speak, that grand old man whose counsel was always thought the best. He spoke with honesty and good courage, setting out his thoughts neat and clear, like a weaver weaving a pattern upon his loom. This is what he said:

"My lord King Agamemnon, I will begin with your gracious majesty, and I will end with you; for you are lord of many nations, and Zeus has placed in your hands the sceptre and the law, that you may take counsel on their behalf. Therefore it is your duty above all both to speak and to listen, and to act for any other who may have something to say for the com-mon good: another may begin, but the rest depends upon you. Then I will declare what seems best to me. For no one will think of a better plan than this which I have had in mind ever since that day when your Grace took away the girl Briseïs from Achillês, and he was angry. That was not what we wished, not at all. You know I spoke strongly to dissuade you; but you gave way to your proud temper, and insulted a great man whom the gods delighted to honour, for you took and you still keep his prize. But even at this late hour let us con-sider how we can appease him, and win him with gentle words and kindly gifts."

The King answered:

"Sir, you speak only the truth about my blind madness. I was blind, I do not deny it. Worth more than many thousands is the man whom Zeus loves and honours, as he now has hon-oured this man and humiliated the Achaian nation. Then since I was blinded and gave way to my wretched passion, it is my wish to appease him and to offer anything in redress.

"Before you all I will proclaim what I have to offer: seven tripods untouched by the fire, ten ingots of gold, twenty bright cauldrons, twelve horses, grand creatures which have won prizes in the race. No man who owned all that my racers have won, could ever be called penniless or pinched for a bit of gold!

And I will give seven women skilful in women's work, Lesbians whom I chose when he captured Lesbos himself, the most beautiful women in the world. And along with these I will give back Briseïs, the one whom I took at that time. And I will swear a solemn oath that she has never lain in my bed, and I have never touched her in the way of a man with a woman.

"This is what I offer now. Afterwards, if the gods grant that we sack the city of Priam, let him be there when we are dividing the spoil; he shall load his vessel with piles of gold and bronze, and choose for himself twenty Trojan women, the most beautiful after Helen. Then if we return to Argos, he shall have my daughter to wife; and I will honour him equally with my own son Orestês, my well beloved son, who is now at home living in wealth and luxury. I have three daughters, Chrysothemis, Laodicê, and Iphianassa: any one of these he shall have without bride-price to take to his father's house; and I will give her a dowry greater than ever man gave to a daughter.

"Seven flourishing cities I will give to him, Cardamylê, Enopê, and grassy Hirê, sacred Pherai and meadowy Antheia, lovely Aipeia and Pedasos with its vines. All stand near the sea, on the border of sandy Pylos; and in them inhabit men rich in flocks and rich in cattle, who shall worship him with their tribute and obey his judgments under his sceptre.

"This I will do for him if he will only relent. Let him yield! only Hadês is pitiless and unyielding, and that is why men hate him most of all the gods. Let him give way to me, since I am a greater King, and since I am older than he is."

Gerenian Nestor replied:

"May it please your Grace, my lord King Agamemnon! Such gifts as you offer now to Achillês no one could despise. Then let us choose envoys to send at once—or rather let me look round and choose them. Phoinix first, let him lead the way; then big Aias and Odysseus; heralds—let Odios and Eurybatês go with them. Here, water for our hands if you please, and call a solemn silence, that we may pray to Zeus Chonidês and crave his mercy."

This was approved by all. At once heralds brought the hand-wash, boys filled the mixing bowls to the brim, wine was served all round with the usual solemnity, they poured their drops and drank. Then they separated; and Gerenian Nestor with many a nod and wink told the envoys exactly what to say, especially Odysseus, if they wished to persuade the redoubtable Achillês.

Phoinix had gone on, and the two others paced after him by the sounding sea, with many an earnest prayer to Poseidon Earthholder Earthshaker that they might successfully persuade that strong will. When they came to the lines of the

Myrmidons, they found Achillês amusing himself with his harp; a beautiful thing it was, made by an artist, with a silver bridge and a clear lovely tone, part of the spoils of Thebê.[2] Achillês was playing upon this harp and singing the glorious feats of heroes. Patroclos sat opposite by himself, waiting until his friend should finish. The two envoys came forward, Odysseus first, and stood still.

Achillês jumped up from his seat in surprise, still holding the harp, and Patroclos got up too when he saw visitors. Achillês greeted them, and said:

"Welcome! I am glad to see friends. Just what I wanted! and you are my very best friends, though I am an angry man."

He led them indoors, and found them a comfortable seat with a fine purple rug; then he said to Patroclos by his side:

"A larger bowl, my dear fellow, if you please! stronger wine, and a cup apiece, for very good friends of mine are under my roof."

Patroclos was busy at once. He set a meat-block by the fire, and put on it a shoulder of mutton with another of goat, and the chine of a fine fat hog. Automedon held the meat and Achillês carved. When this was cut up and spitted Patroclos made a good fire, and when the flame had died down, he scattered the ashes, and laid the spits over them on the fire-dogs, sprinkling the grill with salt. Soon all was done brown and set out on platters; Patroclos handed round baskets of bread, and Achillês served the meat.

He sat down himself opposite Odysseus against the other wall, and told Patroclos to do grace to the gods, as he cast the firstlings into the fire.

When they had all had enough, Aias nodded to Phoinix; but Odysseus saw this, and filling his cup with wine he greeted Achillês himself:

"Your health, Achillês! We do not lack good fare and plenty, either at the board of King Agamemnon, or here and now. Indeed you have given us a regular feast.

"But feasting is not our business, bless it! An awful disaster is what we see, my prince, and we are afraid. Life or death is in question for our whole fleet, unless you put on your armour of might. Close beside our ships and wall is the bivouac of the Trojans, with their allies gathered from the wide world, all full of pride. There are the countless watch-fires of their host, and they believe we shall not hold out but be driven

---

[2] This touch will show how intricate the associations are in the story. Thebê in Mysia was sacked by Achillês, and the King and his seven sons were killed. His daughter was Hector's wife, Andromachê. And Chryseïs, the centre of the whole story, was there at the time, and taken with the spoil.

back upon our ships. Zeus Cronidês gives them favourable signs with his lightning; Hector in triumphant pride is like a raging madman—he trusts in Zeus, and cares for nothing in heaven or earth while that strong frenzy possesses him. He prays that dawn may soon appear, and vows he will chop the ensigns from our ships and burn them with ravening fire, that he will smother us in the smoke and destroy us beside them.

"This is what terribly affrights me. I fear the gods may fulfil his threats, and it may be our fate to perish in the land of Troy, far from home and Argos. Up, then! if now at last you have a mind to save our people in their extremity. You will be sorry yourself when it is too late, but when mischief is done there is no cure. Think first while you can how to save our people from the evil day.

"Wake up, man! Remember how Peleus your father warned you, on the day when he said goodbye to you on your journey from Phthia to Agamemnon, 'My son, victory will be yours if Athenaia and Hera choose to give it; but your task is to curb that proud temper, for a kind heart is the better part. Avoid quarrels, which go before destruction, and then all the nation will honour you both young and old.' That was the old King's warning, but you have forgotten it. It is not too late to change; let be that rancour which wrings your heart. Agamemnon offers you ample atonement if you will relent.

"Now then listen to me, and I will tell you what Agamemnon promised in his own quarters: Seven tripods untouched by the fire, ten ingots of gold, twenty bright cauldrons, twelve horses, grand creatures which have won prizes in the race. No one who owned all that those horses have won could ever be called penniless or pinched for a bit of gold! And he will give seven women skilful in women's work, the most beautiful women in the world, Lesbians whom he chose when you captured Lesbos yourself. And along with these he will give back Briseïs, the one whom he took away that time. And he will swear a solemn oath that she has never lain in his bed, and he has never touched her in the way of a man with a woman.

"That is what he offers now. Then if the gods grant later that we sack the city of Priam, you shall be there when we are dividing the spoil, and you shall load your ship with piles of gold and bronze, and choose for yourself twenty Trojan women, the most beautiful after Helen. And if we return to Argos, you shall have his daughter to wife, and he will honour you equally with his son Orestês, who is now at home living in wealth and luxury. Three daughters he has, Chrysothemis and Laodicê and Iphianassa; any one of these you shall have without bride-price, to take to your father's house; and he will give her a dowry greater than any man ever gave to a daughter. Seven flourishing cities he will give to you: Cardamylê and Enopê and grassy Hirê, sacred Pherai and meadowy Antheia, lovely Aipeia and Pedasos with its vines. All stand near the sea on the border of sandy Pylos; and in them inhabit men rich in flocks and rich in cattle, who shall worship you with their tribute, and obey your judgments under your sceptre. All this he will do if you will only relent.

"But if you hate and loathe Atreidês too much, him and his gifts, at least pity all the nations of Achaia in their extremity! They will honour you as if you were a god, and a great name you will get among them. For now you may kill Hector! He will come close enough in that furious madness—for now he says there's not a match for himself among all the Danaäns who came to Troy."

Achillês answered:

"Prince Odysseus Laërtiadês, I must speak out without undue respect to you. I must tell you how I feel and how I am resolved, that you two may not sit cooing at me on both sides. I hate that man like the gates of hell who says one thing and hides another thing in his heart! But I will tell you exactly what I have decided. I am not going to be persuaded by my lord King Agamemnon, or by any one else, because it seems one gets no thanks by fighting in battle for ever and for aye. Stay at home, or fight all day, you get only equal pay. Be a coward, or be brave, equal honour you will have. Death is coming if you shirk, death is coming if you work! I get no profit from suffering pain and risking my life for ever in battle. I am like a bird that gives the callow chicks every morsel she can get, and comes off badly herself.

"Just so I have spent many sleepless nights, I have fought through many long bloody days, all for a man to win back his dainty dear! Twelve cities I have destroyed with my ships, eleven fighting on land. Out of all these I have taken treasures rich and rare, and always brought all to my lord King Agamemnon; this Lagamemnon lags behind and takes it, distributes a few trifles and keeps the rest! Some things he gave as prizes to the princes and great men; the others keep theirs safe enough— I am the only one he has robbed! He has a wife of his own, let him sleep by her side and enjoy her.

"Why must Achaians make war on Trojans? Why did my lord King gather an army and bring it here? Was it not for lovely Helen? Are there only two men in the wide world who love their wives, my lord King and his royal brother? Why, every man who is honest and faithful loves his own, as I loved mine in my heart although my spear had won her. But now he has taken my prize from my hands and deceived me, let him not tempt me: I know him too well, he shall never move me. No, Odysseus, you and the other princes must help him to save the ships from the fire. Certainly he has done plenty of things already without me. Just now he built a wall, and ran a deep moat round it, and set stakes along the edge. Yet even so he cannot hold off Hector.

"But when I was in the field, Hector would not dare to show fight away from his walls; he got no farther than the Scaian Gates and the oak-tree. There he did once face me alone, and hardly escaped my attack. But now I don't want to fight with Hector any more. So to-morrow I will do sacrifice to Zeus and All Gods, and launch my ships, and load them full; and early in the morning if you like you shall see them in full sail over the Hellespont, with my men on board quite willing to row; and if the Earthshaker give us a good voyage, in three days I shall be in Phthia.

"I left great wealth behind when I came on this accursed voyage; there is more from these parts, gold and red copper, women and grey steel, which I shall take with me, my share by lot—but my prize, he who gave has taken away, his majesty my lord King Agamemnon. Tell him all that I say, in public, that the whole world may be indignant if he hopes to deceive some one else. He is always clothed in shamelessness, but the dirty dog will not look me in the face. I will not help him with advice or with action, for he has wholly deceived and beguiled me. Never again shall he deceive me with his words; he has done it once too often. Leave him alone to go to the devil, for Zeus has taken away his sense. I loathe his gifts, I value them not one splinter! Not if he offered me ten times as much, or twenty times, or any amount more, all that goes into Orchomenos, all that goes into Egyptian Thebes, the world's greatest treasure-house,—Thebes with its hundred gates, where two hundred men issue forth from each gate with horses and chariots, not if he gave me as much as the sands on the seashore and the dust on the earth, not even then would Agamemnon move me until he shall pay in full for the insult which torments my heart!

"His daughter! I will not marry a daughter of my lord King Agamemnon, not if her beauty challenged golden Aphroditê, not if her skill were a match for Athena Brighteyes. No, even so I will not do it! Let him choose her another man, one of his own rank who is a greater king than I. For if the gods let me live and return home, Peleus no doubt will find me a wife himself. There are women in plenty all over Hellas and Phthia, daughters of princes who have cities under their protection; I will take one of these to be my wife. When I was there, I often used to wish to marry a lawful wife, a mate well suited to me, and to enjoy the possessions which Peleus had gotten.

For to me life is worth more than all the wealth of that noble city Ilios in peace time, before our armies came, more than the treasures in rocky Pytho within the doorstone of Phoibos Apollo the Archer. You may seize cattle and sheep, you may get tripods and horses, but for a man's life to come again neither seizing nor catching will help, when once it has passed beyond the fence of the teeth.

"My mother Thetis Silverfoot says, that two different fates are carrying me on the road to death. If I stay here and fight before the city of Troy, there will be no home-coming for me but my fame shall never die; if I go home to my native land, there will be no great fame for me, but I shall live long and not die an early death.

"Indeed, I would advise the others to sail away for home, since you will never make an end of Ilios. Clearly Zeus Allseeing has lifted a protecting hand over her, and the people have grown bold.

"But you return now and give your message to the princes openly, your privilege as counsellors; then let them contrive some better plan than this, if they wish to save the ships and the army. For this plan which they thought of is not for them while I am angry. But let Phoinix stay here and sleep with us, that he may go home with us to-morrow, if he likes; there shall be no compulsion."

They remained silent for some time after this vehement speech. Then old Phoinix spoke, with tears in his eyes, for he was full of fear for the fleet:

"If you have really set your mind on going, Achillês, if you will not help at all to keep the fire away from our ships, if your heart is still full of anger, then how can I part from you, dear boy, how can I be left here alone? You were my charge; your aged father sent me with you on that day when he sent you from Phthia to King Agamemnon, just a child, knowing as yet nothing of the combats of war, nothing of debate, where men can make their mark. So he sent me out to teach you all that, how to be a fine speaker and a man of action too. Then I could not part from you, dear boy, I would not be left behind; not if God himself should promise to scrape off my old age and make me young and strong, such as I was when I first left Hellas with its lovely women.

"I was a banished man; I had to escape from my angry father, Amyntor Ormenidês, and his reproaches. It was all about his concubine; he made much of her, and insulted his wife, my own mother, so she begged and prayed me to take the woman first that she might hate the old man. I did as she asked me; my father came to know it, and cursed me, and

prayed the Avenging Spirits that I might never set any son of
my own on my knees. The gods have fulfilled his prayer,
Underworld Zeus and awful Persephoneia!

"But I could not endure to live in that house with my angry
father. Indeed my friends and cousins were all about me, begging me to stay there and trying to hold me back. Many a
plump sheep and many an ox they slaughtered, many a fine
fat hog they singed and grilled over the fire, many a jar of the
old man's wine was drunk. Nine long nights they watched
round me as I slept; they took turns in watching, the fire was
never out, one fire under the open gallery by the courtyard
gates, one in the porch before my bedchamber. But on the
tenth night, in the darkness, I broke open the door of my room
and got out. I leapt over the courtyard fence easily enough,
without being seen by the men on guard or the serving women.
Then I went a long way, across the whole breadth of Hellas,
until I came to Phthia and to King Peleus. He welcomed me
freely, and loved me as a father loves a son, his only beloved
son and the heir to his possessions. He made me rich, and put
many subjects under my charge, where I lived on the border
of Phthia as lord of the Dolopians.

"And I have made you what you are, my magnificent Achillês! I loved you from my heart: you would never go out to dinner without me, or take a bite at home until I sat you down on
my knee, and cut off a titbit for you to begin with, and gave
you a drop of wine. How often you wetted my tunic,
spluttering out drops of wine like a naughty child! Ah yes, I
had much to put up with and I took no end of trouble; but all
the time I was thinking that God had given no son to me. You
were my son, my magnificent Achillês! I made you mine, hoping that you might save me some time from shame and ruin.

"Come, Achillês, tame that awful temper! You must not let
your heart be hard. Even the gods can be moved and they are
greater than you in excellence and honour and might. They
can be turned by the supplications of mankind, with burnt
offerings and tender prayers, and the savour of sacrifice, when
there has been transgression and error. Prayers are the daughters of Zeus Almighty. They are lame and wrinkled, and dare
not look you in the face, and they follow intent close behind
Sin, the spirit of blind madness. But Sin is not lame; she is
strong and swift of foot, so she is there first in every part of
the world ready to make men fall, and Prayers come after to
heal. If any man does reverence to Prayers when they come
near, they bless him and hear his supplication but if any one
rebuffs them and stubbornly denies them, they go to Zeus
Cronion and beseech him that Sin may go with him, so that he
may fall and be punished.

"And now you, Achillês, must see to it that reverence attend these daughters of Zeus, the reverence which bends the minds of other good men. For if Atreidês were not offering many gifts and promising others, if he still kept his swelling anger, I should not ask you to forget your resentment and to help your people, however much they might need it. But now he offers much at once, and promises more to follow; he has sent envoys, the noblest he could choose out of all the nation, and your own dearest friends. Do not despise the feet of those who bring good tidings! But you had reason to be angry before.

"Have we not heard the stories of heroes in times past, when one was possessed of swelling anger? They were moved with gifts, they were reconciled with good words. I remember one thing that happened long ago, no new thing indeed, but I know just how it was. You are all my friends, and I will tell you. Curetians and Aitolians were fighting before the city of Calydon, and killing one another; the Aitolians defending their city, the others trying to destroy it. This trouble Artemis Goldenthrone had sent upon them. She was offended because Oineus had not offered her the firstfruits in his orchards; when the other gods enjoyed their sacrifices, for her alone there was none. He forgot, or he did not notice; some blind madness possessed him.

"So the offended Archeress sent a ravening wild tusker boar, which did great damage among the orchards: tore up tall trees from the roots, and threw them about in heaps with their roots and their blooming fruits. Oineus' son Meleagros collected huntsmen and hounds from many cities, and killed the boar. A few men could never have mastered him, so huge he was; and many a man he did bring to his funeral!

"But the goddess raised a great turmoil and dispute between Curetians and Aitolians, about the boar's head and shaggy hide.[3] So long as Meleagros fought, things went ill for the Curetians, and they could not hold their own outside the wall, though they were many; but anger swells in the hearts of many men, even though they may be sensible enough, and anger took hold of Meleagros.

"So he was angry with his mother Althaia and stayed at home with his wedded wife. She was the beautiful Cleopatra, the daughter of Marpessa Eueninê and Idas, the strongest man on earth in those days—he raised his bow against Lord Phoibos Apollo himself when Apollo wanted his handsome bride![4] The father and mother had a pet name for Cleopatra at

[3] Meleagros gave the spoils to Atalanta, and his mother's brothers quarrelled with him about it; he killed them, and his mother cursed him, so he sulked like Achillês.

[4] Apollo carried her off, and they fought, until Zeus stopped it. Then Zeus told her to choose, and she chose Idas.

home, 'the little kingfisher,' because Marpessa had wept like a mourning kingfisher when Phoibos Apollo Shootafar carried her off.[5]— Well, this was the wife Cleopatra; and Meleagros stayed by her side and nursed his blighting anger.

"He was angry with his mother, because she had cursed him for killing her brother. She beat her hands on the earth, calling upon Hadês and awful Persephoneia, kneeling upon her knees and wetting her bosom with tears, while she prayed them to give him death. The Avenger that walks in darkness, that pitiless spirit, heard her from Erebos.

"So then there was din and tumult about the gates as the walls were assailed; and the Aitolian elders sent the chief priests of the place to beseech Meleagros to come out and help them with great promises. They asked him to choose a plot in the richest part of the Calydonian plain, fifty acres, half vine-land, half cleared arable land, for his own. Earnestly the old King Oineus entreated him, standing on the threshold of his lofty chamber and shaking the two leaves of the door; earnestly his sisters and his mother besought him, but he refused all the more: his companions, the truest and dearest of all, entreated too. But they could not move him until his chamber itself began to be battered, and the Curetians were scaling the walls and setting fire to the great city. Then at last his own lovely wife entreated him with tears, and recited all the horrors of a city taken by storm: how the men are slaughtered, the houses are burnt to the ground, wives and children are driven away by strangers. Now his heart was torn to hear all these miseries: he put on his armour, and went out. So his own feelings conquered him, and he saved his countrymen from the evil day; but he never received those splendid gifts, and he had to defend them after all.

"Now I pray you do not be of that mind yourself, let not fortune turn you into that path, my dear! It would be worse to let the ships burn before you help. While gifts are to be had, come; the people will honour you as if you were a god. But if without gifts you enter the battle, you will not have the same honour even if you do save the day."

Achillês answered:

"Phoinix, dear old daddy, this is not the honour I want. I think I have been honoured by the ordinance of Zeus, and that honour shall be mine in this fleet as long as the breath remains in my body and as long as my limbs can move. But now just listen to me. Don't confuse my mind with lamentations and groans to please the humour of my lord king high and mighty. You ought not to be kind to him or I shall hate

[5] The hen was supposed to utter her mournful cry when she was separated from her mate.

you, and I am kind to you, so you ought to stand by me and vex any one who vexes me. Be a prince with me, and take half my honour! These will take the message, you stay here for the night and you shall have a soft bed. In the morning we will consider whether to go home or stay here."

He nodded silently to Patroclos to lay a nice bed for Phoinix; a hint to the others that it was time to be going. Aias said then:

"Prince Laërtiadês and my very good friend, let us go; for I do not think we shall achieve our errand this time. We must make our report at once, unwelcome as it is, to our people, who still sit waiting for it, I suppose. But Achillês has worked himself into a savage temper. Hard-hearted man! He does not think of his friends' affection and how we honoured him first and foremost. Cruel man! a man will take blood-price from one who has killed his brother or his own son; the slayer remains in his own country by paying a heavy price, the other controls his heart and temper after accepting the price: but you are implacable, your temper is merciless, such is God's will,—and all for one girl! Now we offer you seven of the best, and a heap of treasure with them. Be reconciled, respect your own roof-tree, for we are under your roof, envoys of the Danaän people; and we would be you nearest and dearest friends of all the Achaian nations."

Achillês answered:

"My lord Telamonian Aias, all you have said is very much what I feel myself, but my heart swells with anger when I remember all that—how Atreidês made me contemptible before the whole nation, as if I were an outcast without rights! However, go now and deliver your message. For I will not think of battle until prince Hector comes as far as the ships and camp of the Myrmidons in his career, and sets our ships in a blaze. Here, I say, beside my own hut and my ship, I think Hector will be held, and his fury stayed."

The envoys took cup in hand, and each poured the sacred drops; then Odysseus led the way back. Patroclos gave orders to the servants to lay a bed for Phoinix without delay, and they made him a comfortable pile of fleeces and rugs with sheets of fine linen. There the old man slept; but Achillês slept in the hut, and beside him the rosy-cheeked Diomedê, a daughter of Phorbas whom he had brought from Lesbos. Patroclos lay opposite, and he also had his companion, Iphis, whom Achillês gave him after the capture of Scyros.

When the envoys reached Agamemnon's quarters, all present rose to their feet, and holding up their cups of gold pledged them standing each in his place. Then they asked what had happened. Agamemnon began:

"Do tell me now, Odysseus—we are most grateful to you, sir—is he willing to defend our ships from the fire, or does he refuse—is he still in the same proud temper?"

Odysseus answered:

"May it please your grace, my lord King Agamemnon, the man will not quench his anger; he is even more full of passion, and rejects you and your gifts. He bids you consider for yourself with your people how you may save the ships and the nation. He threatens to launch his own ships with to-morrow's dawn. He advises us all to sail home, since you will never see the end of Troy city; for Zeus has lifted a protecting hand over it and given courage to the people. That is his message, and here are those to tell you the same who were with me there, Aias and the two excellent heralds. But old Phoinix has stayed behind for the night. Achillês told him to stay, that he might go away with him to-morrow, if he likes, but there shall be no compulsion."

All heard this aghast, in dead silence; it was a heavy blow. They were long silent, but at last Diomedês broke the silence, as usual:

"May it please your Grace, my lord King Agamemnon! It was a great pity to ask Peleion at all or to offer your heaps of treasure. He is always a proud man, and now you have made him prouder than ever. Very well, let us leave him to stay or go as he likes; he shall appear in battle once more whenever he feels inclined or when God makes him go. Now then this is my advice. Let us all have a good meal and a good sleep,—sound sleep and wine and food make the heart and muscles good, you know. And when the dark no longer lingers, but Dawn puts out her rosy fingers, marshal your men and horses betimes, and lead them yourself in the van!"

This pleased them, and all applauded heartily. So they dispersed to their quarters, and enjoyed the boon of sleep.

BOOK X

How Diomedês and Odysseus went on a night raid and how they fared

THE OTHER CHIEFS AND PRINCES SLEPT SOUNDLY ALL THE night long: but not Agamemnon. No sleep visited his eyes; the lord and commander of that great host had too much to make him anxious. He groaned again and again from the bottom of his heart, and his spirit trembled within him. There was storm in his mind; as when Zeus Thunderer flashes the lightning and sends torrents of rain or hail, or covers the fields with snow, or when he opens the mouth of ravening war. So we may imagine the King puffing and groaning as thick as hail, when he looked out over the plain. He was amazed at the countless fires of the Trojan bivouac, the piping and the trumpeting and the stir and bustle of men. But when he turned to his own people and the ships, he tore the hair from his head and groaned, praying to Zeus on high.

The best thing he could think of was to seek out Nestor Neleïdês, and see whether they could contrive some plan between them to defend their people from destruction.

So he sat up, and put on tunic and boots, and threw over all a tawny lionskin that reached to his feet; lastly he took spear in hand.

So also Menelaos was too anxious to get a wink of sleep. He too feared what might happen to the Danaäns, since he was himself the cause of their long voyage over the sea, and the long struggle of the war. He threw a dappled leopard-skin over his shoulders, and set a bronze helmet upon his head, and seized a spear. Then he went out to wake his brother the king. He found him beside his vessel just putting on his armour and glad indeed was Agamemnon to see him.

Menelaos said:

"Why are you arming, my dear fellow? Do you think of sending out a spy? I'm dreadfully afraid you will not find a man ready for that job—to go out all alone in the depth of night and spy in the enemy camp! He will be a plucky man!"

Agamemnon answered:

"We must find some plan, you and I, my dear Menelaos, something useful, to save our people and our ships, now Zeus has changed his mind. Hector's offerings, as it seems, are more to his mind than ours. For I never saw or heard in my life that one man in one day did so much mischief as Hector has done against us, just by himself! He's no son of a god or goddess. But he has done things that our nation will lament for ever and ever. What a mess he has made! Come along, run as fast as you can and call Aias and Idomeneus; I will look up Nestor, and see if he will come with us to the young fellows on outpost duty, and tell them what to do. They will listen to him more than any one, for his son is in command of the outposts, he and Merionês, the friend of Idomeneus. We put them in general charge."

Menelaos said:

"Then what do you want me to do? Shall I stay there with them, and wait for you? Or shall I call them first and then come back to you?"

Agamemnon answered:

"Stay with them, and then we shall not find a miss of each other; there are so many pathways in this camp. Call out wherever you go, and tell them to get up; but address them with proper politeness, name and surname for each, and don't be too proud. We must do the work of menials ourselves. Such indignity was ordained for us, it seems, by Zeus, on the day we were born!"

So his brother departed on his mission. Agamemnon himself made his way to old King Nestor. He found him beside his ship, on a soft bed in his hut. Beside him lay his armour, shield and helmet and a couple of spears; and there was the fine girdle which the old man used to wear when he led his people to battle, for he never thought himself too old. He lifted his head and raised himself on his elbow, calling out:

"Who is this who comes along through the dark night, when all others are sleeping in our camp? Some one hunting for his mules, or hunting for his friends? Speak out! speak or don't come near me! What do you want?"

Agamemnon answered:

"May it please your Grace, my lord Nestor Neleïdês! You will know Agamemnon Atreidês, one whom Zeus has plunged in trouble everlasting beyond all men, as long as the breath remains in my body and my knees can move! I wander here because I can't get a wink of sleep, I am so concerned for the war and the dangers of our people. I am terribly afraid about them; I am all a-dodder, my heart will not keep still, it fairly jumps out of my body, my limbs are all of a tremble. If you fare to do something, now that you are awake too, come with me to the outposts; let us see if they have forgotten all about their watch, dead tired, and fast asleep. Here's the enemy sitting close at hand, and we do not know whether they have a night attack in mind."

Then Nestor said:

"My lord King Agamemnon, I am sure that Zeus Allwise will not accomplish all the purposes of Hector, as Hector now seems to expect. I think he will have troubles worse than ours, if Achillês once changes his mind and forgets his resentment. I will go with you by all means.

"But let us wake up some of the others, Tydeides with his spear, and Odysseus, and Aias—the one who can run, and Phyleus' son, that stout fellow. Yes, there are others we might send some one for—big Aias and King Idomeneus; their ships are farther away, the others are near. But our dear friend Menelaos,—I have great respect for him, but I'll scold him well, even if you don't like it, and I tell you so. Why is he asleep? why has he left all this trouble to you? He might take a little trouble himself to go round calling people. We need it badly enough!"

Agamemnon said:

"My dear lord, there are times when I will tell you myself to give him a scolding. He is often slack and will not take trouble, not because he grudges it, not because he is careless, but because he keeps his eye on me and waits till I begin. But this time he awoke long before me and came to me himself; then I sent him to call the very men you mention. But let us go. We shall find them all outside with the watch, where I directed them to meet."

Nestor answered:

"Then no one will blame him, and they will all do what he tells them."

He put on tunic and boots, and taking a purple robe of fluffy wool, he folded it spreading across and buckled it over his shoulders. Then picking up a strong spear, he went out along the line of ships.

First he wakened Odysseus with a loud call. Odysseus came out when he heard the cry, and said:

"What's the matter now? Why are you wandering about the camp in the darkness?"

Nestor answered:

"My lord Odysseus Laërtiadês, do not be angry, when such dangers beset our people. Come with us, and let us wake some one else who may be able to advise us whether to fight or to retreat."

Odysseus at once went into his hut, and threw a shield over his shoulders. He followed them to Diomedês, whom they found in the open air with his armour. The men of his company were sleeping round him, each with a shield for a pillow; their spears stood upright with the butt-spikes driven into the ground, and the blades sparkling; you could see it a long way off, like lightning in the sky. Diomedês was asleep upon an oxhide with a bright-coloured rug under his head. Nestor stirred him up with his foot, and said in reproachful tone:

"Get up, my dear man! Why do you sleep all night? Don't you know that the Trojans are close by, on the spring of the plain, with ever so little space between us?"

Diomedês was awake and up in a moment, and called out plainly:

"You are a hard one, old gentleman! You never rest. Are there no other men younger than you, who might have gone the rounds to wake people up? There's no dealing with you, aged one!"

Nestor answered:

"Quite true, my friend, quite right and proper. I have sons, and excellent boys they are; there are plenty of people who might go round with a summons. But we are all in very great danger. Fate stands now upon the razor's edge: ruin and destruction for our nation, or life and breath. Come along, wake up running Aias and Phyleus' son—you are a younger man: do have some pity on me!"

Diomedês threw round his shoulders a tawny lionskin that reached to his feet, and grasped his spear. He went off at once and woke the two warriors and brought them along.

When they all came to the outpost, they found the captains of the watch by no means asleep, but all wide awake and fully armed. There was no more sleep in their eyes than if they had been watchdogs in a sheepfold, when they hear some fierce wild beast moving through the hills and woods, and the noise of pursuing men and dogs. There was no sleep for them, as they watched through that awful night; their faces were turned to the plain, while they listened for the coming enemy. The old man was pleased with what he saw, and praised them:

"That's the way to watch, my dear boys! Don't let sleep get a grip of you, or we shall bring glee to our enemies!"

With these words he crossed the moat, followed by the other captains who had been summoned to council. Merionês and Nestor's son went also by their invitation. They sat down in an open space which was free from dead bodies, the very place where Hector had turned when night came on. They talked for a while together, and then Nestor addressed them:

"My friends, I wonder if there is a man who can trust his own pluck enough to go among the enemy? He might get hold of some straggler, or he might hear some gossip and find out what is in their minds; whether they mean to stay out here near the ships, or to retire into the city now they have beaten us. He might find out all that and come back without a scratch. That would be a great credit to him; the world would ring with his praises; and he shall have a fine reward. Every prince in this fleet shall give him a black ewe with a suckling lamb—a priceless prize in all men's eyes! And he shall always be one at our dinners and feasts."

Nothing was said for a while, but then Diomedês spoke up:

"Nestor, I'm your man, ready and willing to visit the enemy camp. But if one more would go with me, that means more courage and more comfort. Two heads are better than one, to see what ought to be done, and double the chance to win: one man alone may find, but one's but half a mind, and one man's wits are thin."

Many wanted to go: big Aias was ready and running Aias was ready, Merionês was ready, Nestor's own son was more than ready, my lord King Menelaos was ready, patient Odysseus who loved a bold adventure—all were ready and eager to go scouting. Agamemnon said:

"Diomedês Tydeidês, you are a man after my own heart! Choose your comrade, choose any òne you like, the best of these who offer—you see there are plenty of them! Have no respect of persons; don't leave the better man behind for respect of high birth or royal rank."

He said that because he was afraid for his brother Menelaos. Diomedês answered:

"If I may really choose my own comrade, how could I think of any one but prince Odysseus, the best man of all, ready heart and high temper in every enterprise, and beloved of Pallas Athena! If he goes with me, we should both come safe out of a burning fiery furnace, for he is the past master of stratagems!"

Odysseus said to this:

"Tydeidês, don't praise me too much; every one knows me, for better or for worse. Let us go, then. Night is passing, and dawn is near; see, the stars have moved onwards, and more than two parts of night are gone, so there is only one left."

Then both men armed themselves. Tydeidês had left his own sword behind, so Thrasymedês gave him one, and a shield; he put on a leather headpiece without boss or plume, what the lads wear—they call it a skullcap. Merionês gave Odysseus bow and quiver and sword, and a well-made headpiece of leather; this was stiffened inside with a strong web of leather laces and padded with felt, and outside rows of boars' tusks were fixed in a pattern.

This fine piece was one of the thefts of Autolycos; he took it once in Eleon, after breaking into the house of Amyntor Ormenidês, and gave it to Cytherian Amphidamas, who took it home to Scandeia; Amphidamas gave it to Molos his guest, and Molos gave it to his son Merionês to wear. Now it was fitted upon the head of Odysseus.

So now then they were both well armed; and away they went. A good omen came to them as they set out—a heron on the right (Pallas Athena sent it); they could not see the bird in the darkness, but they heard it honking. Odysseus was glad at this, and uttered a prayer to Athena:

"Hear me, O daughter of Zeus Almighty! thou who art ever by my side in all enterprises, thou who seest me wherever I move! Now again be gracious to me, Athena. Grant that we may do some great thing to distress our enemies, and bring us back safe."

Diomedês after him also made his prayer:

"Hear me also, daughter of Zeus, Atrytonê! Go with me as thou didst go with Tydeus my father to Thebes, when he was sent there as envoy of the Achaians. He left them beside the

Asopos, and bore a friendly message to the Cadmeians; but on the way back he did doughty deeds with thy help, goddess divine, when thou didst stand by his side. So now let it please thee to stand by me and keep me safe. Then I will sacrifice to thee a yearling heifer, broadbrowed, unbroken, which no man yet has brought under the yoke, and I will overlay the horns with gold."

And Pallas Athena heard their prayers. Then they went on like a pair of lions through the black night, over carnage and over bodies, through arms and armour and red blood.

Meanwhile the Trojans were not asleep; Hector would not let them rest, but called an assembly of all the great men, the princes and leaders. Then he set his proposal before them:

"Who will do something for me?" he said. "He shall be well rewarded. I will give a car and a pair of horses, the best in the Achaian camp, to any one who will dare—and it will make him famous too! any one who will go close to the ships, and find out whether the guards are carefully set as usual, or if they are quite beaten and meditating flight—if they are dead tired and can't keep guard."

There was silence at this. But there was a man among them, the son of Eumedês the herald, named Dolon—rich in gold, rich in bronze. He was a poor creature to look at, that is true, but a quick runner. He was an only son, with five sisters. This man spoke up and said:

"Hector, I'm your man! ready and willing to visit the enemy ships, and spy. Now then, lift up your staff and swear an oath to give me the fine chariot and horses which belong to Achillês Peleion, and I will be your spy, not unsuccessful, not inglorious! I will go right through until I come to Agamemnon's vessel, where the great men are sure to be in council whether to fight or fly."

Then Hector took up his staff and swore an oath:

"Witness Zeus himself, the Thundering lord of Hera! No other man of Troy shall drive those horses, but they shall be your pride for ever!"

This oath was never kept, but it made Dolon go. Then and there he slung bow and arrows over his shoulders, and wrapt about him a grey wolfskin, put on a cap of polecat-skin, took a sharp spear, and away he went towards the ships. But he was never to come back from those ships with news for Hector.

When he had got clear of the crowds of men and horses, he went on full of eagerness. Odysseus saw him coming, and said to his companion:

"Some one there, Diomedês, coming from the camp; a spy perhaps or a man who wants to rob the dead, I don't know which. Let him pass by us a bit, and then we can jump on him and catch him quickly. If he is too fast for us, drive him in upon our ships away from his camp. Charge him with your spear, and don't let him get back to the city."

So they lay down among the dead bodies just off the path, and the man ran past quickly without seeing them. But when he had got as far away as the width of a day's work with mules[1]— they are better than oxen to plow the deep fallow—the two ran after him, and he stood still, hearing a noise. He thought some one had come from the camp to fetch him back, and Hector wanted to retreat. But when they were a spear's throw distant or less, he knew them for enemies. Then he put on his best speed to escape, and they pursued at once, like a couple of savage dogs on the hunt chasing a fawn or a hare through the woods, while the creature runs whimpering before them. So Tydeidês and Odysseus cut him off from his people and chased him on and on, until he nearly reached the watchmen beside the ships. Then Athena gave strength to Tydeidês, that he might come first, and no other man might have the credit of striking him down.

Diomedês charged with ready spear, and called out:

"Stop, or I'll have you with this! and there will not be much chance for you then!"

As he spoke, he cast the spear, but he missed the fellow on purpose, and it passed over his right shoulder and stuck in the ground.

The man stood still, staggering, his teeth chattering, pale with fear. The others came up panting, and seized both his arms. He burst into tears and cried:

"Spare my life! I will pay ransom—there is bronze and gold and wrought iron at home; my father would be glad to give a rich ransom, if he could hear that I am alive and your prisoner!"

Odysseus answered:

"Don't be afraid, don't worry about death. Just tell me, and tell the truth: where are you going like this, towards our ships and away from your camp, alone in the darkness of night when others are asleep? Do you want to strip the bodies of the dead? or did Hector send you to spy out our doings? or is it just a whim of your own?"

Dolon answered trembling in every limb:

"A vain delusion, sir—Hector drove me out of my senses— promised to give me the horses of your illustrious Achillês and his magnificent chariot, told me to march through this black night into your camp, and find out whether the guard was set over your ships as usual, or whether you were quite beaten and talking of flight and too tired to keep a proper watch."

[1] The furrow is constant, the measure is the headland after a day's work.

Odysseus said with a smile:

"Upon my word, that was a great prize to covet, the horses of Achillês! They are not easy for a mortal man to drive, except Achillês himself, who had an immortal for his mother. Now then tell me this, and tell me the truth: Where did you leave prince Hector? Where are his arms and armour, where are his horses? How are the guardposts placed and the sleeping men? Tell me what their plans are—to stay out here before our ships, or to retire into the city, now you have beaten your enemy?"

Dolon answered:

"Indeed I will tell you the truth. Hector and his council are deliberating near the tomb of Ilos, away from the noise; as to the guardposts, sir, there is no special guard at all on watch in the camp. Wherever there is a fire, those who can't help it are awake, and telling each other to watch; but our allies of many nations are asleep, for they leave watching to the Trojans. Their own wives and children are not within reach."

Odysseus went on:

"Well then, are they sleeping mixed up with the Trojans, or apart? Tell me, I want to know all about it."

Dolon answered:

"Indeed I will tell you that, sir, you can rely on me. Towards the sea are Carians and Paionian archers and Lelegans and Cauconians and Pelasgians; towards Thymbrê the lot fell to Lycians and Mysians, Phrygians with horses and chariots, Meionians with horses and chariots.

"But why do you ask me all this? If you wish to get into the Trojan lines, there are the Thracians far away at the very edge, newly come, and among them Rhesos their king. His horses are the finest and tallest of all—whiter than snow, go like the wind! And his chariot is adorned with gold and silver, golden armour he has brought with him, prodigious, a wonder to behold! Too good for a mortal man!

"But what about me? Take me in as your prisoner, or tie me up and leave me here, and then go and see whether I have told you the truth or not."

At this Diomedês said with a frowning face:

"No escape for you, Dolon, don't imagine such a thing, now you are in our hands, although we are much obliged for your information. If we set you free now and let you go, you will come another time to spy upon us, or to fight; but if we kill you while we have you, then you will not trouble the Achaians any more."

Dolon tried to put up his hand and caress his captor's chin, and beg for mercy, but Diomedês gave him no time; he ran his sword through Dolon's neck and cut through both the sinews—

even while he spoke, his head rolled in the dust. They pulled off his leather cap, wolfskin, bow and spear; and Odysseus held them up high, and gave thanks to Athena Spoilgatherer:

"Accept these, O goddess, with our thanks! Thee first of all gods in Olympos will we invoke. Now send us on again to the Thracian horses, and the place where the Thracians lie."

He lifted the spoils and hung them on a tamarisk; after that he grasped a handful of twigs and sprouts and tied them over, as a sign to mark the place, that they might not miss it in the darkness on the way back.

Then they went on, picking their way through the relics of the fight and the pools of blood. Very soon they came upon the Thracians. They were in three ranks, all dead tired and asleep, and their gear was arranged in orderly fashion beside them; near each man was his pair of horses. Rhesos slept in the middle, his horses tethered by the reins to the handrail of the car.

Odysseus saw him first, and pointed him out to Diomedês:

"There's the man, Diomedês, there are the horses, just as Dolon told us before we killed him. Now then, pluck up your courage. You must not stand idle in your armour. Loose the horses—or you kill the men, and I'll look after the horses."

Then Athena breathed strength into Diomedês. He struck right and left; there were ugly groans and cries as the sword went home, and the ground was reddened with blood. As a lion leaps furious on sheep or goats without a shepherd, so Tydeidês went up and down among the Thracians until he had killed twelve; Odysseus went behind him, and every time he struck one of them took hold of a foot and pulled him out of the way, so as to leave a clear space for the horses to pass without being scared by trampling on dead bodies, for they were not used to them yet. Lastly Diomedês came to his thirteenth, the King, and killed him panting and gasping; Diomedês was a nightmare for him, by grace of Athena! Meanwhile Odysseus loosed the horses and tied them together by the reins, and drove them out of the crowd, beating them with his bow, for he had not thought to catch up the whip out of the car. Then he whistled to Diomedês.

But Diomedês had paused to think what was the most audacious thing to do. Should he take the chariot with the fine armour in it, and pull it out by the pole, or lift it off the wheels and carry? or should he kill some more Thracians? As he stood thinking Athena was there and said to him:

"Better go back now, or you may have to run for it, if some other god sends the Trojans to chase you home!"

He obeyed, and quickly leapt on horseback; so did Odysseus, and beat both the horses with his bow, as they flew towards the ships.

But Apollo Silverbow kept no blind man's watch. He saw Athena busy with Diomedês, and this provoked him. At once he plunged into the Trojan camp, and woke Hippocoön, a kinsman of King Rhesos and a councillor among the Thracians.

The man leapt up from sleep, and saw the place empty where the horses had stood, and the men gasping and bleeding. He cried out, and called his friend by name. Then there was a great disturbance and uproar, and people came running up wildly when they saw the devastation which the two men had made and got off clear.

When they reached the place where they killed the spy, Odysseus checked the horses; Tydeidês jumped off and put the spoils in the other's hand, and got on again: he touched up the horses and they were off like birds for the ships as happy as could be.

Nestor first heard them coming, and said:

"My friends! my lords and captains! Can I be wrong—can it be true—Yes, I think so! Horses galloping is what I hear! I only hope it may be Odysseus and Diomedês driving from the Trojan camp, and so soon!—But I am terribly afraid something may have happened to those fine fellows."

Before he had well finished, they were there, the very men. No sooner were they down on their feet than the others gave them a hearty welcome and shook them by the hand; and Nestor said:

"Do tell me about it, Odysseus! I can't praise you enough, this *is* a feather in your cap! How did you get those horses? Did you really get into the Trojan camp, or did some god meet you and make you a present? Like the shining sun, I do declare! I am always about in the battle, and I don't bide in the rear, old as I am; but I have never set eyes on any horses like these. I suppose a god met you and gave them to you; for you are both well loved by Almighty Zeus Cloudgatherer and his daughter Athena Brighteyes!"

Odysseus answered:

"Nestor Neleïdês, most illustrious King! It is easy for a god, if he will, to bestow even better horses than these; for the gods are almighty. But these horses which you ask of, sir, are newly come. They are Thracians, and the Thracian King has been killed by Diomedês, and twelve of his best men by his side. Then for a thirteenth we killed a scout near our lines, who had been sent to spy out the camp by Hector and his princes."

Then laughing aloud for joy, he drove the horses across the moat. They went on to Diomedês' quarters, and tethered them in the stable with his other horses, and gave them a feed of corn. Odysseus hung up the blood-stained spoils of Dolon on the stern of his own ship, until he could prepare a sacrifice for Athena.

Now he and Diomedês waded into the sea, and washed off the sweat from shins and thighs and neck. Then clean again, and refreshed, they bathed in their stone tubs. So bathed and well rubbed with oil they sat down to dine, and dipping their cups in a well-filled bowl of delicious wine, they poured the sacred grace for Athena.

BOOK XI

*How the battle turned, and the captains were
wounded, and Achillês began to take notice*

NOW DAWN AROSE FROM BESIDE HER LORD TITHONOS, TO bring light for gods and men; and Zeus sent Discord towards the Achaian ships, carrying in her dreadful hands a portent of war.

She came to a stand beside the huge black hull of Odysseus' ship, which lay in the middle, from which a voice could reach to Aias Telamoniadês and to Achillês at the two farthest ends. There she stood, and uttered a loud and dreadful warcry, which put strength into the heart of every man in that host for battle and war unceasing. In a moment, battle seemed to them sweeter than a happy voyage to their native land.

Atreidês shouted orders to arm, and he armed himself.

First he buckled on his fine greaves with silver anklets. Next he donned the corselet which Cinyrês had given him as a guest-gift; for the great rumour had come to Cyprus that the fleet was about to sail for Troy, and therefore he gave him this gift to please him.[1] There were ten stripes of dark blue enamel upon it, twelve of gold, and twenty of tin; blue dragons reached up towards the neck, three on each side, like the rainbow which Cronion sets in the cloud to be a portent for mortal men.

Over his shoulders he threw the sword, with shining knobs of solid gold, and a silver sheath with golden slings.

He caught up a brave shield of fine workmanship, covering the body on both sides. Ten circles of bronze ran round it, and it had twenty bosses of white tin with one of blue enamel in the middle. Upon this boss was the grim-faced Gorgon glaring horribly, and on either side Terror and Panic. The shield-strap was of silver, and a blue dragon was twining upon it, with three heads twisted together and growing from one neck.

[1] To square him really, instead of coming himself.

Upon his head he put a helmet with two horns and four bosses and a horsehair plume. How terrible was that nodding plume!

He took a pair of sharp spears with blades of bronze, which sent their glittering gleam high into the air.

Then Athenaia and Hera thundered in honour to the King of rich Mycenê.

Now each man ordered his driver to keep back the horses in due order near the moat; the fighting men fully armed moved forward, and unquenchable rose the warcry to meet the morning. They were in place long before the chariots, which came and stood behind at a little distance.

Then Cronidês made a dreadful noise on them, and let fall a shower of bloody drops from the sky, since he was about to send to Hadês many a mighty head.

The Trojans were over against them upon the rising of the plain, ranged about Hector their great leader, and Polydamas the immaculate, Aineias whom the people honoured as more than man, and Antenor's three sons, Polybos and noble Agenor and young Acamas, glorious heroes all.

Hector was to be seen holding his round shield, now in front, now behind, giving his orders like a shining star of doom, which flashes out of a cloud and then dives again into the darkness: the metal of his armour gleamed like the lightning of Zeus Almighty.

The hosts were like two opposite lines of reapers driving their swathes in the wheat or barley of a great farm, while thick the handfuls fall. So Trojans and Achaians leapt at each other, and neither side thought of giving way: two equal ranks of heads, they were like raging wolves.

Discord Manymoan was joyful at the sight. She alone was present out of all the gods; the others remained quietly in their own abodes on high Olympos. They all blamed Cronion Thundercloud, because it seemed that he meant to give triumph to the Trojans. But the Father cared nothing about them, as it seemed. He sat apart by himself in great satisfaction, as he watched the Trojan city, and the Achaian ships, and the flashing arms, men slaying and men slain.

So long as it was early and the day was growing, the volleys flew from both sides and the men fell; but at the time when a woodman's hands are weary with felling trees on the mountains, and he has had enough of it, when he begins to want a bite of sweet bread and gets ready his meal, at that time the Danaäns called a charge and broke the enemy ranks, shouting loudly to one another.

Agamemnon was the first to charge his man and kill—he struck down Biënor, and after him his driver Oïleus, who had jumped out of the car to face him; but as he came the King drove his spear through helmet and forehead and spattered bone and brain inside. He stript off the dead men's tunics, and left them there with their skin shining white.

Next he went after Isos and Antiphos, two of the sons of Priam, one bastard and one not, both together in one car. The bastard was driving, and Antiphos was his fighting mate. Achillês had once caught them both while keeping sheep on the foothills of Ida, and tied them up with young withies, but he freed them for ransom. That time my lord Agamemnon struck Isos on the breast with his spear, and knocked Antiphos out of the car with a sword-stroke under the ear. Quickly he stript off their armour, and then he knew them; for he had seen them in camp when Achillês brought them in. None of the Trojans could save them, but they were all driven away. They were helpless as a deer, when a lion visits her lair and crunches up her young in his strong teeth. Their dam may be near, but she cannot help; she trembles herself in every limb, and dashes away through the bushes and trees, all of a sweat in her haste to escape the mighty beast.

Two others Agamemnon caught in one chariot, Peisandros and Hippolochos; their father Antimachos was one who most strongly urged Alexandros not to surrender Helen to Menelaos (he expected gold from Alexandros). These two young men were both trying to hold the horses, but the reins slipt from their hands and they were in confusion. Agamemnon leapt on them like a lion, and they cried for mercy.

"Spare us, Prince! you shall have a good ransom for us! There is plenty of treasure in the house of our father Antimachos, bronze and gold and wrought iron——he would gladly give any amount of it if he could hear that we are alive, and your prisoners!"

But he answered their piteous words without pity:

"If you are the sons of Antimachos, he got up in public assembly and told them to kill Menelaos then and there, when he had come on embassy with Odysseus to your city——told them not to let him go now they had him! Now then, you shall pay for your father's abominable outrage!"

With these words he struck Peisandros on the chest with his spear and tumbled him out on his back. Hippolochos jumped down, and Agamemnon killed him there on the ground, and cut off his hands and head, and sent the body trundling along like a roller.

He left them both there, and leapt to the place where the throng was thickest. His men backed him up, and now they were killing the enemy in their headlong rout, horsemen against horsemen, footmen against footmen, while the thundering hooves of the horses drove up clouds of dust from the plain—Agamemnon slew, and slew, shouting, "Come on! come on!" How a devouring fire falls on a thick forest, how the wind carries it rolling along, how the trees fall tearing out their roots as the flames blast them! So the Trojans in rout fell headlong before my lord King Agamemnon; so the rearing horses rattled the empty chariots behind with no ready master to guide them; for the masters lay dead on the ground, the vultures' darlings now.

Hector was out of reach, out of the dust, drawn away by the hand of Zeus from carnage and blood and tumult; but Atreidês was after him, fiercely cheering on his men. The rushing rout went past the ancient tomb of Ilos Dardanidês, past the wild fig-tree in the midst of the plain, making for the city; Atreidês followed and followed shouting aloud, his invincible hands bedabbled in gore.

But when they were near the Scaian Gates and the oak-tree, both armies came to a stand and faced each other. Some were still scattering over the plain, like cattle scared into flight by some lion in the evening dusk—all but one who stares death in the face; for the lion catches her and breaks her neck with his strong teeth, then laps up the blood and guts. So followed Agamemnon Atreidês, ever slaying the hindmost among the scattering herd; many a man fell from his chariot under the hands of Atreidês, face down or face up, as his mad spear drove on and on.

Up to the city, up to the steep walls he would have pushed; but now the Father of gods and men strode down from heaven and took his seat on Ida's peaks among the fountains, holding his thunderbolt. He called his messenger Iris, and said:

"Off with you, Iris, my quick one, and give this message to Hector. So long as he shall see Agamemnon full of fury dealing death in the forefront of his host, let him command his army to fight and keep away himself. But as soon as he sees Agamemnon wounded by spear or arrow and mounting his car for retreat, I will give him power to kill until he drives them upon their ships, when the sun shall set and the darkness come."

Swift as the wind, quick Iris did his bidding. She flew from the heights of Ida down to Ilios; there she found Hector standing in his car, and alighting beside him she said:

"Hector, most sapient prince! I have a message for you from Father Zeus. So long as you shall see Agamemnon full of fury dealing death in the forefront of his host, command your army to fight, and keep away from the battle yourself. But as soon as you see him wounded by spear or arrow, and mounting his car for retreat, Zeus will give you power to kill until you drive them upon their ships, when the sun shall set and the darkness come."

Swiftly sped Iris away: Hector leapt from his chariot, and rallied his men, shaking the spears in his hand as he showed himself here, there, and everywhere, urging all to fight. There was a dreadful conflict: they wheeled about and faced the Achaians, who formed a strong front against them. There stood the two armies face to face: this was the turning-point of the battle.

Agamemnon, as ever, was in the front; and the first to stand against him was the redoubtable Iphidamas Antenor's son. This man was bred and born in Thrace, the fat-loam country, mother of sheep, as they call it. Bonnyface Theano was his mother, and her father Cisseus brought him up from a little tot; but when he grew to the heyday of life, Cisseus married him to his daughter and would have kept him there. But he, just wedded, went from his bridal chamber to follow the rumour of the great war with twelve ships. These he left in Percotê, and came to Ilios by land; so that day he found himself face to face with Agamemnon. When they met, Agamemnon cast a spear first, and missed; Iphidamas stabbed him under the corselet, on the belt, and put all his great weight into the blow. But the spear-point did not go through; it was turned by the silver, and bent like a lump of lead. Agamemnon seized the spear and pulled it with all his lion's strength out of the man's hand; then he struck the man's throat with his sword and killed him.

So Iphidamas fell, and slept as in hoops of steel, unhappy man! fell fighting for his people, far from his bride so newly wed, of whom he had small comfort—and what a world of bridal gifts he had given! a hundred cattle then and there, and a thousand promised, goats and sheep also, all those countless flocks! But then Atreidês Agamemnon stript him of his fine armour and carried it away.

Coön saw this, Coön his eldest brother; and his eyes grew dim to see his brother fall, his own father's son. He stood where Agamemnon could not see, and stabbed him broad-side-on, piercing the arm just below the elbow, right through the flesh. Agamemnon shivered, but he did not stop; he leapt upon Coön with his windseasoned spear. At that moment Coön was busy dragging away his brother's body by the foot, and calling for help; but as he dragged him along Agamemnon struck under the shield and killed him, then sheared off his head over the dead body. So two sons of Antenor there met their deaths and went down to the house of Hadês.

So long as the blood ran hot from the wound, Agamemnon

was fighting everywhere, with spear and sword and great stones. But when the blood ceased to flow, and the wound began to dry, it became very painful; cruel pains took hold upon him, piercing him through like a woman in labour, when the Eileithyiai Hera's daughters deal out their bitter pangs. He mounted his car in agony, and called out loudly:

"My friends! My lords and captains! I leave you to defend our ships and bear the brunt of the battle—for God who knows best would not let me see the day out with you!"

Then he told the driver to make for the camp, for he was in great pain. The driver whipt up his team to a gallop, and away they flew in a cloud of dust, flecking their chests with foam, and carried their wounded king into safety.

Hector saw the retreat of Agamemnon; and he shouted for all to hear:

"Trojans, Lycians, Dardanians! Fight the good fight! Be men, my friends, strain every nerve! He's gone! their best man is gone! Zeus has given the victory to me! Drive straight for the enemy, strike them down and win!"

As a hunter hies on his hounds against a wild boar or lion, Prince Hector hied on his Trojans and gave them new courage and new strength, Hector, prince of Troy, like the god of war himself: ever in the front, ever falling on like a furious typhoon that lashes the lurid seas from above.

Who first, who last fell before the devastating onslaught of Hector Priamidês, when God gave him victory?

Asaios first and Autonoös and Opitês, Dolops Clytidês and Opheltios and Agelaos, Aisymnos and Oros and brave Hipponoös: these were the Danaän captains whom he slew, and after them a multitude, like the tempest striking the crests of the waves—West Wind buffeting the clouds of the white South Wind, beating them off with a heavy squall, rolling up ranks of swollen waves, tearing the heads into flying foam and scattering all abroad into the sky: so the heads of men fell in heaps before Hector.

Now had been ruin utter and desperate, and the Achaians had been routed and rolled back upon their ships, but for Odysseus. He called to Diomedês:

"Tydeidês! what's the matter with you and me? Have we forgotten how to fight? Come here, you laggard, stand by me. It will be a shame indeed if Hector takes our ships."

Diomedês answered:

"Of course I'll stand and see it out. But we shan't do much good, when Zeus Cloudgatherer means to let them beat us, as you can see."

Then he knocked Thymbraios out of his chariot with one thrust of his spear, and Odysseus did the like for his driver

Molion. Having put these out of the fight, the two men left them and ran wild among the throng, and dealt death around, like a couple of wild boars at bay venting their fury on a pack of hounds. Thus they gave a welcome breathing-space to the Achaians as they ran before Hector.

Next they took a chariot and two men, Hippodamos and Hypeirochos, the best of their nation, the two sons of Percosian Merops. He was a great seer and diviner, and he had told his sons not to go to the war and risk their lives. But they would not listen, for the doom of death drove them on; and now they were robbed of life and breath by Diomedês, and Odysseus stript them of their armour.

Now Zeus Cronion stretched equal the cords of battle, as he watched from Mount Ida, and the slaughter went on for both sides. Tydeidês wounded Agastrophos Paion's son on the hip-joint; he went blundering about blindly through the crowd until he fell dead, for his man was not near with the horses to save him.

But Hector saw this, and rushed on the two men shouting, at the head of the pursuing enemy. Diomedês shivered, and called at once to his neighbour:

"Our turn now! Here is ruin rolling upon us both, Hector himself. Hold your ground, let us stand and defend ourselves."

With the words, he poised and threw his spear, and hit—no miss this time! aimed at the head, hit the top of the helmet: metal glanced off metal, and did not go through the three layers of that vizarded morion, the gift of Phoibos Apollo. But the blow drove Hector far back into the crowd; he fell on his knees with one hand resting upon the ground, stunned and dizzy. Tydeidês saw where the spear ran into the ground some way off, and followed up; meanwhile Hector came to and found his car again, and got away with his life. But Diomedês recovered the spear and followed, crying out:

"You have escaped once more, you cur! It was a nice thing that time, but Apollo saved you again. No doubt you remember your prayers before you go where spears are flying. I fancy I'll finish you off next time we meet, if I have a god or so to help me too. For the moment, I will take any one else I can find."

Then he went on with the stripping of Agastrophos. He pulled the corselet from the man's body, and the shield from his shoulders; but as he was taking off the helmet, Alexandros took aim at him from the tomb of Ilos Dardanidês, where he stood with his bow and arrows behind the pillar. He drew bow and shot, and this shot did not miss Diomedês! It ran through the flat of his right foot as he knelt, and pinned it to the ground.

Then Alexandros came out of hiding, and laughed aloud with glee as he cried:

"A hit! This time it was no miss! I only wish it had gone into your belly and killed you! Then our people could have a little rest from their troubles, instead of shivering and bleating like a lot of goats before a lion!"

Diomedês answered him quite composed:

"Hide yourself and pull your bow! Come and steal a wife and go! Frizzle-head with pretty curls, you can make eyes at pretty girls!—Stand up and fight like a man, and much good will your bow and arrows be. This time you have just grazed my foot, and listen to the boasts! I care no more than if a woman shot me, or some fool of a boy—Blunt, I tell you, is the shot of a coward good-for-naught! Mine is quite another thing—one touch, and death is in the sting!—Then the man's wife will have to tear her two cheeks, and his children will be orphans, while his blood reddens the earth and his body rots. More vultures than women about him then!"

As he spoke, Odysseus came and stood in front to protect him, while Diomedês sat down behind him and pulled the arrow through his foot, with dreadful pain. Then he got into his car, and told the driver to take him away to the ships.

Now Odysseus was left quite alone; the others were too much afraid to stand by him, and he said within his unconquerable soul:

"This is a bad business. What will become of me? If I show fear and run away from this mob, that is bad enough. But it is worse to be caught alone, and Cronion has put all the rest into a panic. But what's the use of such arguments? I know only cowards vanish out of the battle, but a brave man must stand his ground and either kill or be killed."

While he was deliberating, the Trojans came up in great numbers and crowded all round him. But they had placed their own destruction in their midst. They harried him from all sides, like a pack of hounds and huntsmen harrying a wild boar from the forest. He comes out of the deep thicket, whetting the white tusks in his slathering jaws, they hear the gnashing sound, they dash forward from both sides, but soon have to meet his terrible onset. So the Trojans dashed upon Odysseus.

And Odysseus first leapt upon Deïopitês and wounded his shoulder, then killed Thoön and Ennomos, then stabbed Chersidamas under the shield upon the midnipple as he stept out of his chariot—down he fell in the dust and clutched the earth. These he left and wounded Charops Hippasidês, own brother to Socos. Then Socos ran up to defend his brother, and called out:

"Odysseus! your name is great in the world, you glutton

for tricks and fighting! This day either you shall boast that you have killed and stript both sons of Hippasos, a great thing indeed, or my spear shall pierce you and rob you of life!"

Then he struck his shield. Right through the shield went the heavy spear, through the belt it forced its way, and tore all the skin from his flank: but Pallas Athenaia would not let it run into his body. Odysseus knew it was no mortal wound, and stept back, saying:

"Fool, death has surely found you. It is true you have ended my fighting for the present; but you shall die here I tell you, this very day, and my spear shall lay you low. You shall give victory to me, and your soul to Hadês."

The other had already turned to retreat; but Odysseus drove his spear through the man's back between his shoulders and out at the chest. He fell with a thud, and Odysseus cried out in triumph:

"There, Socos Hippasidês! Death has been too quick for you, and you could not escape. Poor fool! Your father and your mother shall not close your eyes in death; carrion birds shall flap their wings about you and tear you to pieces. But when I die, my people will give me honourable funeral."

He pulled the spear of Socos from his own body, and out of the shield. The blood now ran and distressed him; and when the Trojans saw the blood of Odysseus flow, they called to each other and advanced all together.

Odysseus began to retreat, and called for help. Three times he shouted as loud as the man's head could hold; three times Menelaos heard the shout. He said at once to Aias beside him:

"Aias Telamonian, my noble prince! The voice of Odysseus is ringing in my ears! It sounds as if they had cut him off alone, as if they were crushing him with numbers! Let us get there through this crowd; we ought to save him. I fear something may happen to him, among the enemy alone. He is a fine fellow, and we should miss him greatly."

So they made their way to Odysseus. They found the Trojans worrying him all round like a pack of grimy jackals round a wounded stag. You have seen such a thing on the mountains. A huntsman has hit the stag with an arrow; the stag gets away, and keeps a good pace as long as the blood is warm and his knees are nimble; but when the arrow is too much for him, the carrion jackals tear and crunch him under the trees—then chance brings up a ravening lion: away go the jackals, and the lion gorges himself. So the Trojans were worrying Odysseus, strong men and many of them, while the warrior lunged out with his spear and kept them off. Then Aias marched up with that great shield like a tower, and stood by his side: away went the Trojans higgledy-piggledy. So Menelaos led him by the hand out of the crowd, until the man came up with his chariot.

But Aias leapt on the Trojans, and killed Doryclos Priam's bastard son, wounded Pandocos, wounded Lysandros and Pyrasos and Pylartês. The mighty man pressed them hard as he drove the whole field in rout, cutting down the horses and men. He was like some mountain torrent in flood, which driven by tempestuous rain pours over the land, carrying many a dry oak tree and many a pine, until it casts a mass of flotsam into the sea.

Hector had not yet heard of this, for he was fighting away on the left of the battle, near the banks of Scamandros. There, most of all, men's heads were beaten down, and uproar unquenchable was rising about Nestor and Idomeneus. Hector was having his talk with these, making a great mess with his spearplay and horsemanship, as he devastated the young men in troops.

Yet the Achaians would never have given way, but that Alexandros stopt the exploits of Machaon [2] with a three-barbed arrow in the right shoulder. The Achaians highly excited were very much afraid that he might be caught if the battle turned; and Idomeneus said:

"Nestor Neleïadês! My lord King! Do get into your chariot and take Machaon away to the ships as quickly as you can. A surgeon is worth many men, when it comes to cutting out an arrow or putting on soothing simples."

Nestor did so at once. He got in, and the surgeon got in— was he not the son of the great healer Asclepios? And the horses galloped away, not sorry to go.

But Cebrionês saw where the Trojans were being driven back, as he stood beside Hector in the chariot; and he said to him:

"Hector, we two are having a nice talk with the Danaäns here on the fringe of the battle; but the others are being driven pell-mell, horses and men. Telamonian Aias is routing them. I know him well by the broad shield on his shoulders. Let us go there ourselves, where all that furious fighting is going on and that terrific uproar."

He touched up the horses, and when they heard the whistle of the whip they sped away among Trojans and Achaians, trampling on shields and dead bodies, until the axle under them was soaked in blood, and the handrails were sprinkled with showers of drops from the horses' hooves and the wheels. Hector longed to get into the throng of men and to break it up; a terrible tumult he brought with him, and little spared

2 One of the two surgeons.

his spear. With spear and sword and great stones he was everywhere, except that he kept clear of Aias Telamoniadês.

But Father Zeus now made Aias think of retreat. He stood still, dazed, and shifted his great shield to his back. Then he retreated slowly and watchfully step by step towards his friends, looking round again and again like a wild animal.

So the lion retreats from the cattle-pen, driven away by dogs and farm-hands, who keep awake all night long to save their fat cattle from his jaws. Greedy for meat he goes straight on, but he gets none; for showers of javelins meet him thrown by strong arms, and burning fagots which frighten the bravest beast. Then in the morning he leaves the place in gloomy mood.

And Aias was gloomy enough as he retreated before the enemy, much against his will, since he feared greatly for the Achaian ships. You have seen a stubborn ass in a cornfield, who is too much for the boys. They may break many sticks on his back, but he goes on cropping the corn; they beat away with their sticks, but what is the strength of a child! They can hardly drive him out when he has eaten all he wants. So the crowds of Trojans hung upon the heels of mighty Aias, poking his shield with their poles all the time. Every now and then he would wheel about and drive off his assailants; then he turned and went on. But all the while he stood alone between the two armies, beating back the Trojans and barring the way to the ships. His great shield was stuck full of spears that strong hands had thrown; and many more stuck in the ground between, still greedy for a taste of flesh.

Retreating thus amid showers of missiles, Eurypylos saw him and came to his side; and with a cast of his spear he brought down Apisaon Phausiadês. The blow pierced the liver and killed him. Eurypylos began to strip off his armour, but this caught the eyes of Alexandros, who let fly at once. The arrow pierced his right thigh and the shaft broke. Dragging his heavy leg Eurypylos hobbled away, shrieking out:

"My friends! My lords and princes! Face about and stand! Here is Aias fighting against heavy odds—he will be shot to death! Stand and defend him, rally round Aias Telamoniadês!"

Then they formed round the wounded man, crouching on the right knee with their grounded shields resting against the left shoulder, and their spears sloped forward at the ready. Aias came towards them, and there he faced about and stood by their side. So they stood fast, and fought like blazing fire.

Meanwhile Nestor's horses were sweating and steaming, as they brought in Nestor and Machaon to the camp. Achillês was standing on the poop of his great ship, and watching the lamentable rout. He saw the chariot come, and noticed who it was, and shouted from the ship for Patroclos. In their hut

Patroclos heard the call and came out—a splendid figure, but
for him this was the beginning of evil things. Patroclos said:

"Why do you call me, Achillês? what do you want with me?"

Achillês said:

"Menoitiadês, friend of my heart! Now I think I shall have
the Achaians at my knees! Dire necessity is upon them now.
Make haste, my dear Patroclos, go and ask Nestor who is this
wounded man he is bringing out of the battle. His back looks
just like Machaon Asclepiadês, but I could not see the man's
face. The horses were going too fast."

Patroclos at once went off at a run into the camp.

By this time the party had reached Nestor's hut. They got
out; Eurymedon took out the horses, and the two men stood
on the beach to dry the sweat off their garments in the sea-
breeze. Then they went in and sat down, and Hecamedê set
about making them a posset. She was a woman from Tenedos,
the daughter of Arsinoös; when Achillês sacked the place, she
had been chosen as a special prize for old Nestor, in honour
of his wisdom and good advice at all times.

Hecamedê set before the two men a fine polished table with
feet of blue enamel, and put on it a bronze basket, with an
onion as a relish for the drink, and pale honey, and ground
barley-meal.

Beside them she placed a splendid goblet which the ancient
man had brought from home, studded with golden knobs; it
had four ears, and each ear had a pair of golden doves pecking
their food, one on either side. Under it were two supports. Another man would hardly move it from the table when it was
full, but old Nestor could lift it easily.

In this goblet the woman mixed them a posset with Pram-
nian wine, grating in goat's cheese with a grater of bronze, and
sprinkled over it white barley-meal. Then she invited them to
drink of her posset. So they drank, and slaked their parching
thirst.

While they were talking together comfortably, Patroclos appeared at the door. The ancient man sprang up from his chair,
and led him in and bade him be seated. But Patroclos declined:

"No sitting for me, my lord! I can't think of it. Formidable,
hot-tempered, is he that sent me, to ask who the wounded
man was that you were bringing in. But I know him myself, I
see it is his honour Machaon. Now I will go back and tell
Achillês. You know well enough, reverend sir, what he is like.
A terrible man! He might easily find fault where there is none."

Nestor answered:

"Indeed? Why is Achillês crying about a wounded man?
Doesn't he know the trouble that has come upon the whole
army? The best men are lying here in camp, wounded and

stricken! Diomedês Tydeidês is shot, Odysseus has a spear-thrust, and so has Agamemnon; and here is this man I have just brought from the field, shot with an arrow from the bow-string. But Achillês, brave man, cares nothing and pities none. Is he waiting until all the ships along the shore are well warmed by a general conflagration, and we ourselves are killed in a row?

"Ah, my strength is not what it was when my limbs were supple. If I were only young and strong now, as I was when that quarrel came up between Elis and our people over cattle-lifting, when I killed that brave man Itymoneus Hypeirochos' son, who lived in Elis!

"I was driving away our reprisals; he was defending his flocks from seizure, and I struck him with my spear—down he fell, and all the clowns ran away in terror. We collected a world of spoil from that countryside—fifty herds of cattle, as many flocks of sheep, as many droves of swine, as many solid flocks of goats, bayards one hundred and fifty, all mares, many with foals at foot. All these we drove through the night to Pylos; and Neleus was a glad man that I had taken a great prize, when I went as a green hand into battle. Criers went out in the morning to noise abroad, that all those who had a claim on Elis should come in. The leading men of our people assembled and did the dividing; for we Pylians were few in number and much aggrieved, and many of us had claims on the Epeians. You see Heraclês had come in former years and done a great deal of damage, when our best men were killed; for Neleus had twelve sons, and all perished but me alone. So the Epeians got above themselves and did us mischief in their impudence.

"The old King chose out carefully a herd of cattle and a large flock of sheep, three hundred, with the drovers. For a great debt was owing to him in Elis, a chariot and four horses, prize-winners, which had been sent there to the games: they were to run for a tripod. These Augeias the King held fast, but he let the driver go and mourn for his horses. So the old man took his revenge for their deeds and their words, and chose a mort of stuff himself, but left the rest to be divided up, that every one might have his rights.

"So we arranged the business and held our sacrifices all over the city. But three days later the Epeians came in full force, men and horses. With them came the two Molions, armed like the rest though they were only boys and knew nothing of battle. There is a city called Sedgetown on a steep hill, far away on the Alpheios, right at the end of sandy Pylos; they set their camp all round this place, intending to raze it to the ground.

"But when they had scoured the plain, Athena came running from Olympos in the night with the news, telling us to arm, assembling the people all over Pylos—and they were glad to come, eager for battle. Neleus forbade me to join them, and hid my horses; he said I knew nothing yet of regular war. But that was no matter; I went on foot, and yet I was to be seen among our horsemen, by providence of Athena!

"There is a river Minyeïos that empties into the sea not far from Arenê. There we horsemen waited for dawn, while the companies of footmen came pouring up. From that place our army in full force came at midday to the river Alpheios. There we sacrificed victims to Zeus Almighty, a bull to Poseidon, a heifer of the herd to Brighteyes Athena. We took our meal in messes, and slept under arms beside the river.

"The Epeians meanwhile were all round the city which they meant to destroy; but the God of War came first in his might! For when the sun rose bright above the earth, we joined battle with them calling upon Zeus and Athena. I was the first to bring down my man, Mulios the spearman, and I took his horses. He was husband of Augeias' eldest daughter Agamedê, a woman who knew all the drugs and simples in the wide world. He drove at me, I struck with my spear, he fell in the dust: and I leapt into his car and took my stand in the front. The Epeians scattered higgledy-piggledy when they saw the leader and chief of their horsemen fall. I swept on them like a thunderstorm and took fifty chariots—two fellows tumbled out of each, right and left, by the thrusts of my conquering spear, and bit the dust!

"Then I should have destroyed Actor's sons [3] the Molions themselves, but their father the mighty Earthshaker carried them out of the battle in a cloud, and saved their lives.

"Then Zeus gave signal victory to the Pylians. We chased them over the wide plain, slaying and spoiling, until we drove our horses to the wheatfields of Buprasion and the Olenian Rock and the hill of Alision, where Athena made us turn. There I slew the last man, and left him; the army drove back to Pylos from Buprasion, and all gave thanks to Zeus among the host of heaven, and to Nestor among men.

"Such was I, a man with men, as truly as I live. But the valour of Achillês will profit Achillês alone—profit! no, repentance will be his lot, when our people are all destroyed. And you, laggard! What did Menoitios say to you, when he sent you from Phthia to Agamemnon? We were there in the house, I and Odysseus, and heard all he said.

"We had been gathering recruits over the whole country, and we came to the palace of King Peleus. Then we found Menoitios and you also, and Achillês was with you. The old king was making sacrifice to Zeus Thunderer in the courtyard: he held a golden cup, and poured wine over the burnt-offer-

[3] Reputed sons of Actor.

ings. You two were busy with the meat, and there we were in the doorway; Achillês sprang up excited, and led us in, bade us be seated, and gave us the guest's due honours. When we had eaten and drunk, I began by inviting you to come with us; you were both ready and willing, and the others laid many injunctions upon you. Peleus told his son to be first and foremost in the field, and this is what Menoitios said to you:

" 'My son, Achillês is above you in rank, and he is stronger than you, but you are the elder. You must give him good advice and tell him what to do; he will obey you for his own good.'

"That was your father's bidding, and you have forgotten it. Yet even now you should remind Achillês of this and see if he will listen. Who knows whether you may have the good luck to move him by your persuasions? The persuasion of a friend is a blessing in the end. If there is some oracle from Zeus he is shy of, something his gracious mother has told him, well then, let him send you out with the Myrmidons, and you may show us light in the darkness. Let him lend you his armour to wear, and then the Trojans may take you for him; they may leave us alone to have a breathing-space from the battle. Hardly time to take your breath in the face of sudden death! But your men are all fresh, and they could easily beat a weary enemy back to their city!"

This touched the heart of Patroclos, and he set off at a run. But as he was passing the ships of Odysseus, close to the place of public meeting and the altars, he met Eurypylos limping out of the battle with the arrow in his thigh. Sweat poured over head and shoulders, and the blood still ran from his cruel wound, but he was undaunted. Patroclos was very sorry to see this, and he spoke out his feelings plainly:

"Oh you poor captains and princes! So you were to die far from home, your white fat to be gorged by the dogs of Troy!— But my dear man Eurypylos, tell me—will they keep off this fiend Hector, or will he make an end of us all?"

The wounded man answered:

"Nothing can save us now, Patroclos. They will soon be upon our ships. All our best men are laid up here already, some shot with arrows, some stabbed with spears: the enemy grow stronger and stronger. But you can save my life—just help me to my ship, and cut out this arrow, wash the blood off with warm water, put on a soothing plaster, that good stuff you learnt about from Achillês, which he got from Cheiron the Centaur, bless him! he was a gentleman. You know our surgeons, Podaleirios and Machaon—one is in camp, I think, wounded, and wants a good surgeon himself, the other is on the battlefield!"

Patroclos said:

"What will come of it? What are we to do, my dear man? I am in a hurry to give Achillês a message from Gerenian Nestor, but I can't help that, I will not desert you in this dreadful state."

He put his arm around Eurypylos and led him to his quarters. His man saw them coming, and made a bed of hides on the ground. There Patroclos laid the wounded man; he cut out the arrow, and washed the place with warm water, and crumbled a bitter root between his fingers, letting the shreds drop into the wound. This was a bitter root which cures all pain, and it took away all his pain; the blood was staunched and the wound dried.

BOOK XII

How the two armies fought before the wall, and how Hector broke down the gate

WHILE PATROCLOS WAS LOOKING AFTER THE WOUNDED MAN, a massed fight was going on outside, and it seemed that the moat was not to keep out the Trojans: that moat with the wall above it which the Danaäns had made to protect themselves and their ships, but forgot the sacrifices which were due to the gods.

The gods did not consent to the building; and therefore it did not stand long. While Hector lived, and Achillês nursed his anger, and the city of Priam was unsacked, so long that great wall stood. But when the best men of Troy were killed with many of the Achaians, and those who were left sacked the city of Priam in the tenth year, and the Achaians had sailed away, then Poseidon and Apollo determined to smother the wall. All the rivers which flow down from Ida to the sea, Rhesos and Heptaporos, Caresos and Rhodios, Grenicos and Aisepos, Scamandros and Simoeis, where shields and helmets had fallen in heaps and the bodies of brave men—all these rivers they led upon it, turning their streams together. For nine days the flood poured over the wall, and torrents of rain fell unceasing, that the sea might sooner swallow it up. Earthshaker himself guided the waters with his trident, until he had swept away all the foundations of logs and stones which the Achaians had laid with such labour; then he made smooth the shore of the Hellespont, and covered it over with sand again. When he had smothered the wall, he turned back the rivers into the courses where they had run before.

But that was to come in the future: for the time being, war and uproar blazed about the strong-built wall, and spears rattled against the stones. The Argives driven by the whip of Zeus were cooped up among their ships, for fear of Hector, that great master of panic; and he fought on and on like a furious tempest.

You have seen a lion or a wild boar in a crowd of dogs and huntsmen, turning to bay in desperate fury, while they stand like a long wall and let fly their spears in volleys; the stout heart of the beast neither fears nor trembles, but his own courage is his death. He wheels round again and again, and tries the line of men; wherever he charges, the line gives way.

So Hector ranged along his lines, hieing them on to cross the moat; but the horses would not go, they stood whinnying on the edge, for they feared that wide ditch. It could not be jumped, and it could hardly be crossed; for both banks were steep, and sharp stakes were set along the edge, many stakes, thick stakes, to keep the enemy away. A horse with a car to pull could hardly get within, but the footmen were all eager to do it.

Then Polydamas came to Hector's side and spoke:

"Hector, and you the leaders of our armies! It is madness to drive horses across a moat. This moat can hardly be crossed at all; the sides are set with sharp stakes, and there is the wall beyond. No chariots can go down there or fight there; the place is too narrow and we shall only be hurt. If it is the will of Zeus Thunderer to destroy the enemy out and out, that would be just my own wish—that the Achaians might perish inglorious far from their home. But if they turn upon us and drive us back from the ships, and if we get entangled in that deep ditch, I do not think one will be left to take the news to Ilios.

"Very well then, listen to my advice. Let our men keep the horses ready beside the moat, and let us all follow Hector in a general attack. The Achaians will not stand, if the bonds of death are really made fast upon them."

This advice seemed good to Hector, and he leapt from his car in his armour. So did all the others; each told his driver to keep his team ready in its place near the moat. Then the fighting men sorted themselves into five divisions, each under its own leaders.

With Hector and Polydamas went the largest party and the best men, fully determined to break down the wall and to attack the ships. Cebrionês was a third, for Hector had left a weaker man with his chariot.

The next party was led by Paris and Alcathoös and Agenor; the third by Helenos and Deïphobos, two sons of Priam, with Asios as third—Asios Hyrtacos' son, who had driven his pair of tall chestnuts from the river Sellëeis. The fourth was under Aineias Anchises' son, with the two sons of Antenor, Archelochos and Acamas, both masters of warfare.

Sarpedon led the allied troops, and he chose to help him Glaucos and Asteropaios, for he thought them the pick of all others. He was conspicuous himself above all.

All these ranged themselves side by side behind their shields, and marched straight for the enemy, determined not to desist until they fell upon the ships.

Only one would not follow the profitable plan of Polydamas, and that was Asios Hyrtacos' son. He did not leave driver and horses behind, but took them with him towards the ships. Poor fool! He was not to escape a cruel fate! He was not to return to Ilios in triumph with horses and car! Before that could be, his unhappy portion was to fall by the spear of Idomeneus Deucalidês. He aimed at the left of the camp, where the Achaians used to drive in and out.

The gates were not closed and bolted, but men were holding them wide open for any of their friends who might be seeking refuge. This place he chose on purpose, followed by his party, shouting and cheering; for they thought that nothing would stop them now from falling upon the ships. Poor fools! Two of the best men were in charge of the gates, Polypoitês and Leonteus, both sons of formidable Lapithans—one was the son of Peirithoös himself.

These two stood in front of the gates, like tall oak trees in the mountains firm on their deep strong roots, which face rain and tempest every day. There they stood firm in their strength to face the attack of Asios. The Trojans marched towards the wall with a loud clamour, holding up their oxhides about prince Asios and Iamenos and Orestês, Adamas Asios' son, Thoön and Oinomaos.

Meanwhile the two guardians from their post inside had been calling on their countrymen to repel the attack; but when they saw them beaten off and the Trojans coming on, they dashed in front of the gate like a pair of wild boars which receive a rout of men and dogs in the mountains. How they charge from both sides, and crush the brushwood all round, tearing it up by the roots! What a clatter of tusks is heard, until they are struck down and killed! So their armour clattered about their breasts as the blows met them; for they fought desperately, trusting in their own strength and the men on the walls. These were throwing great stones upon the enemy, which fell like showers of hail when a boisterous wind drives the dark clouds before it. So the volleys were showered by defenders and assailants alike; helmets and shields rang dry, battered by those millstones!

Then Asios groaned and smacked his two thighs, as he cried fretfully:

"I do declare, Father Zeus, you are only another lover of lies! I did not think the Achaians were brave enough to check our fury, and stop our invincible hands! And here they are like a swarm of wasps or bees in a nest on a mountain path! They won't come out of their holes unless huntsmen come by, and then they defend their young ones. These men are only two, but they will not leave that gate till they kill or be killed!"

But Zeus paid no attention, for he meant to give Hector the credit of victory.

Other parties were attacking the other gates; but I am not a god to tell the whole story, for the fire blazed all round the stone wall, and the Argives defended themselves desperately. All those gods who favoured the Danaäns were deeply distressed.

Meanwhile, the two Lapithans were making a great fight. Polypoitês ran his spear through the helmet of Damasos, and tore through the skull and scattered the brains: so his fighting days were done. Next he killed Pylon and Ormenos. Leonteus hit Hippomachos through the belt; then he drew sword, and dashing through the throng struck first Antiphatês man to man and laid him flat; Menon, Iamenos, Orestês, one after another he brought to the ground.

While these two were stripping the slain, Hector's party were standing in doubt on the edge of the moat. This was the largest party, you remember, and the best men, and most determined to make a breach and burn the ships. But they had seen an omen as they were about to cross: an eagle flying high skirted the army on the left, holding in his talons a serpent alive and panting, dripping blood as it struggled. The serpent curved back his head and struck the eagle in the breast near the neck; the sharp pain made the eagle drop him, and he fell in the crowd of men, while the eagle shrieked and flew away on the wind.

The Trojans shuddered when they saw the snake wriggling in their midst, and took it for a portent from Zeus. Then Polydamas said:

"Hector, you always find fault with me in our assemblies when I give good advice. No man of the people is allowed to disagree by any means in council or in war, he must always support you: but now again I will tell you what I think best.

"Don't let us go forward to fight these men for the ships. I think it will turn out like this omen, as surely as this was an omen meant for us. Here is an eagle flying high, skirting the army on the left, carrying a huge serpent in his talons, alive and dripping blood: drops him at once and can't take him home for his young ones. Just so we, if we do breach the wall and the enemy give way, still we shall travel back in disorder the same road. And we shall leave many of our people behind killed in the fight. That's how a diviner of any credit would interpret this omen, if he knew anything about omens."

Hector frowned at him and said:

"I don't like that way of speaking, Polydamas. You know better than that. But if you really mean what you say, you have simply gone out of your wits. Forget the commands of Zeus Thunderer; is that your advice? Forget the promise he gave me himself? Your advice is to obey a flying bird! What is a bird to me? I care nothing for birds, whether they fly east to the rising sun, or whether they fly west to the darksome gloom. We had better obey the counsels of Zeus Almighty, who rules over mortals and immortals both. The only bird that's always right, is Fight for home and country—fight! Why are you afraid of a fight? If all the rest of us are killed in this battle, there's no fear that you will be killed; you have not the pluck to stand and fight. But if you shirk your part, or if you try to persuade any one else to shirk, you shall die on the spot—here is my spear ready!"

So Hector led the way, and his men followed shouting and cheering. Then Zeus Thunderer sent forth from Ida a blast of wind which carried the dust into the faces of the Achaians. The Achaians were bewitched by this; and it brought success to Hector and the Trojans. Trusting to his omens and his strength, they assailed the wall. They tore out the stones, they dragged down the breastworks, they levered up the buttress-beams which had been sunk in the ground to support the walls, and dragged them out, and then they expected to make a breach. But the defenders would not give way: they put up their ox-hides for new breastworks, and met the enemy with volleys as they tried to climb the wall.

Aias big and Aias little were everywhere, urging the men on the wall to resist, and cheering them on. If they saw any one weakening, they were ready with kind words or hard words:

"Now my good fellows, there's work for all—the best men, the middlings, the not-so-goods! for we are not all alike, you know that yourselves. Let no man turn his back because he hears a shout—forward, all! Cheer one another on! Then Zeus Olympian with his thunder and lightning may help us to drive back the enemy to their city!"

So they went shouting along the line, and the air was full of stones hurled by both armies, Trojans against Achaians,

Achaians against Trojans, and there was a terrible din along the wall.

It was like a storm on a winter's day, when Zeus has brought up a dense cloud and showers upon mankind his volleys of snow. He lulls the winds and pours and pours, until he covers high mountains and cliffs, clover crops and the fat plowland. Down it pours on harbour and beach and sea as far as the place where the wave beats up and stops it; but all else is covered with a heavy sheet of fallen snow.

Yet the Trojans would never have made their breach, had not Zeus sent his own son Sarpedon like a lion pouncing on the cattle. He held his shield before him—a round shield of hammered bronze, lined with several layers of hide which were fastened to the rim all round with gold wire—holding this, with his two spears in hand, he moved forward like a mountain lion, long starved and now greedy to leap into the fold and try the taste of mutton. Even if he finds the drovers there with dogs and spears defending their charge, he is determined not to leave that place without one try—either he gets in and catches one, or the quick hand comes first with a lance.

That was the spirit of Sarpedon, and he said to his friend Glaucos:

"Why have you and I the seat of honour at home, Glaucos? Why have we the best portions, cups always full, and all treat us like something greater than men? And that fine estate on the banks of Xanthos, orchards and wheatlands of the best? For that, we are bound to stand now before our people in the scorching fires of battle, and then the brave men in the ranks can say—'Sure enough there is nothing mean in our kings and governors! They eat the best of meat and they drink the best of wine, but there is strength in them too, that's clear, for they always fight in front!'—We must not be laggards. If to escape from this battle meant that we should never grow old and never die, I should not be fighting here in front, and I would not send you forward to win your name. But now, since whatever we do ten thousand chances of death are about us, which no mortal man can escape or avoid—Forwards! whether we are to give fame to another, or he to us."

Glaucos was no less ready then he, and the two marched on leading their men. Menestheus was the man in charge of that part of the wall, and he shuddered to see them come in that grim fashion. He looked along the wall to see if one of the captains was there to help them; and then he saw standing Aias big and Aias little, with Teucros just arrived from the camp close by. But he could not make them hear, there was such a din, the whole air full of noise from battered shields and helmets and gates—for the gates were shut fast and the enemy up

against them trying to break them down. So he sent his herald
Thoötes to Aias:

"Off with you, Thoötês, run, and call Aias—or rather both
of them—that would be the best thing of all, or we shall all be
destroyed here before long. The Lycian chiefs are here against
us in force, and they are a real hurricane as we know from
experience. If they are pressed hard yonder let Telamonian
Aias come alone, yes and let him bring Teucros to do the
shooting."

Off ran the messenger along the wall until he found his men,
and said quickly:

"You sir, my lord Telamonian, and you sir, Oïliadês, my
commander begs you to come there if only for a little while,
both of you if you can—that will be the best thing of all, or
they will all be destroyed there before long. The Lycian chiefs
are there against them in force, and they are a real hurricane
as you know from experience. But if you are hard pressed
here also, at least let Telamonian Aias come alone and bring
Teucros to do the shooting."

Aias was quite ready, and said without wasting words to
little Aias:

"You two stay here, you and Lycomedês, and take command; I will go there and support them. I will come back at
once when I have done what I can for them."

He set out at once, with his brother Teucros, and Pandion
carried the bow. They passed within the wall to Menestheus'
tower, and found them hard pressed, for the Lycian leaders
were climbing the breastworks like a black tornado.

The newcomers joined in, and then there was a noise! Aias
killed his man first—Epiclês, a companion of Sarpedon. He
took a huge jagged stone, which lay on the top of the heap
which was ready for use inside the breastwork. A man could
not easily lift that stone with both hands, such as men are to-
day, were he ever so strong; but Aias lifted it high and swung
it, smashed the horned helmet and broke the bones of the
man's head into a mess—the breath left his bones, and he took
a header off the wall.

Glaucos in climbing the wall exposed one shoulder—Teucros let fly at him and put an end to his fighting: he went to the
rear as quietly as he could, that no enemy might notice and
boast over his defeat. But Sarpedon did notice, and it grieved
him greatly. Yet he did not forget his battle. He stabbed Alcmaon Thestor's son, and pulled out the spear; Alcmaon followed
the spear and fell flat under his clashing armour. Then Sarpedon grasped the breastwork with his strong hands, and pulled it
right down, leaving a wide gap where many men could pass.

There Aias and Teucros met him together. Teucros hit the

shield-sling which ran over his breast, but Zeus saved his son from instant death in that place. Aias leapt at him and stabbed at the shield; the point did not go through, but made him stagger and check. He moved back a little bit, but he did not leave the battle, for he still hoped for victory: he wheeled about and shouted:

"Men, why do you hold back? I may be strong, but it is hard for me to make a breech and clear the road all by myself! Come along, men! More hands make better work!"

The men were ashamed at their great leader's reproach, and pushed on harder than ever.

On the other side, the Argives strengthened their forces within the walls, and it was a desperate business. The Lycians were not strong enough to make a breach and clear the way to the ships; the defenders could not repel them from the wall now they had got a footing there. It was like a quarrel about boundaries on a common field, when two men with measuring-rods in a narrow space are disputing for their shares. So these two parties stood with the breastwork between them, beating over the top with shields and bucklers and fringe-fluttering leather targets. Many a thrust pierced the flesh, right through the shield or when one turned and showed a bare back. Everywhere wall and breastwork were bespattered with blood of Trojans and Achaians, inside and out.

But nothing could drive the Achaians back. The battle hung in the balance as truly as when an honest workwoman holds her scales in hand, weight in one and wool in the other, to earn a meagre wage for her children.

At last Zeus gave the upper hand to Hector Priamidês, who was to be first man within the Achaian wall. Hector shouted in a great voice to his men:

"Up now, Trojans! Break down this wall and set fire to the ships!"

All heard the cry, and charged the wall in a body: in a moment they were climbing over the top spear in hand.

But Hector seized a stone that lay before the gates, thick at the butt and running to a point. Two men could not easily lever that stone from the ground into a cart, not two of the strongest as men are now, but he managed it easily alone—Zeus made it light in his hands. As a shepherd easily carries a ram's fleece in one hand, and makes little of the weight, so Hector lifted that stone and carried it to the gates. There were two tall wings, strongly built and held fast within by two crossbars moving round on a central bolt. Hector stood close, setting his legs well apart to get good purchase for his blow, and drove the stone at the middle. Both hinges broke; the stone fell within by its weight, the two wings groaned and the crossbars could not hold them, but they were thrown apart by the blow.

Then Hector leapt within, his face like sudden night, his eyes blazing; light flashed from his armour, two spears were in his hands. No man alive could have checked that rush. He wheeled about, and called his men to come on: some climbed the wall, some poured in by the gate; the Danaäns fled to their ships, there was turmoil and uproar unceasing.

BOOK XIII

The battle among the ships

N OW THAT ZEUS HAD BROUGHT HECTOR AND HIS TROJANS AS far as the ships, he left them to hard fighting and endless misery. He turned his bright eyes away, and fixed them in the far distance upon the horsemaster Thracians, and the close-fighting Mysians, and the proud Hippemolgoi who drink mares' milk, and the Abioi, most gently bred of all mankind. He looked no longer on Troy; for he thought that none of the immortals would step in to help either Trojans or Danaäns.

But my lord Earthshaker kept no blind man's watch. He had come out of the sea, and climbed to the highest peak of Samothrace; from there he could see the whole of Ida, he could see the city of Priam and the Achaian ships. There he sat, amazed at the battle. He pitied the Achaians in their defeat, and great was his indignation against Zeus.

Down from the mountain he came in long strides; hills and forests trembled under the immortal feet of Poseidon Earth-shaker. Three strides he made, and the third brought him to his goal, Aigai; for there is built his famous palace in the depths of the water, all of shining gold, incorruptible for ever. There he harnessed the brazenfoot horses to his chariot, swift fliers, with manes of golden hair; he clothed himself in gold, and caught up the whip of wrought gold, and mounted the car. Then he set out over the waves; the monsters of the deep knew their master well, and gambolled about him on all sides, the sea parted before him in gladness. The horses flew quickly along, and there was no wet on the bronze axle; bounding over the waves they brought him to the Achaian ships.

There is a vast cave at the bottom of the deep sea, midway between Tenedos and rocky Imbros. There Poseidon Earthshaker stabled his horses, and gave them ambrosial fodder; then he shackled them with fetters of gold, which nothing could break or loose, and left them to await their master's return, while he went to visit the Achaian army.

The Trojans like fire and tempest were following close upon Hector, one roaring and yelling mass. Now, they thought, they would take the ships, now they would lay low their enemies beside them! But Poseidon Earthholder Earthshaker was there, come up out of the sea to put courage into the Achaians. He took the shape of Calchas with his great voice, and first he addressed the undaunted pair of namesakes:

"Aias Telamonian! Aias Oïliadês! You two must save your nation—fight away, men, never think of flight! Indeed I have no fear for the other places—let the Trojans get over the wall, our people will hold them. But I am terribly afraid something may happen where that madman is leading like a flame of fire —Hector, who boasts he is the son of Zeus Almighty! Now then you two—may God put it in your heart to stand firm and encourage the others to hold out. Then you can keep him away from the ships, try as he may, even if the Olympian himself drives him on!"

As he spoke, Earthshaker gave each a tap with his wand and filled them with stern courage. He made their limbs light, the feet and the hands upon them. Then he left them in a flash, like a hawk which hovers awhile over some lofty cliff, then darts to earth after a bird.

Aias the runner knew him at once, and said to his friend:

"That was one of the gods of Olympos, in the shape of our diviner, telling us to fight! That was not Calchas our interpreter of birds. I knew him at once by the way his feet and legs moved from behind—the gods are easy to know! He tells us to fight, and my own heart makes me want to fight more than ever. My legs are marching underneath, my arms are moving up above!"

The Telamonian answered:

"The same with me! My hands are gripping the spear, my heart is beating high, my feet are dancing along, one two, one two! I'm ready to stand alone and fight Hector Priamidês at his maddest!"

See the joy of battle which the god had put into their hearts!

While these two were talking thus, Earthshaker was in the rear, where the defeated men were having a little rest. They lay about by their ships, exhausted by the hard struggle. It was cruel pain to see the enemy swarming over the wall! Tears filled their eyes, for they hoped no longer to escape destruction. But Earthshaker passed quickly through the ranks, and tried to rally them. Teucros first and Leïtos, Peneleos, Thoas, Deïpyros, Merionês, Antilochos—all the leading spirits he whipt up with reproaches, and did not spare them:

"Shame on you, men! Are you only a lot of boys? You were my trust for defending our ships—and if you are going to shirk from the struggle, the day of defeat has dawned! Here I do declare is a miracle wrought before my eyes, a dreadful thing which I never thought to see—Trojans marching upon our ships! All this time they have been like fidgety fawns in flight, dinner for jackals and panthers and wolves, scampering about anyhow, cowards with no fight in them. All this time they would not stand up against our strong hands and stout spirit, not a bit. Now they have left their city behind! Now they fight in the middle of our camp! All because of an incompetent leader and slack followers. The men quarrel with their master, and will not defend their own ships—the enemy kill them among their own ships! Even if Agamemnon our King is really and truly to blame, because he insulted prince Achillês, it is our duty to fight, and fight we must!

"Come now, let us atone—good men are ready to give way when the offender wants to pay. It is an ugly thing that you go neglecting your duty, and you the best men in the army! I would not quarrel with a wastrel who didn't want to fight, but you make me indignant from the bottom of my heart. You sluggards! you will soon make bad worse by your slackness. Find a place in your hearts for shame and regret, for here is a great struggle upon us. Here is Hector fighting among our ships, Hector the hero has broken down our gates and their crossbars!"

Such was the Earthshaker's rousing speech. The battalions soon rallied about Aias and the Runner, strong again now and such as neither Arês nor Athena could decry. There the best men, the pick of the army, awaited Hector and his Trojans, spear against spear, shield against shield in one long fence, man pressing on man, helmet on helmet, buckler on buckler: the helmets with nodding plumes and horns touching together, so close they stood, their spears interfolded and balanced, like warp and weft on the loom.[1] The men looked straight to their front, impatient for the fray.

But the Trojans came battering on in a great mass. Hector led them with irresistible rush, like a boulder torn from the brow of a cliff by a swollen torrent, which eats under the stubborn stone and sends it bounding up and down, tearing through the trees: unswerving it rolls and rolls until it reaches the level plain, and there it comes to a standstill and rolls no more. So

---

[1] The men were standing up and the spears poised across them like the warp across the woof on the upright loom. This seems to be the meaning of the strange word "folded."

Hector threatened to traverse camp and ships right down to the sea, slaying as he went, but when he met those massy battalions he came to a standstill close against them. The Achaians faced him, stabbing with swords and spears, and thrust him from them: he gave way staggering.

Then he shouted aloud to his Trojans in piercing tones:

"Trojans! Lycians! Dardanian men of war! Stand fast! Not long shall the Achaians bar my way, although they have made themselves like a stone wall! They will yield to my spear, I think, since I am sent indeed by the greatest of the gods, the loud-thundering lord of Hera!"

Each man felt his spirit rise at these words. Then Deïphobos Priamidês in proud confidence advanced with light easy step, under cover of the tall shield which he balanced before his feet. Merionês made a cast at him and hit the great ox-hide fair and square, but the blade did not go through; the shaft broke off at the socket. Deïphobos braced the shield away from his body, daunted at this blow; but Merionês retired in dudgeon, both for the lost victory and the broken spear. He went away to fetch another spear which had been left in his hut.

The fight went on, with incessant cries and shouts. Teucros was the first to kill his man, Imbrios the spearman, whose father Mentor was famous for his horses. He lived in Pedaion before the war, and had to wife Medesicastê, a bastard daughter of Priam. But as soon as the Achaian fleet arrived, he came back to Ilios and lived with Priam, who treated him like his own sons. He had distinguished himself in the field. Teucros stabbed him under the ear, and pulled out the spear; he fell as a mountain ash is felled on a far-seen summit, and brings its soft leafage upon the ground—so he fell in his clashing armour. Teucros sprang forward to strip off the spoils, but Hector cast a spear at him as he came on. Teucros had kept him in his eye and dodged the cast by a slight movement; but the spear hit Amphimachos in the chest as he was entering the battle, and he fell with a thud in his clanging armour. This man was the son of Cteatos Actorion. Hector was advancing to pull the helmet from his temples, when Aias lunged at Hector; but none of his flesh showed, he was all covered with armour, and Aias hit only the boss of his buckler. However, the heavy blow pushed him back behind the two bodies, and the Achaians drew them away. Amphimachos was taken to rear by two Athenians, Stichios and Menestheus; Imbrios was carried off on the shoulders of Aias Telamonian and the other one. They were like a pair of lions which have torn a goat from the sharp teeth of a pack of dogs, carrying it in their jaws well above the thick bushes. So these two men carried off the dead body, and spoiled it of arms and armour. Then Oïliadês in revenge for the death of Amphimachos cut off the head, and with a swing sent it rolling through the crowd like a ball; it rolled up to Hector and lay before his feet in the dust.

Amphimachos was Poseidon's grandson; and his death made Poseidon very angry. He ranged through the Danaän ships and camp, spurring them on to fight and make trouble for the enemy. It happened that Idomeneus met him on his way from a friend who had just been brought in with a wound in the ham. Idomeneus had given charge to the surgeons, and he was now going to his own hut, for he meant to return to the battle. Then Poseidon spoke to him in the voice of Thoas, who was the lord of all Pleuron and hilly Calydon in Aitolia, and a man highly honoured by his people. He said:

"Idomeneus, my lord of Crete! Where are your threats, where are the boasts of the Achaians against Troy? Vanished into thin air!"

Idomeneus answered:

"No man is to blame, so far as I see, Thoas, for we all know how to fight. No one fears, no one plays the coward, no one shrinks or slinks away. This must be the pleasure of Cronion Almighty, as I take it; he wishes the Argives to perish here, far from Argos, without a name. But you were always indomitable, always rallying the laggards. Keep it up then, and let your voice be heard!"

Earthshaker said:

"Idomeneus, may that man never see his home again who this day shall shrink from fight of his own will—may he be sport for carrion dogs in this place! Come on now, take your arms and come with me. We must do our best together, although we are only two, and see whether we can help. Union is strength, even with poor creatures: and we two could show fight against the best!"

Then he went back to join the mellay, a god among the men. But Idomeneus equipt himself in the hut and took his two spears. He strode out in shining armour, like a thunderbolt falling from high heaven with flashes of lightning, a portent for mankind. His attendant, Merionês, met him as he left the hut, for he had come back to fetch a spear: and Idomeneus said to him:

"My good Merionês, why have you left the battle? Is that what your quick feet are for, my good friend? You must be wounded—is there an arrow hurting you somewhere? Or is there a message for me? I don't want to dawdle in the hut, I can tell you; I want to fight."

Merionês answered:

"My lord Idomeneus, I have come to find a spear if I can; I have broken the one I had against the shield of Deïphobos."

Idomeneus said:

"Spear is it? You will find one spear, or twenty spears, standing in a row in my hut—Trojan spears which I take from their dead. It is not my notion of fighting to stand half a mile away. So I have quite a stock of spears and shields and shining corselets!"

Merionês said to this:

"So have I! Plenty of Trojan spears in my hut and in my ship! but all a long way off. I don't forget my duty any more than you do, let me tell you! Whenever there is a fight, there I am in front. Perhaps some of our people may not notice me, but I am sure you know it."

Idomeneus answered:

"I know your courage—what is the use of saying that? If the best men were being picked now for an ambush—that shows who has courage and who has not! The coward changes colour flitter-flutter, he can't sit quiet with a firm spirit, shuffles from one knee to the other or squats on his two hams, his heart goes pit-a-pat and his teeth go chitter-chatter as he thinks of death. The brave man does not change colour; he is not too much afraid when he finds himself in the ambush, he prays they may come on soon. In that case, no one could think little of your courage or your hands. If you were hit in the fight by blade or by arrow, the wound would be in breast or belly—you would be prattling sweet nothings in the front rank, not running away to be shot in the neck or back!

"But come on, don't let us stay talking like children, or they will be really too hard on us—do go in and get your spear."

Merionês lost no time; he got the spear and went after Idomeneus in high spirits. When Arês the pest of mankind marches out to war from Thrace, with Panic his mighty indomitable son, who scares the strongest men to flight—they may join the Ephyrans or they may join the Phlegyans, but they do not listen to both sides; they give the victory only to one. Such another pair were Idomeneus and Merionês, as they marched out to join the battle armed from head to foot.

Merionês said to his friend:

"Where do you think we had better go, my dear fellow? Right, or centre—or left? I think that is the place where they most need help."

Idomeneus said:

"In the centre there are others to defend the ships, Aias and his second, and Teucros, the best archer we have and good also in a stand-up fight. They will harry Hector Priamidês till he has enough of it, however strong he may be. It will be a steep climb for him to beat men like those and burn the ships, fight as he will, unless Cronion himself throw a blazing torch upon them.

Telamonian Aias would yield to no man alive, if he's a man and lives on bread, if steel or stones can break his bones! Even Achillês could not beat him, that is in stand-up fight, for Achillês could beat any man in chasing a flying foe. But for us— keep to the left, this way, and we shall soon know whether we are to win name and fame or some one else."

Accordingly they moved to the left. When the Trojans saw Idomeneus blazing in his armour, and his friend with him, they shouted to one another and rushed at them all together. Then there was a furious conflict under the sterns of the ships. It was like a storm of shrieking winds when the dust on the roads is thickest, blowing up the dust in great whirling clouds. The battle bristled with spears as they hacked and killed; their eyes were dazzled with the sheen of glittering helmets and burnished corselets and shining shields in wild confusion. Hard would the heart be that could see such a conflict without pity!

Such were the calamities which the two mighty sons of Cronos brought upon the fighting hosts by their conflicting wills. Zeus willed victory to Hector and the Trojans to magnify the name of Achillês; yet he did not desire the whole Achaian race to perish before Troy, but only wished to magnify Thetis and her heroic son. Poseidon was for the Argives; he slipt out secretly from the sea and supported them because he was grieved at their discomfiture and indignant against Zeus. Yet both came of one father and one family, although Zeus was older and had more experience. Therefore Poseidon did not openly help them, but secretly always encouraged them in the form of a man. So the two gripped the rope of war and tugged away over both armies with strong pulls, never breaking or loosing it while they loosed the knees of many a man.

Then Idomeneus though grizzled with years, calling his people to follow, leapt on the Trojans and drove them back. He killed Othryoneus of Cabesos, a sojourner in the land, who had lately come to join the war. He had asked in marriage the most beautiful of Priam's daughters, Cassandra, bringing no marriage gifts, but promising to drive away the Achaians by force of arms—a great feat indeed! Priam betrothed his daughter to him, and he was fighting in faith; but as he swaggered forward Idomeneus hit him—drove his spear through the man's corselet into the belly, and he fell with a thud.

Then Idomeneus called out:

"I congratulate you, Othryoneus, as the happiest man in the world, if you really contrive to do what you promised to Priam Dardanidês! He has promised his own daughter to you, and now hear what we would offer, and do it too—we will bring the most beautiful of Agamemnon's daughters from Argos, and you shall have her, if you will join us in sacking the city of Priam. Come

along to the ships and let us make a contract of marriage—we
will not be greedy in the matter of marriage gifts!"

Then he began to drag him away by the leg. But Asios came
to defend him: he was on foot in front of his car, and the driver
kept the horses close behind breathing upon his shoulders. He
fully meant to bring down Idomeneus, but the other was first,
and ran him through the throat under the chin. He fell as an
oak tree falls, or a poplar, or a tall pine felled by shipwrights
in the forest to make a ship's mast; there he lay stretched before
his chariot, groaning and clutching at the blood-stained dust.
The driver was frightened out of what wits he had, and durst
not turn the horses to drive away; so Antilochos pierced him
also through corselet and body. He rolled out of the car gasping, and Antilochos drove the horses away.

Deïphobos now came up to revenge Asios, and made a cast
at Idomeneus; but Idomeneus had his eye on the man, and
crouched down behind his shield, a great shield of oxhide, like
a figure of eight, with two rods to hold it in shape. [2] The spear
grazed it with a dry clang, and passed over; but the cast was not
fruitless, for it struck Hypsenor Hippasidês in the liver under
the midriff and laid him low. Then Deïphobos cried out exultant
in a terrible voice:

"Not unavenged lies Asios there! And he will be glad, I think,
that I have sent an escort with him, if he must go down to Hadês
the Keeper of the Gates!"

The boastful words were bitter to the Argives, most of all to
Antilochos. But he did not forget his friend. He straddled across
the body and covered it with his shield, while two of his companions stooped and carried him away groaning, Mecisteus and
Alastor.

Idomeneus went on wild as ever, ready to die himself or to
send his enemies down into the dark. Next he brought down
Alcathoös, the son of King Aisyetês. His wife was Anchisês'
eldest daughter, Hippodameia, one very dear to her parents.
She excelled all her yearsmates in beauty and intelligence and
clever handiwork, and so she had the best man in Troy for a
husband. This man Poseidon gave into the hands of Idomeneus.
He enchanted his eyes and shackled his limbs, so that he could
neither move away nor move aside; but he stood still like a stone
pillar or a tall tree, while Idomeneus ran his spear crashing
through the corselet of bronze which had saved his body so long
—but now the metal rang dry as the spear went through into
his heart: he fell, and as the heart beat the shaft quivered. Then
at last Arês suffered the blade to abate its fury.

---

[2] There were several shapes: among them the round buckler; the tall
tower shaped like a scoop which covered the whole body; and the
figure of eight with a waist, as tall but more handy.

But Idomeneus cried out exulting in a terrible voice:

"Shall we call that a fair deal then, Deïphobos, three dead men for one? That was your boast, I think. Well, come on yourself and stand up to me, my man, and let me teach you how true a son of Zeus confronts you! Zeus first begat Minos to be warden of Crete; Minos begat Deucalion, and Deucalion begat me to be King of broad realms in Crete; and now here I come over the sea with destruction for you and your father and your countrymen!"

Deïphobos hesitated whether he should try alone, or go back to find some one to support him. It seemed best to look for Aineias.

He found him behind the rest, nursing his everlasting grudge against Priam because Priam paid no honour to so valiant a man. He told him his mind without more ado:

"Aineias, my noble prince, if you care anything for your kith and kin, now is the time to show it! Save your goodbrother! Come with me and let us rescue him! He was no more than your sister's husband, yet he brought you up from a little tot in his own house—and Idomeneus has just killed him!"

This aroused Aineias, and he rushed on Idomeneus in fury. But Idomeneus did not run away like some pampered boy. He stood his ground like a wild boar in the mountains, which awaits a rabble of men in a lonely place; the bristles shiver on his back, his eyes flash fire, he whets his tusks to beat off men and dogs. So Idomeneus stood his ground spear in hand, awaiting the assault of Aineias; he looked round for his companions, Ascalaphos and Aphareus and Deïpyros, Merionês and Antilochos, and called to them in plain words:

"This way, my friends, and help me—I am alone, and I see Aineias coming on at a great rate! He is a terrible man, a rare killer, and he is young and strong which is the greatest thing of all. If we were of one age we should soon see who would win, he or I!"

They all came at once, and stood by him, grounding their shields and leaning them against their shoulders. Aineias called to his own friends, Deïphobos and Paris and Agenor, captains like himself in the Trojan army; and their men followed, as sheep follow the wether to water from the grass. And as that sight warms the shepherd's heart, so it warmed the heart of Aineias to see the men following him.

So they rushed into conflict about Alcathoös with their long spears, and the metal of their armour rang ding-dong with the dints. The two champions Aineias and Idomeneus furiously attacked each other. Aineias cast first, but Idomeneus had his eye on him and dodged the spear—it struck in the ground quivering—a strong throw but a miss. Idomeneus pierced

Oinomaos through the plate of his corselet and spilt his bowels; he fell, clutching at the earth. Then Idomeneus pulled the spear out of the body, but he could not strip the arms; there were too many shots flying about. His knees and ankles were not firm as they used to be, and he could not charge after his own throw or get out of the way. So he stood where he was and defended his life; he could no longer leap nimbly out of danger. As he moved slowly away, Deïphobos—who was full of undying hate against him—cast again; he missed again, but hit Ascalaphos, piercing the shoulder, and Ascalaphos fell in the dust, clutching handfuls of earth. He was the son of Arês, but Arês did not yet know that his son had fallen: his uproarious voice was silent, his strong arm was still, he sat on Mount Olympos under the golden clouds held fast by the will of Zeus, with the other immortals who were there restrained from taking part in the battle.

Now there was a general scrimmage over Ascalaphos. Deïphobos tore off his helmet, but Merionês leapt forward and cast —the spear ran through his upper arm—the helmet fell banging to the ground. Merionês pounced on him like a vulture, pulled the spear out of his arm and ran back. Politês the brother of Deïphobos threw his arms round his waist, and helped him out of the mellay to the place where his chariot was waiting in the background with the driver. They drove him back to the city, groaning in pain as the blood ran from the wounded arm.

Amid the din and confusion Aineias found himself opposite to Aphareus Caletor's son, and ran his spear through the man's throat; his head drooped to one side, shield and helmet collapsed over him, and death ravished his spirit. Antilochos watched until Thoas turned his back, and lunged at him, cutting through the vein which runs up the back to the neck; he fell flat in the dust stretching out both hands to his friends. Then Antilochos leapt on him and stript off his armour, looking round as he did so under the shelter of his great shield; the Trojans struck at the shield from all sides, but they could not touch his body, for Poseidon Earthshaker protected old Nestor's son amid the shower of blows. Indeed he was never free from his enemies, but turned on them again and again; his spear had no rest, but shook and stabbed for ever; he was ever ready to cast or to attack.

Now Adamas Asiadês noticed what he was doing. He drew near and struck the shield in the middle, but Poseidon Seabluehair grudged the life and confounded the spear: it broke in half, and one part stuck in the shield like a charred stake,[3] one part fell to the ground. Adamas retreated among his friends to save his life, but Merionês followed up and stabbed him between

[3] A stake set in the ground and charred at the end to prevent rotting.

midnipple and groin, the most painful wound for miserable mortals in the changes and chances of war. The man bent over the spear struggling, as a bull struggles when bound and dragged with twisted ropes by his keepers in the highlands. So for a little while he struggled and gasped, until Merionês came up and pulled the spear out of his body; then darkness came over his eyes.

Next Helenos in close fight struck Deïpyros on the temple with his great Thracian sword, and smashed off the helmet; it was dribbled about among the feet of the fighting men until one of them picked it up. The owner was dead by this time.

This infuriated my lord Menelaos. He shouted defiance and made for Helenos, balancing his spear, and Helenos drew his bow. So both let fly at the same time, one the spear and one the arrow. Helenos hit the plate of his enemy's corselet, but the arrow glanced off; as black beans or chickpeas jump off a broad shovel on the threshing-floor from the winnower's fling in a stiff wind, so the arrow glanced off the breastplate and fell far away. But Menelaos hit the hand which was holding the bow and ran through hand and bow together; Helenos escaped to his friends, dangling his arm and dragging the spear after him. Agenor drew out the spear, and bound up the hand with a twist of sheep's wool, which his man happened to have with him for a sling.

Now Peisandros made for Menelaos—but fate was leading him straight to his end, to be brought low by your hand, Menelaos, in that dreadful battle! They approached—Menelaos cast wide, Peisandros hit his shield; the spear did not go through but snapt off at the socket. Peisandros was glad and thought he had won, but Menelaos drew sword and leapt on him. Peisandros pulled out from under his shield a fine axe with a long handle of polished olive-wood, and they came to handystrokes. Peisandros hit the other's helmet on the end of the horn just below the plume; as he came on Menelaos met him with the point, which pierced his forehead above the base of the nose. The bone broke, and both eyes fell bleeding in the dust beside his feet. He doubled up in a heap: Menelaos set one foot on his chest and stript off the armour, crying out in triumph:

"That's the way you shall say good-bye to our ships, I think, you presumptuous Trojans! Never satisfied with your violence, after all the insults and outrage you have done to me, you dirty dogs! And you did not fear the wrath of loud-thundering Zeus, the protector of the hospitable house, who shall yet destroy your city utterly. You robbed me of my wedded wife, after you had been guests in her house, and away you sailed with my wealth, quite reckless: and now you want to set fire to our ships and slay us all. No, somewhere you shall be stopped, fight as you will! O Father Zeus! Thy wisdom they say is above all, both men and gods, yet from thee come all these things! See what grace thou showest to violent men, these Trojans, whose spirit is ever ungovernable, who cannot have enough of battle and warfare! Sleep and love are very sweet, song and dance with trippling feet, yet a time comes when they pall, you can have enough of all—but these Trojans never can have enough of war!" [4]

While he said this he was stripping off the armour and giving it to his companions; when all was done, he went forward again to the fighting line.

There another man leapt at him—Harpalion, the son of King Pylaimenês, who had come to the war with his father but never went home to his native land. He struck the shield of Menelaos at close quarters, but he could not drive the spear through. He was retiring to shelter among his friends, glancing watchfully on every side, when Merionês let fly an arrow at him and hit the right buttock; the arrow went through under the bone to the bladder. He sat down where he was and breathed his last in the arms of his Paphlagonian comrades. There he lay stretched out like a worm, and his red blood soaked into the ground. His friends took charge of him and drove him back to the city, mourning; behind them came his father weeping bitter tears, and no blood-price was paid for his dead son.

But his death moved the heart of Paris, since the man had been his friend and host among the Paphlagonians; and he took a shot in revenge. There was a man there, the son of Polyidos the diviner, one Euchenor of Corinth, a man both wealthy and brave. He knew well what his fate would be before he embarked; for the good old man Polyidos had told him often enough, that he was either to die of a cruel disease in his own house, or to fall by a Trojan hand in the great war. So he avoided two evils at the same time, the fatal disease and a heavy fine,[5] and saved himself a great deal of discomfort. Paris hit this man near the jawbone under the ear: a quick death for him when the darkness took him.

So the battle went on like blazing fire. But Hector heard nothing of it; he did not know that his people were being beaten on the left of the ships. And soon the Achaians would have won the victory, such was the help that Poseidon Earthholder Earthshaker gave to them, by encouragement and by his own strength. But Hector kept where he had first entered

[4] This last sentence is condemned by critics as something that "cannot be defended" (Leaf): but it is exactly in keeping with the character of Menelaos. He cannot keep his proverbial saws even out of his prayers. By-and-by we shall hear him quoting another on the battlefield in a scene of dreadful danger (page 207).

[5] He would be fined if he refused to serve.

the gate and broken the Danaän battalions. That was the place
where the ships of Aias and Protesilaos were drawn up in
close lines along the shore; there the wall was lowest, and
there was the most desperate contest of men and chariots.

There Boiotians and Ionians, Locrians and Phthians and
redoubtable Epeians, hardly kept off his furious assault from
the ships, for he was like a flame of fire. They could not
push him back and get themselves clear, not even the picked
men of Athens. Their commander was Menestheus the son
of Peteos, and under him Pheidas and Stichios and sturdy Bias.
The Epeian leaders were Megês Phyleus' son and Amphion
and Dracios. The Phthians were led by Medon and Podarcês.
Medon was a bastard son of King Oïleus, and so he was a
brother of Aias; he lived in Phylacê, having left his country
because he killed a brother of his stepmother Eriopis. The
other was the son of Iphiclos Phylacidês. These two then were
in charge of the Phthians and attached to the Boiotians on
this day, but Aias the runner, also the son of Oïleus, would
not stir one inch from the Telamonian. They stuck together as
close as a pair of oxen breaking the fallow and pulling at the
plow like one; the sweat oozes and trickles at the roots of
their horns; only the yoke holds them apart, as they pull
might and main and cut their furrow across the field to the
headland. There is the very picture of big Aias and little Aias
keeping close side by side. Telamoniadês indeed had plenty
of strong men behind him, to relieve him of the weight of
the shield when he was tired and the sweat ran down to his
knees. But there were no Locrians with plucky Oïliadês. They
were not the men for close fighting; they wore no bronze
helmets with plumes, they had no round shields or good ashen
spears, but bows and slings of twisted yarn were their trust.
With these they shot thick and fast to repel the Trojan
battalions.

So then the front ranks met Hector and his Trojans behind
their armour, while the others volleyed from shelter; the Trojans thought no more of fight, for the arrows threw them
into disorder.

Then the Trojans would have been driven back in this ignominious way from ships and camp, but Polydamas again
offered advice to his bold leader.

"Hector," he said, "you are an obstinate man, you will never
listen to persuasion. Because God has given you prowess in
war above all others, therefore you will be wise above all
others. But you can't have everything at once. To one God
gives prowess in war, to another he gives an understanding
mind: this brings profit to many men, this saves many, as
one who has it knows best himself.

"Well, I will tell you what seems best to me. Here is all this ring of war blazing around you. Our people have got over the wall; some of them stand off armed and idle, some still fight against odds, scattered among the ships. You should go back and summon all the best men; let us discuss every plan, whether we should fall on the ships and trust God for victory, or retire while we can. Indeed I am afraid myself that the Achaians may pay back the debt of yesterday, since that insatiable glutton for war is still there, and I think he will not hold quite aloof from this battle."

This advice seemed good to Hector, and he said simply:

"Very well; I will go to the front and send back the chief men; you keep them here as they come. Then I will come back at once."

Away he went through the ranks, towering above them like a mountain, and calling for the men he wanted, who came back to Polydamas as they were told. He went on looking for Deïphobos and Helenos, Adamas and Asios. But these he could not find; they were no longer safe and sound. Two were lying dead, slain by the Achaians in front of the ships; two were in the city wounded or shot.

But one he did find soon, on the left of that lamentable battle, prince Alexandros, encouraging his men to fight. As he drew near, he reproached him bitterly:

"Damn you, Paris! you handsome coward, you woman-mad seducer—what have you done with heroic Deïphobos, and princely Helenos, and Adamas Asiadês, and Asios Hyrtacidês? What have you done with Othryoneus? Now the tall castle of Troy is ruined out and out! Now dire destruction is sure!"

Alexandros replied:

"You are blaming an innocent man now, Hector. I may have shrunk back once from the battle, but not now, for my mother's son is not quite a weakling. Indeed, from the time when you began this attack upon the ships, we have been enjoying the society of the Danaäns all the time. Our companions whom you ask for are dead. Only Deïphobos and Helenos have gone off, I think they both had spear wounds in the arm, but Cronion spared their lives.

"Now then give your orders, just as you wish. We will follow with all our hearts, and I don't think fight will be lacking so far as our strength goes; but a man cannot fight beyond his strength, try as he will."

He calmed his brother's mind with these words, and they passed on to the thickest and hardest of the fray, round about Cebrionês and Polydamas, Phalcês and Orthaios, heroic Polyphetês and Palmys, Ascanios and Morys, two sons of Hippotion, who had come from Ascania in relief the morning before.

Then Zeus gave them spirit to fight. They moved like a tempest of stormy winds that swoops on the earth under the thunder of Father Zeus, and mingles with the waters amid tumultuous noise, the waves dashing and splashing over the roaring seething sea, curved and crested, first one line and then another line—so rolled the Trojans on, first one serried line and then another line, a sea of metal flashing and crashing as they marched behind their leaders.

Hector Priamidês was in front, looking like man's evil genius, the god of war himself. Before him he held his well-balanced shield, made of thick oxhide and overlaid with bronze. On his temples was a shining helmet with nodding plumes. At every point he tested the opposing battalions, advancing under cover of his shield to see if they would give way; but the Achaians undaunted stood their ground.

Aias first came striding out, and challenged him:

"My dear man, come close! Why do you try to frighten Argives? That is useless: we are not unacquainted with battle, although the cruel scourge of Zeus has humbled us. I doubt not it is your hope to destroy our ships; but we also have hands to defend them. Before that, I tell you, that noble city of yours is like to be taken and sacked by our hands. For yourself, I say, the time is near, when in flight you shall pray to Father Zeus and All Gods, that your horses may be swifter than falcons and carry you into your city over the dusty plain."

As he said this, a lucky bird appeared on the right, an eagle flying high. The Achaian army took heart at the omen and cheered loudly. Then Hector answered:

"What nonsense you do talk, Aias, you blundering lout! I wish I were as certain to be the son of Zeus Almighty with Queen Hera for my mother, and to be worship like Athenaia and Apollo, as this day now here is certain to bring ruin for the Argives one and all! And among them you shall die yourself, if you dare to face my long spear, which will tear your lily-white skin. You shall feed the carrion dogs and vultures of Troy with your fat and your flesh as you lie in front of your Achaian ships!"

Then he led the way, and his people followed with loud cheering, while all the army behind cheered loudly. The Achaians raised their answering cheer, and stood to await the Trojan champions, ready for the contest. The noise of the two hosts resounded to the glorious heavens of Zeus.

BOOK XIV

*How Hera deluded Zeus and sent him to sleep; and
how in consequence the tide of battle turned*

WE LEFT NESTOR IN THE HUT OVER HIS WINE. ALTHOUGH
he was busy with this, he did not fail to hear the uproar
outside, and he said to the wounded man bluntly:

"Machaon, my dear sir, what do you think is going to come
of all this? There's more noise over there by the ships with
these young hotheads shouting. You just sit and drink your
wine until Hecamedê warms the water and washes your wound.
I'll find a gazybo somewhere and have a look round."

He picked up the shield of his son Thrasymedês which lay
in the hut (he had taken his father's), and chose a good
sharp spear, and went out. But standing where he was he
could easily see the shameful sight—the wall knocked down
and men in rout, and Trojans chasing at their heels! The old
man's mind was now heaving blindly, like the sea when it
purples with a long ground-swell, foreboding the shrill courses
of whistling winds, but uncertainly, for the waves do not roll
forward either way until some decided blast comes down. So
he was in doubt between two, whether to join the Danaän
mass, or to seek out King Agamemnon.

At last he decided for Agamemnon, and left the men killing each other, while the hard metal cracked and rang under
the dint of swords and spears.

On his way Nestor met the princes who had been wounded
coming up from the ships, Tydeidês and Odysseus and King
Agamemnon—for their ships were a long way off from the
battle, drawn up in lines near the sea. But they had run the
first ships high and dry, and the wall had been built close
under the sterns. For no beach however wide could have
held all the ships, and the army had not much room; so they
had arranged them in lines, and filled the whole width of the
shore which the headlands of the bay enclosed.

The princes then were coming up together leaning on their
spears, to see how the battle was going, and they were deeply
despondent. There the ancient man met them and filled them
with consternation. Agamemnon said:

"My lord Nestor Neleïdês, why have you left the battlefield, why are you here? I fear that terrible Hector will fulfill the boast he made to his Trojans, that he would never return to Ilios until he had burnt the ships and killed us all! That is what he said, and here it is coming true. I do declare the whole nation have a grudge against me like Achillês, and they will not fight even before the sterns of their own ships!"

Nestor said:

"Yes, here it is plain before our eyes, and not even Zeus Thunderer himself could undo it. The wall is in ruins, and we thought it would be an impregnable defence for ships and men. Here's the battle beside our ships—no rest, no pause; stare as hard as you like, you can't tell which way the Achaians are being driven—nothing but a muddle and men being killed, and the noise resounds to heaven. Do let us consider what is to be done, if wits are any good; but the battle is no place for us—a wounded man cannot fight."

Agamemnon said:

"Nestor, there they are, fighting close under our ships; the wall we built was of no use, nor the moat where every one worked so hard. We did hope it would be an impregnable defence for ships and men! But it must be the will and pleasure of Zeus that the Achaian nation should perish, far from Argos, without a name. I knew it when he was ready to defend the Danaäns, I know it now when he magnifies the enemy as if they were very gods, and shackles our hands and spirits as he has done.

"Well then, this is my advice. Let us launch the first ships that lie near the sea, and moor them afloat by anchor-stones, and wait for the blessed night, if that will make them cease fighting. Then we can draw down all the other ships. Yes, to flee from trouble is quite right, even if you flee by night. Better fight and run away than tarry to be caught next day."

Odysseus said to him with a frown:

"Curse you, Atreidês! What a saying to let slip between your teeth! I wish you had some other army to command, some contemptible army instead of us! Zeus it seems has given us from youth to old age a nice ball of wool to wind—nothing but wars upon wars until we shall perish every one. Is that how you mean to leave the great city of Troy, for which we have suffered such hardships? Be silent, and let no other Achaian hear these words which no man ought to let pass his lips, if he knows what decent talk is like, much less a sceptred king, and one who is at the head of all these nations that you are lord of.

"What you said just now seems to me simple nonsense. Here in the middle of battle and war you tell us to launch our ships, that you may give the enemy their hearts' desire: they are victorious already, and you want to destroy us utterly. For our men will not keep up the fight while the ships are being launched. They will be always looking behind their backs and slinking to the rear. Then your plan will destroy us, most potent captain!"

Agamemnon answered:

"Oh Odysseus! you have cut me to the heart by that cruel reproach! If the people do not wish to launch the ships I do not ask them to do it. I only wish some one could tell us of a better notion, let him be young or old; I should be glad indeed."

Then Diomedês spoke up:

"The man is near—we shall not have far to look—if you will only listen and not be offended because I am the youngest in this company. But I come of good blood; I am the son of Tydeus, who lies in his grave in Thebes. I am descended from Portheus lord of Pleuron and Calydon; he had three sons, Agrios and Melas and Oineus my father's father, the most valiant of them all. My father left home and settled in Argos, by the will of heaven. He married a daughter of Adrestos; he had a rich estate, plenty of wheatlands, plenty of orchards, plenty of flocks and herds. He was the most notable spearman in the nation; you must know whether I tell the truth.

"So you cannot call me lowborn or weakling as any reason for disregarding what I say. Come on! Let us go to the battlefield! If we are wounded we can't help that. We must keep out of range ourselves, or it may be one wound upon another; but we can rally the others and encourage them, I mean those who pleased their temper and would not fight."

All agreed to this; and Agamemnon led the way to the battlefield.

But the famous Earthshaker kept no blind man's watch: he saw them go, and went after, taking the shape of an old ancient gaffer. He took hold of Agamemnon's right hand, and said in plain words:

"Your Grace, now I guess Achillês is reet fain in that cruel heart of his, when a sees blood and rout among us, for a has no sense in his head, not a jot. May a be damned so, may God whistle him down! But tha'rt a' reet, the blessed gods bain't angered wi' thee, not they. Do 'ee bide a bit, and thast see yon gurt lords and captains dusten across the plain to home!"

Then with a great shout he scampered away. The voice of Lord Earthshaker sounded from his chest as loud as the noise of nine or ten thousand men shouting in hot battle; and every man of the Achaian host as he heard felt the strength increase within him to fight on and never yield.

But Queen Hera stood on a peak of Olympos, watching. She knew him at once, her own brother and her husband's, and glad she was to see him so busy in the battle. She saw Zeus also, seated on Ida among the mountain brooks, and a hateful sight she thought him. She began at once to scheme how she might beguile him; and this seemed the best plan. She would prink herself out for a visit to Mount Ida, and entice him to lie by her side in love, so that quiet and balmy sleep might drown his eyes and mind.

So she went to her chamber—which her own son Hephaistos had built for her, with doors closed by a secret lock which no other god could open. She closed the doors, and first she washed every speck and stain from her lovely body with a bath of ambrosia. She anointed her body with oil, ambrosial, soft, scented with perfumes—do but stir it, and the fragrance fills the whole palace of Zeus with its brazen floor, heaven above and earth beneath! She combed her shining hair, and plaited long ambrosial braids to hang from her immortal head. About her she draped an ambrosial robe, which Athena had made so smooth and embroidered with beautiful patterns; she fastened this with golden pins at the breast. She put a girdle round her waist with a hundred dangling tassels, and hung in her dainty ears earrings with three mulberry-drops, delicate and graceful. She spread over her head a new and beautiful veil, white as the sunlight, and upon her feet she laced her shapely shoes.

When all was done, she issued from her chamber, and called Aphroditê apart to tell her a secret:

"Will you do something for me, dear child, if I ask you? Or are you too angry with me for favouring the Danaäns, and will you say no?"

Aphroditê replied:

"Say what you want, my gracious Queen! I will do it with all my heart, if I can do it, and if it is doable."

The artful Queen answered:

"Give me now your charm of love and desire, with which you subdue both mortal men and immortal gods. I am about to visit the ends of the earth, to see Oceanos the father of the gods, and Tethys their mother. You know they took me from Rheia's hands, and brought me up and cared for me in their own house, at the time when Zeus Allseeing thrust Cronos down below the earth and the unvintaged sea. I want to see them and make up their old standing quarrel. They have been at odds for a long time, separate in bed and board, because of some grudge or other. If I can persuade them and bring them together again as loving as before, they will love me and make much of me for ever."

Aphroditê said with a smile:

"I could not say no to that, and I ought not, for you sleep in the arms of almighty Zeus."

So saying, she took out of her bosom the broidered strap with all the charms worked in it: there is love, there is desire, there is lovers' tender prattle, the cajolery which deceives the mind of the wisest. She dropt it into Hera's hands and said:

"Here you are, tuck this into your bosom, this embroidered strap in which everything is worked. I do not think you will fail in winning your heart's desire."

Queen Hera smiled with her lips and her limpid eyes, and smiling she laid it in her bosom.

Aphroditê returned into the house, and Hera sprang from the heights of Olympos. One step to Pieria, one step to Emathia, she sped over the snowy mountains of the Thracian horsemasters, stepping on the topmost peaks, for her feet did not touch the level ground; from Athos she stept over the sea to Lemnos, the realm of princely Thoas.

There she met Sleep, Death's brother, and grasped him by the hand as she said:

"My dear Sleep, you are lord of all gods and all mankind! This is not the first time you have done something for me—listen to me once more! and I will be grateful to you all my days. Lull me the bright eyes of Zeus under his brows as soon as I shall have lain by his side in love. I will reward you with a fine throne, incorruptible, made of solid gold; my son Crookshank Hephaistos shall make it with all his best craftsmanship, and a footstool underneath to rest your soft feet upon while you drink your wine."

Sleep answered:

"My most gracious and honoured Queen! Any other of the immortal gods I could easily put to sleep, even the stream of Oceanos who is father of all—but Zeus Cronion I would not dare to come near, nor could I put him to sleep unless he should himself command me. I have learnt a lesson from your requests once before, that time when the ambitious son of Zeus sacked Troy and sailed away.[1] Then I did indeed lay the mind of Zeus Almighty by drowning him in deep slumber; and you made a dangerous plan—you raised a tempest upon the sea, and drove Heraclês far away from his friends to Cos.

"When Zeus awoke he was very angry, and knocked the gods all over the place. But he wanted me most of all; and if he had found me, he would soon have got rid of me—thrown me out of heaven into the sea, if Night had not saved me! She can

---

[1] Heraclês, the son of Zeus, had attacked Troy to punish King Laomedon for breaking his promise. Hera had always been the enemy of Heraclês; and she persuaded Sleep to make Zeus unconscious while she raised a storm against Heraclês. Zeus punished her as is told in the fifteenth book, and Hephaistos tried to help her; for which Zeus threw him out of heaven. The whole story is given under Heraclês in Smith's *Dictionary of Biography and Mythology*.

tame both gods and men! I took refuge with Night, and by and by he was pacified, for he was loth to offend Night.

"And now you tell me to do another desperate thing!"

Queen Hera said again, with a look from her limpid eyes:

"My dear Sleep, why do you worry about all that? Do you think Zeus will be as angry about Trojans as he was about his own son? Look here, I will give you one of the young Graces, you shall woo her and wed her! You shall have Pasithea, whom you have always wanted!"

Sleep was delighted, and said:

"Very well, swear me an oath by the inviolate water of Styx, touching mother earth with one hand and the glittering sea with the other; call to witness the gods below with Cronos; and swear on your honour that you will give me one of the young Graces, Pasithea to wit, whom I have wanted all my days!"

Hera swore the oath as he asked, and called to witness all the gods under Tartaros who are called the Titans.

When the oath was finished, the two passed swiftly through the air clothed in mist, leaving Lemnos and Imbros behind, on their way to Ida. mother of wild beasts, among the mountain brooks. They left the sea at Lectos, and passed over the dry land with the treetops waving under them.

There Sleep waited, before Zeus could see him. He took the shape of a whistling bird, which the gods call chalcis, but mortals call cymindis; and he perched on a lofty pine, tallest of all the trees which then grew on Ida; it pierced through the mists into high heaven. There he stayed hidden among the foliage.

Hera walked quickly up to Gargaros on the top of Mount Ida, and Zeus Cloudgatherer saw her come. When he saw her, what love filled his heart! He felt then as he did when first they mingled in love, that time when they had gone to bed and their parents knew nothing about it.

He rose and stood before her, saying:

"Why, Hera, whither away so fast? What brings you here? I don't see the chariot and horses!"

His artful queen answered:

"I am going to visit the ends of the earth. I want to see Oceanos, the father of all the gods, and their mother Tethys, who brought me up and cherished me in their own house. I want to reconcile their old quarrel; for they have been at odds this long time, and keep apart in bed and board for some grudge or other. My horses are down at the foot of the mountain, ready to carry me over moist and dry. You are the reason why I came here. I was afraid you might be angry with me afterwards if I go to the house of Oceanos without telling you."

Zeus Cloudgatherer answered:

"My dear, you can go there by and by, but now let us to bed and take our joy! Indeed, no love of goddess or woman has ever come over me like this in a flood and possessed my heart—not when I was in love with Ixion's wife who brought me the wise Peirithoös: not when I was in love with beautiful Danaë Acrisios' daughter, who brought me the glorious Perseus; not when I was in love with the daughter of famous Pho'nix, who brought me Minos and Rhadamanthys; not when I loved Semelê or Alcmenê in Thebes, and one brought me mighty Heraclês, one Dionysos the darling of the world; not when I loved glorious Leto, nor indeed yourself—never was I in love so deeply as I love you now and sweet desire holds me captive!"

His artful queen said:

"You dreadful creature! What a thing to say! You want to make love on the top of a mountain where any one can see! What if one of us gods should see us asleep and go and tell tales to the whole family? I couldn't get up from this bed and go straight home, I should be ashamed. If it is really your wish, if you are bent upon it, there's my room for you, built by Hephaistos with good strong doors. Let us go and lie there, since you are pleased to desire bed."

Zeus Cloudgatherer answered:

"My dear, you need not be afraid that god or man will see. I will gather about us such a golden cloud that Helios himself could not see through, and his sunlight is the strongest light there is."

As he spoke, he took his wife in his arms: and under them the earth divine made a bed of fresh new grass to grow, with dewy clover and crocus and hyacinth soft and thick, which raised them high above the ground. There they lay, and a beautiful golden cloud spread over them, from which fell drops of sparkling dew.

While the Father lay motionless on the top of Gargaros, mastered by love and sleep, with his wife in his arms, Sleep ran quickly to the Achaian ships with news for Poseidon Earthshaker. As soon as he came near enough he blurted out:

"Have your way now, Poseidon! Help the Danaäns, give them victory just for a little, while Zeus is still asleep! I have drowned him in soft slumber myself—Hera has enticed him to bed with her!"

Then he was gone to his work among the nations of mankind.

But he left Poseidon more eager than ever to support the Danaäns. He leapt to the front and shouted:

"Look here, men! Are we going to let Hector Priamidês beat us again? Is he to take our ships and triumph? That's what he says, that is his boast, because Achillês is in the sulks and keeps out of it. We shall not miss the man much if we do our best to help ourselves.

"Listen to me now and do what I tell you. Let us take the best and biggest shields in the camp, and put on the most shining helmets, and seize the longest spears we can find, and then forwards! I will lead you, and I don't think Hector Priamidês will stand before my charge. If there is a staunch fighting man who has only a small buckler, let him give it to some worse fellow with a larger shield and take his."

So Tydeidês and Odysseus and King Agamemnon marshalled them in spite of their wounds, and went about everywhere changing the gear. The good man took the good armour, and gave his worse gear to a worse man. When all were properly arranged, they marched forward. Poseidon Earthshaker led them like a thunderbolt of war, holding a terrible sword long and sharp. No man may meddle with him in the deadly combat, but fear holds them back.

On the other side Hector marshalled his forces. Then came the most dreadful tug of war between Seabluehair Poseidon and Hector the brilliant hero, the Trojans behind one, the Argives behind the other. The sea rolled up to the Argive camp and ships, and the armies met with deafening warcries. Not so loud are the waves of the sea booming against the land, when it rolls in from the deep before the blusterous northeaster; not so loud is the roar in the glens of a blazing mountain, when fire leaps upon the forest; not so loud is the shrieking wind in the treetops, the angriest wind that roars, as the terrible noise of Trojans and Achaians shouting and yelling while they leapt to their struggle for life and death.

Hector first cast a spear at Aias, who was turned full towards him. That cast was no miss—he struck his chest in the place where the shield-strap and sword-strap crossed. They saved his body from a wound; Hector was angry that his cast had no effect, and stept back into safety. As he retired, Aias picked up a large stone—there were many such knocking about under the feet of the men, mooring-stones for the ships—one of these Aias lifted high and threw it at Hector. The stone went over the shield-rim, and striking his chest near the neck sent him spinning like a top with the blow—round and round he went all over the place, and fell flat in the dust. He was like a tree struck by lightning and torn up by the roots with a vile smell of sulphur—enough to daunt any one who saw it close, for dangerous is the thunderbolt of Zeus! The spear fell from his hand, helmet and shield collapsed over him in a heap, his armour crashed and clanged about him.

Then the Achaians ran at him shouting, volleying, stabbing, hoping to drag him off; but no one could touch him, for there were good men about him by this time—Polydamas and Aineias and Agenor, Sarpedon the Lycian and Glaucos, and the others also did their parts, holding their round shields before him. His friends lifted him with their hands and carried him out of the battle to the rear, where the driver was waiting with horses and chariot. So he was driven back towards the city, groaning heavily.

When they reached the ford of the river Xanthos, they laid him on the ground and poured water over him. Upon this he came to himself and opened his eyes. He sat up on his knees and vomited blood; then he fell back upon the ground, still dazed from the blow, and his eyes closed again.

The Argives assaulted more furiously than ever when they saw Hector retire. Aias the Runner first of all leapt upon Satnios, the son of a water-naiad who was born while his father was tending herds beside the river Satnioeis. Aias caught him up and stabbed him in the flank, which laid him flat, and there was a general combat about his body. Polydamas Panthoïdês defending him threw his spear at Prothoënor: it ran through the right shoulder, and Prothoënor fell, clutching at the earth. Polydamas shouted loud in triumph:

"Lo and behold! there's one more spear not wasted, when it leaps from the firm hand of Panthoïdês! One of the Argives has caught it in his body, and he will have something to lean on as he hobbles down to Hadês!"

This taunt infuriated the Argives, and Aias in particular, the Telamonian I mean, who was close by where the man fell. Quickly he made a cast while Polydamas was moving back. Polydamas dodged aside and saved himself, but it caught Archelochos Antenor's son, who was doomed by providence to die as it seems. The point struck where head and neck join at the top of the spine and cut through both sinews. Head and nose and mouth hit the ground before legs and knees came near it.

Then Aias shouted out:

"Think a moment, Polydamas, and answer me truly: Is not that man's life a fair price for Prothoënor? He does not seem to me a common man, or a son of common people; he must be Antenor's brother, or his son, he is exactly like him in looks."

He knew him well all the while, but his taunt provoked the Trojans. Then Acamas straddled across his brother and stabbed Boiotian Promachos, who was trying to drag the body away by the feet. Acamas shouted out triumphantly:

"Champion bowmen[2] you Argives are, and too fond of boasting! I don't think we shall be the only ones to suffer and sorrow:

[2] A taunt: you hide behind and shoot instead of fighting man to man.

some of you shall die here beside us. See how your Promachos lies asleep—and my spear brought him down. I would not have my brother's blood-price long unpaid. That is why a man prays to have one of his kinsmen left, that he may save the family from disgrace."

This boasting speech enraged the Argives, and Peneleos most of all. He rushed at Acamas, but Acamas did not wait for him, so he attacked Ilioneus. This man was the only son of Phorbas, whom Hermês loved most of all the Trojans, and blessed his wealth, so that his flocks were many. Peneleos stabbed him at the root of the eye, under the brow, and tore out the eyeball; the spear went through the eye and out at the nape of the neck, and the man sank down stretching out both hands. Peneleos drew his sword and cut right through the neck; head and helmet fell to the ground with the spear still sticking in the eye. Then Peneleos held it up for the Trojans to see, like a poppy-head on a long stalk, and cried exulting:

"Kindly send word to the father and mother of his honour Ilioneus to arrange for the mourning of their son at home. For the wife of Promachos Alegenoridês is in the same case; she will not have the joy of meeting her beloved husband, when we Achaians return home from Troy."

They trembled in every limb to hear these words, and each man looked about to see how he might escape death.

Now the battle had turned, and many of the Achaians lifted the blood-spoils of their enemies. Telamonian Aias stabbed Hyrtios Gyrtiadês the Mysian captain; Antilochos despoiled Phalcês and Mermeros; Merionês killed Morys and Hippotion; Teucros brought down Prothoön and Periphetês. Then Atreidês stabbed prince Hyperenor in the side and let out his bowels; his soul flew quickly out of the wound, and darkness covered his eyes. But Aias Oïliadês killed more than any other; for he was a quick runner, and no man was like him for running down those who ran away when Zeus put fear into their hearts.

BOOK XV

How Zeus awoke, and what he said to Hera;
how Hera took his message to the divine family and
what they all said to it; and how the two armies
fought among the ships

THUS THE TROJANS WERE DRIVEN OVER THE MOAT AND stakes, and many had fallen; now they halted beside their chariots, pale with fear, terror-stricken.

But Zeus awoke on Mount Ida by the side of Hera his consort. He sprang up and stood, looking at the battlefield. There were the Trojans in rout, there were the Achaians pelting in pursuit with Lord Poseidon among them; there was Hector lying on the plain, and his companions sitting around him—and he dazed, breathing heavily, vomiting blood, for no weak hand had dealt that blow.

The Father of gods and men was moved with pity to see the man, and he said to Hera with an angry frown:

"This is another of your evil schemes, you unmanageable creature! Your trick has driven him from the battle and routed his people. I should not be surprised if you were sorry by-and-by for your wicked web-spinning, when you get the first taste of the fruit, and a good thrashing from me. Don't you remember how I hung you up with two great stones tied to your feet and a golden chain round your wrists, too strong for any one to break? There you dangled in the clouds! The gods were indignant, but they could not go and set you free. Any one I caught I picked up and hurled from the threshold, and down he came to the earth with very little breath left in his body! Even that could not console me for my intolerable anxiety about Heraclês, when you seduced the storms to send him before the north wind over the sea, and then landed him in Cos—another of your mischievous plots! I saved him from Cos indeed, and brought him back to Argos after many hardships. I'll give you cause to remember all this and stop your deceits. You shall soon find out if you get any good by your loving and your bedding and by coming all this way to deceive me!"

Hera shivered at these words, and protested:

"I call on Earth to witness, and the broad Heavens above, and the force of Styx, which is the most solemn oath for the blessed gods, and your sacred head, and our own marriage bed which I would never lightly name, it is not my doing that Poseidon Earthshaker plagues Hector and the Trojans and helps the other side! I suppose his own temper moves him, and pity for the Achaians hard pressed beside their own ships. Why, if he would take my advice, he would follow wherever you lead, Thundercloud!"

The Father of gods and men smiled and answered, very much to the point:

"Ah yes, my dear lady, if only *you* could have one mind with me as you sit in our family circle, Poseidon would soon change his mind to suit yours and mine, however much he might want something else.——But if you are really speaking the truth, go home and tell Iris and Archer Apollo to come here.

"I want to send Iris to tell Poseidon that he must stop meddling in the war and go home; and I want Apollo to breathe courage into Hector again, and make him forget the pain that torments him, and send him back to the battle. The Achaians are to be turned again in headlong flight, and to fall back on the ships of Achillês; he is to put up his friend Patroclos; and Hector is to kill Patroclos under the walls of Ilios, after he has killed many other fine fellows, and among them Sarpedon my own son. Then Achillês in revenge for Patroclos is to kill Hector.

"After that I will make the Achaians sweep the Trojans away from their camp completely, and they shall take the city according to Athena's plans. But meanwhile I will not relent, and I will not allow any other of the immortals to help the Danaäns here, until I fulfil the desire of Peleidês, as I promised to do and bowed my head to confirm it, on that day when Thetis embraced my knees and prayed to me to give renown to Achillês."

Hera durst not disobey. As quickly as the mind of a man can move, when he had travelled far over the wide world, and remembers many places as he thinks "I would be there, or there," and there he is—so Hera flew quick as thought from Ida to high Olympos.

She found the immortal gods assembled in the hall of Zeus. All rose and held up their cups in welcome; she took no notice of the others, but she accepted the cup from Themis, who had run first to meet her, saying without ceremony:

"My dear Hera, why have you come? You seem upset. I'm sure your lord and master has given you a fright."

Hera replied:

"Goddess alive, don't ask me! You know yourself what his temper is, the hard-hearted tyrant! Just sit down and take charge of this meal. I'll tell you about it, and every one shall hear what wicked things he talks of doing! I don't think it will be equally pleasant to every one, man or god, if there is any one of our party who still feels comfortable."

Hera sat down as she spoke. Every one in that hall was disquieted now; Hera laughed with her lips, but there was no warmth on the forehead above those black brows, as she turned towards the whole company and said with indignation:

"We are fools to harbour rebellious thoughts against Zeus, just silly. We still want to walk up and put a stop to him by main force—or by plain talk! and he sits by himself and takes no notice—simply doesn't care. He says he is the best god among us, and the strongest, yes decidedly! So you had better keep whatever nasty little gift he sends each of you. There is one parcel of trouble, I believe, ready for Arês. His favourite son has been killed in battle, Ascalaphos, at least Arês calls him son."

At this Arês slapt his two thighs with his open hands, and cried out in dolesome tones:

"Now don't be surprised, my good Olympians, if I go and pay out those Achaians for my son's death! Yes, even if my fate is to be struck by a thunderbolt from on high, and I have to lie with a heap of corpses in the blood and dust!

"Here, Terror and Panic!" he shouted, "my horses!" and proceeded to put on his armour.

And now there would have been another quarrel between Zeus and the whole family, worse and more dangerous than the quarrel in the Achaian camp, but Athena saw the danger for their own peace—left her seat, dashed out of the door after Arês, tore the helmet off his head and the corselet off his shoulders, pulled the spear from his fingers and put it back in the stand, and rated him roundly:

"You're mad, you're crazy, you're done for! You have ears but you can't hear, you have no sense or decency! Don't you take in what Hera says, straight from Olympian Zeus? Do you want to do no end of mischief and then come home miserable as you'll have to do, and bring disaster on all the rest of us? He will leave Trojans and Achaians on the spot, and go for us, ramping into Olympos, grabbing one after another innocent and guilty. Forget your son, I tell you. Many a better man and stronger man than he has perished, or will perish as time goes on. It is a difficult thing to save the whole human race!"

As she spoke, she pulled Arês back to his seat still furious. But Hera called Apollo outside, with Iris, who was the errand-girl in the divine household, and said without more ado:

"Zeus says you must go to Ida as quick as you can. When you have entered the presence, do what his lordship commands you."

Hera went back to her seat, and the other two went flying to Mount Ida, where the wild beasts breed among the running brooks. There they found Cronidês Allseeing seated upon the heights of Gargaros in the midst of sweet-scented clouds.

They came and stood before Zeus Cloudgatherer, and he was not displeased that they had so quickly obeyed the summons. And first he told Iris her mission in a few plain words:

"Off with you, Iris, my quick one! Give this message to Lord Poseidon, and be no untruthful messenger.

"Tell him to stop fighting, to leave the war and join the divine family, or go down into the sea. If he disregards my words and will not obey, tell him to consider carefully whether he is strong enough to stand up against me: remind him that I am far more powerful than he is, and elder born, yet he does not shrink from calling himself equal to me whom the others fear."

Iris obeyed: swift as the wind she flew from Ida to Ilios, swift as the snow or hail which falls from a cloud when the cold blast of Boreas blows. She alighted beside the Earthshaker and spoke:

"A message for you, Earthholder Seabluehair! I bring a message from Zeus Almighty. He bids you stop fighting and leave the war, to join the divine family or go down into the sea. If you disregard his words and will not obey, his lordship threatens to come to this place and fight you force against force. He bids you keep clear of his hands, for he says he is far more powerful than you are and the elder born, yet you do not shrink from calling yourself equal to him whom the others fear."

The Earthshaker angrily replied:

"Confound it, that is a tyrant's word, though he may be strong! I am his equal in rank and he will constrain me by force! We are three brothers, the sons of Cronos and Rheia—Zeus, and I, and Hadês who rules the lower world. All was divided among us in three parts, and each has his prerogative. We cast lots, and I got the sea, Hadês the gloomy darkness, Zeus the broad heavens high amid the clouds: earth and Olympos were left common to all. Therefore I will not live at the beck and call of Zeus; let him enjoy his own share in peace, even if he is a strong one. But let him not think to scare me with his strong hands as if I were something contemptible. He would do better to try scolding and scaring his own sons and daughters, who must obey whether they like it or not."

Iris said:

"Then that is your answer which I am to report to my master, Earthholder Seabluehair? so stubborn and stiff? or will you change a bit? The noblest natures you will find are not too stiff to change their mind. You know how the Avenging Spirits always attend the elder born."

Then Poseidon Earthshaker answered:

"Iris, my dear goddess, you are quite right. A messenger with news to bring should understand the proper thing. But I tell you it hurts me through and through, when I am his partner, and I have an equal share, and yet he wants to scold me with angry words. Look here, I will give way, though it makes me indignant. But let me say something more—here is a threat which I mean to carry out. If he goes against me and Athena and Hera and Hermês and Hephaistos, and spares Ilios, if he will not destroy the city and give victory to the Achaians, between us two there will be hatred which nothing can heal."

With this the Earthshaker left the battlefield and dived into the sea; and the Achaians missed him badly.

Then Zeus Cloudgatherer said to Apollo:

"Now my dear Phoibos, you go to Hector. Earthshaker has disappeared into the sea at the threat of my wrath, or others would have heard of our feud, I mean the gods in the underworld, Cronos and the rest. But it is much better for us both that he kept clear of my hands, or the matter would not have been settled without sweat!

"Here, take my tasselled aegis-cape, shake it well over the Achaians and put them to flight. Your business, Shootafar, will be to take care of Hector. Inspire him with courage and strength, until the Achaians are driven right down to the Hellespont. After that I will consider what is necessary to do and say that they may recover from their defeat."

Apollo shot down from Ida like the dove-killing falcon, the swiftest of winged things, and alighted near Hector, who was sitting up now. He had come to himself and knew his friends round him; the heavy breathing and sweating ceased when the will of Zeus revived him. Apollo said:

"Prince Hector, why are you here fainting and far behind the others? Are you in trouble of any sort?"

Hector half dazed replied:

"And who are you, most potent god, who stand before me asking these questions? Do you not know that Aias knocked me down with a big stone in front of the ships, and drove me out of the battle, when I was killing his comrades? I really thought I was going to breathe out my last breath to-day and go down among the dead men."

Apollo said:

"Take courage, when you see what a helper Cronion has

sent from Ida to stand by you, Phoibos Apollo Goldensword—
the same who has long protected you and your city. Now command your chariots to drive in a body upon the enemy ships.
I will go before you and turn back the Achaians, and make a
smooth road for your horses."

At once Hector was filled with new spirit. Like a stallion
horse which has fed his fill at the manger, and breaks the
halter—off he goes clattering over the plains, head high and
mane flowing over his shoulders, while proudly he gallops
along to the mares' feeding-ground, so nimblefoot nimbleknee
Hector hurried about ordering his men to do as the god commanded. And what of the battle? As countrymen with dogs
hunt a horned stag or a wild goat, but steep rocks or dark
thickets save him, since to catch him was not their lot; then
a bearded lion disturbed by their cries appears on the path, and
suddenly drives them back from the chase—so the Danaäns
all this while had been hunting their enemy in packs and stabbing with spears and swords, but when they saw Hector ranging
the ranks they were afraid, and their hearts sank down to their
heels.

Then up spoke Thoas among them—the best man of the
Aetolians, one who knew his spear-craft, and a good man also
in stand-up fight, in conference too there were few of the whole
nation better when the young fellows debate together—Thoas
kept his head and cried out:

"Upon my word, here is a miracle which I see with my own
eyes! Hector has escaped, and here he is risen again! We all
hoped he was really and truly dead, and Aias Telamoniadês
had killed him! But some god has saved him again. He has
killed many of our people, and I expect it will be the same now;
the hand of Zeus Thunderer is in this, or he would not appear
now full of fight in the front rank.

"Listen and I will tell you what to do. We will order the main
body to retreat towards the ships; and pick out the best men,
to make a stand and try to hold him off with spears in rest. I
don't think even that furious man will be bold enough to plunge
into a Danaän square!"

Accordingly Aias and his pair, and Idomeneus, Teucros and
Merionês and Megês, and their followers summoned all the
best fighting men to face Hector, while the main body began
to retreat behind them.

The Trojans thrust forward in a body, led by Hector in fine
form; before them went Phoibos Apollo with a cloud about his
shoulders, holding the aegis-cape, shaggy, conspicuous, terrible,
made by Hephaistos for Zeus to carry and to confound mankind. Holding this in his hands, Apollo led the advance.

The Argives stood in a mass to meet them, and a piercing

war-cry arose from both sides. Arrows leapt from the bow-string, spears shot from steady hands—some to pierce the bodies of strong young men, many to fall between ere they could taste the white flesh, and to stick in the ground greedy for a taste.

So long as Apollo held the aegis-cape unmoving, the volleys hit their mark on both sides and the people fell. But when he looked the Danaäns full in the face and shook it, with a loud and terrible shout, he melted their hearts within them and they forgot their courage. Then like a herd of cattle or a great flock of sheep chased by a couple of wild beasts in the murk of night, with a sudden attack when the keeper is away, so fled the Achaians in panic; for Apollo put fear into them and gave victory to Hector and his Trojans.

Then man struck man in the scattering battle. Hector killed Stichios and Arcesilaos, one of the chief of the Boiotian captains, the other the great friend of Menestheus. Aineias brought down and stript Medon and Iasos. Medon was a bastard son of Oïleus and brother of Aias, as has been told before; Iasos was the leader of the Athenians, the son of Sphelos Bucolidês. Polydamas took Mecisteus, Politês took Echios in the front rank, Agenor took Clonios. Paris struck Deiochos from behind in flight, and ran him through the end of the shoulder.

While they were stripping the armour from these men, the fugitives were tumbling over the stakes and moat, and running in all directions, and getting behind the wall as they could. So Hector shouted loudly to his men:

"Leave the spoils, and make for the ships! If I see any man anywhere else, and not by the ships, I will kill him on the spot! His family shall never give him his due with fire, but carrion dogs shall tear him under the walls of our city!"

Then down from the shoulders he put the lash to his horses, and called out to the ranks. All cheered and drove on with him with a devil of a din. Before them Phoibos Apollo levelled down the sides of the ditch with a touch of his feet, and filled the hollow; thus he built a long dam across, as wide as a strong man's spear-cast. The men poured over it in mass, Apollo in front holding the precious aegis; and he threw down the wall as easily as a boy playing on the beach, who builds his toy-castles in the sand and shuffles them down again with his feet. So easily didst thou, O glorious Apollo! confound all the toil and travail of the Argives, and turn them to rout!

So the Argives came to a halt beside their ships, appealing to one another, and lifting up their hands to All Gods, they prayed earnestly every man; Gerenian Nestor most earnestly of all raising his hands to heaven offered his prayer:

"O Father Zeus! if ever a man of us in Argos has made burnt

offering of bulls or sheep, and prayed for a safe return, remember that, Olympian! Save us from this cruel day, and let not Achaians be thus conquered by Trojans!"

Zeus Allwise thundered loud, hearing the prayer of old Neleidês.

But the Trojans attacked still more furiously when they heard the thunder of Zeus Almighty. As a great billow from the open sea rolls over the bulwarks of a ship, when a strong wind piles it up as the winds do pile the waves, so the Trojans with a mighty noise came rolling over the wall; and driving their horses to the ships they fought with spears hand to hand—they from their chariots, the others from the ships where they had climbed, using the long jointed poles shod with bronze which were there at hand.

All this while, as long as the battle was outside the walls and far from the ships, Patroclos had been in the hut of gentle Eurypylos, amusing him with talk, and soothing the pain of his wound with plasters of his healing herbs. But when the Trojans came pouring in and when he heard the noise of the Danaäns in rout, he groaned and slapt his thighs, saying in distress to his friend:

"I can't stay here any longer, Eurypylos, although you need somebody with you, but just listen to this battle going on! Your man shall attend to you—I must hasten to Achillês and try to make him fight. Who knows whether I may not persuade him, with good luck? The persuasion of a friend often brings a happy end!"

So saying, he went off as fast as his feet would carry him.

The Achaians held their own before the attack, but they could not push off the Trojans though they were fewer; nor could the Trojans break the ranks in front of them and get among the ships and huts. The battle was evenly balanced, and kept as straight as a master carpenter's line in cutting a plank.

There was fighting in many places; but Hector found himself opposite the ship of Aias. They fought a duel for the ship, but one could not get the other out and use his fire, and the other could not drive him back now his luck had brought him there. Caletor, Hector's cousin, brought up a torch to fire the ship, but Aias knocked him down with his pike and the torch fell from his hand. When Hector saw his cousin down in the dust beside the ship, he called out:

"Trojans! Lycians! Brave Dardanians! Don't give way in this narrow place—at least save Caletor who has fallen here among the ships, or the Achaians will get his armour!"

Then he cast a spear at Aias—missed him, but hit his man Lycophron (he lived with Aias at home, being banished from Cythera after killing a man)—the spear struck the man's head over the ear as he stood beside Aias, and he tumbled out of the ship to the ground. Aias shivered and said to his brother:

"Don't be lazy, Teucros! Here is our faithful friend Mastoridês dead, who was as dear to us as our own parents and lived in our house. Hector has killed him! Where are your arrows of death, where is the bow that Phoibos Apollo gave you?"

Teucros heard and ran up with bow and quiver. He shot arrow after arrow quickly against the attackers. One hit Cleitos Peisenor's son, the comrade of Polydamas, as he held the reins in his hands. He had trouble with his horses, for he was driving them where the fighting was thickest to win favour with Hector, but a blow came upon him that no one could help, however much he might wish. For the arrow fell on the back of his neck; he tumbled out of the car, and the horses shied and ran away with the empty car rattling. Polydamas saw this at once, and he was first to stop them. He gave them over to Astynoös, with strict orders to keep them near and watch him; then he went back to the fighting.

Teucros picked out another arrow for Hector; and he would have put an end to the fighting if he had shot the champion. But Zeus was on the watch—he was protecting Hector, and he robbed Teucros of his victory—he broke the bowstring as Teucros drew it at Hector: the bow fell from his hand, and the arrow went off somewhere else. Teucros shivered, and said to his brother:

"Confound it, look there! How God cuts our plans to pieces! he knocks the bow out of my hand, and he breaks my bowstring, which I put in fresh this morning to stand the strain of all these arrows."

Aias replied:

"Don't waste time. Let the bow and arrows lie there, since God has made a mess of them out of spite against our people. Take a long spear and a shield, fight yourself and make the others fight. Aye, make them pay dear for their victory if they do take our ships, and let us remember our duty."

So Teucros put away the bow in his hut. He slung over his shoulders a shield of four hides, and put on a good helmet with a nodding plume of horsehair, and took up a sharp spear; then he ran quickly to the side of Aias.

Hector had seen how the shots had been cut short, and he called out loudly:

"Trojans! Lycians! My brave Dardanian friends! Here we are among the ships! Be men, remember your duty and fight! I have just seen the arrows of a champion brought to nought! It is easy to see the mighty hand of Zeus among men, and to discern whom he makes victorious and whom he weakens and will not help—as now he weakens the spirit of our enemies and helps us. Fight one and all for the ships! If a man dies by shot or stab, let him be dead. It is no disgrace for him to die fighting for his native land. At least wife is safe and his children after him, house and estate are unhurt, if once the Achaians go away to their own country."

These words put courage into all. Aias on his part addressed his companions and roused them to new efforts:

"Shame, Argives! Now it is certain we must either drive these men back from the ships or perish. If Hector takes our ships, do you expect to walk all the way home on foot? Don't you hear Hector exhorting all his people to burn our ships with fire? This is a battle, not a dance! For us there is no better plan and no better notion than to have at your enemy man to man. To die at once and have done with it, is better than a lingering death—to be squeezed like this among these ships by poor creatures like these!"

Then Hector killed Schedios Perimedês' son, the Phocian captain, and Aias killed Laodamas Antenor's son, captain of the foot. Polydamas brought down Cyllenian Otos, the Epeian prince and friend of Megês Phyleidês. Megês saw it and leapt upon him, but Polydamas slipt from under him and Megês missed his thrust (for Apollo would not allow the son of Panthoös to be killed there) but he drove the spear full into the chest of Croismos. He fell, and Megês began to strip off his armour, but Dolops leapt upon him (the bravest of men, son of Lampos, and grandson of Laomedon, a man who could use a spear and knew all the art of war): he struck Phyleidês at close quarters full on the shield, but he was saved by the plates of his good corselet. This corselet Phyleus had brought out of Ephyra from the river Sellëeis; his guest-friend King Euphetês had given it to him for the war, and this now saved his son's life. Megês next made a stab at the ridge holding the horsehair plume of his helmet, and cut off the whole plume: down came the plume and lay scarlet in the dust.

While Megês lingered over this fight, hoping to win, Menelaos came to help. He stood behind unseen and got Dolops broadside on, then struck at the shoulder; the spear ran through and showed on the other side, as if struggling to get out of his chest, and he fell on his face. The two men dashed forward to take his spoils. Then Hector called on all his brothers, but first he reproached his cousin Melanippos Hicetaon's son. This man used to keep his herds of oxen in Percotê before the enemy came, but as soon as the fleet arrived he returned to Ilios and made his mark. He lived in the palace, and Priam treated him

like one of his own sons. Hector called him by name with reproaches, as he led the way:

"What's this, Melanippos? Are we to let him go? Aren't you
a bit sorry that your cousin Dolops is killed? Can't you see
them fingering his armour? Come along—we can't stand off
any more, we must fight till we kill them or they take Ilios and
destroy us all!"

They were away in a moment, while Telamonian Aias exhorted his own side:

"Be men, my friends! Remember your honour, remember
what your fellows will think of you and your doings in this
battle! A little sense of shame will give a better chance for
all to live; but he that runs away, that same will do no good
and get no fame!"

They were full of high spirit as it was, but his familiar saws
took their fancy: they fenced in their ships with a paling of
hard metal, while Zeus excited the Trojans against them. Now
Menelaos called to Antilochos:

"You are younger than the rest of us, Antilochos! No one
is quicker on his feet or stronger in the fight. Won't you jump
out and have a shot at somebody!"

Then he was at it again, while Antilochos jumped out of the
first rank and looked round. The Trojans all shrank back, as
he cast a lance—and that was no miss; Melanippos was then
just coming into the battle, and it struck him on the breast.
Down he fell with a thud, and Antilochos was upon him in a
moment to strip him—like a dog pouncing on a wounded fawn
when the hunter has shot it jumping out of its harbourage.
There was a pounce, Melanippos! But Hector saw it and came
up at a run. Antilochos did not stay, but used his own quick
feet: he was off like a wild beast which has done something
naughty, killed a dog or a herdsman, and then runs before the
men come up in a pack—yes, that was how Nestoridês ran,
with Hector and all the Trojans coursing after him shouting
and volleying like the devil! When he was safe with his friends,
he turned and stood.

The Trojans rushed at the ships like ravening lions, fufilling
the will of Zeus, who drove them furiously on and on, and took
all the heart out of the Achaians, as their hope of victory faded.
For his will was to give triumph to Hector Priamidês, to let him
make a burning fiery furnace of the ships and fulfil the un-
reasonable prayer of Thetis. He watched for the glare of a
burning ship; for at that moment he meant to roll the Trojans
back from the ships and give the victory to the Achaians.

That was why he urged Hector to attack, when he needed no
urging. Hector was mad as spear-shaking Arês, mad as a con-

flagration in some thick forest upon the mountains. There was foam on Hector's lips, his eyes blazed under the shaggy brows, the helmet shook violently on his temples; for Zeus himself helped him from heaven, and brought him honour and glory fighting alone amid a host of foes. For his life was to be but a tiny span; already the day of fate drew near, when Pallas Athenaia was to bring out Peleidês in his might.

He tried again and again to break the enemy ranks, where he saw the men thickest and the armour strongest, but break them he could not for all his ardour. They stood close like great stones in a wall, or like a steep cliff over the sea, which endures the swift courses of whistling winds and the swelling breakers that burst against it. So stood the Danaäns fast, and would not yield. But Hector shining fiery all about was dashing against the mass, falling upon it as a billow swells up to the clouds before the wind and falls on a ship: she is swallowed up in foam, the dreadful blast roars against the sail, the mariners tremble with fear, for only a hair's-breadth saves them from death. So the Achaians' hearts were torn within them.

But Hector was like a savage lion after the cattle, while they graze along a marshy bottom in thousands, and among them a herdsman not certain how to tackle the beast over a mangled heifer: the man keeps pace with the first or last of the herd, but the beast leaps into the middle and gorges his kill, while the rest scamper away. So the Achaians made a rare scampering before Hector and Father Zeus, all but one whom Hector slew, Mycenaian Periphetês, the son of Copreus, who used to take the messages from King Eurystheus to Heraclês the great hero. That mean father begat a son more excellent in every way, fleet of foot and strong to fight, first of his people for intelligence; so Hector's victory was the more honourable. The man carried a tall shield that reached to his feet; when he turned shifting the shield about he caught his foot in the rim, and fell backwards with the helmet banging about his head. Hector heard the noise, and ran up and killed him with a thrust in the chest, close beside his friends; but they could do nothing to help him, for they were too much afraid themselves.

They were now in among the ships, and the sterns enclosed them, that is the front line: the enemy kept pouring in. Now the Argives were forced to retire and leave their front ships. They remained all together and did not disperse; both shame and fear restrained them, and they kept calling to one another. Most of all Gerenian Nestor besought every man to listen as he loved his parents:

"My friends," he cried, "play the men! have some respect for the opinion of the world, remember your wives and children, your property, your parents, alive or dead! Let every man remember! In their names, as you think of them far away, I beseech you to stand firm and not to give way to panic!"

While he thus tried to encourage them, Athena dispersed the rare great mist which blinded their eyes: now it was bright light on both sides, both about the ships and in the hard-fought battle. They could all see Hector and his companions, both those who were fighting a long way off, and those who were near the ships.

But Aias did not choose to remain standing with the other Achaians in groups; so he went up and down over the decks of the ships, carrying a huge pike used for sea fighting, several lengths jointed together, two-and-twenty cubits. He jumped from deck to deck with long steps like a skilful horse-rider. When such a one has picked out four horses from the rest and tied them together, see him drive them along the highroad towards the city! How the men and women run together and stare, as he bounds up and down from horse to horse, quite safe all the time, while they gallop along! So Aias bounded along up and down from deck to deck in long jumps, while his voice resounding filled the sky and he roared to the Danaäns, "Defend your fleet and your camp!" [1]

Hector also could not keep still amid his followers; but he swooped upon the black hull of a ship, as a brown eagle swoops on a flock of birds feeding by a river, geese or cranes or long-necked swans—and Zeus pressed him from behind with his mighty hand, and brought the army with him.

Again a bitter fight arose by the ships. You would say they were fresh unwearied troops now first in the field, so furiously they fought. But the thoughts of the two armies were very different. The Achaians feared they could never escape destruction; the Trojans hoped one and all to burn the ships and to kill the men.

Hector now caught hold of the stern of a fine ship, the one which had brought Protesilaos to Troy, but never carried him home again. Achaians and Trojans fought for possession of that ship, all close work; no waiting now to be shot at with arrows and spears, but all stood close together with one absorbing passion, and they fought with axes and choppers and swords and spears. The ground was covered with fine-wrought blades, dropt from fighting hands, unslung from shoulders: blood ran in streams. Hector would not let go of the stern, but kept hold of the ensign,[2] calling to his men:

"Fire, this way! and cheer all together! Now Zeus has given us a day which is worth everything! He has given us the ships

[1] The tumbler does not jump from horse to horse, but down to the ground and up again; so Aias.

[2] A stern ornament, not a flag.

which came here against the will of heaven, and brought us so many troubles—all because the old men were cowards, and kept me back and wouldn't let the men go when I wanted to attack the ships. But if Zeus Allseeing made us stupid then, now he encourages us and commands us himself!"

They attacked more violently than before. Aias could no longer stand, for he was overwhelmed with volleys. He left the deck, expecting death at every step, and retired a little way along the seven-foot bridge that led fore and aft. There he remained on guard, repelling any one who tried to board with fire, and he never ceased roaring:

"My friends! brave hearts! true sons of war! Prove yourselves men, my friends! Remember your duty! Do we think there is any one behind to help us? Or any better wall to save a man from destruction? We have no city near with ramparts to defend us, we have no reserves! We are on the plain of Troy, with an armed enemy in front, and the sea behind, and our native land far away! Hard hitting must save us—war is no place for kindness!"

All the while he kept vigorously driving with his pointed spear. Whenever a man rushed at the ship with his fire alight, Aias was ready with a prod of the long spear. Twelve men he wounded in the fight around the ship.

BOOK XVI

*How Patroclos took the field in the armour of Achillês,
his great feats of war, and his death*

WHILE THIS BATTLE WAS GOING ON ROUND THE SHIPS, PAtroclos appeared before Achillês with tears pouring down his cheeks—a veritable fountain, a mountain brook running over the rocks! Achillês was deeply grieved, and spoke to him plainly:

"My dear Patroclos, why are you crying like a baby? You might be some little girl running to her mother, and pulling at her apron, and keeping her from her work, and blubbering and looking up and saying, Nurse me mammy dear! That's what you look like, my dear man, crying like that. Have you some news for the men, or just for me, or is it a special message from home to you? Why, your father Menoitios is still alive, for all we know, and Peleus Aiacidês is alive and on his throne; we should be sorry indeed to hear of their deaths. Are you really lamenting for the Achaian people, can't endure to see them falling thick and fast among the ships? It's their own fault, their own tyrannical dealings. Speak out, don't hide it, then we shall both know."

Patroclos answered with a groan:

"Don't be angry, Achillês my prince, our strong deliverer! Such misfortune has come on our people! There they are, all who used to be best in the field, lying wounded, shot or stabbed, somewhere among the ships! Diomedês Tydeidês is wounded, Odysseus is wounded, Agamemnon is wounded, Eurypylos is wounded too—shot in the thigh with an arrow. They have the surgeons busy about them with all their medicines curing the wounds—but there's no curing you, Achillês! I pray I may never have such a grudge in my heart as you have. Curse your courage! What good will you be to any one from now to the end of the world, if you will not save the nation from destruction? Cruel man! your father was not Peleus nor your mother Thetis—you are a son of the green sea and the stony rock, with that hard heart!

"If there is some prophecy you are afraid of which your mother told you from the lips of Zeus, let me go at least and take out our Myrmidons, to see if there is any hope in that way! Put your armour upon my shoulders, and perhaps the Trojans may think it is you, and give a little rest to our tormented people. Little time to take your breath face to face with sudden death! And it will be easy for us coming into the battle fresh, to drive weary men from our camp away to their city!"

So he prayed, poor fool! for his prayer was destined to bring death and destruction for himself. Achillês replied in hot anger:

"Ah, what have you said, Patroclos, my dear friend! I care for no prophecy, if I do know any; my mother has told me none from the lips of Zeus. But I feel bitter grief in my heart, when here is a man who will rob his equal and take back his prize because he is the stronger. This is a terrible grief to me, and this has been my torment. The girl that the army chose out for my prize, whom I made my own by force of arms when I took that city—that girl my lord King Agamemnon tore from my hands as if I were a foreigner without any rights!

"But we will let bygones be bygones. I see it was impossible to bear resentment for ever and ever. I did think I should not forget my resentment until fire and battle came to my own ships.—You go then; put on my armour and lead our brave men into the field, now the enemy have swallowed up the Achaian ships like a great cloud, now that our people have their backs to the sea and only a small space is left them to hold, now that all Troy is here confident—for they see not the face of my helmet shining near them!—that would soon rout them and fill the gullies with their dead, if my lord King Agamemnon were kind to me!

"But now they are fighting round our camp! There is no spear in the hands of Diomedês Tydeidês, furiously raging to defend the Danaäns from ruin. I have not heard yet the voice of my lord King shouting out of his hateful head! But Hector's words of command are breaking upon me all round, his Trojans cover the whole plain with their clamour—they vanquish the Achaians in fair fight!

"Never mind—fall on them and beat them, Patroclos! Save our ships, or they will burn them and we shall never see home again. But listen carefully while I tell you exactly what to do, that you may win honour and glory for me from the whole nation, and they may send back that lovely girl and handsome gifts besides.

"When you have cleared them away from the ships, come straight back. If after that the loud-thundering lord of Hera gives you a chance of triumph, never think of fighting on your own account without me, you will steal my honours in that way. Don't be excited by fighting and victory so as to lead our men as far the city walls, or one of the Olympian gods may meddle; Apollo Shootafar is very fond of them. You must turn back as soon as you have saved the ships, and let them ravage the plain.

"O Father Zeus, Athenaia, Apollo! If only not one single Trojan could be left alive, and not one Achaian, but you and I might be left, that we alone might tear off the sacred diadem of Troy!"

By this time Aias was at the end of his endurance under the showers of blows: he had two forces against him, the will of Zeus and the volleys of the Trojans. The metal of his helmet rang and rattled as the blows beat and beat upon the knobs; his left shoulder was tired with bearing the heavy shield so long. But nothing could shake him, stab and strike as they would. His breath came hard, sweat poured in streams over every limb, he had not a moment's rest: nothing but trouble upon trouble everywhere.

O ye divine Spirits that inspire the songs of men! Help me to tell how the fire first fell upon the Achaian ships!

Hector drew near, and struck the ashen pike of Aias with his great sword, at the end near the socket, and cut it right through. Aias brandished the useless pole, and a blade fell on the ground with a clang a long way off. Then Aias shuddered, for he saw in this the act of God. He knew that Zeus Thunderer was foiling his plans of battle and meant to let the Trojans win; and he retired out of reach. Then they cast fire upon the ship; it lapped round the stern and blazed up at once all over the ship.

And then Achillês slapped his two thighs, crying out:

"Hurry, Patroclos, my friend, be off with your horses! I see fire sweeping about the ships! I fear they may take the ships and then we shall never get away. On with your armour, and I will wake up the men!"

Patroclos lost no time. He put on his legs the greaves with silver anklets, next covered his chest with the star-bespangled corselet of Aiacidês. Over his shoulders he slung the sword, with bronze blade and silver knob, and then the great strong shield. Upon his head he set the helmet with its plume nodding defiance. He took two lances that fitted his grip, but not the spear of Aiacidês; for only Achillês could wield that huge heavy pike, not another man in the Achaian host. This was the strong ashen spear from Mount Pelion, which Cheiron had given his father to be the terror of his enemies.

The horses he put in charge of Automedon, whom he thought more of than any one except Achillês himself, and he trusted him best to be ready at his call in battle. So Automedon harnessed the horses, chestnut Xanthos and piebald Balios, swift as the winds: west-wind Zephyros was their sire, and their dam the harpy Podagra, got in foal while grazing in a meadow beside the stream of Oceanos. In the side-traces he put one mortal horse with the pair of immortals, Pedasos the incomparable, which Achillês had brought back from captured Thebê.

Meanwhile Achillês had got the men under arms and marshalled in their camp. They were like a pack of ravening wolves ready for the hunt. How the savage beasts bring down a great antlered stag in the mountains and tear him to pieces with blood-dripping jaws!—then off goes the whole pack to a brook, and they lap up the clear surface-water with long, thin tongues, belching out clots of gore. Their courage is high as ever, though their bellies are stuffed. So the Myrmidon leaders and captains bustled about Patroclos, while Achillês was among them, marshalling the chariots and ranks of armed men.

Fifty ships of war was the fleet which Achillês had brought to Troy; in each were fifty stout fellows on the benches; five officers he appointed to command them, under himself commanding in chief.

One division was led by Menesthios in his resplendent corselet. His mother was Peleus' daughter the fair Polydora, a mortal woman; his father the river-god Spercheios, but by repute one Boros Perieres' son, who brought his bride-gifts and wedded her in due form.

The second was led by warlike Eudoros, a girl's love-child. His mother the dancing-beauty Polymelê, was daughter of Phylas. Hermês Argeiphontês caught sight of her, when the girls were singing on the dancing-ground of Goldenreed Artemis, Lady of the noisy hunt. Hermês at once fell in love; climbing to her chamber he lay with her secretly, and she gave him a splendid son Eudoros, fleet of foot and strong to fight. When at last our Lady of Childbirth had brought him to the light and he saw the rays of the sun, Echeclês Actor's son paid his court and made her his wife. Old Phylas brought him up with the same love and kindness as if he were his own son.

The third was led by Peisandros Maimalidês, who was the most renowned spearman in the country after Patroclos. The fourth was under Phoinix, the fifth under Alcimedon, the son of Laercês.

As soon as Achillês had arranged them all in their ranks, he gave his last orders in these stern words:

"Myrmidons, do not forget all those threats of yours against the Trojans here in camp, and how you have reproached me while my resentment lasted. Would you not say—'Hard-hearted man! You must have sucked bile from your mother's breast! Cruel man, to keep us here against our will! At least let us sail away and go back home, since this poisonous bile is in your heart!' How often you came crowding to talk at me like that. Now here is the great battle you were enamoured of, plain to see. Then let every man keep a stout heart and fight!"

As they heard this rousing speech from their King, they closed their ranks more firmly; helmets and shields were packed together, like the squared stones of a wall, which a man builds to keep the strong winds outside his house. Shield pressed on shield, helmet on helmet, man on man; the horsehair plumes on the shining horns nodded and touched, so close they stood. In front of all two men made ready for battle, Patroclos and Automedon, two men with one mind, to lead the Myrmidons forward.

Achillês returned to his quarters, and opened the lid of a fine carven chest, which Thetis Silverfoot had put on board ship for him, full of shirts and woollen rugs and cloaks to keep off the wind. In this was a goblet of fine work; no other man but he ever drank wine from it, no god was honoured with libations from that goblet save Zeus the Father alone. This he took out, and first cleansed it with sulphur, then washed it in clean water, and washed his own hands. Last he ladled wine into it, and stood in the midst of the courtyard, and prayed as he spilt the wine looking up into heaven—Zeus Thunderer saw him without fail:

"O Lord Zeus, Dodonaian, Pelasgian, whose habitation is far away! O thou ruler of tempestuous Dodona! and about thee the Selloi dwell, thy interpreters, foot-unwashen, ground-bedded! Once indeed thou didst hear the words of my prayer; thou didst honour me, and thou didst strike hard upon the Achaians. Then grant me now also the boon I crave. I will remain myself where the ships are gathered together; but I send my comrade with many men to fight. Send victory with him, Zeus Allseeing! Make bold the heart in him, that Hector may learn whether my man knows how to fight alone, or whether his hands are invincible only when I go myself into the maul of war!

"But when he has driven the battle away from the ships, I pray that he may come back unscathed, with all his armour and his warlike companions."

Such was his prayer, and Zeus Allwise heard him: half he granted, and half he refused. To drive the battle away from the ships he granted; to return safe out of battle he refused.

Achillês after his libation and prayer went into the hut, and put away the goblet in the chest. Then he went outside and stood. He still longed to see the battle himself.

Patroclos and his force marched on until they found the Trojans. They were like a swarm of wasps with a nest by the road, which boys have been teasing and poking in their way. The poor little fools only stir up trouble for everybody; and if a wayfarer disturbs the wasps by accident, they pour out in fury and defend their home. Just as furious were the Myrmidons when they poured out of their camp with a great noise. Patroclos cried out in a loud voice:

"Myrmidons! Fellow-soldiers of our prince! Be men! remember your old valour! Let us win honour for Peleidês, who is the best man in this army and his soldiers are second to none! Let my lord King Agamemnon know his blind madness, when he made no account of the best man of all our nation!"

Then with courage refreshed they fell on the Trojans in a swarm, and the ships around resounded with the noise of their shouting.

But when the Trojans saw Patroclos and his companions in their shining armour, they were amazed, and the ranks wavered; for they believed that Achillês had thrown off his resentment and made friends again. Every man looked about him for some escape from certain death.

Patroclos first cast a spear into the thick of the struggle near the stern of Protesilaos' ship, and hit Pyraichmês; this was the leader of the Paionians, who came with chariots from Amydon on the Axios. The spear went into his right shoulder, and he fell on his back groaning, while his Paionians fled in all directions; for they were panic-stricken when Patroclos brought down their leader and champion. He drove them away from the ships and quenched the fire. The Trojans fled in rare confusion, leaving the half-burnt ship, and the Danaäns poured in among the ships with a deafening din. As the fire was quenched and the smoke dispersed, it seemed as when Zeus disperses a thick cloud from a mountain top and light breaks through from the infinite air of heaven, showing the peaks and pinnacles of the rocks. Then the Danaäns had time to breathe for a little, but the battle was not over; the Trojans still held their ground, although they had been forced to leave the ships, and they were not yet running pell-mell in rout.

There were a number of scattered combats here and there. First Patroclos pierced the thigh of Areïlycos at the moment he turned to fly: the spear broke the bone, and he fell flat on his face. Next Menelaos wounded Thoas where his chest showed over the side of the shield, and he collapsed. Phyleïdês watched his moment as Amphiclos ran at him, and lunged at him first— hit the bulging thigh where the muscle is thickest, and cut through the sinews, and darkness came over his eyes.

Nestor's two sons each brought down his man. Antilochos drove his spear into the flank of Atymnios; his brother Maris ran in front of the body and made a thrust at Antilochos; but Thrasymedês got in first before he could strike, and tore the upper arm from the muscles, breaking the bone, and killing the man. So the two sons of Nestor sent down to Erebos the two valiant sons of Amisodaros, the man who bred that raging destructive monster the Chimaira; they were Sarpedon's men.

Aias Oïliadês leapt at Cleobulos, and took him alive when he was hampered in the crowd; but he cut his throat with his sword and killed him on the spot—all the blade grew hot with the blood as death took him.

Peneleos and Lycon cast at each other at the same time and both missed; they ran together and fell to with swords. Lycon sliced at the horn of the other's helmet, and his sword broke off at the hilt; Peneleos struck his neck under the ear, and the blade cut so deep that the head hung over to one side held only by the skin.

Merionês ran and caught Acamas as he was mounting his chariot, and stabbed him in the right shoulder; he fell off, and his eyes were dimmed.

Idomeneus stabbed Erymas in the mouth. The point came out under the brain and broke the bones; his teeth were knocked out, and both his eyes filled with blood, which spurted up through nostrils and mouth as he gaped. Then the dark cloud of death spread over him.

These Danaän leaders got each his man. The rest of the Danaäns pounced on their enemies, as ferocious wolves pick out lambs and kids from the flock and pounce on them, when a careless shepherd has let them go straying over the hills; they tear the poor timid creatures to pieces at sight, and so did the Danaäns, while the Trojans forgot they had ever been brave, but remembered to run as if flight had no disgrace.

Big Aias made a dead set at Hector, determined to spear him; but Hector knew all the tricks of war—he kept his broad shoulders covered with the good oxhide, and watched the whizzing arrows and thudding spears. He knew well enough that the tide had turned, and victory was lost; all the same he stood firm and saved his companions.

But now the rout and confusion spread from the ships, as when Zeus spreads the tempest and a cloud comes into the open from the upper air. Now they were all pouring back in a rabble. Hector in his galloping car left the Trojan army, as they were trying to get over the moat which was in their way. Many a team galloped off, leaving their masters' chariots in the ditch with broken poles. But Patroclos was close behind, loudly crying "Kill! Kill!" as the broken hordes filled every path with noise and confusion. The dust rose in clouds, the horses tugged and strained to get clear of the camp. Patroclos drove shouting wherever he saw the thickest crowd; men kept falling out of their cars under his axle-trees, the cars tumbled over clittery clattery. Straight over the moat galloped the horses, on and on; "Down with Hector!" was the cry of his heart. To strike down Hector was his one passion; but Hector was far ahead. Panting horses were everywhere running loose, like a roaring torrent, when a thundercloud in the autumn pours heavy cataracts on the black earth, the rivers rise in flood, crundels and dimbles are full and ravines are cut in the mountains: down come the torrents tumbling criss-cross out of the hills, and destroying the works of men, until they fall roaring into the sea. Such is the vengeance of Zeus, upon men who give unrighteous judgments and drive justice far from them, having no regard for the wrath of heaven.

Patroclos cut off the front of the routed army, and then drove them back towards the ships. He would not let them get back to their city, but kept them in the space between the ships and the river and the city walls, charging and slaying, until he had exacted the price of many lives.

First he struck Pronoös and killed him, when the shield uncovered his chest. Next he drove at Thestor, who was crouching down in his chariot dazed with terror, the reins dropt from his hands. Patroclos came quite close and stabbed him in the right jaw through teeth and all, then dragged him gaping over the rail by the spear, and threw him down on his face, as a man sitting on a rock lands a big fish with hook and line. Erylaos rushed at him, but Patroclos smashed his head to pieces in the helmet with a stone and brought him down. Then he attacked one after another Erymas and Amphoteros and Epaltês, Tlepolemos Damastoridês, Echios and Pyris, Ipheus and Euippos and Polymelos Argeadês, and laid them all flat on the ground.

Sarpedon saw his countrymen falling—he knew them by their dress, for they wore no loin-guard—and he called to them in reproach:

"Shame, Lycians! Where are you running? Play up, men! I will meet this man myself, I want to know who he is that sweeps everything before him. Look how many good men and true he has killed!"

Then he jumped out of the car in his armour; and Patroclos when he saw did the same. They leapt at each other yelling, like a couple of vultures on a high rock shrieking and fighting with beak and claw. When Zeus saw them he said to Hera:

"This is very sad! Sarpedon, whom I love best of all men, is fated to be killed by Patroclos Menoitiadês. I really don't know what to do. Shall I pick him up out of the battle alive, and put him down in his own country? Or shall I let him be killed by Menoitiadês?"

Hera said:

"O you dreadful creature, you mustn't say that! A mortal man, doomed of old by fate, and you want to rescue him from death? Do as you like; but you cannot expect the rest of us gods to approve. Think for a moment. If you send Sarpedon home alive, some other god may want to take his son out of the battlefield. He loves his son too, you know! Many of the immortals have sons fighting before Troy, and you will make them all very jealous. But if you do love him, if you are sorry for him, just let him be killed by Patroclos Menoitiadês; but as soon as he is dead and done for, send Death and Sleep to carry him back to Lycia, where his family and friends will do the funeral honours with barrow and pillar, for that is the privilege of the dead."

The Father of men and gods agreed that this was right. But he sent a shower of bloody raindrops upon the earth in honour of his dear son, whom Patroclos was destined to kill on Trojan soil, far from his native land.

When they were within reach, Patroclos struck Thrasymelos Sarpedon's man in the lower belly, and brought him down. Sarpedon cast at Patroclos and missed, but he hit the horse Pedasos in the right shoulder. The horse fell crashing in the dust, and gasped out his life with a moan; the other two sprang apart with a crack of the yoke, entangling the reins above them. Automedon mended matters by drawing his sword and cutting loose the trace-horse; then the others were righted and drew the reins taut.

The two men now came together again for their battle. Sarpedon cast, and the spear passed over Patroclos' left shoulder without touching. Patroclos followed up, and there was no mistake about his cast: he struck where the midriff encloses the beating heart. Sarpedon fell, as an oak tree falls or a poplar, or a tall pine felled by a woodman to make a ship's mast: so he lay in front of his horses and chariot, moaning and clutching at the bloody dust. Like a bull that a lion kills—he tracks a herd and leaps on the bull, and the strong-hearted creature groans in his death between the lion's jaws, so under the blow of Patroclos the strong heart of the Lycian warrior struggled with death, and he called his comrade by name:

"Waste no time, Glaucos! You are a warrior among men—now ply your spear and show yourself a warrior! Now let dreadful war be your heart's desire, if you are good at need! First bring up all our best men to fight for Sarpedon; than fight yourself with your own blade. I shall be your shame and disgrace all your days for ever, if the Achaians strip me fallen before their own ships .Stand firm and bring up our people all!"

Even as he spoke the end came, and death closed his eyes and nostrils. Patroclos set foot on his breast and pulled out the spear, bringing the midriff with it; he dragged out life and blade together. His Myrmidons caught the panting horses, which would have run away now that the chariot had lost its masters.

But Glaucos heard these last words with bitter pain; his heart was wrung that he could not help. He took hold of his arm and pressed it, for he was in great pain from the arrow where Teucros shot him in his attack on the wall. And he prayed aloud to Apollo Shootafar:

"Hear me, Lord, in the happy land of Lycia or in Troy! Thou hast power everywhere to hear an afflicted man, as I am afflicted now! Here I have a cruel wound: my arm throbs from side to side with sharp pains, the blood will not dry, my shoulder is heavy! I cannot hold a spear steady or go and fight with my enemies. A man is slain, the best of men, Sarpedon the son of Zeus, but the father helps not the son. I beseech thee, Lord, heal this cruel wound, lull the pains, give me strength, that I may summon my comrades and make them fight, and fight myself for the body of my dead!"

Apollo heard his prayer. In a moment he stilled the pains, he dried the blood that ran from the wound, he put courage into the man. Glaucos knew it in his heart, and he was glad that the god had quickly heard his prayer.

First he went round urging the Lycian leaders to fight for Sarpedon. Then he repaired at a good pace to the Trojans, Polydamas and Panthoïdes and Agenor, Aineias and Hector the mighty man himself, calling upon them in plain words—

"Look here, Hector! you have quite forgotten your allies. They wear themselves out for your sake, far from home and friends, and you will not help them. Sarpedon lies dead! the leader of the Lycian spearmen, who ruled his country with justice and his own strong arm. Brazen Arês has brought him down by the spear of Patroclos! Do stand by us, friends! Let your hearts be moved with indignation! Do not suffer the Myrmidons to strip him and maltreat his body, in revenge for the Danaäns whom we have killed in fair fight beside their own ships!"

The Trojans were thrilled with grief every inch of them, pangs intolerable, unendurable; for he was the mainstay of their city although a foreigner. There was a large force with him, and he was ever their champion in the field. They went straight for the enemy at full speed, led by Hector eager for revenge.

But the Achaians were set on by the rousing voice of greatheart Patroclos Menoitiadês. He began by calling Aias and his namesake, who were ready enough:

"Now then, Telamonian! Now then, Runner! Let it be your pleasure to have at the enemy. Be as good as you ever were, or better! Sarpedon lies dead—the first man who jumped upon our wall! Come along—if only we can revenge ourselves on his body and strip the armour from his shoulders. If any of his friends try to help him, we can give them our spears!"

This was no more than they wished themselves. When both sides were there in force, Trojans and Lycians against Myrmidons and Achaians, they joined battle with terrible shouts, and how their weapons crashed and smashed! Then Zeus drew a dreadful darkness over the conflict, that the battle for his son might be dreadful and desperate.

At first the Trojans drove back their enemies. For a man was struck down who was by no means the least among the Myrmidons—Epeigeus, the son of prince Agaclês. Epeigeus once had been ruler of Budeion, but he had killed one of his cousins and took refuge with Peleus and Thetis Silverfoot. They sent him to the war at Ilios along with Achillês. He was taking hold of the dead man, when Hector smashed skull and helmet with a large stone; he fell dead over the body.

Then Patroclos provoked by his comrade's loss rushed at him straight, like a hawk scattering daws and starlings. That was a fine pounce of yours, Patroclos, my leader of chivalry, straight for Lycians and Trojans, to avenge your comrade's death!—He struck Sthenelaos on the neck with a stone and tore the sinews out.

Then Hector and the front rank fell back, as far as a man casts a long goatspear in practice or in games, or in war when he faces murderous foemen; and so far the Achaians pushed forward. Glaucos first wheeled about and killed Bathyclês, Chalcon's son, who lived in Hellas, a man notable among the Myrmidons for riches and wealth. Bathyclês nearly caught him, but Glaucos turned suddenly and stabbed him in the chest. The Achaians were infuriated at the fall of so good a man; the Trojans were glad, and rallied round the body, but the Achaians came on unshrinking.

Then Merionês got another Trojan, the brave soldier Laogonos, a son of Onetor, who was priest of Idaian Zeus and highly honoured. He struck him under jaw and ear; the spirit of life quickly left him, and darkness covered him up. Then Aineias let fly his spear against Merionês, in the hope to hit him as he advanced under his shield. But he kept a steady eye and stooped forwards, avoiding the spear, which dumped into the ground behind: there it stood with quivering butt, until Arês took its fierceness away. Aineias was furious, and called out:

"Merionês, you do know how to dance! But my spear might have stopped your dancing for good and all if it had only hit you!"

Merionês answered:

"Aineias, you do know how to fight! But you are a mortal man after all, and you will not find it easy to kill every man alive who defends himself. I might hit you myself, and then where would your strong hands be? You would give the victory to me, and your soul to Hadês!"

Patroclos rated him for this:

"My good man, why do you bandy words like this? You are wasting time. Taunts and jibes will not drive the Trojans away from the dead body. Many a man will fall before that! Words are potent in debate, deeds in war decide your fate. Then don't go on piling up words, but fight!"

So Patroclos hurried him off to the thick of the action, and the noise rose far and wide, thudding and thumping of swords and spears on metal and leather, on shields and bucklers, as the thuds of the axes are heard afar when workmen fell the trees in the mountain forests. Now not even a man who knew him well could have known the noble Sarpedon, smothered from head to foot in blood and dust and showers of shafts. The crowds of men struggled about the body, like a swarm of flies buzzing about a farmyard in spring-time, when the milk runs over the pails and the bowls are doused with milk.

And all the while Zeus did not turn away his eyes from the battle, but gazed at them, musing in his mind on Patroclos and his bloody deaths: should Hector kill him there over Sarpedon's body and strip him of his armour; or should he add yet more to the number of the dead. At last he thought it best that Patroclos should kill yet more, and drive Hector back to the city walls.

So first he made Hector's courage fail. Hector entered his car and turned to retreat, calling on the Trojans to follow—he knew the sacred scales of Zeus! Then not even the brave Lycians stood firm, but all fled away, now they had seen their king lying pierced through the heart in the heap of corpses—for many had fallen over him at the time when Cronion tightened the strife. But the others tore the shining armour from his shoulders, and Patroclos sent it away to the camp.

Then Zeus Cloudgatherer said to Apollo:

"Make haste now, my dear Phoibos, take Sarpedon out of range and cleanse him of the black blood, carry him far away and wash him in the river; anoint him with ambrosia and clothe him in raiment incorruptible. Then give him to those two swift carriers, Sleep and Death, and they shall quickly set him down in the happy land of Lycia, where friends and kinsmen shall do the last rites with barrow and pillar; for that is the honour due to the dead."

Apollo did not neglect his father's bidding. He went down from Ida into the battlefield; he carried the body of Sarpedon out of range, and took it far away and washed it in the river; he anointed it with ambrosia and clothed it in raiment incorruptible. Then he gave it to the two swift carriers, Sleep and Death, who quickly set it down in the happy land of Lycia.

Now Patroclos ordered Automedon to drive him after the Trojans and Lycians. Poor fool! he was quite blinded. If he had done as Achillês told him, he could have escaped black death. But always the will of Zeus is stronger than man; and Zeus put that temper into his heart.

Who was the first, who was the last you killed, Patroclos, now the gods had summoned you to death? First Adrestos and Autonoös and Echeclos, Perimos Megadês and Epistor and Melanippos, then Elasos and Mulios and Pylartês—all these he killed; and the others were glad to escape.

And then the Achaians would have taken the proud city of Troy by the valour of Patroclos, for he went onwards like a storm: but Apollo stood on the wall to help the Trojans, intent upon his death. Three times did Patroclos set his foot on a corner of the wall, three times Apollo dooled him back, rapping the shield with his immortal hands. When he tried the fourth time like one more than man, Apollo shouted at him and said in plain words:

"Back, prince Patroclos! It is not fated that proud Troy shall fall to your spear, nor to Achillês, who is a much better man than you."

Then Patroclos fell back a long way, in fear of the wrath of Apollo Shootafar.

But Hector checked his horses at the Scaian Gate; for he was in doubt whether to drive into battle again, or recall his army to take shelter within the walls. As he was considering, Apollo appeared by his side, in the form of a lusty young fellow Asios, who was Hector's own uncle, being brother of Hecabê, and the son of Dymas who lived near the Sangarios in Phrygia. Apollo said then, in the shape of this man:

"Why have you left the battle, Hector? You ought not to do it. I wish I were as much better than you as I am worse; you should soon be sorry you shirked. Hurry—make for Patroclos, and you may get him—Apollo may give you victory!"

As Apollo disappeared into the mellay, Hector told Cebrionês to whip the horses into battle. Apollo turned the Argives to flight and made the Trojans prevail; but Hector left the others alone and drove towards Patroclos. Then Patroclos leapt out of his car, holding the spear in his left hand; he picked up with his right a sharp shining stone just large enough to fill his hand. He did not try to keep clear of the fellow now—he threw with all his might, and his shot was not wasted, for it hit Cebrionês (himself a bastard son of Priam) on the forehead, as he held the reins. The stone crushed both brows into one and smashed the bone, and both eyes fell down in the dust in front of him. He rolled out of the car like a tumbler, and Patroclos said in mockery:

"Bless my soul, there's a springheel! What a neat header he takes! If he were at sea he could fill many hungry bellies by diving for sea-urchins. He would jump overboard in any weather, to judge from that excellent dive overcar on land! I didn't know there were divers in Troy!"

He pounced on Cebrionês like a lion which ravages the fold, until he is run through the chest and his own courage is his destruction: ah Patroclos, that was what came of your leap! And Hector leapt from his car to meet him: and there they fought as two lions fight over a deer's body, both hungry, both furious—there Patroclos Menoitiadês and glorious Hector were ready to tear each other to pieces. Hector laid hold of the head and would not let go, Patroclos held fast by the foot—and the two armies behind them were fighting too. It was like the struggle of East Wind and South Wind to shake the trees in a mountain dimble—oak and ash and smooth-barked cornel. How they beat the long boughs together with a rare great noise! What a crashing of cracking trunks! So Trojans and Danaäns dashed together, dealing death, and neither thought of retreat. Round the body of Cebrionês the sharp spears fell thick, the winged arrows flew from the string; showers of big stones battered the shields of the fighting men: and the dead man amid the whirlwind of dust lay grand in his own grandeur, forgetful of his horsemanship.

So long as the sun bestrode the middle sky those death-dealing showers went on from this side and that; but when the sun took his turn to ox-loosing time, the Achaians became stronger beyond measure. They dragged away the body of Cebrionês and stript his armour, and Patroclos turned upon the Trojans again. Thrice he leapt on them like another god of war with awful shouts, thrice nine men he killed: but at the fourth furious attack—ah then, Patroclos, the end of your life was in sight! for Phoibos was there in all his terrors.

Patroclos did not see him coming, for the god was hidden in mist. He stood behind Patroclos: his eyes rolled in rage, and he slapped him between the shoulders with the flat of the hand. The helmet was knocked from his head, and went rolling and rattling under the horses' feet; the plumes were dabbled in blood and dust. Never before had it been God's will that this plumed helmet should be fouled in the dust, when it covered the head and brows of a man of the blood divine. Achillês; then Zeus granted that Hector should wear it, yet death was coming near him. Patroclos felt the spear in his hand broken to pieces, the great strong heavy-bladed spear; the tasselled shield with its belt fell from his shoulders; the corselet was stript off his body by the great son of Zeus. His mind was blinded, his knees crickled under him, he stood there dazed.

Then from behind a spear hit him between the shoulders. A Dardanian struck him, Euphorbos Panthoïdês, best of all his yearsmates in spearmanship and horsemanship and fleetness of foot. He had already dismounted twenty since he drove out to learn his first lesson of war. His was the first blow, but it did not bring down Patroclos, and Euphorbos pulled out the spear and mixed again with the crowd; he could not stand up to Patroclos even when naked and bare. But the god's blow and the spear together were too much for Patroclos, and he sought safety among his friends.

When Hector saw him retreating and wounded, he came near and stabbed him in the belly: the blade ran through, he fell with a dull thud, and consternation took the Achaians. So fell Patroclos, like a wild boar killed by a lion, when both are angry and both are parched with thirst, and they fight over a little mountain pool, until the lion is too strong for the panting boar. Patroclos Menoitiadês had killed many men, but Hector Priamidês killed him: and then he vaunted his victory without disguise:

"So Patroclos, you thought that you could sack our city! you thought you would rob our women of the day of freedom, and carry them off to your own country! Fool! In front of them are the horses of Hector prancing out to battle. My spear is well known among my brave Trojans, for I defend them from the day of fate: here you shall stay and feed the vultures! Ah, poor wretch, your Achillês is a good man, but he was no help to you, although no doubt he warned you earnestly when you started (and he stayed behind)—'Don't come back to me, my brave Patroclos, until you have stript the blood-stained shirt from Hector's body!' No doubt he must have said that, and you thought you could do it—no more sense in you than that!"

Patroclos replied, half fainting:

"For this once, Hector, make your proud boast; for you are the victor, by help of Zeus Cronidês and Apollo, who mastered me—an easy thing: they stript off my armour themselves. But if twenty men like you had confronted me, my spear would have slain them all on the spot. No, it was cruel fate that killed me, and Leto's son, and of men Euphorbos; you come third and take my armour. One thing I tell you, and you should lay it up in your mind: you have yourself not long to live. Already death and fate are beside you, and Achillês Aiacidês shall lay you low."

Even as he spoke, the shadow of death covered him up. His soul left the body and went down to Hadês, bewailing his lot, cut off in his manhood and strength. But Hector answered him though dead:

"What is this prophecy of certain death to me, Patroclos? Achillês may be the son of the divine Thetis, but who knows if I may not strike him with my spear, and he may be the first to die!"

Then he set one foot upon the body, and treading it away from the spear, pulled out the spear, and went at once with the spear after the driver Automedon. He wanted to kill him too, but the immortal horses which the gods had given to Peleus were carrying him out of the way.

BOOK XVII

How they fought over the body of Patroclos

MENELAOS HAD NOT FAILED TO MARK THE DEATH OF PATRO- clos. He came up at once and bestrode the body, like a cow standing over her calf, the first she ever bore, with plaintive lowing. He held spear levelled and shield before him, ready to kill any one who should attack. Euphorbos also was not indifferent to the hero's fall; he presented himself before Menelaos, and said:

"Go back, my lord King Menelaos! Go back, leave the body, leave the spoils! I was first to strike him—not a man of Trojans or allies comes before me. Then leave me my triumph, or I will kill you—and life is sweet!"

Menelaos cried out in hot anger:

"Father Zeus! how ugly is a vainglorious boast! There's not as much pride in a panther, or a lion, or a wild boar—and a boar's the most blustering swaggerer on earth—as there is in these sons of Panthoös with their ashwood poles![1] Hyperenor was a strong man, but he had small joy of his strength when he made light of me, and stood up to me, and thought I was one to be despised. I don't think he walked home on his own feet to make his wife and parents happy! I fancy I'll quench your pride too if you stand up to me. I advise you to go away and hide yourself. You had better not come near me or you'll be sorry for it. When a thing is done and past, even fools are wise at last!"

Euphorbos did not care; what he said was:

"Now indeed, my lord Menelaos, you shall pay in full for my brother whom you killed—and here you are boasting how you made his wife a widow in her new bridal chamber, and brought mourning and lamentation upon his parents! I might console those unhappy creatures if I could bring your head and your armour, and lay them in the hands of Panthoös and lady Phrontis. But it shall not be long before we put our quarrel to the test of life or death!"

With that he struck a blow on the shield; the point bent and did not go through. But Menelaos with a prayer to Father Zeus lunged, and as the man stept back struck him on the root of the throat, putting his weight into the blow: the blade cut through, and he fell with a dull thud in his rattling armour. That hair lovely as the Graces, those tresses tight-pinched with gold and silver wire, were drenched with blood. He lay like a tall stem of olive, which a man keeps in a private garden where plenty of water flows, growing fair and high; it sways in the breath of all the breezes, heavy with the white flowers, until suddenly a storm-wind roots it out of the trench and lays it along the ground. And so lay he, when Menelaos had killed him and stript his armour.

When a mountain-bred lion, proud in his strength, ravishes the best cow from a grazing herd, he takes the neck in his strong teeth and breaks it, then gulps down blood and bowels,

1 Euphorbos, Hyperenor, and Polydamas.

tearing savagely: dogs and herdsmen hoot loudly from a distance and dare not come near, for they are all afraid. Just so none of those men dared to come near Menelaos.

Then he would have carried off the spoils without trouble, but Phoibos Apollo grudged it to him. So the god took the shape of Mentês the Ciconian, and spoke to Hector in plain words:

"Hector, you are chasing what you will never catch, when you run like this after the horses of Achillês. It is not easy for a mortal man to master them and drive them: that is only for Achillês, whose mother is herself an immortal. Meanwhile King Menelaos has been defending Patroclos, and he has killed your best man Euphorbos Panthoidês." Then he went back into the mellay.

Hector looked round angrily and saw them at once, the body lying on the ground with blood flowing from the wound, and Menelaos stripping off the armour. He shouted, and hastened towards them like a flame of fire. Menelaos heard the shout and said to himself:

"What shall I do! If I leave the spoils, and if I leave Patroclos who lies here for my sake, not a Danaän but will hate the sight of me. If I stand and fight Hector and the Trojan army alone, to save my honour, I shall be surrounded—for here comes Hector with all his army!

"No, no, all that is nonsense. When one fights a fellow that finds favour in the sight of God, he simply tempts providence and brings tribulation rolling upon himself. Then no Danaän will hate the sight of me, if he sees me retreat before Hector, because Hector has heaven to help him. But if I could hear anything of that redoubtable man Aias, we might even tempt providence a bit, and strike a blow to save this dead man for Achillês Peleidês. That would be the best choice of evils."

While he was deliberating, Hector and his Trojans had come near. Menelaos left the body and retreated, turning again and again—like a bearded lion chased from the farmyard by dogs and men with shouting and spears: his stout heart freezes within him, and sorely against his will he leaves that farm. So in a slow reluctant pace, Menelaos went on until he found his people. Then he faced about, and looked everywhere for Telamonian Aias. He soon saw him on the left of the battle rallying the men, who were in mortal fear of Phoibos Apollo.

He went off at a run and soon reached him, and said:

"Aias! This way, don't waste time! Hurry up for Patroclos! He's dead, but we may bring back the body to Achillês—the armour is lost, Hector has it."

This did arouse Aias. He and Menelaos together made their way through the press. Hector had taken the armour, and now he was dragging away the body, intending to cut off the head and throw the body among the carrion dogs. But now comes Aias behind that great shield like a stone wall! Hector retreated and leapt into his car; he gave the armour to be carried back to the city and to be his chief pride.

Aias now covered the body with his broad shield. He stood as a lion stands over his young, when huntsmen meet him leading his cubs through the woods: with a defiant swagger he draws down the eyelids to hide his eyes. So stood Aias, with his legs across the body of Patroclos. By his side was Menelaos, ever more and more anxious.

Now Glaucos with a frown reproached Hector for his delay:

"You are handsome enough, Hector, but there is a good deal lacking in you as a soldier. You have a great name for nothing, you are a regular shakeleg! You had better consider now how you and your people alone are going to save Ilios. None of the Lycians at least will fight for you, since we get no thanks it seems for these everlasting battles. How are you likely to save an ordinary man, when you deserted Sarpedon in this heartless way? and he was your friend and comrade, and you left him to be the Argives' prey and plaything! He did good work for you and your city while he lived, and now you have not the pluck to save him from the dogs.

"If any Lycians will listen to me, it's homeward we will go, and that means certain destruction for Troy. For if the Trojans had now real bold undaunted courage, such as men feel when they fight for home and country, we should very soon drag Patroclos into Ilios. If we could drag him away and get him into the city dead, the Argives would very soon release the armour of Sarpedon, and we should bring him too into Ilios—for the master of Patroclos is one who is chief champion of the Argives, he and his men. But you would not stand up to Aias and look in your enemy's eyes, or fight it out with him, for he is a better man than you."

Hector looked angrily at him and said:

"How could a man like you, Glaucos, say such an outrageous thing? Damn it all, I thought you were the most sensible man in Lycia. I don't think much of your sense now, when you say such a thing. I would not stand up to that monster Aias, so you say! Battles and trampling horses don't make me shiver; but the will of Zeus Almighty must always prevail, and he can make the strongest man take to his heels, and robs him of victory easily, or again he sends him forward to the fight. Pray come this way, sluggard, stand by my side and see my work! See whether I shall be a coward all the day long, as you declare, or if I shall stop the fighting of a Danaän or two, however fierce they may be over dead Patroclos!"

With this he called to the Trojans at the top of his voice:

"Trojans! Lycians! My brave Dardanians! Be men, my friends, don't forget your duty! fight your hardest until I put on the armour of Achillês, which I have torn off the back of Patroclos after I killed him!"

He hurried away out of the battle, and ran as fast as he could to the men who were carrying the armour—they were not far away, and he ran like the wind. There behind the battle he stood and changed; he gave his own gear to the carriers, and put on the incorruptible armour of Achillês Peleidês, which the heavenly ones had given to his father, and his father had given to him in old age: but the son never grew old in his father's armour.

When Zeus Cloudgatherer saw him behind the battle, arming himself in the gear of Peleidês, he shook his head and said to himself:

"Ah, poor creature! You have no thought of death in your mind, and death is very near. You don the incorruptible armour of a mighty champion whom others do tremble at. His comrade you have slain, that man so gentle and so strong, and torn his armour brutally from head and shoulders. Yet I will put great strength into your hands, to set off against this—that you shall never return out of this battle, or give to Andromachê the famous armour of Peleion."

Over these words he bowed with his black brows. But he made the armour fit the body of Hector; and the dreadful spirit of war entered into him, and filled every limb with power and strength. He came back to his allies shouting: there they all saw him shining in the armour of the great Achillês. Then he appealed to each in turn, Mesthlês and Glaucos, Medon and Thersilochos, Asteropaios and Deisenor and Hippothoös, Phorcys and Chromios and Ennomos the bird-diviner, and said plainly without wasting words:

"Hear me now, you thousand tribes of my allies from the country round about! I did not want numbers, and I was not looking for numbers, when I sent round to your cities to invite you here. What I wished was, that you of your own generous hearts might save the women and children of Troy from the Achaian invaders. That is my thought when I exhaust my people with supplies and food for you, and try to content you all. Then let each man turn straight to the front, come death, come life—that's how war and battle kiss and prattle! The man who succeeds in driving back Aias and gets Patroclos into Troy, dead as he is, half of the spoils I will allot him and keep half myself: he shall have as much pride as I have!"

Straight for the Danaäns in a heavy mass they marched, with spears at the ready. They expected soon to drag away the corpse from Aias Telamoniadês. Fools! he killed many of them over that corpse.

At last Aias was convinced, and said to his companion:

"We are wasting time, my dear prince. I cannot believe any longer that we shall get safely out of this by our two selves. I am not so much worried about this dead corpse of Patroclos, which will soon be a good supper for dogs and vultures, as I am worried about my own live head which may come to grief, and for yours too, when I see battle all round us like a cloud—Hector himself, and certain death once more manifest for us. Look sharp, call some of our good men if you can make one hear."

Menelaos shouted for help loud and clear:

"Friends! captains and princes! You guests of our royal house, who drink free at the board of Agamemnon and Menelaos! Captains in high command!—But Zeus gives rank and honour still to every creature at his will.—I really can't make out where they all are, there is such a blaze of battle hereabouts.—But do come, if I don't mention your names, come everybody, you ought to be ashamed to let Patroclos be just a toy for dogs to play about with!"

Aias the Runner heard him clearly enough, and came running up first, then Idomeneus and his formidable retainer Merionês. But who could ever remember the names of all who came after these to reinforce the fighting?

Then the Trojans rushed on in a mass, roaring and shouting, like a great wave roaring against the swollen stream at a river's mouth, when the foam flies high and the headlands boom. The Achaians stood firm and determined round the body, fenced by their metal-plated shields. Cronion also covered their shining helmets in a thick cloud. He had no feeling against Menoitiadês when he was alive, and when dead he hated to let him be mauled about by Trojan dogs, and so he helped the defenders.

At first the Trojans pushed the Achaians back, and they left the body. The Trojans hurt none of them in the retreat as they would have liked to do, but they began to drag the body away. But the Achaians were not likely to be long in rallying when Aias was there—Aias, the finest man and the strongest man in the army after Achillês! He soon swung them round again, and charged like a wild boar twisting about in the woods, which easily scatters huntsmen and dogs and all. So Aias scattered the Trojans who were crowding about Patroclos, determined to drag him away and cover themselves with glory.

Now Hippothoös (the son of Pelasgian Lethos) had tied up the ankles of Patroclos with his swordbelt, hoping to gain credit with Hector. He was dragging the body away, when a blow fell on him irresistible. Aias was upon him, and drove the great spear crashing through his helmet, and the brains ran out along the socket. The man dropt the foot of Patroclos and let it lie, as he fell prone over the corpse, far from fertile Laris; few and short had his days been when Aias laid him low, and he never paid to his parents the debt of a grateful son.

Then Hector cast a lance at Aias, but Aias was watching his eye and dodged a little aside; the blade hit Schedios and ran under his collar-bone and stuck out of the shoulder, bringing him down with a bang and a clang in his armour. Schedios was the son of Iphitos and the best man among the Phocians; he came from Panopeus, where he was king.

Phorcys Phainops' son now straddled across Hippothoös, but Aias stabbed him right in the belly. The blade pierced the corselet-plate and his bowels gushed out; he fell in the dust, clutching at the earth.

Then Hector and his front men fell back, and the Achaians with shouts of triumph dragged away the bodies of Phorcys and Hippothoös, and stript off their armour.

And now the Trojans would have lost heart, they would have been driven behind the walls of their city, and the Achaians would have prevailed by their own strength and courage even against the decree of Zeus, but Apollo made Aineias take part. He assumed the shape of the herald Periphas Epytidês, a faithful old servant of the family, and said:

"Aineias, I wonder how you could defend Ilios if a god were against you! Why, I have seen other men who trusted in their numbers and the strength of their manhood, and kept their realm even against Zeus; but in our case Zeus wishes victory for us rather than for the Danaäns. Yet you all run away for ever and will not fight!"

Aineias knew Apollo Shootafar at a glance, and called out to Hector:

"Hector! and your other captains, Trojans and allies! This is really a disgrace, if we are to be driven into the city like beaten cowards! But one of the gods has just come and told me, that Zeus the God of battles is still on our side. Then let us have at the enemy! Don't suffer them tamely to rescue the body of Patroclos dead!"

Then he dashed through the front ranks and stood before them; the others wheeled about and faced the Achaians. Aineias struck down a man, Leocritos Arisbas' son, the trusty comrade of Lycomedês; then Lycomedês came up to the body and cast his spear. The blade struck Apisaon Hippasidês in the liver, and he collapsed. This man came from Paionia, and he was their best man after Asteropaios. Then Asteropaios rushed forward at once to avenge his friend, but he could do nothing; the shields all stood like a fence about Patroclos, and the spears stuck out. Aias was everywhere, keeping the men in hand; he would not let any one move back, or go out in front, but made them stand close round the body and lunge when they could. Such were the tactics of that prodigious man. The ground was red with blood, men were falling one after another among the assailants; and the Danaäns too, for they did not fight without bloodshed, although they lost fewer men, because they were careful to keep together and defend one another.

As they fought in this fiery conflict, you could not suppose there was either sun or moon in the sky; for a thick cloud covered all the place where the fighting men stood about the body of Patroclos. But the rest of the two armies fought at their ease in the open air; the sharp clear sunlight spread everywhere, and not a cloud was to be seen on earth or mountains. All these fought with pauses for rest, avoiding the shots which came from either side with plenty of room between; but the group in the middle had a hard struggle against both cloud and battle, and even the best of them were worn out with their efforts.

But two men, Thrasymedês and Antilochos, had not yet heard that Patroclos was dead. They thought he was up at the front and still fighting. They were in a place apart where Nestor had sent them, watching the carnage and rout of their people.

All day long there were hard times for those who were fighting round the body of Patroclos. Their desperate struggle covered them with sweat, knees and legs and feet, hands and eyes. They tugged and pulled at the dead body, like a party of men who have to stretch an oxhide soaking with grease, and pull away standing in a ring till the natural moisture runs out and the grease runs in—the hide is well stretched with all those men pulling! So they pulled that body against one another in the narrow space, the Trojans towards Troy and the Achaians towards the ships. That was a savage maul! Neither Arês nor Athena would have thought it something too small to glut their anger. See what a bitter struggle of men and horses Zeus kept on the stretch about Patroclos!

But Achillês did not know yet, as it seems, that Patroclos was dead. For the battle was far away from the ships under the walls of Troy. Achillês never expected that he was killed; he thought that if he got as far as the gates he would return alive, for he never expected at all that Patroclos would take the city without him, nor with him indeed: so much he had often been told by his mother, when she spoke privately of the will of Zeus. Certainly his mother told him nothing of all the misfortune which had now come about, and how the dearest of all his companions had been killed.

So they went on without ceasing to grapple with one another in deadly strife over the body; and you might have heard the Achaians saying:

"Ah, my good friends! There's no doubt we could not retreat

with honour, and let the Trojans drag away this man in triumph. May the black earth swallow us first! That would be better."

And the Trojans would say:

"Ah, my friends! not a man must give way, not if we are all doomed to die together over this body!"

So they encouraged one another, and so they fought, while the iron din resounded through the unvintaged air to the brazen sky.

But behind the battle the horses of Achillês had been weeping, ever since they heard that their driver was low in the dust, struck down by Hector's blood-stained spear. What could Automedon do? Often he touched them with a quick lash, often he cursed and often he coaxed—but go they would not, neither back to the sea nor forward to battle: they stood with the car steady behind them, moving no more than a stone pillar on a tomb. They drooped their heads till they touched the ground, hot tears ran from their eyes and fell, as they mourned the driver whom they had loved and lost; their thick manes hung from the yoke-pad over both sides of the yoke.

Cronion was grieved as he saw their mourning, and shaking his head he said to himself:

"Ah, poor things! Why did we give you to a mortal man like Peleus, when you are immortal and never grow old? To share the sorrows of miserable mankind? For I think there is no more unhappy thing than man, of all creatures that breathe and move on the earth. Nevertheless, you and your splendid chariot shall never be driven by Hector Priamidês—that I will not suffer. Is it not enough that he has the arms, and utters vainglorious boasts? You shall have strength from me in your knees and your spirit. You shall bring Automedon to the ships and save him from the battle; for I will still give them victory, and they shall slay until they reach the ships; then the sun shall go down and sacred night shall come."

Then he breathed courage into the horses. They shook the dust from their manes, and brought their car swiftly to the battlefield. Automedon swooped as a vulture on the geese, fighting for all his sorrow: lightly he charged into the thick of the throng, lightly he left pursuing Trojans behind. But he killed no creature whom he pursued; for alone in that sacred chariot he could not both hold the swift horses and attack with a spear.

At last a friend saw him, Alcimedon, son of Laercês Haimon's son. He stopped behind the car and called out:

"Automedon! has some god robbed you of your good sense, and put this useless notion into your head? There you go out in front fighting the Trojans alone! But your comrade is dead. Hector himself has the armour of Aiacidês on his back, and mighty proud he is!"

Automedon answered:

"Alcimedon, you're the man for me! There's no one else in the whole army who can manage these fiery horses, only Patroclos, that heaven-born genius! while he was alive. But now he is dead and gone. Come on, take whip and reins, I'll get out and fight."

He leapt out as he spoke; Alcimedon got into the welcome car and took over whip and reins. This Hector saw and called out:

"Aineias, my stand-by! I have just seen those two horses of Achillês suddenly appear in the battle! And drivers who are no good! I could take them, I hope, if you'll help. I don't think they would dare to stand up to you and me!"

Aineias was ready, and they advanced together under their trusty shields—good oxhide with a thick facing of metal. Chromios and Aretos went with them. They felt sure they would kill the men and drive off those splendid horses—poor fools! Not without bloodshed were they to part company with Automedon.

But Automedon commended himself to Father Zeus, and full of confidence he turned to his faithful friend:

"Alcimedon," he said, "don't keep the horses too far from me—let me feel their breath on my back. I believe Hector will stick at nothing until he has killed us both and got hold of these horses, and routed our people, unless he is killed himself."

Then he called the Aias pair and Menelaos:

"Aias! You two and Menelaos! Leave the body to the best men you have, and let them see to the defence, but here are we two alive! Help us and save us! Hector and Aineias are on us with all their weight, and they are the most dangerous of the Trojans. Ah well, all is on the knees of the gods. I will have a shot myself, and the lord of heaven shall decide."

He cast his spear and hit the shield of Aretos: the blade went through the shield and through the belt and pierced his belly. Aretos gave a leap forward and fell on his back, as an ox leaps forward and falls, when a strong man strikes wtih a sharp axe behind the horns and cuts the sinew. The sharp spear turned in his bowels, and he was still. Hector made a cast at Automedon, but Automedon was watching his eye and stooped forward; the spear flew over him and stuck in the ground behind, quivered and was still. Then they would have fallen to with swords, but Aias and the Runner came to their comrade's call, and parted the fighters. Their coming alarmed Hector and Aineias and Chromios, who retired leaving Aretos dead on the spot. Automedon quickly stript off the armour, and said triumphantly:

"There now, I have eased my sorrow a little for my friend's death, although the man I killed is worth less!"

He took up the blood-stained spoils and put them in the car, then got in himself with blood all over feet and arms, like a lion that has gorged a bull.

The strife round Patroclos now became more bitter and desperate than ever; Zeus had sent down Athena to encourage the Danaäns—he had changed his mind, no doubt. She wrapt herself in a lurid cloud, like the cloud about a rainbow which Zeus stretches across the sky to be a portent of war, or the chilly storm which drives men from their work upon the earth and distresses their flocks; then she dashed among the Achaians and pressed them on to the fight one and all. She began with Menelaos who happened to be near, and said in the shape and voice of Phoinix:

"You, Menelaos, will certainly have shame and disgrace, if the great friend of Achillês is worried by dogs under the walls of Troy. Stand firm, be brave, and keep the men at it!"

Menelaos said:

"O Daddy Phoinix, dear old ancient! Let Athena give me strength, and keep the shots away, and I would gladly stand firm and defend Patroclos; for his death has touched my heart indeed. But Hector is furious as blazing fire. He kills and kills without ceasing, and Zeus gives him the victory!"

Athena Brighteyes was pleased that Menelaos had prayed to her first of all. She strengthened his back and knees, and put in his inmost heart the courage of a fly: beat him off from your skin as often as you like, he goes on biting, and human blood is his dainty dish.

So Menelaos was filled with the irrepressible audacity of a fly. He stood over the body and cast his spear. There was a man Podês among the Trojans, Eëtion's son, a rich man and a brave man. Hector thought more of him than any man of the nation, for he was his comrade and boon-companion. The spear struck this man on the belt as he started to escape; it pierced him and brought him down. Then Menelaos pulled the body among his people.

Now Apollo did his part for Hector. He took the shape of Phainops Asiadês from Abydos, who was dearest of his guest-friends.

"Hector," he said, "what Achaian will ever fear you again, now you have run away from Menelaos, who used to be a flabby spearman? Now he has killed your true friend and good soldier Podês, and picked him up by himself, and dragged him from under your noses, and got away with him!"

This made Hector furious, and he pressed forward: at the same moment Cronidês turned the battle. Thick clouds covered Mount Ida, lightning flashed and thunder rolled, the mountain quaked; Zeus took up his tasselled aegis-cape shining bright, and shook it at the Achaians. They turned in panic flight, and the Trojans began to prevail.

Boiotian Peneleos began the retreat; moving slowly backwards, he had a shoulder grazed and cut to the bone by Polydamas who was close upon him. Next Hector struck Leïtos Alectryon's son on the wrist, and disabled him; Leïtos made haste to escape looking about him watchfully, for he knew he could not handle the spear now. Hector pursued, but Idomeneus hit him on the corselet over the breast; the spear broke at the socket, and the Trojans raised a shout. Idomeneus was now disarmed, and he would have been a dead man, for he had come on foot from the ships; but help was at hand. For Coiranos of Lyctos in Crete had brought his master Meroinês into the battle, and he kept the horses near while his master was fighting on foot as usual. Idomeneus got into this car, and as he stood there Hector cast at him. He just missed him, but hit Coiranos under the ear, cutting through the tongue and spilling his teeth. Coiranos tumbled out dropping the reins, but Merionês stooped and picked them up from the ground, saying:

"Whip 'em up and away to the ships! You see yourself that we are losing now."

So Idomeneus whipt them up and got away; and Coiranos saved Idomeneus, but not his own life.

Aias and Menelaos also saw that the victory was passing from them, and Aias said:

"Damn it, any fool can see that Father Zeus is helping the other side. All their shots hit, whether a good man throws or a bad man—Zeus makes 'em all go straight! And all ours miss and stick in the ground. Well, we must look after ourselves. What is the best thing to do? We want to bring off this body, and get back to our friends too. They will be glad to see us! I think they are sorry enough if they look in this direction. They cannot expect us to keep off Hector the invincible: he'll soon be upon our ships.

"I wish some one would go at once and tell Achillês. I don't believe he has even heard the bad news that his dear friend is dead. But I cannot see such a man anywhere; men and horses are all swallowed up in this mist. O Father Zeus, save the Achaians out of this mist! Make the sky clear, grant us to see with our eyes! Kill us in the light, since it is thy pleasure to kill us!" [2]

[2] "I did not go right in. It was indeed a Head-House, and I came to the sudden conviction that if I were to die I would much rather it were in the clear and open air."—Jack McClaren, *My Odyssey*, page 29. This natural wish has been expressed by other men in like case.

The Father pitied him, as he prayed with tears in his eyes. In a moment he scattered the mist and the dust, the sun shone above, all the scene of the battle was disclosed. Then Aias said:

"Look about now, my lord Menelaos, if you can see Antilochos alive still, and send him to tell Achillês that his dearest friend is dead."

So Menelaos moved away, as a lion retreats from a farmyard, tired with fighting off dogs and men: he leapt in greedy for meat, but got none; for they have been awake all night to save their fat cattle from his jaws, and he is met with showers of lances thrown by strong hands, and burning brands which terrify him, so when the dawn comes he must depart disappointed. No less unwilling was Menelaos to leave Patroclos a prey to the Trojans, as he feared he would be now all the army was in rout. Before he went, he said earnestly:

"Be careful, you two, and Merionês: You are in charge here, and you must not forget the gentle Patroclos, poor fellow. He was kind and pleasant to all in his life, but now death and fate has found him."

Then he moved away glancing watchfully all round, like the eagle which is said to have keenest sight of all birds that fly in the heavens. High in the air he spies the quick-footed hare lying under a thick bush, stoops in a flash and kills him. So Menelaos cast sharp glances around among the throng of men, to see if he could spy the son of Nestor alive.

Suddenly he saw him away to the left, rallying the men as well as he could, and he called out as soon as he was near enough:

"Antilochos! This way, my dear man, I have bad news for you, I am sorry to say. I think you can see already for yourself that God is rolling up trouble for us, and the Trojans have the best of it. But we have had a terrible loss—Patroclos is dead. Now then run as quick as you can and tell Achillês—he may be able to save the body, but that is all; his armour is gone— Hector has it."

Antilochos was shocked to hear the news. He was struck dumb; his eyes filled with tears, and his voice was choked. But he did what he was told; gave his arms to Laodocos, who was following him with the horses, and ran off at full speed.

This left the Pylians without a leader. They were hard pressed, and looked for another, but Menelaos did not care to stay there and take the place of their leader. He put Thrasymedês in charge, and ran back himself to defend the body of Patroclos. As soon as he reached Aias he said:

"I have just sent your man at full speed to tell Achillês. But I don't believe he will come just now. He may be furious against Hector, but he could not fight naked and bare. We must do

what we can for ourselves, and see if we can save the body and
our own lives too."

Aias said:

"Quite right, Menelaos. Be quick—you and Menelaos put
your arms under the body and lift it. You carry it away, and
we two will protect your rear against Hector and all the rest.
We have one name and one heart, and we are well used to
stand side by side and face the foe!"

So they hoisted the body with a great effort. The Trojans
raised a yell when they saw them lifting the body, and rushed
at them like dogs that run before their masters upon a wounded
boar: they run furiously, until he turns on them in defiance,
then they scurry back all over the place. So the Trojans would
come on in a body stabbing at them with spears and swords,
but whenever the doughty pair turned on them and stood, their
colour changed and not one would dare to advance and show
fight.

In this way they carried the body to the ships, fighting as
they went; while the battle spread round them like wild fire
which suddenly rises and spreads over a city, blown before the
wind, until the houses fall in ruins amid the blaze. So as they
moved on, the ceaseless din of horses and fighting men rose all
about them; and the two did their task like mules putting forth
all their dogged strength, to drag a baulk or a ship's mast down
a rocky path, worn out with sweat and weariness. Behind them
the two namesakes held off the battle, as a woody ridge right
across the plain holds a flood, holds the torrents of mighty
rivers, and drives off their waters over the plain for all their
impetuous force.

But the Trojans pressed them hard, and especially two, glorious Hector and Aineias Anchisiadês. The Achaians fled before
them with death-shrieks, and forgot how to fight; as daws or
starlings fly in a cloud with death-shrieks when they see a falcon, who is certain death for small birds. Many a fine spear and
shield was thrown away and left around and about the moat
in the Danaän rout, for there was never a moment's peace.

BOOK XVIII

*How Achillês received the news, and how his
mother got him new armour from Hephaistos*

WHILE THE BATTLE WENT ON LIKE BLAZING FIRE, ANTILOCHOS had been running at the top of his speed to Achillês.

He found Achillês in front of the ships anxious and thoughtful. He feared what had really happened, and he was saying to himself:

"Ah, what can this mean? Here are our people again rushing in a rabble towards the camp. I fear the gods may bring bitter grief on me, as my mother told me once. She declared that the best man of the Myrmidons would be killed in battle while I yet lived. It must be the brave Menoitiadês who is dead. Headstrong man! I ordered him strictly to come back as soon as he had got rid of the fire, and not to fight with Hector."

As these thoughts were passing through his mind, there was Antilochos. When he was near enough he told his cruel news, with tears running down his cheeks:

"Bad news, my lord prince! I have very bad news for you, I am sorry to say. Patroclos is dead, they are fighting for his body, only the body, for the armour is lost—Hector has it!"

Sorrow fell on Achillês like a cloud. He swept up the dust with both hands, and poured it over his head and smirched his handsome face, till the black dirt stained his fragrant tunic. He tore his hair and fell flat in the dust, grand in his grandeur. The captive women also whom he and Patroclos had taken, wailed in grief, and ran out to where he lay, beating their breasts and half fainting. Antilochos had taken the hands of Achillês and stood weeping beside him, while he moaned heavily; for he feared Achillês might put the steel to his own throat.

His gracious mother heard his terrible cry, sitting by her old father deep down in the sea. She shrieked, and all the Nerëid nymphs gathered about her in the deep sea: there came Glaucê and Thaleia and Cymodocê, Nesaia and Speio, Thoê and round-eyed Haliê, Cymothoê and Actaia and Limnoraia, Melitê and Iaira, Amphithoê and Agauê, Doto and Proto, Pherusa and Dynamenê, Dexamenê and Amphinomê and Callianeira, Doris and Panopê and famous Galateia, Nemertês and Apseudês and Callianassa; there came Clymenê and Ianeira and Ianassa, Maira and Oreithyia and curly-headed Amatheia, and all the other Nereïds of the deep sea.[1] All beat their breasts and wailed, as Thetis led off the lament:

"Hear me, sister Nereïds, and you all shall know the sorrow of my heart. Woe is me! unhappy mother of a noble son! I bore a lovely boy, perfect and strong, a hero above heroes. He ran up like a slim tree, I tended him like a choice plant in the garden, I let him go in the fleet to fight against Ilios: but I shall never have him back again, he will never return to his father's house. As long as he lives and sees the light of the sun he has only sorrow, and I can do nothing to help him.—But I must go and see my dear child, and hear what trouble has come to him so far from the battle."

She left the cave, and her sisters went with her weeping, through the water, until they came to the Trojan strand. There they stept out upon the beach one after another, not far from the place where the Myrmidons had drawn up their ships, and Thetis sought her son.

She found him groaning, and clasped his head with a sorrowful cry, saying simply:

"My child, why do you weep? What is your trouble? Tell me, don't hide it. Zeus has done all that for you, all you besought him to do, the whole army has been brought to disaster for want of you and huddled up under their ships!"

Achillês said with a deep groan:

"Yes, my dear mother, the Olympian has done all that for me. But what good do I get of all that now, if my dear friend Patroclos is dead? I cared more for him than all my companions, as much as for my own life. He is lost! my armour is Hector's! Hector killed him, Hector stript off that miraculous armour, that beautiful armour, that wonder of wonders, which the gods gave to Peleus on the day when they laid you in a mortal's bed. I wish you had gone on living with your immortal sisters of the sea, and Peleus had married a mortal wife! But now—it was all to bring a thousand sorrows on you too, for your son's death! You will never have me back again, I shall never go home—for I have no desire myself to live and remain among men, unless I may kill Hector first with my own

---

[1] All these names, like other Greek names, have meanings, many of them connected with the sea. But the effect is very different from the list of Phaiacians in the eighth book of the *Odyssey*. Those are all invented by Homer, with a comic effect, for a company in high spirits. These are traditional, and the effect in this scene of mourning is a soothing echo from the beautiful songs of fairyland. The meaning matters nothing to us, only the sound.

spear and make him pay the death-price for Patroclos Menoiti-adês!"

Thetis answered weeping:

"You have not long to live, my child, if you say that. Quick after Hector fate is ready for you!"

Achillês burst out in anger:

"Quick let me die, since it seems my friend was killed and I was not there to help him! He perished far from his native land, and I was not there to defend him!

"But now, since I am never to return home, since I brought no hope to Patroclos or my other comrades whom Hector killed, and how many they are! since I only sit idle beside the ships a burden to the earth, although there is none like me in battle—as for debate, others are better there—O that discord might utterly cease to be in heaven or earth! and anger, that makes even the prudent man take offence—anger that is far sweeter than trickling honey, and grows in men's hearts like smoke—just as I was made angry now by my lord King Agamemnon.

"But I will let bygones be bygones, although I am indignant; I will rule my temper because I must. Now I will go and find the destroyer of that dear life, Hector! Fate I will welcome whenever Zeus and All Gods may choose to bring it. Not even the mighty Heraclês escaped fate, and he was one that Lord Zeus Cronion loved best of all; yes, fate brought him low, and the implacable anger of Hera. So with me; if a like fate has been ordained for me, there I shall lie when I am dead; but now may I win a glorious name! May they know that I have been long away from the battle! May I bring sobs and groaning to some wives of Troy and Dardania, and tears to their tender cheeks, which they shall wipe away with both hands! Don't try to keep me from the battle; you love me, I know, but you shall never persuade me."

Silverfoot Thetis answered:

"Yes indeed, my child, that is true, it is no bad thing to defend comrades in distress and danger of death. But your armour is in the enemy's hands. Hector is wearing that fine shining gear on his own shoulders. He is proud enough, yet I don't think he will have it long to boast of, for death is near him! But I do beseech you not to enter the battle until you see me here again. To-morrow I will come back at sunrise, with new armour from Hephaistos himself."

She turned from her son, and said to her sisters as they went away:

"Now you must return to our father's house and tell all to the Old Man of the Sea. I am going to Olympos, to ask

Hephaistos the master craftsman if he will kindly make new armour for my son."

And so they dived again into the sea, and Silverfoot Thetis set out for Olympos, to fetch new armour for her dear boy.

But all the while the Achaian rout went on, as Hector chased the fugitives with a terrible noise, until they came to their ships on the Hellespont. They could not get the body of Patroclos clear away; for Hector was on them again with horses and men like a consuming fire. Three times Hector caught him by the legs to drag him away, calling on his men; three times the doughty pair were strong enough to beat him off. Now Hector would make a rush through the press, now he would stand and shout to his men, but never one step backward. Like shepherds who try to keep off a starving lion, the formidable pair could not scare him away from that body.

Indeed, he would have dragged it away in triumph, if Iris had not appeared—Hera sent her to Achillês without a word to Zeus or any other god. She gave her message clear and plain:

"Up, Peleidês! Show them you terrors! Go and help Patroclos! His body is the prize of this awful struggle—Trojans charging to drag him away to Troy, Danaäns fighting to hold him, all killing each other! And Hector most of all—he means to cut off his head and fix it upon the stakes! Up with you, don't lie there! You should be ashamed to let Trojan dogs tumble and tear Patroclos. Yours is the disgrace, if the body is brought in mangled and mutilated!"

Achillês answered:

"My dear goddess, who sent you with this message?"

Iris said:

"Hera sent me—our gracious Queen herself. Cronidês knows nothing about it, nor any other god in Olympos."

Achillês answered:

"And how can I go into the maul? My armour is in the hands of those men, and my mother forbids me to arm until I shall see her again between my eyes. She has promised to bring me fine new armour from Hephaistos. I don't know any other that I could use except the great shield of Aias Telamoniadês. But he is there in the front himself, I believe, using his spear to defend Patroclos."

Iris said:

"We know well enough that they hold your armour. But just go and show yourself at the moat, that the Trojans may be startled into quiet, and your people may have a breathing space. There's little time for breath in face of sudden death!"

Away went Iris at speed, and Achillês rose up. Over his broad shoulders Athena draped the tasselled aegis-cape: over his head she spread a golden haze; from his body shone a white-hot glow. We have seen a city on some island far away in the sea, besieged by enemies: all day long as they fight smoke rises to the sky, but when night falls we can see the beacons one after another signalling to the world for help with fires blazing high. So the light rose from the head of Achillês shining up to the sky, as he stepped from the wall and stood beside the moat. He did not mingle with his people, for he remembered his mother's strict command, but there he stood and shouted, and from far away Pallas Athena lifted up her voice; great was the confusion among the Trojans. The voice of Aiacidês sounded loud and clear, like the loud clear voice of a trumpet when fierce enemies beleaguer a city all about.

The Trojans heard the brazen voice of Aiacidês, and their hearts were filled with consternation. The horses turned away, foreboding evil to come. The charioteers were dumbfounded to see that bright and terrible light blazing above his head, the light which Athena had kindled. Thrice did Achillês shout aloud from the brink of the moat; thrice were confounded the Trojans and all their host. There also perished twelve men of their best, speared upon their own chariots by their own spears.

Then the Achaians were glad indeed to draw back the body of Patroclos out of the turmoil and lay it upon a bier. His companions trooped around it mourning; Achillês followed, weeping hot tears, when he saw his faithful friend stretched on the bier and torn with cruel wounds. He had sent him forth to the war with chariots and horses, hoping to welcome a safe return: but what a return was this!

The sun set unwearied, for Hera sent him unwilling down under the Ocean stream, and the Achaians at last had rest from their desperate struggle.

When the Trojans on their part had left the field of battle and unyoked the horses, they gathered in conference before they thought of food. All stood as they held their debate, none could endure to sit; for all were dismayed now Achillês had shown himself, after he had remained so long far from the battlefield.

Polydamas Panthoös' son was the first to speak, for he alone could look both before and behind. He was Hector's close friend. Both were born in one night; but one was first in debate, the other in battle. This man now addressed the assembly.

"Look well about you, my friends," he said. "My advice is to retire now to the city, and not to spend this night in the plain before the enemy camp. We are a long way from our walls. So long as yon man was incensed against King Agamemnon, the Achaians were easier to fight. I was glad myself to sleep near their ships, when I hoped we should take them. But now I am terribly afraid of Peleion. With his overbearing temper, he will never be content to stay in the middle plain where both sides share the battle; for him the stake is our city and our women.

"Then let us retreat to the city; listen to me, for this is what will happen. Just now the blessed night has checked his pursuit; but if he finds us here to-morrow when he sallies forth armed, many a man shall know him well. Many a Trojan shall be gnawed by dogs and vultures, and he that escapes will be glad of a refuge in Ilios—I only pray that the tale may be far from my ears!

"If we do as I say, with regret I am sure, we will keep our forces assembled, and the city will be safe behind walls and lofty gates and high doors well barred. To-morrow at dawn we will arm ourselves and take post along the walls. It will be the worse for him if he comes out and fights for our fortress! Back to the ships he will go, when he has had enough of exercising the horses and careering round the city. That temper of his will not give him leave to assault it, and take it he never shall—dogs shall devour him first!"

Hector frowned at him and said:

"I don't like what you say this time, Polydamas. Go back and huddle up in the city? Haven't you all enough of being cooped in behind walls? There was a time when the whole world talked of Priam's town, Troy the great magazine of gold and bronze! But now all our homes are stript of their treasures; many have been sold and gone to Phrygia or Meionia since Lord Zeus has been displeased. But now, you fool, do not publish those notions of yours any longer, just when the great god has granted me to win success before the enemy camp and to crush up the Achaians against the sea! Not a Trojan will listen to you—I will not allow it!

"Come now, all, do as I shall tell you. First let us take a good meal in our divisions, see after the watch, keep awake every man. If any Trojan is worried overmuch about his goods, let him collect them and distribute them to be mob-gobbled—it is better the people should enjoy them than our enemies! To-morrow at dawn we will arm ourselves and make a great attack on the ships. If Achillês has really risen up by the ships, it shall be all the worse for him—just as he likes! I at least will never turn my back on battle! I will stand up to meet him, to win or lose it all. The God of War will see fair play—he's often slain that wants to slay!"

The Trojans cheered this speech, in their folly, for Pallas Athena stole their sense away. Hector's advice was bad, and they praised him; Polydamas offered good counsel, and no one praised him. Then they took their meal where they were.

But the Achaians mourned Patroclos all night long. Achillês

led their lamentations, sobbing and pressing on his friend's breast those hands which had slain so many; groaning like a lion, when some hunter has robbed him of his cubs and he has come back too late—how he scours the glades in search of the robber's track, and hopes to find him, with bitter bile in his heart! So Achillês cried aloud to his Myrmidons:

"What a fool I was! What empty words I said on that day, when I tried to comfort the noble Menoitios in my home! I said I would bring his son back to Opoeis covered with glory, victor over Troy, laden with spoil! But Zeus does not fulfil all the designs of men. Both of us are destined to make the same earth red, here in Troy; for I shall never return to be welcomed by ancient Peleus in our home, or by Thetis my mother, but earth shall cover me in this place.

"But now, Patroclos, since you have gone down into the grave before me, and I am left, I will not give you burial until I shall bring here Hector's arms, and the head of Hector who killed you. Then before your pyre I will cut the throats of twelve noble sons of Troy in payment for your death. Till then you shall lie as you are beside our ships, and round about you shall weep in lamentation night and day Trojan and Dardanian women, whom we have gotten by our strength and by our long spears in sacking many a rich town."

Then he directed that a large tripod should be set over the fire to wash the blood from his friend's body. They set the tripod accordingly with a cauldron, and filled it with water, and kindled the wood beneath. The flames curled about the cauldron; and when the water boiled they washed him, and rubbed him with oil, and filled the wounds with nine-year-old unguent. Then they laid him on a bier, wrapt in fine white linen from head to foot, with a white sheet spread over him. All night long Achillês and the Myrmidons mourned for Patroclos.

Meanwhile the gods in heaven were talking about it. Zeus said to his Queen:

"So you have had your way after all, my queen! You need not open your fine eyes like that. You have got Achillês up on his quick feet. One would think those bushy-headed Achaians were your own children!"

Queen Hera replied:

"What a thing to say, Cronidês! You shock me. I suppose even a mere man will do what he can for a man, even a mortal who has not my experience of life. I am chief of all goddesses on two counts, because I am eldest, and because I have the honour of being your wife and you are king of heaven: ought not I to damage the Trojans when I hate them?"

By this time Silverfoot Thetis had come to the house of

Hephaistos—that brazen starry house incorruptible, preëminent among the immortals, which old Crookshank himself had made. She found him in a sweat, running about among his bellows, very busy; for he had twenty tripods to make which were to stand round by the wall of his room. He put golden wheels under the base of each, that they might run of themselves into any party of the gods and then run back home again. They were a miracle! They were nearly done, only the lugs had to be put on; he was just finishing these and forging the rivets.

While the clever creature was making these, Thetis came up. Charis saw her and ran out at once with her veil flying—pretty Charis whom the famous Crookshank had made his wife. She clasped the visitor's hand and cried out:

"My dear Thetis, what brings you to our humble home in all this finery? This is an honour! I am glad to see you, dear. You don't often come this way! Come in do, and have something to eat."

She led Thetis in and made her sit on a chair covered with silver studs, beautifully carved and inlaid, and set a footstool for her feet. Then she called to Hephaistos:

"Husband! come in here. Thetis wants you!"

The good old hobbler answered:

"Then there's a goddess in our house whom I respect and love. She saved my life when I was laid up after that bad fall I had, all my mother's doing, shameless thing, when she wanted to hide me away because I'm lame. I should have had a bad time of it then, if Eurynomê and Thetis had not taken me to their hearts—you know Eurynomê, the daughter of ebb-and-flow Oceanos. I stayed with them nine years, and I made them no end of lovely things—brooches, twisted spirals, rosettes, necklaces—all in a hollow cave, and Oceanos rolling ever round and round foaming and roaring! Not a soul knew where I was, neither god nor mortal man, only Thetis and Eurynomê, who saved me. And now here she is in our house! I am bound to do anything for Thetis, pretty dear, pretty hair! I have to pay for my life! You just give her something nice to eat and drink while I put away my bellows and tools."

The old nonsuch got up from his anvil puffing and blowing, and limped about on his nimble thin shanks. The bellows he laid away from the fire, and collected all his working tools in a hutch of silver. Then he wiped a sponge over his face and both arms and sturdy neck and hairy chest, and put on his tunic, and limped out leaning on a thick stick, with a couple of maids to support him. These are made of gold exactly like living girls; they have sense in their heads, they can speak and use their muscles, they can spin and weave and do their work by grace of God. These bustled along supporting their master, and he stumbled to a chair beside Thetis, saying:

"My dear Thetis, in all your finery! What brings you to our humble home? This in an honour, and I am glad to see you, my dear; you don't often pay us a visit. Tell me what you want; I shall be pleased to do it if it is doable, and if I can do it."

Thetis answered with tears running down her cheeks:

"My dear Hephaistos, is there any goddess in Olympos who has troubles to bear like mine? Zeus Cronidês has chosen me out of all to make me miserable! Out of all the daughters of the sea he gave *me* to a man, to Peleus Aiacidês, and I had to endure a man's bed against my will. The man lies in his house worn out with the burden of old age, and now there is more for me! He gave me a son to bear and bring up, a hero of heroes. He ran up like a slim tree, I tended him like a rare plant in my garden, I let him go with the fleet to Ilios for the war—but I shall never get him back, he will never come home to his father's house! As long as he lives and sees the light of the sun, he has trouble, and I cannot go to help him.

"There was a girl the army chose for him as a prize—she was taken away from him by my lord Agamemnon! There he was pining away in grief for the girl; then the Trojans drove the Achaians back upon their ships and cooped them up there, would not let them get out; the people sent envoys to him with a petition and promised heaps of fine gifts. He refused to help in the battle himself, but he sent Patroclos in his own armour and strong forces with him. All day long they fought at the Scaian Gates, and he would have taken the city then and there, but Apollo killed Patroclos on the field, after many great exploits though Hector had the credit.

"So now I come to your knees with my prayer for my son, doomed to die so soon—Will you give him spear and helmet and a good pair of greaves with ankle-guards, and a corselet? What he had was lost when the Trojans killed his faithful friend, and there he lies on the ground in misery!"

The famous Crookshank answered:

"Cheer up, don't worry about that. He shall have his fine armour, and every man that sets eyes on it shall be amazed. I wish I could hide him from death as easily when that dreadful doom shall come!"

Without a moment's delay he went off to his bellows, poked them into the fire and told them to get to work. The bellows, twenty in all, blew under their melting-pots, ready to blow or to stop, letting out the blast strong, or weak, or just in any measure he wanted for his work. He put over the fire to melt, hard brass and tin, precious gold and silver. Then he placed a great anvil-stone on the block, and took hammer in one hand and tongs in the other.

First he fashioned a shield large and strong, adorning it with beautiful designs all over. He made a threefold rim round the edge of shining metal, and slung it on a silver baldric. There were five layers of hide in the shield; on the surface he laid his clever designs in metal.[2]

Upon it he wrought the Earth, and the Sky, and the Sea, the untiring Sun and the full Moon, and all the stars that encircle the sky—Pleiades and Hyades, Orion the mighty hunter and the Bear (which men also call the Wain), which revolves in its place and watches Orion, and alone of them all never takes a bath in the ocean.

Upon it he fashioned two cities of mortal men, and fine ones. In the first was wedding and feasting; they were leading brides from their chambers along the streets under the light of blazing torches, and singing the bridal song. There were dancing boys twirling about, pipes and harps made a merry noise; the women stood at their doors and watched. A crowd was in the market-place, where a dispute was going on. Two men disputed over the blood-price of a man who had been killed: one said he had offered all, and told his tale before the people, the other refused to accept anything[3]; but both were willing to appeal to an umpire for the decision. The crowd cheered one or other as they took sides, and the heralds kept them in order. The elders sat in the Sacred Circle on the polished

[2] The facing of the shield was of metal. The simplest plan for the pattern is five concentric circles, separated by narrow rims or flat belts, all surrounded by one broader rim or belt (the Ocean stream) and two other narrow rims.

In the middle is the boss (the Earth) surrounded by a small complete circle, with Sun, Moon, and Stars.

Then the first rim or belt, and beyond it a circle or wide belt with the early scenes, the Two Cities (Peace and War).

Then another rim or belt, and beyond it a circle with Vintage, Plowing, Harvest.

Then a third rim or belt, and beyond it a circle with hunting, Sheep, Cattle, and Huts.

Then a fourth rim or belt, and after it a circle with the Dance.

Then a fifth narrow rim, and a broader belt with the Ocean, and narrower rims to finish.

[3] The aggrieved kinsman might refuse any price, and claim death, or outlawry, when any one might kill the offender without price. The parties pleaded, with or without the help of lawmen, and the meeting decided. The Icelandic Sagas describe a state of society where these customs were in use, and they are the most illuminating commentary upon Homer.

stones, and each took the herald's staff as they rose in turn to give judgment. Before them lay two nuggets of gold, for the one who should give the fairest judgment.

The other city had two armies besieging it round about, all in shining armour. They were divided in plan, whether to sack it outright, or to take half the wealth of the city in ransom. But the besieged were by no means ready to agree, and they were preparing an ambush. The wives and little children were left to guard the walls with the old men; the others sallied out, led by Arês and Pallas Athena, both worked in gold with golden robes, fine and tall in their armour like real gods, conspicuous above the men who were much smaller.⁴ When they arrived at the place chosen for their ambush, near a river where all the animals came to drink, they settled down to wait under arms. Meanwhile they had sent out two scouts, who sat a long way off to see when the cattle and sheep were coming. Soon they came, with two herdsmen playing on their pipes and suspecting nothing. So the men in ambush had good warning and quickly got round the cattle and fine white sheep, cut out the whole convoy and killed the herdsmen. The besiegers were still sitting in conclave when they heard the news—they were off at once behind their prancers, arrived in no time, stopt and fought their battle along the river-banks with volleys of spears from both sides. And there among them was Discord, there was Tumult, there was cruel Fate, holding one just wounded and still alive, and one unwounded, dragging one dead by the feet; and the cloak she wore on her shoulders was red with the blood of men.

They looked like living men as they struggled and fought and pulled back the dead bodies from either side.

Upon it he placed a rich field of soft fallow land, broad acres already thrice plowed; many plowmen were driving their teams up and down with a turn at the end. Whenever they came to the headland after a turn, there was a man to receive them and hand them a mug of wine; then they turned again to their furrows and made all haste to the headland. The soil was black behind them, and looked like soil under the plow, although it was gold. That was a wonderful thing!

Upon it he put a royal demesne, where the hands were reaping with sharp sickles. Gavels were falling in a row along the swathe, others the binders were binding into sheaves with wisps of straw. Three sheaf-binders were standing by, and

---

⁴ I saw long ago a marionette show in a little Indian town, the Siege of Delhi: in which the officers were twice as tall as the men, and the general tallest of all. The Great Mogul stood inside the city, twice as high as the walls.

boys behind them were getting the gavels and bringing them up continually; the king was among them standing staff in hand near the swathe, silent and happy. The heralds were under an oak-tree a little way off; they had killed an ox and were getting it ready for supper, while the women were making barley-porridge for the hands' luncheon.

Upon it he put a vineyard heavy with grapes, all of beautiful gold; the place was thick with standing poles of silver and the grapes hanging on them were black. A ditch of blue enamel ran round it, and a fence of tin; there was one path only across, by which the carriers passed when they gathered the vintage. Boys and girls in merry glee carried the honey-sweet fruit in baskets of wickerwork. In the midst a boy with a melodious harp played a delightsome tune, and sang to the harp a dainty ditty in a sweet little voice; the others trippled along behind him singing and shouting and keeping time by the beat of their feet.

Upon it he fashioned a herd of straighthorn cattle. The cattle were made of gold and tin; they made their way from the midden to pasture along the murmuring river side, along the quivering reeds. Golden herdsmen stalked beside them, four men with nine quick-footed dogs. Two grim lions were among the cows in front, holding a roaring bull; they dragged him away bellowing loudly, dogs and men were after him. The lions had torn open the bull's hide, and they were gorging his red blood and bowels: in vain the men tarred on the dogs, which ran up close and barked and jumped back, but as for biting they kept out of reach.

Upon it he made a pasturage for fleecy white sheep, a wide place in a pleasant dell, with folds and pens and roofed huts.

Upon it he worked a dancing-place, like the one that Daidalos made in Cnossos for curly-headed Ariadnê. There young men and maidens of price[5] danced holding one another by the wrist. The maidens were clad in soft linen, the lads in finespun tunics glossy with a touch of oil. The maidens wore pretty chaplets, the lads carried golden daggers hung from silver straps. Now they circled on practised feet, light and smooth as a potter's wheel when he sits and tries with a touch of his hands whether it will run; now they would scamper to meet in opposite lines. A crowd stood round enjoying the lovely dance; a heavenly ministrel twangled his harp, and two tumblers twirled about among them leading the merry sport.

Upon it he placed the mighty River of Oceanos at the extreme edge of the shield.

When the shield was finished, he fashioned a corselet that

[5] Such as would earn a great bride-price from wooers.

shone brighter than fire, he fashioned a strong helmet with a golden crest, he fashioned greaves of flexible tin.[6]

Then the famous Crookshank craftsman brought all he had made and laid it before Thetis; and she shot like a falcon from snowy Olympos, bearing the bright armour to her son.

BOOK XIX

How Achillês made friends with Agamemnon and armed himself for war

DAWN IN HER SAFFRON ROBE AROSE OUT OF THE OCEAN stream, bringing light for heaven and earth; and Thetis came to the Achaian camp with the god's gifts for her son.

He lay with Patroclos in his arms, weeping bitterly, while his comrades were mourning around. The goddess clasped his hand and said:

"My child, we must let this man be, for all our sorrow. He is dead once for all, since that is God's will. Now for you: accept these fine gifts from Hephaistos. See how fine they are. No man has ever worn them!"

She laid them before Achillês in a rattling pile. The Myrmidons were too much startled to look at them and shrank back; but Achillês looked, and when he saw them, how his anger swelled, how his eyes blazed as if with some inward flame! But he was glad when he held in his own hands the glorious gifts of the god.

When he had enjoyed this pleasure for a while, he told her plainly what he meant to do.

"Mother," he said, "this armour is indeed the work of immortal hands, such as no man could make. Now I will get ready at once. But I am very much afraid the flies may get into my dear friend's wounds; worms will breed and make the flesh nasty—there's no life in it—the body will rot."

Thetis answered:

"Do not trouble about that, my child, I will see what I can do to keep off those savage tribes of flies which batten on those killed in war. Even if he lies here a whole twelvemonth

---

[6] The greaves were not meant to keep off a spear-thrust, but to prevent the edge of the shield from chafing the leg as the man walked. So they were short and pliable.

his flesh will be as sound as ever, or sounder. What you must do is to call a meeting of the princes, and denounce your feud against King Agamemnon. Then you may arm yourself at once, and clothe you in your valour!"

Then she dropt into the dead man's nostrils red nectar and ambrosia to keep the flesh wholesome.

Achillês felt new courage after his mother's words. He paced along the shore calling aloud in a great voice, and summoned the Achaian princes. Even those who used to stay always about the ships, the pilots who kept the steering-oars, and the stewards who gave out the food, even these came to the assembly; and the two doughty men of war, Tydeidês the indomitable and prince Odysseus, they also came limping and leaning on their spears, for their wounds troubled them still, and then sat down in front. After them came my lord Agamemnon, still suffering from the wound which he owed to Coön Antenor's son.

As soon as the assembly was full, Achillês rose to his feet and spoke.

"Atreidês, what good was it to us both, you and me, to take things to heart so, and to fall into a soul-devouring feud for a girl? I wish Artemis had shot her dead with an arrow on that day when I took Lyrnessos! Then all those brave men would have been saved who bit the dust in battle because I was angry! Hector and the Trojans got all the good there was; and I think the Achaian nation will not soon forget my feud and yours. But we must let bygones be bygones; we must forget our sorrow and control our temper, for we cannot help it. Then here is the end of my resentment, for I must not be angry for ever and ever. Come then, make haste and tell the army to get ready for battle. Let me meet the enemy face to face once more, and see if they would like to spend a quiet night near our ships. But I think there are some who will be glad to bend the knee in rest, if they escape from the battle when my spear shall drive them!"

The assembly was glad indeed to hear Achillês denounce his feud. Then King Agamemnon answered from the place where he was sitting, without coming forward to the front:

"My friends, my brave Danaäns——"

Here he was interrupted by cries and disturbance:

"My friends! it is right to give a hearing to any speaker who rises, it is not fair to break in. That makes it hard for the best of speakers. (Further disturbance.) With all this noise in the crowd how can a man speak? How can you hear? It is too much for the loudest voice.—Peleidês is the man—I want to explain things to him, please listen the rest of you and take note of what I say. (Loud cries: "It was all your fault!") People have said that to me often enough, and reproached me, but it was not *my* fault! Zeus—fate—the Avenger that walketh in darkness—it was *their* fault! *They* put that blind madness in my heart amongst you all, on that day when I robbed Achillês of his prize myself. But what could I do? God bringeth all things to pass! Eldest daughter of Zeus is Atê, the blindness that blindeth all, accursed may she be! Tender are her feet; for she touches not the ground, but she walks upon the heads of men to their harm, and binds fast many a one.

"Aye, before now Zeus himself was blinded, he that is chief of gods and men as they say; yet even he as it seems was deceived by Hera with her woman's wiles, on the day when Alcmenê was to bring forth mighty Heraclês in wall-crowned Thebes.

"Zeus made his boast before the assembled gods. 'Hear me,' he said, 'gods and goddesses all! I have something that I wish to announce. To-day the Lady of Travail will bring a man to the light, one who shall rule all the people round about, one of those men who are sprung from my blood and lineage.'

"Hera made answer in the cunning of her heart, 'You shall prove a liar! Time will show that you cannot make good your words. Swear to me now, Olympian, a solemn oath, that that man shall rule the people round about who this day shall fall between a woman's feet, being of your blood and lineage.'

"Zeus did not understand her cunning; he was wholly blinded, and swore that solemn oath.

"Then Hera darted down from the heights of Olympos, and quickly sped to Achaian Argos. There as she knew was the wife of Sthenelos Perseïadês, seven months gone with child, and she brought forth a son to the light though he lacked the full tale of months. As for Alcmenê, Hera delayed the birth and held back the Ladies of Travail. Then she went herself with tidings to Zeus Cronion:

" 'Father Zeus, fiery Thunderbolt! I have news for you. Already the strong man is born who shall rule the people of Argos—Eurystheus, the son of Sthenelos Perseïadês; he is your child, it is unbecoming that he should rule the people of Argos.'

"These words cut him to the heart. Forthwith he seized Atê by the hair of her head in his wrath, and swore a solemn oath that Atê the Blinder who blinds all should never again enter Olympos and the starry sky. He swung her round and cast her out of heaven; quickly she fell down into the world of men. To think of her made him groan, whenever he saw his own son toiling and moiling in disgrace for Eurystheus.

"So it was with me; when now again Hector dealt destruction among our people beside our own ships, I could not forget Atê the Blinder who at the beginning made me blind. But since I was blinded and Zeus took away my sense, I wish to make amends, and to pay anything in atonement.

"To the battle then, sir, I pray! Lead the army to battle! Treasures in plenty are here, and here am I ready to offer all that Odysseus promised you yesterday in your quarters. If you wish, wait now, though you are so fervent to begin. I will send servants to bring the treasures here, and you shall see that they are enough to content you."

Achillês answered:

"My lord King Agamemnon, as for treasures, they are yours to give, if you will, which is right and proper, or to keep; but now let us think of battle and at once. We must not waste time jabberwinding[7] here. There is a great work yet undone. To see Achillês once more in the field and striking down the battalions of Troy with the spear—let each of you remember what that was, and fight his man!"

Odysseus said to this:

"Wait a bit, Achillês—we know your quality, but do not drive out the army to battle fasting. Fighting lasts a long time, when once the battalions meet, and God breathes courage into both sides.

"First order them all to take food and drink here in camp. Strength and courage both are mine when I have my bread and wine! No man can fight all day from dawn to sunset on an empty belly. Even if his spirit is ardent for battle, yet his limbs grow heavy unawares, hunger and thirst come on him, his knees stagger as he goes. But after plenty of food and wine a man can fight all day; his heart is brave, his limbs are not weary until all take their leave of the battlefield.

"Then dismiss, and tell them to make a proper meal. But first let my lord Agamemnon bring his treasures into this assembly, that every one may see them and you may be consoled yourself. Let the King stand up before all, and swear that he has never gone into that woman's bed, or had to do with her. Be gracious and forgiving yourself, sir, and let him make friends with you in his own quarters over a handsome banquet, that you may lack nothing which is due.

"My lord King, you will be a juster man to others after this. It is no shame for a king to make amends, when he has wronged a man without provocation."

The King answered:

"I am glad to hear what you have said, Laërtiadês. It was all true, and excellently put. I am ready to take my oath, it is my own wish, and I will not speak falsely before God.—But

---

[7] κλοτοπεύειν, apparently a word invented for the occasion, in mockery of τολυπεύειν, the women's yarnwinding, which Homer uses regularly in the phrase "winding up the war."

let Achillês wait awhile, wait all the rest of you, until what I offer is brought before you and we swear friendship together.

"For you, sir, this is my request: choose out the first of our young princes to carry the treasures from my ship which I promised yesterday, and to bring the women. My herald Talthybios shall find a boar-pig somewhere for the sacrifice to Zeus and Helios."

Achillês answered at once:

"My lord King Agamemnon Atreidês, another time will do better for that matter, when there shall be some pause in the battle and when there is less passion in my heart. Those men are still lying mangled on the field—the men Hector killed while Zeus gave him victory, and you two are sending us to dinner! What I would say is—Fight, men, fasting and foodless! at sunset we will have a great supper, when we have wiped out our disgrace. Till then not a drop of drink or a bit of food shall pass down my throat; for my friend is dead, he lies in my hut, mangled with spear-thrusts, his feet turned to the door; my friends are mourning around, and I care for no such things, only death, and blood, and the heavy groans of men!"

Odysseus now spoke:

"Prince Achillês," he said, "you are the greatest man in our host, stronger than I am and better far in the field of battle; but I would put myself before you far in judgment, for I am your elder and my experience greater. Then bear with me, and give me a hearing.

"Men soon grow sick of battle; when Zeus the steward of warfare tilts the scales, and cold steel reaps the fields, the grain is very little but the straw is very much. The belly is a bad mourner, and fasting will not bury the dead. Too many are falling, man after man and day after day; how could one ever have a moment's rest from privations? No, we must harden our hearts, and bury the man who dies and shed our tears that day. But those who survive the horrors of war should not forget to eat and drink, and then we shall be better able to wear our armour, which never grows weary, and to fight our enemies for ever and ever.

"Now no one must hang back expecting another summons. This is the summons! There will be trouble if any one stays behind. Let us march all together and waken up war against our enemy!"

No sooner said than done. He called Nestor's two sons, with Megês Phyleus' son, Thoas and Merionês, Lycomedês Creiontiadês and Melanippos, and they went to Agamemnon's quarters, and collected the seven tripods which he had promised, and the burnished cauldrons, and the twelve horses; then they led out the seven skilful work-women, and eighth, beautiful Briseïs. Odysseus weighed out ten nuggets of gold; and carrying these he led the way, followed by the other young princes with their burdens.

These treasures were laid before the assembly; and Agamemnon rose to his feet. Talthybios the herald stood by his side holding the boar in his arms. Then Agamemnon drew out the knife that used to hang by the sheath of his great sword, and cut the firstling hairs from the boar; he lifted up his hands to Zeus and prayed, while the people all sat silent listening, as is meet. He prayed in these words, looking up into the broad heavens:

"Witness first Zeus, highest and greatest of the gods, witness Earth and Sun, and the Avengers who below the earth punish all men that take a lying oath: Never have I laid my hand on the maiden Briseïs, neither desiring her for my bed nor for any other thing. She has remained untouched under my roof. If any word of this is false, may God send upon me all the afflictions which he sends upon one who swears a lying oath."

As he spoke he cut the boar's throat. Then Talthybios swung it round his head and threw it into the deep sea, food for fishes.

Achillês now rose and spoke:

"O Father Zeus, great is the blindness thou sendest upon men! Never would Atreidês have stirred up my temper to last all this time, never would he have carried off the girl against my will deaf to everything, but Zeus I supposed wished to bring death on many of our people.—Now go to your meal, and then we will fight."

Thus he dismissed the assembly, and they were soon dispersing to their ships. The Myrmidons took charge of the treasures and brought them to the ships of Achillês. They put away the goods in his quarters, and found a place for the women, and the grooms drove off the horses to join the rest.

But when Briseïs, radiant as golden Aphroditê, caught sight of Patroclos mangled and pierced with spears, she threw herself on the body and shrieked aloud, tearing her breast and tender neck and lovely face, and cried out through her tears:

"O Patroclos! best beloved of my unhappy heart! Alive I left you when I went from this place, and now I find you dead, my prince of men, when I return! So my life is trouble upon trouble without end. My husband who took me from my father's hands I saw mangled and pierced with spears before the walls; three brothers dear to me, all my own mother's sons, these also met their doom. And when Achillês killed my husband and took the city of prince Mynês, you told me not to weep; you promised that Achillês should take me to Phthia and make me his wedded wife, and hold our wedding feast in the Myrmidons' country! Therefore I weep without ceasing for you dead, since you were always kind!"

She wept, and the women wailed with her, in show for Patroclos, but each also for her own woes.

Round about Achillês was a group of Achaian elders, who begged him to eat, but he refused, groaning:

"I beg you, if any of you my dear comrades will listen, do not ask me to touch food or drink, for I am in deep sorrow. I will wait for sunset and bear it as best I can."

Most of the princes dispersed at this, but the two kings remained, and Odysseus, Nestor and Idomeneus, and the old man Phoinix, trying their best to comfort him in his sorrow; but he would not be comforted before he could plunge into the maw of bloody battle. He could not forget; heaving a deep sigh he said:

"Ah me, time was when *you*, my dearest comrade, now so cruelly lost, when you with your own hands would lay me a tasty meal, quickly and neatly, while all was hurry to get into the battlefield! Now you lie there mangled, and I have not the heart to touch food and drink though there is plenty, because I miss you so. For nothing worse could ever happen to me, not if I heard of my father's death—and now I suppose he is shedding tears in Phthia for want of a son like me, and here I am in a foreign land, battling with Trojans for the sake of that horrible Helen. Or it might be the boy in Scyros, my dear son, if Neoptolemos is still alive. Once I hoped and wished that I alone should perish here far from home, and that you would return to Phthia. You could have picked up my boy at Scyros and taken him home, you could have showed him my estate and the servants and my stately house. Peleus would have been dead and gone by that time—and I think he must be dead already, or perhaps just alive and unhappy in his old age, always waiting for the cruel news that I am dead."

He wept as he spoke, and the old men mourned with him, each thinking of what he had left behind.

It was a pitiable sight for Zeus also, and he spoke in his usual downright way to Athena:

"My dear girl, you have quite deserted your hero. Has Achillês gone clean out of your mind? There he sits, in front of the ships, mourning for his friend, without a bite or sup— all the rest have gone to their dinner. Go along and drop nectar and ambrosia into his breast, or he will starve."

This was just what she wanted to do. Like a harpy, long-winged, shrill-screaming, she dived out of heaven through the air. The Achaians were then making ready for battle; she dropt the precious ambrosia and nectar into his breast to save

him from the pangs of hunger, and returned to her great
Father's house.

Now they were all pouring out from the camp, thick and
fast, helmets gleaming bright, bossy shields, strong-plated
corselets, lancewood spears; their sheen filled the sky—all the
earth laughed with the glittering metal, the tramp of men resounded under their feet. It was like one great snowstorm,
when the flakes fly thick and fast through the air, icy cold in
the clear blast of Boreas. In their midst was Achillês, arming
himself in the armour that Hephaistos had made, while grief
intolerable sank deep into his heart: he gnashed his teeth, his
eyes flashed fire, his mind was upon the enemy. First he
clasped over his legs those fine greaves with their silver ankle-
guards. Next he put the corselet about his chest and slung
the silver-studded sword over his shoulders. Then he took up
the great shield, which gleamed like another moon with a light
which filled the place: as the light that burns in a lonely
farmstead up on the mountains, seen from the open sea by
mariners when a gale has blown them out of their course far
away. Then he lifted the strong helmet and set it upon his
head, shining like a star and nodding its golden plumes.

Achillês tried himself in the armour, to see if it fitted and if
his limbs had easy play—it seemed to lift him up in the air
like wings! He raised his father's spear from the stand—that
spear, long, heavy, strong, which no other man in the Achaian
host could wield, but only Achillês knew how to handle; that
ashwood spear from Pelion, which Cheiron got from the
mountain top and gave his father to be the terror of his foes.

The horses were harnessed and put to by Automedon and
Alcimos. They settled the breaststraps about them, they put
the bits in their mouths, they drew back the reins to the car.
Automedon took whip in hand and jumped in; Achillês fol-
lowed, armed for war, and shining like golden Hyperion.
Then he called to his father's horses:

"Bay and Piebald, you famous colts of Quickfoot! Find some
better way to bring your driver off safely, when we have had
enough of fighting! Don't leave him there dead like Patroclos."

Then bonny Bay spoke out from under the yoke, for Hera
gave him speech: he suddenly bowed his head till his mane fell
under the yoke-pad and swept the ground, and spoke in a
human voice:

"Sure enough we will save you yet this time, mighty Achillês. But the day of your death is near. We are not to blame,
but a great god and compelling fate. No slowness or tardiness
of ours let the Trojans tear the armour from Patroclos; but
that most powerful god, the son of beauteous Leto, slew him
in the forefront of the fray and gave Hector his triumph. We

could run swift as the west wind, lightest of all the winds that
blow; but it is your own fate to fall by the strength of a god
and a man."

He said no more, for the Avengers checked his speech. But
Achillês answered him angrily:

"Why do you foretell death for me, Bay? You need not. I
know well myself that it is my fate to die here, far from my
father and my mother. Still I will never cease driving the
Trojans until they have had enough of war."

With these words he shouted, and drove his team to the
front.

BOOK XX

*How Achillês swept the battlefield, and how the gods
helped on either side*

WHILE THE ACHAIANS WERE ARMING WITH ACHILLES, EAGER
to fight once more, and the Trojans awaited them on the
rising of the plain, Zeus commanded Themis to summon the
gods to assembly on Mount Olympos. She hastened over
heaven and earth to do his bidding, and they all came; even
the rivers, except Oceanos, even the nymphs who inhabit the
groves and grassy dells and the springs and fountains. They all
came to the house of Zeus Cloudgatherer, and took their seats
in the galleries of polished stone which Hephaistos had built
for them by his clever art.

So there they were assembled in the palace of Zeus. Not even
Earthshaker was deaf to the summons; he also came out of
the sea, and as he sat down among them he wanted to know
what Zeus had in mind.

"Why have you summoned the gods again to conclave,
Fiery Thunderbolt? Are you a bit anxious about Trojans and
Achaians? Certainly this war is blazing up very close to us now."

Zeus Cloudgatherer answered:

"You know what I have in mind, Earthshaker, you know
why I have summoned you. I do care about their killing one
another like that. But this is what I want to say. I mean to
stay here, and sit in a sheltered spot, and amuse myself by
watching them. The rest of you may go where you like, join
the Trojans or the Achaians, help them both just as you
fancy. For if Achillês is left alone to fight the Trojans, they

will not stand one minute before Peleïon's pursuing feet! Why, the sight of him was always enough to make them tremble! And now that he is furious for the death of his comrade, I fear he may storm the city, fate or no fate."

This was enough to raise war to the death at once. The gods were off to the battlefield on both sides. To the Achaian camp went Hera and Pallas Athena, Poseidon Earthshaker, Hermês Luckbringer the masterpiece of cunning wit; Hephaistos swaggered beside them hobbling along with his thin shanks moving nimbly. To the Trojans went Arês in his grand helmet, and with him Phoibos with his long hair waving, and Artemis Archeress, Leto and Xanthos, and smiling Aphroditê.

When Achillês appeared after his long absence, and the Trojans saw him sweep into the field with gleaming armour like a very god of war, their knees trembled beneath them in dismay, and for a long time the Achaians carried all before them. But as soon as the gods showed themselves, up rose Discord the mighty harrier of nations, loud shouted Athena, standing outside the wall on the edge of the moat, or moving upon the seashore: Arês shouted aloud from the other side, black as a stormcloud, crying his commands from the citadel of Troy, or speeding over Callicolonê by Simoeis river.

So the blessed gods drove the two hosts together and made the bitter strife burst forth. The Father of men and gods thundered terribly from on high, Poseidon made the solid earth quake beneath, and the tall summits of the hills; Mount Ida shook from head to foot, and the citadel of Ilios trembled, and the Achaian ships. Fear seized Aïdoneus the lord of the world below; fear made him leap from his throne and cry aloud, lest Poseidon Earthshaker should break the earth above him, and lay open to every eye those gruesome danksome abodes which even the gods abhor—so terrible was the noise when gods met gods in battle. For against Lord Poseidon stood Phoibos Apollo with his winged arrows, against Enyalios glaring Athena stood; Hera was faced by Shootafar's sister, Artemis Archeress, with her rattling golden shafts, Leto was faced by Luckbringer Hermês in his strength; and Hephaistos had before him that deep River, whom the gods call Xanthos, but men Scamandros.

Achillês longed most of all to meet Hector Priamidês. Hector he sought amid the press; with Hector's blood most of all he longed to glut the greedy god of war. But Apollo sent Aineias against him. He said to him in Lycaon's voice and shape:

"Aineias, you are a good one to make speeches, but where are those threats you made over the wine, when you promised the princes of Troy to fight Achillês Peleidês man to man?"

Aineias said:

"My dear Priamidês! Why do you tell me to tackle that

proud man, when you know that is the last thing I want? It wouldn't be the first time I have faced Achillês. Once before he chased me off Ida with his spear, when he had come out for our cattle, the time when he ravaged Lyrnessos and Pedasos. Zeus saved me, Zeus gave me strength and a nimble pair of legs, or I should have gone down before Achillês—and Athena, for she was always in front of him to show the light of safety, while she told him to kill Trojans and Lelegans. It's no good for a mere man to fight Achillês; he's always got some god to protect him. And even without that his cast goes straight and does not stop till it runs through human flesh. But if only God would give me a fair chance he wouldn't beat me so easily, not if he claims to be made of solid brass!'

Apollo said:

"You should pray to the everlasting gods yourself. You are no mere man. They say Aphroditê was your mother; she is a daughter of Zeus, and Achillês comes from a lower god, just a daughter of the Old Man of the Sea. Go straight for him with the cold steel, and don't let him frighten you with sorry things like curses and threats."

These words inspired Aineias with new courage, and he went in search of his adversary. But Hera saw him! She called her allies to her and said:

"Now then, Poseidon and Athena, just consider what we had better do. There is Aineias in full panoply marching to meet Achillês—and Apollo made him go! Very well, let us turn him back again—or else we must take a hand—one of us might stand by Achillês; he must keep up his strength, he must not lose heart. We will show him that his friends are the best of the immortals, and the others are just windbags, the same who tried to defend the Trojans before. All we Olympians have come into this battle to save Achillês from harm for this day: what will happen afterwards is only what Fate spun for him with her thread when he was born. But if Achillês does not learn this from the voice of some god, he will fear when he finds himself face to face with a god. For gods are dangerous when they show their presence openly."

Poseidon said to this:

"Now Hera, that's all nonsense, don't lose your temper. I should not like to make gods fight with one another. Then let us get out of the way to some place where we can sit down and see. Let us leave the matter there, battle is the men's affair. But if Arês begins it, or Phoibos Apollo, if they get in the way of Achillês and won't let him fight, then we are in it on the spot, hammer and tongs! I think they will soon turn their backs and return to the family in Olympos, when once we have them under our compelling hands!"

He led the way to the high ruins of that ancient wall, which the Trojans had built with Athena's help for Heraclês, to keep off the sea-monster which used to come up and ravage the land. There they sat down hidden from the world in a thick mist; Arês and Apollo and the rest were on the brows of Callicolonê. So the two parties confronted each other, waiting to see what would happen. Neither wished to begin the fray; and Zeus sat on high commanding in chief.

The plain below was crowded with horses and men; the sheen of their armour gleamed bright, the ground rattled and shook under their feet, as the two armies met.

Charging into the space between, two champions came, Aineias Anchisiadês and Prince Achillês. Aineias first stept out of his car defiant, the heavy helmet nodding upon his head; he shook the sharp spear, and guarded his breast with the shield. Peleidês moved forward to meet him, like some wild lion when a crowd of men has come out to destroy him, a whole village; at first he moves unheeding, but as soon as some bold lad casts a lance and wounds him, he crouches down with open jaws, foam gathers about his teeth, he growls in rage and flogs flanks and ribs with his tail to excite himself, glaring at his foes—then a leap and a furious charge upon the mass, either to kill or to die. So rage and fury stirred Achillês to meet his enemy face to face.

When they were near enough, Achillês first spoke.

"Aineias," he said, "why have you come out so far in front of your lines? Have you a mind to fight with me? Do you hope to make yourself lord of Priam's honour, in the midst of his Trojans? Yet even if you kill me, that will not make Priam lay his prerogative in your hand; he has sons, and himself he is firm, no windy-minded man. Can it be that you have a demesne parcelled out for you by the Trojan nation, prime fruit-land and cornland, ready for you to live in if you can kill me? That will not be so easy as you think.

"Why, I made you run with my spear once before! Don't you remember how you were alone with your cattle, and I chased you off the mountains at a racing pace? You did not turn once to look back that day! But you got off clear to Lyrnessos. I was after you, and I sacked the town, thanks be to Athena and Father Zeus! I carried off all the women with my booty; but Zeus and All Gods saved you then! I don't think they will save you now, as you imagine. So I advise you to go back to the ranks and not to stand before me, or something may happen to you. When a thing is done and past, even fools are wise at last!"

Aineias answered:

"Don't think you will scare me with words, Peleidês, as if I were a little child. I can use taunts and abuse quite well if I like. We know each other's lineage, we know the names of our fathers, household tales among the children of men; but you have never set eyes on my parents, nor I on yours. Men say the admirable Peleus is your father, and your mother is Thetis the lovely daughter of the sea; for myself, I am proud to be the son of noble Anchisês, and my mother is Aphroditê. One of those two houses will mourn a son this day; for I tell you, childish words will not be enough to part us.

"But if you care to know more of my lineage, that is no secret. First, Zeus Cloudgatherer begat Dardanos. He founded Dardania, and lived on the skirts of Ida among the running brooks, for sacred Ilios was not yet built upon the plain, and there was no city as yet. Dardanos was father of King Erichthonios, the richest man on earth. He had three thousand mares with young foals at foot, which grazed on the marshy land. Boreas the North Wind saw them grazing and was enamoured. He took the shape of a blue roan stallion, and served some of them; they conceived and dropt twelve foals. These could scamper over a cornfield and never break a stalk, touching only the tops of the ears; they could scamper over the broad back of the sea, and touch only the crest of the waves.

"And Erichthonios begat Tros King of the Trojans. Tros again had three admirable sons, Ilos and Assaracos, and Ganymedês, who was the most beautiful of mortal men; he was rapt away by the gods for his beauty, to be cupbearer to Zeus and live among the immortals. Ilos again begat Laomedon; and Laomedon begat Tithonos and Priamos and Lampos and Clytios, and that sprig of Arês, Hicetaon. Assaracos begat Capys, and he begat Anchisês. I am the son of Anchisês, and Hector is the son of Priam.

"Such is the lineage that I can boast; but courage—Zeus increases that in men or diminishes, according to his will, for he is lord of all.

"Now let us stand no more talking like children in the midst of a battle. We could load one another with curses enough to sink a ship as big as a mountain! A rare runner is the tongue, with tales of all sorts in stock, and an infinite crop of words growing all round. Whatever kind of words you speak, such you will hear. But why must we bandy curses like a couple of scolding wives, who have some spite gnawing at their hearts till they run out and scold in the middle of the street, true and false together—the spite brings that in too! Your words will not turn me away from deeds when I mean battle. Come along now quickly, let us each taste what our mettle is like."

He let drive his good spear against that dreadful shield: the blade struck with a loud crash. Peleidês held the shield well away, for he thought the spear of Aineias would pierce through—foolish man! Had he not the sense to know that it is not easy for mortal man to master or escape the glorious gifts of the gods! And so then, the good spear of Aineias did not break the shield; the god-given gold was proof against it.

Achillês now cast his spear, and struck on the outermost ring, where the metal was thinnest and the hide thinnest behind. The Pelian lancewood ran through with a ringing sound. Aineias had crouched down holding up the shield; so the shaft passed over his back and stuck in the ground, still fast in the shield with the two layers torn apart. But he had escaped: he stood up dizzy and shaken when he saw that shaft sticking at his elbow. Achillês then drew sword and leaped at him with a shout. Aineias lifted a great big stone in his hand such as two men could not carry, as men go now, but he managed it easily alone. And now Aineias would have crashed down that stone on his helmet, or on that shield which had saved him before, and Peleidês would have chased and killed him with that sword; but Poseidon Earth-shaker thought his time was come, and said to the others:

"Confound it! I am sorry for that brave Aineias. He will be killed very soon and go down to Hadês, because he listened to Apollo Shootafar. What a fool! Apollo won't save him. But why should this poor innocent suffer for some one else's griev-ances? There's no sense in that, and he always is most gener-ous in his offering to the gods who rule the broad heavens.

"Come along, let us save him ourselves, or Cronidês will be angry if Achillês lays him low. And it is ordained that he shall escape, that the lineage of Dardanos may not perish with-out seed and disappear. Cronidês loved Dardanos more than all the sons he had of mortal mothers. He has already come to hate Priam's family, and now indeed Aineias shall be King of the Trojans, and his son's sons after him."

Hera replied:

"Settle it as you please, Earthshaker, about Aineias, whether you will save him or leave him alone. But remember that we two have sworn again and again, I and Pallas Athena, before all the company of heaven, never to stir a finger to help the Tro-jans, not even when Troy shall be consumed in blazing fire by the victorious Achaians!"

So Poseidon left them, and passed through the battle to the place where Aineias and Achillês were face to face. He drew a mist over the eyes of Achillês; he pulled out the spear from the shield of Aineias and laid it before the other's feet, whisked up Aineias off the ground and hurled him through the air. Over the ranks of fighting men Aineias flew from the god's hand, over the lines of horses, and alighted on the outskirts of battle where the Cauconians were getting ready for action. Poseidon was there by his side, and said at once:

"Aineias, what god tells you to stand up in this mad way

against Peleion the invincible? He's a better man than you are, and more in favour with the gods. Just retreat whenever you see him, unless you want to take lodgings in Hadês before your time. But when Achillês meets his death, you may confidently come to the front, for no other Achaian shall kill you."

After these plain words he left him, and scattered the mist from the eyes of Achillês, who opened his eyes wide and said to himself angrily:

"Confound it all, here's a miracle done before my eyes! There lies my spear on the ground, and not a trace can I see of the fellow I meant to kill! Aineias must have some friends in heaven. And I thought his boasting was all stuff and nonsense! Let him go to the devil. He won't have a mind to try me again after this happy escape from death! All right, I will round up our people and have a try for some other Trojans."

So he went along the lines, calling out to each man:

"Don't wait any longer, my brave Achaians, but have at 'em man to man! It's too much for me—I may be strong but I can't tackle the whole army! Not even Arês could do it, and he is a god immortal! Not even Athena could manage the mouth of a battle like this! But as far as my power goes, with hands and feet and strength, I swear I will never pause or rest one instant! Straight through their line I will go, and I don't think the man will be happy who comes within reach of my spear!"

As he encouraged his men thus, Hector called to the Trojans and told them he was about to meet Achillês:

"My brave Trojans!" he cried, "have no fear of Peleion! If words were weapons, I could face the immortal gods; but the spear is less easy—the gods are too strong for us! Not even Achillês will bring all his words to pass; some he will do, some he will cut in the middle. I will meet him face to face, even if his hands are like fire and his spirit like flashing steel!"

The Trojans heard his rousing appeal; they lifted their spears and moved to meet their foes. Soon the war-cry was raised and the confusion of battle began. Then Apollo appeared by Hector's side, and said:

"Hector, you must not stand out yet and fight with Achillês alone. Watch him in the throng amid the surging mass, and do not let him cast at you or come close to strike you with the sword."

Hector was alarmed by these words, and plunged into the mellay.

But Achillês leapt on the Trojans in fury, with terrible shouts. First he got Iphition Otrynteïdês, the valiant leader of a strong force. A Naiad nymph was his mother, and his father

Otrynteus lived under snowy Tmolos in the rich town of Hydê. He was rushing straight at Achillês, when Achillês cut his head clean in two, crying out as he fell:

"There you lie, Otrynteïdês, my terrible foe! Here is your deathplace, but your birthplace was by the Gygaian Lake near your father's demesne, beside fish-giving Hyllos and eddying Hermos!"

Darkness covered his eyes, and the tires of Achaian wheels tore his body; and over it Achillês brought down that doughty man Demoleon Antenor's son, stabbing him through helmet and temple: the helmet did not save him, but the blade went through and broke the bone, scattering his brains. Hippodamas next leapt out of his car and tried to escape, but Achillês stabbed him through the back. He died gasping, with a bellowing sound, as a bull bellows when the young men drag him about the altar of Heliconian Poseidon, and Earthshaker is glad. Next Achillês went after Polydoros Priamidês. His father would never let him fight, because he was youngest of all his sons, and dearest. But he beat the world in running; and that day in his childish vanity he would come out to show off his paces, until he died for it. He was running by when Achillês hit him on the back, where his belt was fastened with golden clasps and the corselet doubled over. The point came out through his stomach, and he fell on his knees groaning, as he clasped his bowels with his hands.

When Hector saw his brother clasping his bowels and sinking to the earth, his eyes grew dim. He could not keep away any longer, but went straight up to Achillês like a flash of fire, balancing his lance. Achillês saw him—sprang to meet him and cried out in defiance:

"Near is the man of all others who has struck me to the heart! The man who killed my precious comrade! Now we need not shirk each other along the lanes of battle!"

Then he said to Hector frowning:

"Come nearer, that you may die quicker!"

Hector answered boldly:

"Don't think you will scare me with words, Peleidês, as if I were a little child. I can use taunts and abuse myself if I like. I know you are a stronger man than I am, but all that lies on the knees of the gods. If I am the weaker man, yet I may take your life with a cast of my spear, for my blade also has a sharp point!"

He poised and cast his spear. But Athena turned it back from Achillês by a gentle puff of breath, and it fell at Hector's feet. Achillês leaped at him furiously with a shout—Apollo caught him away softly (as a god can do) and hid him in mist. Thrice

Achillês leapt at him—thrice the spear struck a cloud of mist. When for a fourth time he would have struck, he cried out angrily with brutal frankness:

"Again you have just missed death, you cur! that was a nice thing, but again Apollo saved you! Of course you say your prayers to him whenever you go where spears are whizzing. I dare say I shall finish you next time I meet you, if I can find a god of my own to help me. Meanwhile I will try to find somebody else."

Then he pierced the throat of Dryops, and left him lying before his feet, as he brought down a big strong man, Demuchos Philetor's son; this man he struck on the knee with a spear-cast and finished him off with the sword. He rolled out of a car the two sons of Bias, Laogonos and Dardanos, one with spear and one with sword. Tros Alastor's son ran up to clasp his knees: perhaps he might have mercy and spare a young man like himself. Poor fool! He did not know that man would never listen: no sweet temper was here, no soft heart, but plain madness. Tros clasped the knees—the sword ran under his liver, the liver slipt out, a stream of blood poured over it into his bosom, he fainted. On went Achillês: ran his spear through Mulios, in at one ear out at the other—cut down through the head of Echeclos with one blow of the sword, and warmed it in his blood—ran his spear through Deucalion's elbow where the sinews hold it—the man with arm hanging heavy saw death before him, a sword sliced off his head and sent it flying helmet and all, he lay with the marrow spurting out of the spine. On went Achillês: Rhigmos was the next, the son of Thracian Peiros—a lance caught him in the middle and stuck in the body rolling him out of his car—the driver turned the horses, a spear stabbed him in the back and rolled him out of the car, the horses ran away.

On went Achillês: as a devouring conflagration rages through the valleys of a parched mountain height, and the thick forest blazes, while the wind rolls the flames to all sides in riotous confusion, so he stormed over the field like a fury, driving all before him, and killing until the earth was a river of blood. As broad-browed oxen tread the white barley on a threshing-floor and quickly crush the husks under their feet, so under Achillês the horses trampled with their feet dead men and broken shields; the axle was soaked with blood, and the handrail of the car was red with spatterings from the horses' hooves and the running wheels. On went Achillês, with spatters of gore upon his invincible hands.

BOOK XXI

The battle by the river

WHEN THEY CAME TO THE FORD OF XANTHOS, ACHILLÊS CUT the Trojans into two parts. One he drove on to the plain towards the city, over the ground where the Achaians had been routed the day before by the furious assault of Hector. These poured flying before him, but Hera spread a thick mist to baffle them. The other half were crowded into the river. They threw themselves into the rolling eddies with a great noise, which echoed along the water and the steep banks; there they were, swimming and tumbling about in the water with shouts and cries. The din and confusion of horses and men in the eddies of the deep-roaring river seemed like some great swarm of locusts taking refuge in the water when a sudden fire breaks out.

Achillês left his spear on the bank leaning against a tree, and leapt among them like a fury, sweeping his sword round him, striking right and left: blows and blows and piteous groans, the river red with blood. The Trojans huddled crouching under the banks of that dreadful river, like shoals of fish scattering into the holes and crannies of some bay before a monstrous dolphin that swallows all he can catch. Achillês cut them down till his arms were tired. Then he picked out a dozen lads alive, to be the death-price for Patroclos Menoitiadês. He dragged them out bewildered like so many fawns, and tied their hands behind them by their own belts. These he sent back to the camp, and returned to the work of carnage.

He met first one of the sons of Priam trying to escape from the river, Lycaon. Achillês had taken him once before on a night-raid. The boy was out in his father's park, cutting the young shoots of a wild fig-tree to make into chariot-rails, when Achillês came on him with sudden disaster. That time he sent him across the sea to Lemnos, and sold him to Euneos the son of King Jason, for a fine silver cup. A family friend, Eëtion of Imbros, ransomed him for a great price and sent him to Arisbê; but he left that place secretly and got home safe. For eleven days he was happy with his friends after the return from Lemnos, and on the twelfth day God let him fall again into the hands of Achillês, who was to send him to Hadês, much loth to

245

go. Now he was defenceless, without spear or shield or helmet; he had thrown all that away, sweating and weary, stumbling in his flight. So Achillês knew him at once, and he stood still awhile as he thought angrily to himself:

"Damn it, here's a miracle done before my eyes! I shall see next the Trojans I have killed rising up out of their graves. Here's this fellow escaped the day of doom! I sold him into Lemnos. The wide sea keeps back many from the road they would go, but it couldn't keep him. Very well, he shall have a taste of my spear-blade. I'll see whether he will come back from that place too, or if mother earth will hold him as she holds many a strong man."

The young man had been trembling and hoping for mercy; and as Achillês lifted the spear he ran up, so that the spear missed his shoulder and stuck in the ground; with one hand he embraced the knees of Achillês, with the other he caught hold of the spear and would not let go, as he spoke out his simple prayer:

"I beseech you, Achillês! Have mercy and spare me! I am as good as a suppliant, noble prince, and the suppliant claims respect! At your table first I broke bread on the day when you took me in the park, when you parted me from father and friends, and sold me into Lemnos for the price of a hundred oxen. Now I have been ransomed for thrice as much, and this is the twelfth day since I came back to Ilios after much suffering! Now again cruel fate has put me in your hands! I must have offended Father Zeus, that he has given me again to you. Short and sad was my life to be, if my mother had but known it when she brought me forth—my mother Laothoê, the daughter of Altês the venerable king of the Lelegans, in the city of Pedasos upon Satnioeis. His daughter was Priam's wife, with so many others. She had two sons, and you will butcher us both! Already you have killed one in the battle, Polydoros, with that sharp spear, and now here am I for my death, for I don't think I shall escape your hands now my bad luck has brought me near you. But listen, sir, this is something you may have forgotten—don't kill me, I am only half-brother of Hector, who killed your friend so gentle and so strong!"

But Achillês was not to be softened, and this was his answer:

"Fool, don't talk of ransom to me, don't make speeches. Before Patroclos met his doom, mercy was rather more to my mind; I took many Trojans alive and sold them. But now not one shall escape death of all that God puts into my hands, not one Trojan of them all, most especially no son of Priam.— Come, my friend, die too; why do you cry like that? Patroclos died too, and he was a much better man than you. Don't you see me too, a fine big man? My father is a brave man, my mother is a goddess: yet I too have death and fate fast upon me. The day shall come, morning or evening or midday, when some one shall take my life too in battle, with a thrust of the spear or an arrow from the bow."

The young man's knees gave way, his heart failed him; he let go the spear and sank to the ground in a heap, with both hands outspread. Achillês drew the sword from the sheath and thrust it down to the hilt in his neck; he fell flat on the ground, while the blood ran out and sank into the earth. Achillês dragged him away by the leg and threw him into the river, saying with rough plainness:

"Lie there now with the fishes, and they will bloodlick your wound without any trouble. No mother shall lay you out and mourn for you, but Scamandros will roll you in his eddies to the broad bosom of the deep. Many a leaping fish will dart up under the black ripples to eat the white fat of Lycaon.—Perdition to you all, till we come as far as the citadel of sacred Ilios, you fleeing, I cutting down the rearmost! Not even that River shall help you, the river with his deep stream and silver eddies, the river to whom you have sacrificed so many bulls for so many years, and thrown so many horses alive into his eddies! For all that you shall perish miserably, until you all shall pay for my friend's blood, and the lives of those whom you slew before our ships, while I was away from the battle!"

The River had been growing more and more angry, and he began to consider how he could stop Achillês from his carnage and save the Trojans from destruction. Meanwhile Achillês had attacked Asteropaios. He was a son of Pelegon, himself the son of the river Axios and Periboia, the eldest daughter of Acessamenos. With one leap Achillês was upon him, and the other came out of the river to meet him holding two spears: for Xanthos put courage into him, being angry because of all those men that Achillês had slain in the water without mercy. Achillês called out:

"Who are you that dare to come and face me? What is your family? Unhappy are they whose sons face my wrath!"

Asteropaios answered:

"Do you want to know my family, Peleidês? I come from distant Paionia at the head of my countrymen. It is now ten days since I reached Ilios. I trace my lineage from the river Axios, who begat Pelegon the famous spearman, and they say he is my father. Now then let us fight, valiant Achillês!"

Then Achillês lifted his spear, and Asteropaios threw both spears at once, for both hands were as the right. One struck the shield, but it did not break through, for the god's golden gift held it off; the other grazed his right forearm and drew blood, but it passed on and stuck in the earth, greedy for more. Then

Achillês cast at him, but missed the man, and the spear ran into the river-bank up to the middle. The other tried to pull it out of the bank; thrice he shook it, thrice gave up, and then he tried to bend and break it, but Achillês was upon him sword in hand and cut across his belly so that the bowels gushed out. He fell panting, and darkness covered his eyes. Achillês knelt on his chest and stript off the armour, crying in triumph:

"Lie as you are! Is it a hard thing to match yourself against a son of Cronion, even for the son of a River. Yes, you called yourself son of a River, but I can boast descent from Almighty Zeus! My father was Peleus Aiacos' son, King of the Myrmidons; and Aiacos was sprung from Zeus. Then as Zeus is mightier than all the rivers that run into the sea, so the lineage of Zeus is mightier than one river! For look—here is a great river beside you, if he can help at all! But there's no fighting against Zeus: neither lord Acheloios is a match for him, nor all the power of deep-flowing Oceanos—from whom come all the rivers, and all the sea, the springs and the deep wells have their source in him. Even he is afraid of the thunder and terrible lightning of Almighty Zeus, when he rattles and roars in the sky!"

As he spoke, he dragged the spear out of the river-bank, and left the man dead in the sand where the water soaked him. Eels and fishes attended to him, gnawing and tearing the kidney-fat.

But Achillês now went on after the Paionians, who were still hurrying away along the river after they saw their chief brought low by the sword of Achillês. There he got Thersilochos and Mydon and Astypylos and Mnesos and Thrasios and Ainios and Ophelestês. He would have slain even more, but the angry river showed himself in human form, and called out from a deep eddy:

"O Achillês! you are too strong, your deeds are too violent! For the gods themselves are always your helpers. If Zeus has granted you to destroy the Trojans, drive them out of my stream and do your mischief on the plain. My bed is full of corpses, I am choked with corpses and I cannot pour my water into the sea, and you go on killing and killing. Let be now, I pray. I am confounded, my lord!"

Achillês answered:

"As you wish, my lord Scamandros, as you say. But I will not cease destroying these Trojans until I can shut them up in their city and try Hector strength to strength, whether I kill him or he kills me."

Scamandros thought of Apollo, and exclaimed:

"Upon my word, Silverbow, you have not done much to keep your divine father's commandments! Didn't he order you strictly to stand by the Trojans and help them, until the late evening sets and brings darkness over the fields!"

Then Achillês was after the Trojans like a fury. He leapt from the bank into the water. At once the River was on him in a wild flood, surging and tumbling the heap of corpses about and pushing them up on the dry land and bellowing like a bull;[1] but those who were still alive he kept safe and hid them in his deep eddies. The waters rose in tumultuous billows all round Achillês, beat on his shield and pushed him so that he could not stand on his feet. He caught hold of a tall elm tree; but the tree tore away its roots and fell from the bank, fell right across the river and dammed the flood with its branches, so that Achillês scrambled out of the water and went off as fast as he could across the plain, frightened. The River would not stop, but rolled after him, a great black surface; he still hoped to get in the way of Achillês and save the Trojans. But Achillês kept a spearthrow ahead, darting like a black hunter-eagle, the strongest and swiftest of birds that fly. His armour brattled and clattered—the River came thundering on behind—he just managed to keep away, and ran! As a gardener brings water from a dark burn to his plants and gardens, and shovels out the dams from the channel, leading the water, as it tumbles all the pebbles about in the bed and runs quickly on down the slope, almost catching its leader, so the River rolled on after Achillês and caught him at every step, fleet-footed though he was. But gods are stronger than men. And if he ever stopt those quick feet, and showed front to see whether all the gods of the broad heavens were hunting him, a great wave would rise and beat over his shoulders. He would lift up his feet high to get clear, quite distracted; the River tired out his legs with its violent rush, eating the ground from under his feet.

Then Peleidês looked up to the heavens and groaned:

"O Father Zeus! to think not one of the gods has a little pity for me, to save me from this river! After that I don't care what happens. But I cannot blame any of the host of heaven so much as my own mother, who cajoled me with falsehoods. She said I should die by one of Apollo's quick shafts under the walls of Troy. I wish Hector had killed me, the best man born and bred in these parts! Then a brave man would have killed, and a brave man would have died. But now my fate is to die an ignominious death, caught in this river, like a boy from the pigsty who tries to cross a torrent in winter and drowns!"

As he spoke the words, Poseidon and Athena stood by his side in the shape of two men, gripping his hand and encouraging him. Poseidon said:

[1] Rivers were personified in the shape of bulls.

"Don't shrink like that, Peïeidês, don't be afraid. Here are two gods to help you with full consent of Zeus—I and Pallas Athena. It is not your fate to be swallowed up by a river. The River will soon give over—you know it without being told. But now we will give you a piece of good advice, if you will listen. Fight away until the Trojans are shut up in their city, all that are left; but you come back to the ships as soon as you have killed Hector. We promise you victory."

Achillês was much encouraged by this advice, and he pushed across the plain. The whole space was covered with water, all sorts of fine armour and weapons floating upon it, and the bodies of young men cut off in their prime. He stumbled along wading through these and lifting his knees high to make way against the running current; Athena gave him strength enough to hold his own.

But Scamandros was angrier than ever against Achillês. He lifted a great crested wave on high and called loudly to Simoeis:

"I say, Brother! This man's too strong—let us both join to stop him, or he'll drive the Trojans before him and sack the city! Help here, quick! Fill up your stream from the springs, bring down all your torrents, raise a flood, roll along trees and stones in confusion—we must stop this wild man who thinks himself as good as any god and sweeps the field! I vow his strength shall do him no good, nor his handsome body, nor his fine armour—which will soon lie at the bottom, I think, buried in mud! I'll slime him over in sand and roll a mountain of shingle on the top! His friends shall not know how to find his bones in all that slough! Here shall be his sepulchre—there will be no need to pile a barrow when the Achaians make his funeral!"

Then the River rose in a mighty towering wave, roaring and swirling with a confused agglomeration of foam and blood and bodies, curving over the head of Achillês, and there he would have caught him: but Hera saw the danger, and called to Hephaistos:

"Up with you, Crookshank, my son! You were to mark River Xanthos, as we arranged. Go and help the man, be quick, raise a conflagration, and I will bring West and Southeast with a heavy gale from the sea to drive the flames and burn up bodies and armour together. You burn the trees along the banks and invade the river. Don't let him move you by prayers or by curses! And don't stop until you hear me calling and telling you to stop!"

Hephaistos at once raised a devil of a fire. The conflagration first swept the plain and burnt up all the heaps of bodies which Achillês had left there. As the wind blows in autumn on an orchard newly watered, and dries it, and the harvester is glad, so the fire dried the water off the plain and consumed all the bodies. Then he turned his flames to the river itself, burnt elms and willows and tamarisks, burnt clover and rushes and galingale and everything that grew along the banks. Eels and fishes dived and darted about in great distress, as Hephaistos directed his fiery blast on the water. The River was burnt himself, and called out:

"Hephaistos! No god alive can stand against you, and how could I fight you, all ablaze with fire like that? Make up the quarrel! Let Achillês drive the Trojans out of their city and have done with it. What are quarrels and succours to me?"

He was well in the fire as he spoke, and his water was bubbling like a copper full of hog's-fat melting over a brisk blaze, with fagots of good dry wood piled all round: the water boiled, and he did not care to run any more while the fiery blast of Hephaistos tormented him. So he appeared to Hera frankly:

"My dear Hera, why has your son pitched on *my* stream? Why trouble *me* out of so many others? You can't blame me more than the others who help the Trojans. Well, *I* will promise to stop if you say so, but let *him* stop too. I give you my oath I will never help Trojans again, not even when the Achaians fire the city and burn the whole place up in the conflagration!"

At once Hera called out:

"Stop, Hephaistos my admirable son! It is not proper to knock about an immortal god like this for the sake of mortal men."

At the word Hephaistos quenched his furious fires, and the river ran down between his banks as before.

So Hera stayed that quarrel, when Xanthos was pacified, although she was still angry. But the other gods were bitter against each other on the opposing sides: they soon fell to it with a great din, until the wide earth rang again, and the high heavens trumpeted. Zeus heard the noise sitting on Mount Ida; his heart laughed with glee to see god meeting god in battle.

Shield-piercing Arês began, with a leap at Athena, spear in hand, shouting insults as he came:

"Why do you pit gods against gods again, you dog-fly, with that bold audacity of yours, that furious temper? Don't you remember how you let loose Diomedês Tydeidês to wound me, how you caught that spear in the sight of all and sent it straight at me and tore my beautiful flesh? You will pay now for what you did then, I think!"

With this threat he lunged his spear against the tasselled aegis-cape, that terrible cape which is proof against the thunderbolt of Zeus. Athena stept back and picked up a great stone that stood in the ground, black and rough, an ancient landmark, and threw it, and hit Arês on the neck. He collapsed and fell in his rattling armour, dabbing his hair in the dust: seven roods of land his great body covered. Pallas Athena triumphant told him her mind in plain words:

"You silly fool, do you think yourself a match for me? You have not found out yet how much stronger I am than you. That may satisfy your mother's curses for deserting the Achaians and taking the Trojan side. She is angry, I can tell you!"

So saying she turned her eyes away. Aphroditê caught him by the hand, and helped him up, groaning heavily and still half dazed; but Hera saw this and called out to Athena:

"Look at that, Atrytonê! Look, you daughter of Almighty Zeus! Here's this dog-fly again, leading the pest of all mankind out of the battle! After her!"

Athena was after her with joy, rushed at her and gave her a push on the breast with her open hand, which brought them both down in a heap. Then she told the pair what she thought of them:

"I wish all those who help the Trojans were like these, when they meet the Achaians in battle—as bold and as hardy as Aphroditê when she confronted me to help her Arês. Then we should long ago have made an end of this war, and we should have sacked the tall fortress of Troy!"

Hera smiled.

My lord Earthshaker was facing Apollo; and he spoke next:

"Phoibos, why are we two out of it? The others have begun, and we ought to do something. It would be a disgrace to return to that brazen house on Olympos without a battle. You begin, you are the younger, and it would hardly be fair for an older god of more experience, like me.—You silly fool, there is not much sense in your head. Do you forget what we two had to suffer at Ilios all by ourselves, when Zeus sent us to serve Laomedon for one year at a fixed wage, when he was master and gave us orders? My job was to build a fine broad wall round the city to make it invincible; yours, Phoibos, was to tend the cattle on the foothills of Ida. But when pay-day came, happy day! that terrible man robbed us of all our pay! Told us to go, threatened to tie us up hand and foot and sell us somewhere among the islands far away! Said he would lop off both our ears! So we came back disappointed, without our pay. He promised, you see, and did not pay up. There's the man whose people you are obliging so kindly! instead of joining us and doing your best to destroy them out and out, women and children and all."

Apollo answered:

"Look here, Earthshaker: you could not call me a sane god if I were really to fight you for the sake of mortal men. Poor things, they are like the leaves of the forest, you know, grow up full of fire and eat the kindly fruits of the earth, then wither away and perish.[2] Come along, let the others fight and we will keep out of it."

So he turned away, for he felt shy of coming to blows with his own father's brother. But his sister the wild beasts' lady, Artemis Huntress, scolded him roundly in no flattering words:

"So you run away, Shootafar? You let Poseidon have all the honours, and give him victory for nothing? Silly fool, what is your bow for? A windbow—useless! Don't let me hear you boasting again in our Father's hall before all the family, how you will stand up to Poseidon and fight him!"

Apollo made no answer to this, but Hera did; and she scolded the Archeress roundly:

"How can you dare to put yourself against me, you bold bitch? You will find it hard to face my wrath, in spite of the bow you carry, for women are your prey; Zeus has made you a lion among the women and lets you kill any you like! You had better go and show your prowess in the mountains by killing savage beasts and wild deer, and leave your betters alone. But if you want to learn the art of war, I'll show you I am the stronger when you set up yourself against me!"

She grasped both the other's wrists in her own left hand, and with her right pulled the quiver off her shoulders and beat it about her ears, smiling at her twists and wriggles, while the arrows fell out in a shower. Artemis was in tears by this time, and she managed to slip away underneath; she was off like a dove chased by a falcon into a cleft of the rocks, where she escapes for once by good fortune. So Artemis escaped weeping, and left the arrows on the ground.

Hermês said to his antagonist:

"I won't fight with you, Leto. It's dangerous to bandy fisti-cuffs with the wives of Zeus Cloudgatherer! You are heartily welcome to boast before the whole family, that you beat me by force of arms!"

Leto just picked up her daughter's arrows lying about in the dust higgledy-piggledy, and went away.

Artemis, however, got as far as the great hall of Zeus, and threw herself on her father's knees weeping, while her soft robe quivered and shook. Her father clasped her close to him and asked, laughing gently:

"My dear child! Who in the heavens has treated you like this?"

She answered:

"Your own wife slapped me, father, with her pretty white

2 This obviously recalls the proverbial tag of Glaucos in Book VI, (page 76), half remembered and quoted without intelligence: a parody, like the whole of this divine battle.

hands! Your wife Hera, who began all this quarreling and
fighting in our family!"

While all this was going on, Phoibos Apollo entered the city
of Ilios. He was anxious about the place, and feared the
Danaäns might take it that very day before its time. The other
gods had gone home, some resentful, some triumphant, to their
places beside their father the Thundercloud. But Achillês was
dealing death on men and horses alike, carrying with him
devastation and woe, as when smoke rises to heaven over a
burning city after the wrath of God has brought upon it devastation and woe.

But the old King Priam was standing on the wall, when he
suddenly saw Achillês like some monstrous portent sweeping
the Trojans before him in rout, and there was no help. Groaning aloud he came down from the wall, and called to the
keepers of the gate as he went along:

"Open the gates wide, and hold them in hand until our people
come in. They are flying before Achillês, and here he is, close
at hand, driving them on. I think this will be a bad business.
But as soon as they are all safe inside, close the gates fast at
once, for I fear that man of destruction may make a dash to
get in too."

They ran back the bolts and pushed back the gates, now the
one hope of safety; and Apollo leapt out to meet them, that
he might save the Trojans from destruction. Straight to the
lofty walls they ran, parched with thirst, smothered in dust;
close behind Achillês plied his spear, his heart possessed with
madness and the lust of victory.

Then the Achaians would have taken Troy, but for Phoibos
Apollo. There was a brave man there, Agenor the stalwart son
of Antenor, and Apollo strengthened his heart with courage
and himself stood by him, leaning against the Oak but hidden
in mist, to keep from him the heavy hands of death. This man,
when he saw Achillês coming, stood still in great perplexity of
mind, and deeply moved he said to his own brave heart:

"Here is trouble for me! If I run before Achillês, along with
this terrified crowd, he will catch me all the same and cut my
coward's throat. If I let the crowd go on in their rout before
Achillês, and use my feet to escape somewhere else in the plain,
I may get into the foothills of Ida and hide under the bushes;
then I may cool off my sweat in the river and come back to
Ilios in the evening—but what's the use of thinking such
things? Suppose he notices me taking myself off towards the
plain, runs after me and catches me with those quick feet of
his! Then there will be no escape from death, for he is stronger
than any man alive. Then what if I stand up to him where I
am! The man's flesh can be cut, I suppose; he has no more than

one life, they say he's mortal, and Zeus Cronidês gives the victory!"

With these thoughts he pulled himself together to await Achillês, firmly resolved to fight for it. He was like some panther in the thick bush before the huntsman, which fears not and flees not when she hears the baying of the hounds. Even if the man gets in first with a stab or a shot, though pierced with a spear she loses no courage until she grapple or die. So this man Agenor, the brave son of a doughty sire, would not think of flight before he could try Achillês. He held the shield ready before him and shouted aloud:

"I suppose you hope, Achillês, this day to take the city of Troy. Silly fool! Much pain yet remains to be suffered for Troy! There are many men within, and strong men, and we stand before our wives and children to defend our fortress. *You* shall meet your fate here, terrible and bold though you are."

Then he aimed the spear and let fly. The blade struck just under the knee with a loud clang, but it glanced off the tin of the shin-guard without piercing the god's masterpiece. Achillês was following up, when Apollo carried off the man in a mist and sent him in peace out of the battle. Then he kept Achillês away from the battlefield by a trick. Achillês saw Agenor as he thought standing before his feet, and rushed after him— chased him over the plain, turned him towards the river Scamandros, always just a little behind; for that was Apollo's trick, so that Achillês always expected to catch him at the next step. Meanwhile the mob of routed Trojans managed to get behind the walls until the place was full of them, and glad they were to get there. They had not spirit left in them to wait for one another, and see who was dead and who was alive; they simply poured into the city, all whose legs were quick enough to save them.

BOOK XXII

Of the last fight and the death of Hector

NOW THE ROUTED MEN WERE HUDDLED TOGETHER IN THE city like a lot of trembling fawns; and while they cooled off their sweat, and drank to assuage their thirst, leaning upon the battlements, the Achaians came near to the walls, and formed up with their shields against their shoulders. But Hector stayed where he was, in front of the Scaian Gate, for the shackles of fate held him fast.

Then Apollo made himself known to the pursuing Achillês.

"Why are you chasing me, Peleidês?" he said, "mortal man chasing immortal god? You never knew that I was a god, I see, you are still as wild as ever. You routed the Trojans, and now you care nothing about them—just look, they are all collected in the city, and you have wandered away here! You will not kill me, for death cannot come near me."

Achillês answered angrily:

"You have baffled me, Shootafar. Cruel god, to draw me here away from the walls! Many more should have bit the dust before I reached Ilios! Now you have saved their lives and robbed me of my victory. Easy enough, since you have no vengeance to fear. I would certainly have my revenge if I had the power."

Then he was gone in his angry pride, like a prize race-horse with a car behind him that gallops over the plain straining every muscle.

The old King Priam was the first to see him speeding over the plain. His armour shone on his breast, like the star of harvest whose rays are most bright among many stars, in the murky night: they call it Orion's Dog. Most brilliant is that star, but he is a sign of trouble, and brings many fevers for unhappy mankind.

The old man groaned, and lifting up his hands beat them upon his head as he groaned, and cried aloud to his son entreating him; but his son was standing before the gates immovable, and determined to meet Achillês face to face.

"O Hector!" the old man cried in piteous tones as he stretched out his hands, "Hector my beloved son! Do not face that man alone, without a friend, or fate will soon find you out! Do not be so hard-hearted! Peleion will destroy you, for he is stronger than you are. O that the gods loved him as I do! Soon would vultures and dogs feast on him lying on the ground! Then this cruel pain would pass from my heart. He has bereaved me of many sons, and good sons, killing and selling to far-off islands.

"Now again there are two sons that I cannot see amongst those who are crowded here in the city—Lycaon and Polydoros; their mother was the princess Laothoê. If they are alive in the enemy camp, they shall be ransomed; there is gold and bronze enough here, for she had plenty from her old father Altês. If they are dead already and in the house of Hadês, there is grief for their mother and me their father; but for the rest of the people the grief will not last so long if only you do not die with them by the hands of Achillês.

"Do come within these walls, my son! Save the men and women of our city; life is sweet—do not let Achillês rob you of life and win glory for himself! Pity me also—an old man, but not too old to know, not too old to be unhappy! A miserable portion indeed Father Cronidês will give me then—to perish in my old age, after I have lived to see many troubles, seen my sons destroyed and my daughters dragged into slavery, my house ransacked, little children dashed on the ground in fury, my sons' wives dragged away by Achaian hands! And my self last of all—some one shall strike me down or pierce my body, and leave me dead at my door for carrion dogs to devour; my own table-dogs, my watchdogs, which I have fed with my own hands, will go mad and lap my blood, and lie sated by the door where they used to watch. For a young man all is decent when he is killed in battle; he may be mangled with wounds, all is honourable in his death whatever may come. But a hoary head, and a white beard, and nakedness violated by dogs, when an old man is killed, there is the most pitiable sight that mortal eyes can see."

As the old man spoke he tore the white hairs from his head; but Hector would not listen. His mother stood there also, weeping; she loosened the folds of her dress, and with the other hand bared her breast, and through her tears cried out the secrets of her heart:

"O Hector my own child, by *this* I beseech you, have pity on me, if ever I gave you the soothing breast! Remember this, my love, and come behind these walls—let these walls keep off that terrible man! Do not stand out in front against him, do not be so hard! For if he kill you, never shall I lay you on your bier, never shall I mourn over you, my pretty bud, son of my own body! Nor your precious wife—we shall both be far away, and Danaän dogs will devour you in the Danaän camp!"

But their tears and their prayers availed nothing with Hector's proud spirit. He stood fast, and awaited the coming of his tremendous foe. Like a serpent of the mountains over his hole, fed full of poisons and imbued with bitter hate, who lies in wait coiled about the hole and fiercely glaring, so Hector imbued with unquenchable passion would not retreat, but stood, leaning his shield against a bastion of the wall. Then deeply moved he spoke to his own heart:

"What shall I do? If I retreat behind these walls, Polydamas will be the first to heap reproaches on me, for he advised me to lead the army back to the city on that dread night when Achillês rose up. I would not listen—it would have been better if I had! And now that I have ruined them all by my rashness, I am ashamed to face the men and women of Troy, or some base fellows may say—Hector thought too much of his own strength, and ruined us all! They will say that: and my better part is to face him for life and death. Either I shall kill him and return in triumph, or I shall die with honour before the gate.

"Shall I lay down my shield and helmet and lean my spear against the wall, and go to meet him alone, and promise to yield Helen with all her wealth, all that Alexandros brought with her to Troy?—yield the woman who was the cause of the great war, let the princes of Argos take her away, offer to pay besides half the treasure of our city, make the elders of the city take oath to hide nothing but to divide honestly all we possess? But what good would that be? Suppose I should approach him, and then he would not have pity and would not spare me? Suppose I should strip off my armour, and then he should just kill me naked like a woman? This is no place for fairy tales, or lovers' pretty prattle, the way of a man with a maid, when man and maid prattle so prettily together! Better get to work at once; we'll see which of us the Olympian makes the winner!"

So he mused and stood his ground, while Achillês drew near, like Enyalios the warrior god, shaking over his right shoulder that terrible Pelian ashplant: the armour upon him shone like flaming fire or beams of the rising sun. Hector trembled to see him. He could stand no longer but took to flight, and Peleidês was upon him with a leap: Hector fled swiftly under the walls of Troy and Peleidês flew after him furiously, as a falcon swoops without effort after a timid dove, for he is the swiftest of flying things, and he darts upon her with shrieking cries close behind, greedy for a kill. They passed the look-out and the wind-beaten fig tree, keeping ever away from the wall along the cartroad, until they reached the two fountains which are the sources of eddying Scamandros. One is a spring of hot water, with steam rising above it as if it were boiling over a fire, one even in summer is cold as hail or snow or frozen ice. Near these are the tanks of stone, where the Trojan women and girls used to wash their linen in peace-time, before the Achaians came.

So far they came in their race, fleeing and pursuing, a strong man fleeing and a far stronger in pursuit: they ran hard, for Hector's life was the prize of this race, not such prizes as men run for, a beast or an oxhide shield. Thrice round the city of Priam they ran, like champion racehorses running round the turning-post for a tripod or a woman or some great stake, when a man is dead and the games are given in his honour. All the gods were watching, and the Father of gods and men exclaimed:

"Confound it, I love that man whom I see hunted round

those walls! I am deeply grieved for Hector, who has sacrificed many an ox on the heights of Ida or the citadel of Troy! and now there is prince Achillês, chasing him round the city of Priam. What do you think, gods? Just consider, shall we save him from death, or shall we let Achillês beat him now? He is a brave man."

Athena Brighteyes replied:

"O Father Flashingbolt, O Thundercloud, you must never say that! A mortal man, long doomed by fate, and you will save him from death? Do as you please, but the rest of us cannot approve."

Zeus Cloudgatherer answered:

"Never mind, Tritogeneia, my love. I did not really mean it and I want to be kind to you. Wait no longer but do what you wish."

Athena was ready enough, and shot away down the slopes of Olympos.

Achillês was now following at full speed and gave Hector no chance. He watched him like a hound which has put up a hart from his lair, and gives chase through the dingles and the dells; let the hart hide and crouch in the brake, the hound tracks him out till he finds. If Hector going by the road made a dash at the city gates for refuge, hoping his friends might help him with a volley from the walls above, Achillês would take a short cut and get before him, running under the walls and turning him back towards the open ground. It was like some race in a dream, where one chases another, and he cannot catch or the other escape; so Achillês could never catch Hector, or Hector escape Achillês. How indeed could Hector have escaped his fleet pursuer so far, if Apollo had not then for the last time been near, to give him strength and speed? And Achillês had signalled to his own men that no one should let fly a shot at Hector, and take his own credit away if he came in second.

But when the fourth time they drew near the two fountains, see now, the Father laid out his golden scales and placed in them two fates of death, one for Achillês and one for Hector. He grasped the balance and lifted it: Hector's doom sank down, sank down to Hadês, and Apollo left him.

At that moment Athena was by the side of Achillês, and she said in plain words:

"Now you and I will win, my splendid Achillês! Now I hope we shall bring great glory to our camp before the Achaian nation, by destroying Hector, for all his insatiable courage. Now there is no chance that he can escape, not if Apollo Shootafar should fume and fret and roll over and over on the ground before Zeus Almighty! Rest and take breath, and I will go and persuade the man to stand up to you."

Achillês was glad of a rest, and stood still leaning on his barbed ashplant.

Athena now took the form and voice of Deïphobos: she went over to Hector and said to him simply:

"Achillês is giving you a hard time, old fellow, chasing you like this round the city. Let us stand and defend ourselves."

Hector answered:

"O Deïphobos, I always liked you best of all the sons of my father and mother! But now I shall think more of you than ever, for daring to come outside for my sake when you saw me here. All the rest keep inside!"

Athena said:

"My dear old fellow, father and mother and all our friends begged and besought me to stay, they are so terribly afraid of him; but I had not the heart to desert you. Now then let us have at him! No sparing of spears—let us see whether he will kill us both and carry off our bloodstained spoils, or if your spear shall bring him down!"

So the deceiver led him towards Achillês; and when they were near him Hector spoke:

"I will fly from you no more, Peleidês. Three times I raced round the city of Priam and would not await your attack; but now my heart bids me stand and face you, for death or for life. But first come near and let us give our troth; the gods shall be the best witnesses and sentinels of our agreement. If Zeus gives me endurance, and if I take your life, I will do no vile outrage to your body; I will take your armour, Achillês, and your body I will give back to your people. You do the same."

Achillês answered with a frowning face:

"Hector, I cannot forget. Talk not to me of bargains. Lions and men make no truce, wolves and lambs have no friendship —they hate each other for ever. So there can be no love between you and me; and there shall be no truce for us, until one of the two shall fall and glut Arês with his blood. Call up all your manhood; now you surely need to be a spearman and a bold man of war. There is no chance of escape now; this moment Pallas Athena shall bring you low by my spear. Now in one lump sum you shall pay for all my companions, whom you have slain and I have mourned."

With the words he poised and cast his long spear. But Hector saw it coming and crouched down, so that it flew over and stuck in the earth. Pallas Athena pulled it out and gave it back to Achillês, but Hector saw nothing. Then Hector said:

"A miss! I am not dead yet as you thought, most magnificent

Achillês! So there was something Zeus did not tell you about me, as it seems. You are only a rattletongue with a trick of words, trying to frighten me and make me lose heart. I am not going to run and let you pierce my back—I will charge you straight, and then you may strike me in the breast if it be God's will, but first see if you avoid *my* spear! I pray that you may take it all into your body! The war would be lighter for Troy if you were dead, for you are our greatest danger."

He poised his spear and cast it, and hit the shield fair in the middle; but the spear rebounded and fell away. Hector was troubled that the cast had failed; he had no second spear, and he stood discomfited. Then he shouted to Deïphobos and called for another, but no Deïphobos was there. Now Hector knew the truth, and cried out:

"All is lost! It is true then, the gods have summoned me to death. Deïphobos was by my side I thought—but he is in the city and I have been deceived by Athena. Now then, death is near me, there can be no delay, there is no escape. All this while such must have been the pleasure of Zeus and his son Shootafar, who have kindly protected me so far: but now fate is upon me. Yet I pray that I may die not without a blow, not inglorious. First may I do some notable thing that shall be remembered in generations to come!"

With these words he drew the sword that hung by his side, sharp and strong, gathered himself and sprang, like an eagle flying high and swooping down from the clouds upon a lamb or cowering hare. Achillês moved to meet him full of fury, covering his chest with the resplendent shield while the thick golden plumes nodded upon his flashing helmet. His right hand held poised the great spear, which gleamed like the finest of all the stars of heaven, the star of evening brilliant in the dark night; he scanned Hector with ruthless heart, to see where the white flesh gave the best opening for a blow. Hector was well covered with that splendid armour which he had stript from Patroclos, but an opening showed where the collar-bones join the neck to the shoulder, the gullet, where a blow brings quickest death. There Achillês aimed, and the point went through the soft neck; but it did not cut the windpipe, and Hector could still answer his foe. He fell in the dust, and Achillês cried in triumph:

"There, Hector! You thought no doubt while you were stripping Patroclos that you would be safe; you cared nothing for me far away. Fool! There was an avenger, a stronger man than Patroclos, waiting far away! I was there behind in the camp, and I have brought you low! Now you shall be mauled by vultures and dogs, and he shall be buried by a mourning nation!"

Hector half-fainting answered:

"I beseech you by your soul and by your knees, by your father and your mother, do not leave me for dogs to mangle among your ships—accept a ransom, my father and my mother will provide gold and treasure enough, and let them carry home my body, that my people may give me the fire, which is the rightful due of the dead."

Achillês said with an angry frowning face:

"Knee me no knees, you cur, and father me no fathers! No man living shall keep the dogs from your head—not if they bring ransom ten times and twenty times innumerable, and weigh it out, and promise more, not if Priamos Dardanidês pay your weight in gold—not for that ransom shall your mother lay you out on the bier and mourn for the son of her womb, but carrion dogs and carrion birds shall devour you up! For what you have done to me I wish from the bottom of my heart that I could cut you to pieces and eat you raw myself!"

Hector answered him dying:

"Ah, I know you well, and I forebode what will be. I was not likely to persuade you, for your heart is made of iron. But reflect! or I may bring God's wrath upon you, on that day when Paris and Phoibos Apollo shall slay you by the Scaian Gate, although you are strong."

As he spoke, the shadow of death encompassed him; and his soul left the body and went down to Hadês, bewailing his fate, bidding a last farewell to manhood and lusty strength. Hector was dead, but even so Achillês again spoke:

"Lie there dead! My fate I will accept, whenever it is the will of Zeus and All Gods to fulfil it."

He drew the spear out of the body and laid it aside. Then he stript off the armour, and the other Achaians came crowding round. How they gazed in wonder at Hector's noble form and looks! Yet no one came near without a stab; they beat him and stabbed him, saying to each other:

"Ha ha! Hector feels very much softer now than when he burnt our ships with his blazing brands!"

Achillês, when he finished stripping the spoils, turned to the crowd, and made them a speech in his downright manner.

"My friends," he said, "princes and captains of the nation, since as you see the gods have granted me to kill this man who has done us more damage than all the rest put together, let us go round the city ready for battle, and find out what they mean to do: whether they will leave their fortress now this man is dead, or whether they will still confront us although they have no Hector.—But stay, what am I thinking about! Patroclos lies beside our ship unmourned, unburied! Patroclos I can never forget so long as I live and move! And even if in the house of

Hadês men forget their dead, yet I will remember my dear comrade even there. Come on, my lads, let us march back to our ships singing our hymn of victory, and bring this man with us. We have won a great triumph; we have killed Hector, to whom the Trojans prayed as if he were a god!"

And then he thought of a shameful outrage. He cut behind the sinews of both Hector's feet from ankle to heel and strapt them together with leather thongs, and fastened them to his chariot leaving the head to drag. Then he laid the armour in the car, and got in himself and whipt up the horses. Away they flew: the dust rose as the body was dragged along, the dark hair spread abroad, there in the dirt trailed the head that was once so charming, which now Zeus gave to his enemies to maltreat in his own native land. And as the head was bedabbled thus in the mire, his mother tore her hair and threw away the covering veil, and wailed aloud seeing her son; his father lamented sore, the people wailed, and lamentation filled the city. Such lamentation there might have been, if all frowning Ilios were smouldering in ashes.

The people had much ado to keep the old King in his frenzy from rushing out of the Dardanian Gate. He rolled in the dung-heap and appealed to all, naming each by his name:

"Have done, my friends! I know you love me, but let me go out alone and visit the Achaian camp—let me pray to this terrible violent man! He may have shame before his fellows, and pity an old man—yes, I think he has an old father like me, Peleus, who begat him and bred him to be the ruin of Troy! And for me more than all he has brought trouble—so many of my sons he has killed in their prime! I mourn for them, but not for them all so much as one, who will bring me down with sorrow to the grave, my Hector. Would that he had died in my arms! Then we could have mourned and wept till we could weep no more, the unhappy mother who bore him, and I his father."

As he spoke, he wept, and the people lamented with him. Then Hecabê led the women's lamentation, herself weeping the while:

"My child, I am desolate: how shall I live in sorrow when you are dead? Night and day you were my boast in the city, and a blessing to all, both men and women, who used to welcome you as one divine. Truly you were a great glory to them also while you lived, but now death and fate has come upon you!"

But Hector's wife had not yet heard anything of her husband; no messenger had told her the truth, that he remained outside the gate. She was busy with her loom in a far corner of the house, embroidering pretty flowers on a wide purple

web. She called to the servants to put a cauldron to boil on
the fire, that Hector might have a warm bath when he came in
from the battle. Poor creature, she knew not that he was far
away from all baths, brought low by the hands of Achillês and
the will of Brighteyes Athena.

But when she heard lamentation and wailing from the wall,
her limbs quivered and the shuttle fell to the ground out of
her hand, and she called to her maids:

"Here, come with me two of you and let me see what has
happened. That was the voice of my honoured goodmother!
My heart is in my mouth—my knees are turned to stone! Some
trouble is at hand for the sons of Priam! Far from my ear be
that word! But I am terribly afraid prince Achillês has cut off
my rash Hector by himself and driven him away to the plain!
Ah, he will put an end to the fatal pride that always possessed
him, for Hector would never stay in the crowd—he would
always run out in front and yield in courage to no man!"

She tore out like a mad woman with beating heart, and the
maids followed. When she came to the crowd of men on the
battlements, she stood peering about—then she saw him dragged
along in front of the city; the horses were dragging him at full
speed towards the Achaian camp, careless what they did. Then
the darkness of night came over her eyes, and she fell backwards fainting and gasping; the coverings fell from her head—
diadem, coif, braided circlet, and the veil which golden
Aphroditê had given her, on the day when Hector paid his rich
bride-gifts and led her away from Eëtion's house. Crowding
round her were Hector's sisters and goodsisters holding her
up, distracted unto death.

When she came to herself and revived, she cried out amid
her sobs:

"O Hector, I am unhappy! So we were both born to one fate,
you in Troy in the palace of Priam, I in Thebê under woody
Placos, in the house of Eëtion who brought me up as a tiny
tot—doomed father, doomed child! Would I had never been
born! Now you have gone to the house of Hadês deep down
under the earth; but I am left in bitter grief a widow in our
home. And our son is still only a baby—O doomed father,
doomed mother! Never will you be a blessing to him, Hector,
or he to you: for you are dead. Even if he escapes from this
miserable war, yet his portion shall be always labour and sorrow, for strangers will rob him of his lands.

"The day of orphanhood makes a child wholly friendless. He
must always hang his head, his cheeks are slobbered with tears,
he goes begging to his father's friends, and plucks one by the
cloak, another by the shirt; if one has pity he puts a cup to his
mouth for a sip, wets the lips but not the palate. The boy who

has both father and mother slaps him and drives him away from the table with unkind words—'Just get out! Your father does not dine with us.' Then the boy runs crying to his widowed mother—yes, Astyanax, who once sat on his own father's knee and ate only marrow and richest fat of sheep! And when he felt sleepy and did not want to play any more; he slept on a bed-stead, with nurse's arms round him, with a soft bed under him, full and satisfied.

"But now he will have plenty to suffer since his father is gone—my Astyanax as they all call him in this city, because you alone saved their gates and walls. And now you are in the enemy camp, far from your father and mother, and when the dogs have had enough, crawling worms will eat your body—naked, although there is nice soft linen in your house made by your own women. But I will make a bonfire of the whole store; it is of no use to you, for your body will not lie out in that, but it will do you honour in the eyes of the people of Troy."

She wept while she spoke, and the women lamented with her.

BOOK XXIII

The funeral rites of Patroclos, and how the games were held in his honour

WHILE THE TROJANS WERE MOURNING WITHIN THEIR CITY, the Achaians made their way to the ships beside the Hellespont. Most of them dispersed to their own vessels, but Achillês would not let the Myrmidons disperse until he had addressed them in these words:

"Your horses have done good service to-day, my brave comrades; but we must not unyoke them yet. Let us go, horses and chariots and all, to mourn for Patroclos, for that is the honour due to the dead. When we have consoled ourselves with lamentation, let us unharness them and take our meal."

Then he led the cavalcade three times round the body, all mourning and crying aloud; and Thetis lamented with them. The sands were drenched with their tears, their armour was drenched, so much their hearts longed for that mighty man. And Peleidês led their lamentations, as he laid his manslaying hands on his true friend's breast:

"Fare thee well, Patroclos, even in the house of death! See now I am fulfilling all that I promised! I said I would drag

Hector to this place and give him to the dogs to devour raw; and in front of your pyre I would cut the throats of twelve noble sons of the Trojans, in payment for your death."

Then he did a vile outrage to royal Hector: he stretched the body on its face in the dirt beside the bier of Menoitiadês.

After that all took off their armour, and unharnessed the loud-whinnying horses, and sat down beside the ship of Achillês in their thousands. There he provided a fine funeral feast. Many bellowing bulls fell under the knife, many sheep and bleating goats; many tusker boars bursting with fat were stretched out to singe over the fire. Around the dead body of the victims poured out in cupfuls was running all over the ground.

Meanwhile Prince Peleion was being led by the Achaian chieftains to Agamemnon. They had trouble to persuade him, so deep was his sorrow for his comrade. At the King's head-quarters orders were given to set a cauldron of water over the fire, that his body might be washed clean of the bloodstains, but he flatly refused and swore to it:

"No, by Zeus highest and greatest of gods! It is not lawful that water may come near my head, before I lay Patroclos on the fire and build him a barrow and cut off my hair! For no second sorrow like this shall come upon me so long as I am among the living. Yet for this present we must consent to the meal which we hate. Then to-morrow, my lord King Agamemnon, shall be for bringing firewood and providing all that is proper to send the dead down into the dark. The fire shall burn him quickly out of sight, and the people shall return to their work."

They did accordingly: the meal was prepared, and all partook and found no lack. When they were satisfied, the others retired to rest; but Peleidês lay with many of his Myrmidons, in the open air on the shore of the sounding sea, while the waves washed on the beach, lay groaning heavily until sleep fell upon him: a deep sweet sleep that soothed the sorrows of his heart, for his strong limbs were weary with that long pursuit after Hector about the city of Ilios.

In sleep came to him the soul of unhappy Patroclos, his very image in stature and wearing clothes like his, with his voice and those lovely eyes. The vision stood by his head and spoke:

"You sleep, Achillês, and you have forgotten me! When I lived you were not careless of me, but now that I am dead! Bury me without delay, that I may pass the gates of Hadês. Those phantoms hold me off, the souls of those whose work is done; they will not suffer me to join them beyond the river, but I wander aimlessly about the broad gates of the house of Hadês. And give me that hand, I pray; for never again shall I come back from Hadês when once you have given me my portion of fire. Never again in life shall we go apart from our companions and take counsel together; but I am swallowed up already by that cruel fate which got me on the day I was born; and you also have your portion, my magnificent Achillês, to perish before the walls of this great city. One thing more I say, and I will put it upon you as a charge if you will comply: do not lay my bones apart from yours, Achillês, but with them, as I was brought up with you in your home, when Menoitios brought me quite a little one from Opoeis to your house, for manslaughter, the day when I killed Amphidamas' son—I did not mean it, we had a silly quarrel over the knuckle-bones. Then Peleus received me, and brought me up kindly in his house, and named me as your attendant. Then let one urn cover my bones with yours, that golden two-handled urn which your gracious mother gave you."

Achillês said in answer:

"Why have you come here, beloved one, with all these charges of this and that? Of course I will do as you tell me every bit. But come nearer; for one short moment let us lay our arms about each other and console ourselves with lamentation!"

He stretched out his arms as he spoke, but he could not touch, for the soul was gone like smoke into the earth, twittering. Achillês leapt up in amazement and clapt his hands with solemn words:

"See there now! So there is still something in the house of Hadês, a soul and a phantom but no real life in it at all! For all night long the soul of unhappy Patroclos has been by my side, sorrowing and lamenting and telling me what to do. And it was mightily like himself!"

All around were moved to lamentation when they heard his words.

They were still mourning when Dawn showed her fingers of light. Then King Agamemnon sent out mules and men from the whole camp to bring firewood, under the charge of Idomeneus's man Merionês. The company set out with their axes and ropes, driving the mules in front: a long journey—upalong downalong offalong and criss-cross. On the foothills of Mount Ida they felled the tall trees busily, down came the trees with a crash, the men split them and tied them on the mules, the mules tore up the earth, hurrying to the flat land, scrambling through the bushes and over the plain. All the woodcutters had logs to carry, under the orders of Merionês. Down on the shore they laid their logs in order, in the place where Achillês designed a great barrow for Patroclos and himself.

When the logs were laid in their places, the men sat where they were, all together. Then Achillês ordered his Myrmidons to don their armour and harness their horses; they mounted the cars, both fighting men and drivers, chariots in front, a cloud of footmen behind, thousands, and in the midst was Patroclos borne by his comrades. They had cut off their hair and thrown it over the body like a shroud. Achillês came behind him clasping the head; his own unspotted comrade he was escorting to the grave.

At the place which Achillês had appointed, they laid him down and piled great heaps of firewood. Then Achillês did his part. He stood away from the pile, and cut off the golden tress which he had kept uncut among his thick hair for the river Spercheios, and spoke deeply moved as he gazed over the dark sea:

"O Spercheios! this is not for thee! That vow was vain which Peleus my father made,[1] that when I returned to my native land I would consecrate my hair to thee, and make solemn sacrifice, and that he would sacrifice fifty rams without blemish into thy waters, at the altar which is in thy precinct at the same place. That was my father's vow, but thou didst not fulfil his hope. Now therefore, since I am not to return to my native land, I would give the warrior Patroclos this to carry with him."

Then he laid the hair in the hands of his well-loved companion. All present broke into lamentation with all their hearts; and they would not have ceased while the sun shone, but Achillês drew near to Agamemnon and said to him:

"Atreidês, you are our lord paramount, and it is yours to command. There is plenty of time for the people to mourn, but just now I ask you to dismiss them from this place and tell them to get ready their meal. All this is the business of those who are nearest akin to the dead; and let the chieftains remain with us."

Agamemnon accordingly dismissed the people, while the mourners remained, and piled up the wood, and made a pyre of a hundred feet each way, and upon it they laid the body. They killed flocks of sheep and herds of cattle in front of the pyre, skinned them and cut them up; Achillês took away all the fat, and covered the dead with it from head to foot, and heaped the flayed bodies about him. Jars of honey and oil he placed leaning against the bier. Four horses he laid carefully on the pyre, groaning aloud. Nine dogs the prince had, that fed from his table; two of these Achillês took, and cut their throats and laid beside him. The twelve noble young Trojans he slew without mercy. Then he applied the relentless fire to

---

[1] A boy kept one part of his hair uncut and this he dedicated to his river-god at puberty: Aeschylus *Choephoroe* 6. Achillês had left home so young that the πλόκαμος θρεπτήριος was still uncut.

consume all, and with a groan he called on his comrade's name:

"Fare thee well Patroclos, even in the grave fare thee well! See, I now fulfil all that I promised you before. Here are the twelve noble sons of Trojans—the fire is eating them round about you! Hector Priamidês the fire shall not have to eat, but the dogs!"

But his threat was vain: no dogs were busy about Hector, for the dogs were driven off by the daughter of Zeus, Aphroditê herself, by day and by night. She washed the skin with rose-oil of ambrosia that it might not be torn by the dragging; and Phoibos Apollo drew down a dark cloud from heaven to earth, and covered the place where the body lay, that the sun might not scorch the flesh too soon over the sinews of his limbs.

But the pyre would not burn, and Achillês did not know what to do. At last he stood well away from the smouldering heap, and prayed to North Wind and West Wind promising them good sacrifices; many a libation he poured from his golden goblet, praying them to come and make the wood quickly catch fire, to burn the bodies.

Iris heard his prayers, and flew quickly to the Winds with her message.

They were all in a party at West Wind's, and having a fine feast, when in came Iris flying and stood on the doorstone. As soon as they set eyes on her, up they all jumped and shouted out, every wind of them, "Come and sit by me!" But she said:

"No thank you, no sitting: I'm bound for the Ocean stream. There is a grand sacrifice in the Ethiopian country for us immortals, and I want to have some too. But Achillês is praying to North Wind and West Wind; he wants them to come and promises a good sacrifice. He wants them to make the pyre burn, where Patroclos lies with the people all mourning around."

Her message given, away she flew, and the Winds rose with a devil of a noise and drove the clouds in a riot before them. They swooped upon the sea and raised the billows under their whistling blasts; they reached the Trojan coast and fell on the pyre till the flames roared again. All night long they beat upon the fire together blowing and whistling; all night long stood Achillês holding his goblet, and dipt into the golden mixer, and poured the wine on the ground, till the place was soaked, calling upon the soul of unhappy Patroclos. As a father laments while he burns the bones of his own son, newly wedded and now dead, to the grief of his bereaved parents, so Achillês lamented as he burnt the bones of Patroclos, stumbling up and down beside the pyre with sobbings and groanings.

But at the time when the morning star goes forth to tell that light is coming over the earth, and after him the saffron mantle of Dawn spreads over the sea, at that hour the flame died down and the burning faded away. Then the Winds returned over the Thracian gulf to their home, while the waters rose and roared.

And then Achillês moved away from the pyre, and sank upon the ground tired out: sleep leapt upon him and gave him peace.

Now the people were all gathering round Agamemnon. They made such noise and uproar that Achillês sat up and said:

"Atreidês, and you other princes, you must first quench the pyre with wine wherever the flames have touched. Then let us gather the bones of Patroclos Menoitidês, and be careful to find the right ones. They are easy to know, for he lay right in the middle and the others were on the edge, horses and men together. His bones we must wrap in a double layer of fat and lay them in a golden urn, until I myself shall be hidden in Hadês. But I do not wish any great mound to be raised for him, only just a decent one. Afterwards another can be raised both broad and high, by those of you who are left behind me."

They did his bidding at once. First they quenched the pyre with wine wherever it had burnt and the ashes were deep; then weeping they gathered the bones of their gentle companion, and laid them covered with fat in a golden urn, which they wrapt up in fine linen and put away safely in the hut. Round the pyre they set up a circle of stone slabs to mark the outside limit, and shovelled earth within.

As they were about to go after finishing this task, Achillês told them to stop, and made them sit in a ring while he sent back for prizes: cauldrons and tripods, horses and mules and fine cattle, women also and grey steel.

For the chariot-race he offered as first prize a woman skilled in women's work, and a tripod of two-and-twenty measures with handles to it. The second prize was a mare, a six-year-old unbroken, heavy with a mule-foal. The third was a cauldron of four measures, brand-new and still white. The fourth, two ingots of gold, and the fifth a brand-new basin with handles. Then he rose to his feet and addressed them:

"My lord King, and gentlemen all, here are prizes ready for the charioteers. If our contests were held in honour of any other I should be sure of carrying home the first prize, since you know how much the best my horses are; for they are immortal—Poseidon himself gave them to Peleus my father, and he lent them to me. But let me say that I and my horses will not come forward. Think of the glorious driver they have lost, how kind he was! How often he would wash their manes in pure water and pour soft oil upon them; and now they stand trailing their manes in the dust and mourning him, now they stand with sorrow in their hearts. The course is open to all the rest of you, whoever believes in his horses and car."

The competitors quickly came up, and first by a long way Eumelos Admetos' son, who was well known for horsemanship. Next came Diomedês Tydeidês, driving the two horses of Tros which he had taken from Aineias (when Apollo saved the man). Next King Menelaos Atreidês with a pair of quick goers, Agamemnon's mare, Sunshine Aithê, and his own horse Whitefoot Podargos. Agamemnon's mare was the gift of Echepolos Anchisiadês,[2] a very rich man who lived in Sicyon, which he offered because he wanted to stay at home happy instead of going to war. The mare was eager for the race. Antilochos was the fourth who brought a team. This was the son of Nestor Neleiadês, and the horses were Pylos-bred. As he was getting ready Nestor took the opportunity to give him some advice (although he was quite able to do without it), and this is what he said:

"Zeus and Poseidon were very kind to you, Antilochos, when you were quite young, and they taught you all the art of horsemanship. Then I don't think there is much need to teach you anything, for you know well how to wheel round the post. But your horses are the slowest of all, and so I fear you will find it a bad job. Their horses are faster, true, but the men could not be more knowing than you are. Well then, dear boy, rub up every trick you can think of, or the prizes will give you the slip and out of sight! The tricks of the trade—and a woodman's made! He does not depend on brute force. The tricks of the trade—and a pilot's made! The winds may blow but on he'll go. And the tricks of the trade make driver beat driver. One man leaves everything to horses and car, wheels wide to this side or that side carelessly, the horses go roaming over the course, he does not hold them in hand; but he that knows his tricks may have inferior horses to drive—yet he keeps his eye always on the post, wheels close in, does not forget how much to stretch the horses at first by the handling of the reins, but keeps them well in hand and watches the man in front.

"Now I will tell you the mark—you can't miss it. There's a dry stump at the turn of the road standing about a fathom above the soil, oak or fir, which does not rot in the rain. Two white stones are set against it, one on each side, and the land round this is smooth for horses. It may be the mark of some man dead long ago, or set up for a post in former days, and now Achillês has fixed it for the turning-point of his race. Drive your car

---

[2] Son of Anchises of Sicyon, not the Anchises of Troy. The old Greek annotator remarks, "The King preferred a good warhorse to a conscientious objector."

close almost grazing the post, and yourself in the basket lean gently to the left: give the goad to the off horse with a call and let him have rein. Let the near horse almost graze the post, so that the nave of the wheel seems almost to touch the surface of the stone, but do not let it touch or you may wreck the car and damage the horses. That will be a disgrace to you and a pleasure to the others! But my dear boy, keep your head and be careful, for if at the turning-post you can cut in and get round in front, no man alive could catch you by a spurt or pass you, even if he were driving Arion, Adrastos' divine thoro-bred racer, or some of Laomedon's fine stock from this part of the world." [3]

Then Nestor returned to his seat, after telling his son all the ins and outs of the matter.

Merionês was the fifth.

When they were all ready, they mounted their cars and threw in their lots. Achillês shook them, and the lot of Antilochos leapt out, next came Eumelos, after him Menelaos Atreidês, then Merionês, and last the best of them all got his place, Tydeidês. They took stand in a row, and Achillês showed them the turning-point in the distant plain. He posted his father's man Phoinix as umpire, to keep an eye on the running and report what happened.

They were all off together at once, whipping up the horses, flicking them with the reins, crying them on furiously: the ships were left behind, and away they galloped—their manes went flying on the wind and clouds of dust rose under their bodies. The cars now ran steady, now bounded high; the drivers stood in their baskets with hearts beating high in hope. Every man called to his horses, and the horses flew over the ground.

But when they had turned back seawards on the return course, then indeed each horse showed his mettle, then indeed they forced the pace. At once Eumelos' mares took the lead, followed by the stallions of Diomedês, the famous breed of Tros—not far behind, indeed quite close—they seemed ever on the point of trampling on Eumelos' car, and their breath warmed his back and shoulders as their heads leaned over his body.

And now Diomedês would have passed, or at least made a dead heat, if Apollo had not been annoyed at his success; so he knocked the whip out of his hand. Tears of anger filled his eyes, as he saw the mares going better than ever and his own team slackening without the prick.[4] But Apollo's cheating did not escape the eye of Athena: she picked up the whip and gave

[3] Of course the cars had to make a loop about the post. The cars were put in a line at scratch, and the best place was on the left hand.
[4] The whip was probably a long pliant rod with spurs at the end.

it back, encouraged the horses, ran after Eumelos furious and broke the yoke of his chariot. His horses ran away off the road, and the pole was left dragging on the ground[5]; the driver was rolled out over the wheel, and barked his elbows and mouth and nose and bruised his forehead. Tears filled his eyes, he choked, and could not utter a word.

Tydeidês kept his team in hand and cleared them, galloping now far in front of the others, for Athena put spirit into the horses and made him win. After him came Menelaos; but Antilochos who was next shouted to his pair:

"Go it, you two! Pull away—there's no time to waste! I don't ask you to beat that pair in front; Athena has made them go like that, and she will make him win. But do catch up Atreidês, don't let his horses beat you. What a shame—let a mare beat a pair of stallions! Why are you behind, my brave boys? I tell you plainly and I shan't forget—there will be no more fodder for you in Nestor's stable, he will just cut your throats at once if we make poor sport by carelessness! After him—put on a spurt! I know what to do—I'll head past him at the narrow way, he shan't escape me!"

They were fairly terrified by their master's shouts, and put on a spurt for a short time until Antilochos saw the narrows. The road here led through a gulley, and in one part the winter flood had broken down part of the road and made a hollow. Menelaos was driving in the middle of the road, hoping that no one would try to pass too close to his wheel, but Antilochos turned his horses out of the track and followed a little to one side. This frightened Menelaos, and he shouted at him:

"What reckless driving, Antilochos! Hold in your horses. This place is narrow, soon you will have more room to pass. You'll foul my car and destroy us both!"

But Antilochos only plied the whip and drove faster than ever, as if he did not hear. They raced about as far as the cast of a quoit swung from the shoulder of a lusty young man who tries what he can do, and then Atreidês fell behind: he let the horses go slow himself, for he was afraid they might all collide in that narrow space and overturn the cars and fall in a struggling heap. But he shouted angrily:

"That was a nasty trick, Antilochos! Damn you, why do we say that Antilochos always plays the game! Far from it! Still you shan't get your prize without taking your oath."[6]

Then he called to the horses:

"Now then, don't be slack, don't stand still there! It's hard on you of course—but you'll see, their feet and joints will fail before yours. Their young days are behind them!"

[5] They were fastened by the yoke only without traces.
[6] He must swear an oath that he had played fair.

The horses took the hint and put on pace, until they caught up the others.

Meanwhile the crowd were looking out for the horses. Soon they came flying along in clouds of dust. Idomeneus the Cretan prince was the first to see them: he was sitting away from the rest on high ground. He heard a shout and knew the man's voice, then he made out a horse clear in front; he was roan so far as he could see with a white full-moon on his forehead. He stood up and shouted to the spectators:

"Hallo, my lords and gentlemen! I spy horses—can you see them too? Another team appears to be in front, looks like another driver. The mares must have come to grief somewhere on the plain, but they were leading on the way out. I certainly saw them first at the turning, but now I can't see them at all—I have looked hard over the whole plain. Did he lose his reins, couldn't hold them and failed at the turn? That's it, I think he was thrown out and wrecked his car and the horses ran away at their own sweet will. Do get up and have a look too—I can't see clearly, but he seems to be that Aitolian prince, you know who, he has the city in Argos—Diomedês Tydeidês."

Aias Oïleus' son laughed scornfully and said:

"Cataracts of talk as usual, Idomeneus. There are the mares yonder, the old high-stepping racers! You are not the youngest man in the army so much as all that, those eyes in your head are not so much the sharpest of the whole nation. But always cataracts of words; you really should not be such a cataract-orator before your betters. The same mares are leading that led before, and the same Eumelos holding the ribbons."

This brought an angry reply from Idomeneus:

"Quarrels are your best line, Aias, for you have not much sense, and for anything else we can all beat you easily. You are a stubborn one! Come along now—let us bet a tripod or a cauldron which team is first, and the umpire shall be my lord Agamemnon! You will learn something when you pay up."

Then Aias the Runner jumped up to make a retort with more angry words, and the quarrel would have gone on, but Achillês stopt them by saying:

"Don't abuse each other like that, you two, Idomeneus and Aias. It is quite out of place here. You would be the first to reprove any one else who did that kind of thing. Sit down in your places and see what happens. They will soon be here themselves, and then every one will know who is first and who is second."

While he spoke Tydeidês had come quite near, at the gallop, plying his whip down from the shoulder, and the horses were bounding along at full speed, kicking up clouds of dust over their driver, and the car with its gold and tin plates gleaming rolled behind: the tires left hardly a trace in the light dust, so quickly they flew.—And now he was there, in front of them, the sweat dripping from the horses' heads and chests! He leapt down from the car and leant the whip against the yoke. Nor was Sthenelos behindhand. He ran up and took the prize, and then loosed the horses; the woman and the tripod were taken in charge by his comrades.

Next Antilochos drove in, after beating Menelaos, by trick not by merit; even so Menelaos was close behind, as near as a horse to the wheel when he trundles his master along at full speed—the tip of the tail touches the tire. That is pretty close, there is not much space between! Menelaos had got as near as that, and when he began there was a quoit's throw between them; but Menelaos soon caught up, for Agamemnon's mare Sunshine was in great form, and if the course had been longer she would have passed and left no doubt as to the winner.

But Merionês was a spear's throw behind Menelaos, for his horses were slowest of all and he was the worst driver for a race.

Eumelos came in last of all, dragging his car behind and driving the horses in front. Achillês was very sorry for him and made no secret of his feelings:

"The best man comes last," he said, "but let us give him a prize, as he deserves. He shall have the second, but Diomedês must have the first."

There was a cheer at this, and he would have given him the mare with general approval, but Antilochos Nestorides pleaded his claim before Achillês Peleidês.

"Achillês, I shall strongly resent it if you do what you have said. For you intend to rob me of my prize, and your only reason is that his horses and car came to grief, and himself too though he is such a good man. Well, he ought to have made his prayers to heaven, and then he would never have come in last at all. If you are sorry for him and want to show your friendship, there is plenty in your quarters—there is gold, there is bronze and sheep, there are captive women and horses: take some of that and give him even a bigger prize by and by, or even now, that every one may be pleased. But the mare I will not give up. If any one wants it let him fight me for it."

Achillês smiled, for Antilochos was his very good friend and he was delighted with him. He answered:

"Very well, Antilochos, if you say I am to fetch out something more to give Eumelos, I certainly will. He shall have the corselet I took from Asteropaios, bronze with a slip of tin running round it. That will be a treasure for him!"

He directed Automedon to fetch it out from the hut. Automedon did so, and handed it to Eumelos, who received it with satisfaction.

And now Menelaos rose in high dudgeon, for he had not forgiven Antilochos. The herald placed the staff in his hand and called silence, and Menelaos proceeded to speak.

"Antilochos," he said, "you were always one for fair play, and now see what you have done: you have disgraced my reputation, and fouled my horses by throwing yours in front, when yours were not nearly so good.

"I appeal to you, my lords and gentlemen. Judge between us without favour, that no one may ever say—'Menelaos compelled Antilochos to give way by false evidence; he leads away the mare, because he is superior in dignity and power, although his horses were not nearly so good.' Or look here, I will decide the matter myself, and I don't think any man will ever reproach me, for it shall be justice.

"Come this way, Antilochos, my young prince, and observe the custom. Stand before your chariot and horses, and take in your hand the whip that you had in the race, lay your hand on the horses and swear by Earthholder Earthshaker that you did not foul my chariot with malice aforethought."

Antilochos, once more the man of fair play, made answer:

"Bear with me now, for I am much younger than you, my lord Menelaos; you are my elder and my better. You know that a young man always goes too far. His mind is too hasty, his wits are flighty. Then let your heart forgive me. I will give up to you willingly the horse I won. And if you demand something of my own besides, something greater, I will give it at once rather than be out of favour with you, my prince, all my days, and offend against heaven besides."

Then he led up the mare and gave her over to Menelaos; and the prince's heart was warmed, like growing corn with the dew upon the ears when the fields are bristling—so, Menelaos, your heart warmed within you!—And he said simply:

"Now, Antilochos, I will put away my anger gladly, for you were never perverse or light-minded before. Just for once boydom was too much for wisdom. Another time don't try to overreach your betters. Not every one, let me tell you, could have made me change my mind; but you indeed have suffered much and worked hard for my sake, and so have your excellent father and brother. Then I will grant your petition; and I will make you a present of the mare, which is my own, that all these here may know that my temper is not tyrannical and harsh."

So saying he gave Noëmon the mare to lead away, and took the cauldron himself.

Merionês took the two ingots of gold in the fourth place, as he came in fourth. The fifth prize was left over, the two-handled bowl; this Achillês carried through the company and gave it to Nestor, saying:

"Here, venerable prince, you shall have something too; let it be a treasure for you in memory of the burying of Patroclos. For you will see him no more in this world. I give you this prize for nothing: you will not box for it, or wrestle, or cast a javelin, or run a race. Already the years are heavy upon you."

He placed the bowl in Nestor's hands, and Nestor received it with pleasure and said with great simplicity:

"Aye, aye, my boy, that's true enough. My joints are not what they were, my dear boy, nor my feet, my hands do not shoot out from the shoulders right and left, touch and go! Ah, if I were young and strong as I was once, when the Epeians were burying my lord Amarynceus in Buprasion, and his sons set up prizes in the King's honour! There wasn't a man to match me, not an Epeian, not a Pylian, not an Aitolian of them all! In boxing I beat Clytomedês Enops' son, in wrestling Pleuronian Ancaios who stood up to me, I outran Iphiclos though he was a good man, with spear I overshot both Phyleus and Polydoros. I only lost with the horses. There the two Actorions beat me by force of numbers! They coveted victory because the biggest prizes were waiting. They were doubles, one took the reins and went bowling along, bowling along, one talked to 'em with the whip.[7]

"Ah yes, once! that's what I was. Now it's the turn of younger men, let them tackle such tasks. Old age is my master now, worse luck, but then I was high among the heroes. Now go ahead, there's your comrade to honour with games like the others. This gift I accept with grateful thanks, and it does my heart good that you remember me your affectionate friend, and you do not forget the honour which is my due among our people. May the gods reward you according to your desire."

Peleidês listened to all the praises of the grand old man, and returned through the throng of spectators to his place.

Next he displayed the prizes for boxing. A hard battle that is! And the prize was a much-enduring mule, a six-year-old yet unbroken, the hardest age to break. The prize for the loser was a two handled goblet. Achillês rose in his place and said:

"Prince Atreidês and gentlemen all, we invite the two best men to put up their hands and box for these prizes. He to whom Apollo shall grant endurance before the face of the whole nation, shall lead away to his quarters this much-enduring mule; and the loser shall carry off this two-handled bowl."

At once a fine big man came forward, Epeios Panopeus' son, a good boxer. He laid a hand on the mule and said:

"This way for any one who wants the bowl! For the mule, no one else shall have it, for no one will beat me in the ring. There

---

[7] Twins, joined in one body. Thus they were "two to one," and they had four arms, two to drive and two to whip, which was not fair.

I claim to be the best man. I lack something in the battlefield, and is not that bad enough? A fellow can't be number one in every kind of work that's done—that is quite true. I tell you plainly and I will make good my words: let him come on—I'll tear his flesh and smash his bones to a pulp. He had better bring his friends and relations in a body to carry him out when I've done with him."

A dead silence followed these words. At last one man Euryalos rose alone, a splendid fellow; he was the son of my lord Longman Standfastson,[8] who came to Thebes for the funeral of Oidipus after he took his deadly dump, and there beat all the Cadmeians. Tydeidês got him ready. He put on his belt, gave him the gloves of good oxhide straps, cheered him up, and wished him luck.

The two men stept forward girt into the ring and put up their hands. Then they fell to it with stout fisticuffs, lead and parry. You might hear their teeth gnashing, and the sweat poured from their bodies! Euryalos watched warily for an opening, but at last Epeios landed him one on the jaw and he did not stand long after that. He was knocked clean off his feet and lifted into the air, curving like a great fish that leaps out of the shallows off the seaweed and through the ripples when Boreas blows, and into the dark waves again. So he came down, but his generous adversary helped him up, and his friends were ready to lead him away, dragging his legs and spitting blood and drooping his head to one side. So they led him away dazed and fainting, and came back for the two-handled bowl.

Without delay Peleidês displayed the third set of prizes, for the wrestling—and a hard bout that is! He showed the prizes all round. For the winner, a large tripod to stand on the fire, which the spectators valued at twelve oxen. For the loser, he brought out a woman well skilled in women's work, valued at four oxen. Then he stood up and said:

"Rise any who wish to compete for this prize."

Up rose that large man Telamonian Aias; up rose Odysseus, the man who was never at a loss, who knew all the tricks of the game. They girt them and stood forth into the ring, and their strong arms took hold of one another with close grip. Their bodies looked like a pair of baulks which a builder leans together to hold up a high roof. Their backs creaked as the hard hands pulled steadily; drops of sweat came out, blood-red weals began to show on ribs and shoulders. Hard was the struggle for that fine tripod; but Odysseus could not bring his man down, nor could Aias, for Odysseus was too strong.

As the spectators began to be bored by this, the large man Aias said to his adversary:

"Prince Laërtiadês, Odysseus never-failing! Either lift me, or I will lift you, and as to the rest Zeus will provide!"

As he spoke, he lifted, but Odysseus knew the trick. He knocked him behind the knee so that his leg gave way and threw him backwards; Odysseus fell on his chest, to the admiration of all. Then Odysseus took his turn and tried to lift Aias, but he could not do it, only moved him a little from the ground. So he hooked his knee round and both fell together in the dirt. Then they would have tried for the third throw, but Achillês rose and stopt them.

"That is enough," said he, "don't tire yourselves out. I declare both men winners. Receive equal prizes, and let us go on to the next event."

They were quite willing, wiped off the dust and put on their tunics.

Achillês now brought out prizes for the footrace. There was a silver mixing-bowl finely wrought, holding six measures. It was the most beautiful bowl in the world, for it was the work of Sidonian artists, and Phoenician merchants had brought it over the sea to the harbour of Lemnos and given it to Thoas as a gift; his grandson Euneos Iasonidês gave it to Patroclos as the price of Lycaon. This bowl Achillês offered as first prize, for the second a great fat ox, and for the last a half-nugget of gold. Then he got up and said:

"Rise any who wish to run for this prize."

Aias the Runner rose, Odysseus rose, then Nestor's son, Antilochos, for he was the best runner among the young men. They stood in a row, and Achillês pointed out the goal. The pace was forced from the start, but before long Aias was leading with Odysseus close behind him, close as the weaver holds the crossbeam to her breast while she pulls the spool across the warp— Odysseus trod in his footsteps before the dust had time to settle, and the breath of Odysseus beat on his head as he ran; the spectators cheered his efforts, but he was doing his very best already. When they came to the last bit of the course Odysseus offered a silent prayer to Athenaia:

"Hear me, my goddess, give thy good help to my feet!"

Pallas Athena heard and made his limbs light, the feet and hands on him. And when they were just on the point to pounce on the prize, Athena tript Aias and made him slip, where the place was covered with offal from the beasts which Achillês had butchered in honour of Patroclos; and down he went, got mouth and nostrils full of the stuff. So Odysseus came in first and lifted the mixing-bowl, and then Aias took hold of the ox. As he stood holding the animal's horn and spitting out the dirt, he said:

"Damn it, that goddess tript me up! She's always by his side like a mother and helps him!"

All burst into a roar of laughter. Antilochos carried off the last prize smiling, and he said to the people:

"You know it quite well, my friends, but I will repeat it: The saying now is true agen, the immortals honour older men. Aias is a little older than I am, but this Odysseus is one of the ancient generation—a green old age is his, as they say. Yet it would be a hard job for any of us to beat him in running, except only Achillês."

So he ended with a compliment to Achillês, and Achillês responded:

"Thanks, Antilochos, your kind words shall not be said in vain. I will add half a nugget of gold to your prize."

He placed it in his hands as he spoke, and Antilochos received it with satisfaction.

Now Achillês brought out the armour of Sarpedon which Patroclos had taken in the field—the long spear and the shield and helmet, and said:

"We invite the two best men to contend for these. Let them arm themselves and take their blades, and try one another before us. Whichever shall first pierce through the armour to what is within and touch the flesh and draw blood, to him I will give this fine Thracian sword silver-bossed which I took from Asteropaios, but the armour both shall hold together; and we will make a good feast to entertain them."

At this invitation up rose Telamonian Aias, up rose Diomedês Tydeidês; and both donned their armour in the rear. Then they came forward to confront each other glaring terribly, to the admiration of all. They drew close—thrice they charged, thrice they attacked, then Aias pierced the buckler: but he did not reach the flesh, for the corselet held the blow. But Tydeidês reached over the great shield and touched the neck with his blade again and again. Then the people were afraid for Aias; they called them to stop and share the prize. But Achillês gave Diomedês the sword with sheath and sling.

Again Achillês brought out a lump of roughcast iron which that mighty man Eëtion used to hurl. When he killed Eëtion, he brought it away with the rest of the spoils. He rose now and said:

"Rise, you who wish to contend for this prize. Any man will have enough here to use for five revolving years, even if his fat fields are far away. No shepherd or plowman will need to visit the city for iron, there will be plenty at home."

At this challenge up rose that redoubtable warrior Polypoitês, up rose Leonteus the strong man, up rose Aias Telamoniadês and prince Epeios. They stood in a row, and Epeios took up the weight, circled it round his head and put it, and the people roared with laughter. Next to put the weight was Leonteus, that veritable sprig of Arês; third Telamonian Aias lifted it and hurled it. The cast from that strong man went beyond the others. But when Polypoitês raised the lump, he threw it as far beyond all the others as a herdsman sends his cudgel flying over the herds of cattle. There was a loud cheer, and his companions got up and carried away the prize to their camp.

Next for the archers Achillês brought forward blue steel— ten axes and ten half-axes.[9] Away on the sand he sat up a ship's mast, with a rockdove tied to the top by a string round its leg. He told them to shoot at this: "Whoever hits the dove shall have all the axes to take home; whoever misses the dove but hits the string shall have the half-axes."

Then up rose prince Teucros, and up rose Merionês that excellent servant of Idomeneus. They shook their lots in a helmet, and Teucros won first shot. He let fly at once a strong shot, but he forgot to vow that he would make due sacrifice of firstling lambs to the Lord. So he missed the dove, since Apollo grudged that to him, he cut through the string close to the bird's foot. Away flew the bird into the sky, and the string fell to the ground amid the cheers of the people. But Merionês instantly snatched the bow from his hand—his arrow had been ready in hand while Teucros aimed. He vowed quickly that he would make due sacrifice of firstling lambs to Apollo Shootafar. High in the clouds he could see the dove: there he shot her under the wing as she circled round. The arrow went right through, and fell down before the feet of Merionês, and stuck in the ground; but the dove settled on the pole, head hanging and wings drooping. Then the life left her, and she fell away from the pole, to the amazement of all who saw it. Merionês took away the ten axes, and Teucros had the half-axes.

Again Peleidês brought out a long spear, and a brand-new cauldron ornamented with flowers, worth one ox; and the spear-throwers came forward. Up rose my lord King Agamemnon, up rose Merionês, the excellent servant of Idomeneus. But Achillês had something to say:

"My lord King, we know how high you are exalted above all, and how you are best in strength and in casting of spears. Very well, pray accept this prize and take it with you; but let us offer

---

[9] "Dark violet-coloured iron" suggests tempered steel. If the meaning is axes made of this metal, possibly half-axes were axes with one blade. But scholiasts tell us that "axe" meant a certain weight of iron. The axe may have been a sort of currency, when there was no coinage, and the name may have been transferred to a given weight. See Ridgeway, *Origin of Coin and Weight Standards,* 40; Rouse, *Greek Votive Offerings,* 389.

the spear to Merionês, if you approve; at least that is what I
should like."

My lord King Agamemnon was content. He gave the spear
to Merionês, and gave the prize into the hands of Talthybios
his herald.

BOOK XXIV

*How Priam and Achillês met, and the
funeral of Hector*

THE ASSEMBLY WAS DISMISSED, AND THE PEOPLE DISPERSED
to their own ships. Their thoughts were on food and
quiet sleep; but Achillês wept, remembering his well-loved
friend, and all-conquering sleep did not lay hold upon him. He
turned this way and that way, thinking what manhood and fine
temper he had lost with Patroclos, how many tasks he had
wound up with him, how many hardships they had suffered together, wars with men, and cruel seas they had cloven. As he remembered these things he shed hot tears, now tossing on his
side, now on his back, now prone; again he would rise up and
roam distracted along the seashore. Never did he fail to see the
dawn appear over sea and shore; and then he would harness the
horses and fasten Hector to drag behind the car. Three times
round the barrow of dead Menoitiadês he would trail him, then
return to rest in the hut leaving him stretched prone in the dust.
But Apollo kept the skin free from defilement, pitying the poor
fellow though dead; he wrapt him all about with his golden
cape, that the dragging might never tear him.

Thus Achillês maltreated Hector in his rage. But the blessed
gods were offended at this pitiable sight, and wished to send
Hermês Argeiphontês to steal him away. Most of the gods approved this; but not Hera nor Poseidon nor the bright-eyed
Maiden. They continued as they had been, when first they came
to hate sacred Troy, and Priam and his people, for the blind
delusion of Alexandros: he had affonted those goddesses,
when they came to his farmyard and he preferred the one who
granted his shameful lust.

But when the twelfth dawn came, Phoibos Apollo said at
last:

"You are hard, you gods, you are torturers! Has not Hector

in times past burnt you thigh-pieces of bulls and goats without blemish? Yet you can't bear to save his dead body for his wife to see, and his mother and his son, and Priam his father and his people, to let them burn him in the fire, and perform the rites of burial. But that abominable Achillês—he is the man you want to help, gods—the man who has no sense of decency, no mercy in his mind! Savage as a lion, which is the slave of his strength and furious temper, and hunts the sheep for a dinner! Like him Achillês has lost all pity; he has in him none of that shame which does great good to men as well as harm. A man may have lost some dear one, I suppose, a brother or even a son, but he weeps and laments and there is an end of it; for the Fates have given mankind a patient soul. But this man, after he has taken the life of noble Hector, ties him behind his car and drags him round his comrade's tomb. I declare that is not right or decent. We may well be shocked at him, though he is a brave man; even the senseless clay he insults in his fury."

This made Hera angry, and she retorted:

"That might be all very well, Silverbow, if you are going to put Achillês and Hector in the same rank. Hector's a mortal and sucked a woman's pap, but Achillês had a goddess for his mother—I brought her up myself from a little one, and gave her away as a wife to a man, to Peleus, who was in high favour with the immortals. You were all at the wedding, gods—and you too, there you sat with your harp—but you prefer low company and no one can ever trust you!"

Here Zeus broke in:

"My dear Hera, don't go and get spiky with the gods. They shan't be in the same rank at all, but Hector really was a prime favourite with the gods more than any man in Troy,—at least, I thought so, for he never failed in his friendly offerings. My altar was never without a good feast, or libations and spicy savours, our special prerogative. But let stealing alone—can't be done—we can't steal away Hector so that Achillês won't see, for there is his mother on guard night and day. No, no, let one of you call Thetis before me, and I will give her some good advice. Achillês must accept ransom from Priam and let him have Hector."

This was no sooner said, than stormfoot Iris was off with her message. Midway between Samothrace and rocky Imbros down she plunged into the dark sea with a splash, plunged into the deep like the leaden plummet on a horn-bait which carries death to the greedy fishes.

She found Thetis in a vaulted cave, and the other nymphs of the sea sitting round her. She was lamenting her perfect son, doomed to perish in Troy so far from his native land. Iris stood before her and said:

"Rise up, Thetis, Zeus Allwise summons you before him."

Silverfoot Thetis answered:

"Why does the great god summon me? I am ashamed to show myself among the immortals when my heart is so full of infinite sorrow. However, I will go. No word that he speaks will be spoken in vain."

She took a dark veil as black as any garment could be, and followed Iris, and the water gave way before them; they stept out on the beach and shot up to heaven.

There they found Cronidês Allseeing, and the deathless gods were seated about him in full assembly. Athena was next to Father Zeus, but she gave up her seat to Thetis. Hera placed a golden cup in her hands with friendly words of welcome and Thetis drank and gave back the cup.

Then the Father of gods and men spoke:

"So you have come to Olympos, goddess Thetis, although you are sad and your heart is full of sorrow that will not be comforted. I know that myself, but still I sent for you, and I will tell you why. For nine days there has been quarrelling in our family about Hector's body and Achillês. They want Argeiphontês to steal the body away, but I want to keep your respect and affection in time to come, and so I propose to raise your son even higher in men's esteem, and this is how it will be done.[1]

"Go straight to the camp. Tell your son the gods are angry with him, and I most of all have been moved to wrath, because in his mad passion he keeps Hector and has not let him go. I hope he will fear me and let him go. I will send Iris myself to King Priam, and bid him to visit the Achaian camp and ransom his son. He shall bring treasure enough to warm the heart of Achillês."

Thetis lost no time. She made haste to her son's hut, and found him there sobbing and groaning. His companions were busy preparing their meal; they had just killed a shaggy ram which lay in the hut.

His mother sat near him and stroked his head, saying:

"My child, how long will you eat your heart out with sorrow and lamentation? Never a thought for bread or bed? Even a woman to love you is some comfort. And I shall not have you long, but death and cruel fate are at hand!

"Now listen to me quickly—I bear a message from Zeus to you. He says the gods are angry with you, and he most of all has been moved to wrath, because in your mad passion you

[1] The heroic point of honour lay in the receipt of a *quid pro quo* (Leaf).

keep Hector and would not let him go. Make haste now, take ransom and let him go."

Achillês answered:

"Let some one come here with a ransom and take the body, if the Olympian himself commands, and really means it."

Long the mother and the son talked together without concealment heart to heart; and at the same time Cronidês was sending Iris to Ilios:

"Off with you Iris my quick one! Leave Olympos behind you, and hasten to Troy; announce to King Priam that he is to go into the Achaian camp, and carry treasure enough to warm the heart of Achillês. He must be alone, not another man of the Trojans must go with him. But a herald may attend him, some old man, to drive the mules and the wagon and also to bring back the body of him that Achillês slew. Do not let him fear death or be anxious at all. I will provide for that by sending Argeiphontês as his escort, to lead him as far as Achillês. And when he shall lead him into the hut, neither Achillês nor any one else shall kill him; for Achillês is not stupid or thoughtless or impious—he will be most scrupulous to spare a suppliant man."

Away went stormfoot Iris on her errand. She came to Priam's, and there she found groaning and lamentation. The sons were sitting in the courtyard about their father, soaking their garments in tears; the old man was in their midst, wrapt closely in his mantle, with muck smeared all over head and neck which he had clawed up in handfuls as he grovelled on the ground. In the house his daughters and his gooddaughters were wailing, as they called to mind all those brave men who lay dead by their enemies' hands.

The messenger drew near to Priam; he fell into a fit of trembling, and she spoke softly to him:

"Fear nothing, Priamos Dardanidês, be not anxious at all. I come here with no evil tidings, but with good in my heart for you. I am a messenger from Zeus, who far away cares for you much and pities you. The Olympian bids you ransom Prince Hector. You are to carry treasure to Achillês enough to warm his heart. You must be alone; no other Trojan must go with you, but a herald may attend you, some old man, to drive the mules and wagon and to bring back the body of him that Achillês slew. You are not to fear death or to be anxious at all. Zeus will provide for that by sending Argeiphontês as your escort, and he shall lead you as far as Achillês. Even when he shall lead you into the hut, neither Achillês nor any one else will kill you, for he will prevent them. Achillês is not stupid or thoughtless or impious, and he will be scrupulous to spare a suppliant man."

She gave her message, and she was gone. The old King gave orders at once to get ready a mule-wagon and put on the top-carrier. Meanwhile he went into his treasure chamber, roofed with sweet-smelling cedar, in which he kept many precious things, and called his wife Hecabê:

"My dear, what a surprise! An Olympian messenger has come from Zeus, that I am to go into the Achaian camp and ransom our dear son! I am to carry treasure enough to warm the heart of Achillês. Now then tell me, what do you think about it? As for me, I am terribly anxious to go and visit the Achaian ships and the Achaian camp!"

The woman shrieked and said:

"O misery! where are your wits flown? Once you were famous for good sense throughout your kingdom and even in foreign lands! How can you wish to visit the Achaian ships alone—to meet the eyes of the man who has killed and stript so many of your brave sons! Your heart must be made of steel. If he sets eyes on you—if he gets hold of you—that is a faithless man, a cannibal! He'll never pity, he'll never have mercy! No, no, let us stay in our own house and lament him far away. As for him—that is how inflexible Fate spun her thread for him when I brought him forth from my womb—to be devoured by carrion dogs, far from his father and mother, in the house of a violent man—ah, I could fix my teeth in *his* liver and devour it! That would be some revenge for my son. The man he slew was not playing the coward's part—he was standing to shield Trojan men and Trojan women, and thought neither of shelter nor of flight!"

The old King answered:

"Don't hold me back when I want to go, don't be a bad omen for me yourself. You will never persuade me. If some one else had bidden me go, a mere mortal man such as a priest or seer or diviner, we might think it falsehood and keep clear of the whole thing. But now—I heard a god's voice with my own ears, I saw with my own eyes! Go I will, and his word shall not be in vain. If it is my portion to die in the Achaian camp, I am willing. Let the man kill me on the spot, when once I have held my son in my arms, and lamented him, as I have so longed to do."

Then he opened the store-chests, and took out twelve resplendent robes and twelve singlet cloaks, as many rugs and white sheets, as many tunics. He took out gold and weighed ten nuggets; next two shining tripods and four cauldrons, and a magnificient goblet which a Thracian embassy had presented, a great treasure—not even this did he grudge, for he greatly desired to ransom his son. Lastly he drove away all the people from the corridor with a good rating:

"Get out for shame—don't make yourselves a nuisance here!

Have you no mourning at home that you come here to vex me? What good have you gained that Zeus Cronidês has sent trouble upon me, and I have lost the best of my sons? You shall find that out yourselves, when you will be easier than ever to kill now that man is dead. O may I go down to the gates of death, before I see the city wasted and sacked before my eyes!"

He hurried among them driving them out with his staff, and then he cried out to his sons—there were nine of them in the place, Helenos and Paris and Agathon, Pammon and Antiphonos and Politês, Deiphobos and Hippothoös and Dios:

"Make haste there, you worthless sons, I am ashamed of you, hangdogs! I wish you had all been killed instead of Hector! How unhappy I am! I had the best sons in the broad land of Troy, and I declare not one is left--Mestor too good for this world, and Troilos the famous chariot-fighter, and Hector who was like one come down from heaven to live on earth—he seemed to be no son of mortal man, as if a god must have been his father! These are all killed in battle and only rubbish is left, cheats and tumblers, heroes of the dancing-floor, grand men to raid their neighbours' cattle and sheep! Get ready a wagon, will you, and be quick about it, and put in all this stuff. We have a journey to make."

They were all startled by their father's outburst, and got to work. So they brought out a fine new mule-wagon with its wheels, and fastened on the top-carrier. They took down from the peg a box-wood yoke fitted with knob and rings for the reins. Then they brought out the yoke with its yoke-band, nine cubits long, and fitted it on the pole at the curving end and the ring over the pin; they tied it over the knob with three turns to left and right, and carried the rope back to the car-post tucking the tongue under the rope.

This done they brought out from the treasury all the precious things for Hector's ransom, and packed them on the wagon. They put to a couple of strong-footed mules broken to harness, which had been a gift of the Mysians to Priam. For Priam, they yoked a pair of horses which he had bred himself and fed at the manger.

As Priam and the herald were about these preparations, and considering how they should behave, Hecabê in deep dejection came near. She held a golden goblet of wine in her right hand, that they might pour a libation before they went; and standing before the car she said:

"Take this, and pour to Zeus the Father, and pray for a safe return from our enemies—since your mind is set upon going, although I wished it not. Now pray to Cronion Thundercloud upon Mount Ida, whose eye can see all the Trojan land, and ask for a bird on the right hand—that swift messenger whom he loves more than all the birds, the strongest bird of all; that you may see him with your eyes, and have him to trust in this journey to the Danaän camp. If Zeus Allseeing shall refuse to send his messenger, I at least would bid you not to go to the place, however you may desire it."

King Priam replied:

"My wife, I will not refuse what you ask, for it is well to lift up our hands to Zeus and pray him to have mercy upon us."

The old King called to a waiting-woman for pure water; she brought jug and bowl and poured the water over his hands. He then took the cup from his wife, and standing in the courtyard poured the wine upon the ground, raising his eyes to heaven as he uttered this prayer:

"O Zeus our Father, most mighty and most glorious, enthroned upon Mount Ida! Grant that Achillês may show me kindness and pity, and send me a bird, that swift messenger whom thou lovest more than all the birds, the strongest bird of all. Show him on my right hand, that I may see him with my eyes and have him to trust in this journey to the Danaän camp!"

So he prayed, and Zeus Allwise heard him. At once he sent an eagle, most unfailing omen among birds that fly, the dark one, the hunter, the one that men also call dapple. The stretch of his outspread wings was as wide as the bolted door of a rich man's lofty treasure-house. They saw him on the right sailing over the city; all that saw him were glad, and their hearts were warmed within them.

Now the old King made haste to mount his car, and drove out of the front gateway from the echoing gallery. The mules went in front drawing their four-wheeled wagon, with Idaios driving, and the horses followed driven by the old King. As they passed quickly through the city, all his kinsfolk followed weeping and wailing as if he were going to his death. But as soon as they had come down from the city upon the plain, these all went back, sons and goodsons together.

Zeus did not fail to see the two men when they appeared upon the plain. He pitied the old King, and said to Hermês his son:

"Hermês, you always like to make friends with a man and have a talk with any one you fancy. Off with you then, and lead Priam to the Achaian camp. Take care that no one sees or takes any notice until you get to Peleion."

Argeiphontês was willing enough. He put on those fine boots, golden, incorruptible, which carry him over moist or dry to the ends of the earth as quick as the wind; and he took the rod that bewitches the eyes of men to sleep, or wakes the sleeping. Holding this, Argeiphontês flew until he reached the Hellespont and the land of Troy. There he took the shape of a young prince with the first down upon his lip, the time when youth is most charming.

The others had just passed beyond the great barrow of Ilos, and they halted by the river to give the animals a drink; for darkness had come by this time. The herald looked out and noticed Hermês not far off, and he said to his master:

" 'Ware man, Dardanidês![2] a wary mind now is what we want. I spy a man! and I surmise he'll soon tear us to pieces. Come, let us take the horse-car and be off—unless you would have us clasp his knees and beg for mercy."

The old man was all confusion and frightened to death; he felt gooseflesh all over his body and stood dazed, but Hermês Luckbringer came up of himself and said, taking him by the hand:

"Whither away, father, with horses and mules in the dead of night, when mortal men are all asleep but you? Have you no fear of the Achaians breathing fury, your enemies, and bad men to meet? If one of them saw you driving all these commodities through the black night, what would you do then? You are not young yourself, and this your follower is old for defence if some one wants to pick a quarrel. But I will do you no harm, indeed I would protect you. You remind me of my own father."

Then the old King replied:

"Things are very much as you say, dear boy. But there is still some god even for me, who stretched a hand over me when he sent a wayfarer like you to meet me—a good man to meet, if I may judge from your handsome looks and shape, and no unmannerly savage. You must come of a good family."

Argeiphontês answered:

"Quite right, sir, that is true enough. But tell me please if I may ask you, are you exporting all these precious goods to a foreign land just to put them in safety? Or are you all deserting sacred Troy in fear? For the great man has perished, the noblest of them all—your son. He never hung back from the battlefield!"

The old King said:

"And who are you, noble sir, what is your family? How truly you have told me the passing of my ill-fated son!"

Argeiphontês replied:

"You are trying me, sir, when you ask about noble Hector. Often I have seen him with my own eyes in the field of glory— then also when he drove the Achaians upon their ships, and slew and slew, making havoc with his blade! We had to stand

---

[2] φράζεο is a hunting term, and very likely φραδής is another. This word is unique in Homer, like so many words of common talk.

and admire, for Achillês would not let us fight because of his rancour against Agamemnon. I am a servant of his, and we came over in the same ship. I am one of the Myrmidons. My father is named Polyctor. He is a rich man, and old just like yourself here; he has six other sons, I was the seventh. We cast lots who should join up, and the lot fell on me. I have just come away from the ships to the plain, for to-morrow the Achaians will open battle against the city. They hate sitting idle, and the princes cannot hold them back.

Then old King Priam said:

"If you are really a servant of Achillês Peleidês, pray tell me the whole truth. Is my son still there by the ships, or has Achillês cut him to pieces and thrown him to the dogs?"

Argeiphontês answered:

"Dear sir, no dogs and vultures have touched him yet, but there he lies beside the ship of Achillês as he was. Twelve days he has been lying there, and his flesh is not decayed, nor do the worms eat him as they eat the dead on the battlefield. It is true Achillês drags him callously round his comrade's barrow at dawn every day, but it does him no harm. You would open your eyes if you could come and see how he lies as fresh as dew, washed clean of blood and nowhere nasty. The wounds have all healed up, and there were many who pierced him. See how the gods care for your son even in death, for he was very dear to them!"

This made the old man happy, and he replied:

"My dear boy, it is good indeed to give the immortals their proper due, for my dead son as truly as he lived never forgot the gods who dwell in Olympos. Therefore they have remembered him, although death is now his portion. But pray do accept from me this pretty cup, and protect me and guide me with God's help, that I may find my way to the hut of Peleidês."

Argeiphontês said:

"You are trying me, sir; you are old, and I am young, but I cannot consent, when you ask me to accept a gift behind the back of Achillês. I fear him, and I should be heartily ashamed to defraud him, or something bad might happen to me. But you shall be my charge. I would guide you carefully as far as Argos, by land or by sea, and no one should despise your guide or attack you."

With this, Luckbringer jumped into the car, and took whip and reins into his hands, and filled horses and mules with spirit. So they went on until they reached the wall and moat. The watchmen were then busy about their supper; but Argeiphontês sent them all to sleep, and in a moment ran back the bars, and opened the gates, and brought in Priam and the wagon with its precious cargo.

They came at last to the hut of Achillês. It was a tall building which the men had made for their prince, walls of fir-planks thatched with a downy roofing of reeds which they had gathered from the meadows. In front was a wide courtyard surrounded by thickset stakes. The door was held by one fir-wood bar; it took three men to push home the bar, and three men to pull it open, but Achillês could push it home by himself. This time, Hermês jumped down and opened the door for the old King, and brought in the precious gifts for Achillês. After that he said:

"I must tell you, sir, that I am an immortal god, Hermês, and my Father sent me to be your guide. But I must go back now, and I must not show myself to Achillês. It would be a shocking thing if a mortal should entertain an immortal god for all to see. You go in and clasp his knees, and beseech him in the name of his father and mother and his son, to touch his heart."

So Hermês took his leave and went back to Olympos.

But Priam dismounted and went towards the house, leaving Idaios where he was, to hold the horses and mules. He found Achillês alone: only two were waiting upon him, Automedon and Alcimos, and he had just finished eating and drinking; the table was still beside him. Priam came in, but they did not see him; he came near Achillês and clasped his knees, and kissed the terrible murderous hands which had killed so many of his sons.

Achillês looked with amazement at royal Priam, and the two men also were amazed and stared at each other, as people stare when some one from a foreign land takes refuge in a rich man's house, after he has killed a man in a fit of madness and has to flee the country.

Then Priam made his prayer:

"Remember your own father, most noble prince Achillês, an old man like me near the end of his days. It may be that *he* is distressed by those who live round about him, and there is no one to defend him from peril and death. But *he* indeed, so long as he hears that you still live, is glad at heart and hopes every day that he will see his well-loved son return home from Troy. But I am all-unhappy, since I had the best sons in the broad land of Troy, and I say not one of them has been left. Fifty I had when the men of Achaia came; nineteen born to me of one womb, the others of women in my household. All those many have fallen in battle; and my only one, who by himself was our safeguard, that one you killed the other day fighting for his country, Hector: for him I come now to your camp, to redeem him from you, and I bring a rich ransom. O Achillês, fear God, and pity me, remembering your own father—but I am even more to be pitied—I have endured to do what no other man in the world has ever done, to lift my hand to the lips of the man who slew my son." [3]

As he said it, he lifted his hand to the face of Achillês, and the heart of Achillês ached with anguish at the thought of his father. He took the old man's hand, and pushed him gently away. So the two thought of their dead and wept, one for his Hector while he crouched before the feet of Achillês, and Achillês for his own father and then for Patroclos. When his agony had passed and he could move again, he got up from his seat and raised the old man by the hand,[4] pitying his white hairs and white beard, and spoke simply from heart to heart:

"Ah, poor man, indeed your heart has borne many sorrows! How could you come to the Achaian camp alone? How could you bear to look on the man who killed all your noble sons, as I have done? Your heart must be made of steel. Come now, sit down upon a seat. We will let our sorrows lie deep in our hearts awhile, for there is no profit in freezing lamentation. This is the way the gods have spun their threads for poor mortals! Our life is all sorrow, but they are untroubled themselves.

"Zeus has two jars of the gifts that he gives, standing upon the floor beside him, one of good things and one of evil things. When the Thunderer mixes and gives, a man meets with good sometimes and bad other times: when he gives all bad, he makes the man despised and rejected; grinding misery drives him over the face of the earth, and he walks without honour from gods or from men. And so with Peleus, the gods gave him glorious gifts from his birth, for he was preëminent in the world for wealth and riches, he was King over the Myrmidons, and although he was mortal they made a goddess his wife. But God gave him evil too, because he got no family of royal princes in his palace, but only one son, to die before his time. And now he is growing old, and I cannot care for him; for I am here in Troy, far from my country, troubling you and your children.

"You also, sir, once were happy, as we hear: upsea as far as Lesbos the seat of Macar, upland to Phrygia, and along the boundless Hellespont, you were paramount with your riches and your sons. But ever since the lords of Heaven brought this calamity upon you, there has been nothing but battle and man-slaughter about your city. Endure it, and let not your heart be uncomforted; for you will have no profit by sorrowing for

---

[3] The suppliants gesture, to touch the chin and caress the lower part of the face. It is clear that Priam does so at this moment, although Homer does not say so; but I have no doubt the minstrel raised his hand, as a Greek would do in reciting such a story, and this would take the place of words.

[4] To raise one by the hand implied accepting him into protection.

your son. You will never raise him from the dead; before that, some other trouble will come upon you."

The old King answered:

"Tell me not yet to be seated, gracious prince, while Hector lies here uncared-for. I pray you set him free quickly, that I may look upon him; and accept the ransom that we bring, a great treasure. May you live to enjoy it and return to your own country, since you have spared me first."

Achillês frowned and said:

"Tease me no more, sir, I mean myself to set your Hector free. Zeus sent me a message by my mother, the daughter of the Old Man of the Sea. And I understand quite well, sir, that some god brought you into our camp. For no mere man would dare to come among us, let him be ever so young and strong. He could not escape the guards, and he could not easily lever back the bolt of our doors. Then provoke my temper no more in my sorrow, or I may not spare even you, sir, although you are a suppliant, and that would be sin against the commands of Zeus."

The old man was afraid, and said no more; but Peleidês leapt out like a lion, and the two attendants followed, Automedon and Alcimos, the men whom he trusted most after the dead Patroclos. They unharnessed the horses and mules, and led in the old King's crier to a seat. Then they unpacked Hector's ransom from the wagon, except two sheets and a tunic, which they left to wrap up the body for its journey home. Achillês called out women to wash and anoint the body, but first he moved it out of the way. He did not wish Priam to see his son, and perhaps burst into anger from the sorrow of his heart when he saw him, for then he feared that he might be provoked himself to kill him and sin against the commands of Zeus.

After the women had washed the body and anointed it with oil, and put on the tunic and wrapt the sheet around, Achillês himself lifted him, and laid him upon the bier, and his attendants carried him to the mule-car. Then he cried aloud and called on the name of his lost friend:

"Don't be cross with me, Patroclos, if you hear even in Hadês that I have given back Hector to his father, since the ransom he paid is not unworthy. You shall have your due share of this also."

Then Achillês returned into his hut, and sat down on the bench where he had been before, against the opposite wall, and spoke to Priam:

"Your son, sir, has been set free now as you asked, and he lies on his bier. At break of day you shall see him yourself, on your journey, but just now let us think of supper. Even beautiful Niobê thought of something to eat, after she had lost twelve children in her own house, six daughters and six sons in their prime. Apollo shot the boys with his silver bow, and Artemis Archeress the girls. They were angry because Niobê compared herself with Leto, said she had borne a dozen and Leto only two, so those only two killed them all. They lay nine days in their blood, and there was no one to bury them, for Cronion had turned the people into pebbles[5]; but after all the heavenly ones buried them on the tenth day. So then she thought of something to eat, when she was tired of shedding tears. Now she is somewhere among the rocks, on a lovely mountain in Sipylos, where the beds of the nymphs divine are said to be, the ones that danced about the river Acheloïos; there, stone though she is, she broods over the sorrows which the gods brought on her.

"Well then, venerable prince, let us two also think of something to eat. After that, you may weep for your son again when you have brought him back to Ilios. Many tears he will cost you!"

Then Achillês got up and killed a white lamb, his comrades flayed it and prepared it, cut it up, spitted and broiled it and laid the meat on the table. Automedon brought baskets of bread, and Achillês served the meat.

When they had eaten and and drunk all they wanted, Priamos Dardanidês gazed at Achillês, admiring his fine looks and stature—indeed he seemed like some god come down from heaven. And Achillês gazed at Priamos Dardanidês, admiring his noble face and speech. They looked at each other a long time, and then the old King said:

"Put me to bed now quickly, my prince, let us lie down and sleep quietly and rest; for my eyes have never closed under my eyelids since my son lost his life at your hands. All this time I have mourned and brooded over my endless sorrow, tossing about in the muck of my courtyard. Now I have tasted food, and I have let the wine run down my throat; until now I had touched nothing."

Achillês gave orders at once to lay beds in the porch, and strew on them rugs of fine purple with blankets above and woollen robes to wear. The women torch in hand went to get ready two beds, and Achillês said a light word or two:

"You must lie outside, my dear sir, for I may have a visit from one of the councillors from headquarters—they are for ever coming and sitting here and counselling their counsels as if it were a public meeting! If one of them should spy you here in the middle of the night, he would go at once and report it to his majesty King Agamemnon, and there would be delay in releasing the dead.

[5] A pun on λαός and λᾶας. Nothing more is known of this part of the story.

"But tell me please, if I may ask the question—how many days do you think of to perform the funeral solemnities? I will stay here and keep the people quiet for that time."

The King answered:

"If you are willing to let me do the funeral rites for prince Hector, you will do that for which I shall be deeply grateful. You know how we are crowded into the city; it is a long way for us to get the wood from the mountains, and the people are very much afraid. We would mourn him nine days in the house, on the tenth we would bury him and feast the people, on the eleventh we would build a barrow, and on the twelfth we will fight, if we must."

Achillês said:

"It shall be as you ask, venerable king. I will hold back the battle for the time you say."

Then he clasped the old man's right wrist, that he might fear nothing, and led him to the porch where he was to sleep with the herald. Achillês himself lay to rest in a corner of the hut, with lovely Briseïs by his side.

All were fast asleep throughout that night both in heaven and on earth, except Hermês, who could not sleep for thinking how he should bring away King Priam out of the camp and keep the watchmen at the gate from seeing. He stood by the old man's bed and said to him:

"Sir! you do not seem to care what happens, sleeping like that in the midst of your enemies because Achillês spared you! Now then: you have redeemed your son, you have paid a heavy ransom: but you alive will cost three times as much for your other sons to get you back, if Agamemnon Atreidês finds out, or the Achaians find out!"

This frightened the old man, and he woke up the herald: Hermês harnessed the horses and mules and drove quickly through the camp, and no one found out.

But when they reached the ford of the Xanthos, Hermês left them and returned to Olympos.

Then the saffron robe of Dawn spread over all the earth, and they drove towards the city mourning and lamenting, while the mules brought the dead. No man and no woman had seen them coming; Cassandra was the first. She had gone up into the citadel, and from there she caught sight of her father standing in his car, and the city-crier, and the other lying on a bier in the mule-wagon. She lifted her voice in wailing, and cried for the whole town to hear:

"Come, all you men and women of Troy! You shall see Hector! Come, if ever you were glad while he lived to welcome his return from battle, for he was a great gladness to the city and all the nation!"

Then grief intolerable came upon every heart. Not a man, not a woman was left behind in the city; all crowded out of the gates and met the dead. First came his wife and his mother tearing their hair; they ran to the wagon and threw their arms over his head, while the people stood mourning around. They would have stayed there all day weeping and wailing, but the old King called out from his car:

"Let the mules pass. When I have brought him into our house you will have plenty of time to lament."

So the people made a way for the wagon to pass.

When he had been brought home, they laid him out on a bier, and posted beside him mourners to lead the dirge, who sang their lamentable dirge while the women wailed in chorus. Andromachê laid her white arms about the head of her dead warrior, and led the lament:

"My husband, you have perished out of life, still young, and left me a widow in the house! The boy is only a baby, your son and my son, doomed father, doomed mother! and he I think will never grow up to manhood; long before that our city will be utterly laid waste! For you have perished, you our watchman, you our only saviour, who kept safe our wives and little children! They will soon be carried off in ships, and I with them. And you, my child!—you will go with me where degrading tasks will be found for you to do, drudging under a merciless master; or some enemy will catch you by the arm, and throw you over the wall to a painful death, in revenge perhaps for some brother that Hector killed, or father, or son maybe, since many a man bit the dust under the hands of Hector: your father was not gentle in the field of battle! Therefore the people throughout the city lament for him,—and you have brought woe and mourning unspeakable upon your parents, Hector! But for me most of all cruel sorrow shall be left. For you did not stretch out to me your dying hands from your deathbed, you said no precious word to me, which I might always remember night and day with tears!"

So Andromachê spoke weeping, and the women wailed in chorus.

Then Hecabê led the lament amid her sobs:

"Hector, best beloved of all my children, dearest to my heart! Living the gods loved you well, therefore they have cared for you even when death is your lot. Other sons of mine Achillês took, and he would sell them over the barren sea, one to Samos, one to Imbros, or to steaming Lamnos; but you—when he had torn out your soul with his sharp blade, he dragged you again and again round the barrow of his comrade whom you slew; but that did not bring him back from the grave! And now you lie in my house fresh as the morning dew, like one that Apollo Silverbow has visited and slain with his gentle shafts!"

So Hecabê spoke weeping, and the women wailed long in chorus.

Helen came third and led the lament:

"Hector, best beloved of all my goodbrothers, and dearest to my heart! Indeed my husband is prince Alexandros, who brought me to Troy—but would that I had died first! Twenty years have passed since I left my country and came here, but I never heard from you one unkind or one slighting word. If any one else reproached me, a sister or brother of yours, or a brother's wife, or your mother—for your father was always as kind as if he were mine—you would reprove them, you would check them, with your gentle spirit and gentle words. Therefore I weep for you, and with you for my unhappy self. For there is no one else in the length and breadth of Troy who is kind or friendly; they all shudder at me."

So she spoke weeping, and the people wailed long and loud.

Then old King Priam said:

"Now, Trojans, fetch wood into the city, and have no fear of any ambush of our enemies. For Achillês in parting from me promised that he would do us no harm until the twelfth day shall dawn."

Then they put oxen and mules to their wagons and assembled before the city. Nine days they gathered infinite quantities of wood; when the tenth day dawned, they carried out brave Hector weeping, and laid the body on the pile and set it on fire.

When on the next day Dawn showed her rosy fingers through the mists, the people gathered round about the pyre of Hector. First they quenched the flame with wine wherever the fire had burnt; then his brothers and his comrades gathered his white bones, with hot tears rolling down their cheeks. They placed the bones in a golden casket, and wrapt it in soft purple cloth; this they laid in a hollow space and built it over with large stones. Quickly they piled a barrow, with men on the look-out all round in case the Achaians should attack before their time.

This work done they returned to the city, and the whole assemblage had a famous feast in the palace of Priam their King.

That was the funeral of Hector.

PRONOUNCING INDEX

PRONOUNCING INDEX

THIS index shows the correct quantities of the vowels in the names, and an accent ' is placed to suggest how the reader may pronounce them as if English names:

c always sounded as k.

ch " " " kh.

a, e, i, o, u as in Italian properly, but they may be sounded as in English (u=oo) for convenience.

Vowels marked ā, ē, etc., are of double length.

The mark on ê means that it is not mute, but forms a syllable.

A-ban'-tes.

A-bar-bar'-e-ê.

A'-bās.

A-blē'-ros.

A-by'-dos.

A'-ca-mās.

A-ces'-sa-me-nos.

A-chai'-ā.

A-che-lō'-i-os.

A-chil'-lēs.

Ac'-ri-si-os.

Ac'-tōr.

Ac'-to-ri-ōn.

Ad-mē'-tos.

A-dres-tei'-a.

A-drēs'-tos.

A'-ga-clēs.

A-ga-mē'-dē.

A-ga-mem'-nōn.

A-ga-pē'-nōr.

A-ga'-sthe-nēs.

A-ga'-stro-phos.

A'-ga-thōn.

A-ge-la'-os.

A-gē'-nōr.

A-gla'-i-ā.

A'-gri-os.

Ai-a-a'-ci-dēs.

Ai'-ās.

Ai'-gai.

Ai-gai'-ōn.

Ai-gi-a-lei'-a.

Ai'-gi-a-los.

Ai'-gi-lips.

Ai-gī'-na.

Ai'-gi-on.

Ai-nei'-ās.

Ai'-ni-os.

Ai'-nos.

Ai'-o-li-dēs.

Ai-pei'-a.

Ai'-py.

Ai'-py-ti-on.

Ai-sē'-pos.

Ai-sy-ē'-tēs.

Ai-sy'-mē.

Ai-sym'-nos.

Ai'-thē.

Ai-thē'-ces.

A-las'-tōr.

Al-can'-dros.

Al'-ca-tho-os.

Al-cēs'-tis.

Alc-mā'-ōn.

Alc-mē'-nē.

A-lec'-try-ōn.

A-le-gē'-no-ri-dēs.

A-lī'-si-on.

A-li-zō'-nes.

A-lex-an'-dros.

A'-lo-pē.

A'-los.

301

Al-pheï'-os.

Al'-tēs.

A'-ly-bē.

A-ma-ryn-ceï'-dēs.

A-ma-theï'-a.

A-mo-pā'-ōn.

Am'-phi-clos.

Am'-phi-da-mās.

Am-phi-ge-neï'-a.

Am'-phi-ma-chos.

Am-phī'-ōn.

Am-phī'-os.

Am'-pho-te-ros.

Am'-phi-tho-ē.

A-my'-clai.

A'-my-dōn.

A-myn'-tor.

An-caï'-os.

An'-chi-a-los.

An-chī'-sēs.

An-draï'-mōn.

An'-dro-ma-chē.

A-ne-mō-reï'-a.

An-teï'-a.

An-tē'-nor.

An-thē'-dōn.

An-theï'-a.

An'-the-mi-ōn.

An'-ti-lo-chos.

An'-ti-ma-chos.

An'-ti-pho-nos.

An'-ti-phos.

An'-trōn.

A-paï'-sos.

A'-pha-reus.

A-phro-dī'-tē.

A-pi-sā'-ōn.

A-pol'-lō.

A-pseu'-dēs.

A-rai-thy'-re-ā.

Ar-ce-si-lā'-os.

Ar'-chi-lo-chos.

A-rē̆'-i-ly-cos.

A-rē̆'-i-tho-os.

Ā-rē̆'-nē.

A'-rēs.

A-re-tā'-ōn.

Ā-rē̆'-tos.

Ar'-ge-a-dēs.

Ar-gei-phon'-tēs.

Ar-gis'-sa.

Ar'-gos.

A-ri-ad'-nē.

A'-ri-moi.

A-ris'-bē.

Ar'-nē.

Ar'-si-no-os.

Ar'-te-mis.

Ā-saï'-os.

As-ca'-la-phos.

As-ca'-ni-ā.

As-ca'-ni-os.

As-clē'-pi-a-dēs.

As-clē'-pi-os.

A'-si-nē.

Ā'-si-os.

Ā-sŏ'-pos.

As'-sa-ra-cos.

As-te'-ri-on.

As-te-ro-pai'-os.

As'-ty-a-nax.

As'-ty-no-os.

As'-ty-o-chē.

As-ty-o-chei'-a.

As'-ty-py-los.

Ā'-tē.

A-thē'-nā, A-thē-naï'-ā.

A'-thōs.

A'-treus.

A-trȳ-tŏ'-nē.

A-tym'-ni-a-dēs.

A-tym'-ni-os.

Au-gē̆'-i-a-dēs.

Au-gei'-ai.

Au-gei'-ās.

Au'-lis.

Au'-to-ly-cos.

Au'-to-no-os.

A'-xi-os.

A'-xy-los.

A-zeï'-dēs.

Ba'-li-os.

Ba'-thy-clēs.

Ba-ti-eï'-a.

Bel-le-ro-phon'-tēs.

Bēs'-sa.

Bi'-ās.

Bi-ē'-nŏr.

Bo-a'-gri-os.

Boi'-bĕ.
Bo'-re-ăs.
Bŏ'-ros.
Bri-a'-re-ŏs.
Brĭ-sē'-is.
Bry-sei'-ai.
Bū'-co-li-ŏn.
Bū-dei'-on.
Bū'-pre-si-on.

Ca-bĕ'-sos.
Cai'-neus.
Cal'-chăs.
Ca-lē'-si-os.
Ca-lē'-tŏr.
Cal-li-a-nas'-sa.
Cal-li-a-nei'-ra.
Cal'-li-a-ros.
Cal-li-co-lŏ'-nĕ.
Ca-lyd'-nai.
Ca'-ly-dŏn.
Ca-mei'-ros.
Ca'-pa-neus.
Ca'-pys.
Car'-da-my-lĕ.
Ca-rĕ'-sos.
Ca-rys'-tos.
Ca'-sos.
Cas-san'-drā.
Cas-ti-a-nei'-ra.
Cas'-tŏr.
Ca-ys'-tros, -trois.
Ce'-a-dĕs.
Ce'-bri-o-nĕs.
Cĕ-phĕ'-sos.
Cĕ-rin'-thos.
Chal'-cis.
Chal-cō-don'-ti-a-dĕs.
Chal'-cōn.
Cha'-ris.
Cha'-rops.
Chei'-rŏn.
Cher'-si-da-măs.
Chro'-mi-os.
Chro'-mis.
Chrȳ-sē'-is.
Chrȳ'-sē, Chrȳ'-sēs.
Chrȳ'-so-the-mis.
Cil'-la.
Ci'-ny-rĕs.

Cis'-seus.
Cle-o-bū'-los.
Cle-ŏ'-nai.
Cle-o-pa'-trā.
Clo'-ni-os.
Cly'-me-nĕ.
Cly-tai-mnĕs'-trā.
Cly'-ti-dĕs.
Cly'-ti-os.
Cnŏ'-sos.
Coi'-ra-nos.
Co'-ŏn.
Cŏ'-pai.
Co'-preus.
Co-ro-nei'-a.
Co-rŏ'-nos.
Cōs.
Cra'-pa-thos.
Cra'-thon.
Crei-on'-ti-a-dĕs.
Crĕ'-thōn.
Crī'-sa.
Cro-cy-lei'-a.
Crŏ'-mnā.
Cro'-ni-dĕs.
Cro'-ni-ŏn, Cro-nī'-ŏn.
Cro'-nos.
Cte'-a-tos.
Cyl-lē'-nĕ.
Cȳ'-mo-do-cĕ.
Cȳ'-mo-tho-ĕ.
Cȳ'-nos.
Cy-pa-ris-sĕ'-eis.
Cy-par-is'-sos.
Cȳ'-phos.
Cȳ'-pris.
Cy-thĕ'-rā.
Cy-tŏ'-nos.

Dai'-da-los.
Dai'-tŏr.
Da'-ma-sos.
Da'-na-ĕ.
Dar-da-ni-dĕs.
Dar'-da-nos.
Da'-rēs.
Dau'-lis.
Dĕ'-i-co-ŏn.
Dĕ-i-o-pī'-tēs.
Dĕ'-i-pho-bos.

Gla'-phy-roĭ.
Glau'-cĕ.
Glau'-cos.
Glī'-sās.
Go-no-es'-sa.
Gor'-gy-thi-ŏn.
Gor'-tӯs.
Grai'-a.
Grē-nī'-cos.
Gū'-neus.
Gyr'-ti-a-dēs.
Gyr-tŏ'-nē.

Hă'-dēs.
Hai'-mōn.
Ha-li-ar'-tos.
Ha'-li-ĕ.
Ha'-li-os.
Har'-ma.
Har-mo'-ni-dēs.
Har'-pa-li-ŏn.
Hĕ'-bĕ.
He'-ca-bĕ.
He-ca-mĕ'-dă.
Hec'-tŏr.
He'-le-nos.
He-li-cā'-ŏn.
He'-li-cĕ.
Hĕ'-li-os.
He'-los.
Hē͏ͤphais'-tos.
Hep'-ta-po-ros.
Hĕ'-rā.
Hĕ'-ra-clēs.
Her-mei'-ās.
Her'-mēs.
Her'-mi-o-nē.
Hi-ce-tā'-ŏn.
Hip'-pa-si-dēs.
Hip-pē-mol'-goĭ.
Hip'-po-co-ŏn.
Hip-po-da-mei'-a.
Hip'-po-da-mŏs.
Hip'-po-lo-chos.
Hip'-po-no-os.
Hip'-po-tho-os.
Hip'-po-ti-ŏn.
Hī'-rĕ.
His-ti-ai'-a.
Hy'-a-des.

Hy-am'-po-lis.
Hӯ'-lē.
Hy-pei'-ro-chos.
Hy-pei'-rŏn.
Hy-pe-rei'-a.
Hy-per-ē-sī'-ē.
Hy-pe-rī'-ŏn.
Hy-po-thē'-baĭ.
Hyp-sē'-nŏr.
Hyp'-si-py-lē.
Hy'-ri-ă.
Hyr-mī'-nē.
Hyr-ta'-ci-dēs.
Hyr'-ta-cos.

I-ai'-ra.
I-al'-me-nos.
I-a-nas'-sa.
I-a-nei'-ra.
I-ă-ōl'-cos.
I-ar'-da-nos.
I-ă'-sŏn, Jā'-son.
I-ă'-so-ni-dēs.
Ī-dai-os.
Ī-dŏs.
Ī-do'-me-neus.
I-ē-lӯ'-sos.
Ī'-li-os.
Ī'-los.
Im-bras'-ĭ-dēs.
Im'-bri-os, Im'-bros.
Ī'-pheus.
Ī-phi-a-nas'-sa.
Ī'-phi-clos.
Ī'-phi-da-măs.
Ī-phi'-no-os.
Ī'-phis.
Ī-phī'-tēs.
Ī-phi-ty-ŏn.
Ī'-ris.
Ī-san'-dros.
Ī'-sos.
Ī-thō'-mĕ.
Ī-tŏn.
Is-ī'-ŏn.

La'-as.
La-ce-daī'-mōn.
Lă-er'-tēs.
Lam'-pos.

Lā-o-da-mei'-a.
Lā'-o-di-cē.
Lā-o'-do-cos.
Lā'-o-go-nos.
Lā'-o-me-dōn.
Lā-o-me-don'-ti-a-dēs.
Lā'-o-tho-ē.
Lā-rī'-sā.
Lei-ō'-cri-tos.
Lē'-i-tos.
Lēm'-nos.
Le-on'-teus.
Lē'-thos.
Lē'-tō.
Leu'-cos.
Li-cym'-ni-os.
Li-lai'-a.
Lim-nō-rei'-a.
Lin'-dos.
Ly-cā'-ōn.
Ly-cas'-tos.
Ly'-ci-ā.
Ly-co-mē'-dēs.
Ly'-cōn.
Ly-co-phon'-tēs.
Lyc'-tos.
Ly-cūr'-gos.
Lyr-nēs'-sos.
Lȳ-san'-dros.

Ma'-car.
Ma-chā'-ōn.
Mai'-ma-li-dēs.
Mai'-ra.
Man'-ti-ne-ā.
Mar-pes'-sa.
Ma'-sēs.
Mē-cis-tē'-i-a-dēs.
Mē-cis'-teus.
Me'-de-ōn.
Mē-de-si-cas'-tē.
Me'-dōn.
Me'-ga-dēs.
Me'-gēs.
Mei'-ōn.
Mē'-i-o-ni-ā.
Me-lan'-thi-os.
Me'-las.
Me-le-a'-gros.
Me-li-boi'-a.

Me'-li-tē.
Me-ne-lā'-os.
Men-es'-thēs.
Me-nes'-theus.
Me-nes'-thi-os.
Me-noi'-ti-a-dēs.
Me-noi'-ti-os.
Men'-tēs.
Men'-tōr.
Mī-lē'-tos.
Mē'-ri-o-nēs.
Mer'-me-ros.
Me'-rops.
Mes'-sē.
Mes'-thlēs.
Mē-thō'-nē.
Mi-dei'-a.
Mī'-nōs.
Mnē'-sos.
Mo-li'-ōn.
Mo'-los.
Mo'-rys.
Mū'-li-os.
My-ca-lēs'-sos.
My-cē'-nai.
My-cē'-nē.
My'-dōn.
Myg'-dōn.
My'-nēs.
My-rī'-nē.
Myr'-mi-dōn.
Myr'-si-nos.

Nas'-tēs.
Nau-bo'-li-dēs.
Nē-mer'-tēs.
Ne-o-pto'-le-mos.
Nē'-re-id.
Nē'-ri-ton.
Nē-sai'-ā.
Nes'-tōr.
Nī'-reus.
Nī'-sa.
Ni'-sy-ros.
No-ē'-mōn.
No'-mi-ōn.
No'-tos.

Ō-ca'-le-ā.
Ō'-ce-a-nos.

Sthe'-ne-los.
Sti'-chi-os.
Stra'-ti-ē.
Stro'-phi-os.
Stym-phē'-los.
Styx.
Sȳ'-mē.

Ta-lai'-me-nēs.
Ta-la-i'-o-ni-dēs.
Tal-thy'-bi-os.
Tar'-phē.
Tar'-ta-ros.
Tec'-tŏm̄.
Te'-ge-ā.
Te'-la-mōn.
Te-la-mŏ'-ni-a-dēs.
Tĕ'-le-ma-chos.
Te'-ne-dos.
Ten-thrĕ'-dōn.
Tĕ-rei'-a.
Tĕ'-thys.
Teu'-cros.
Teu'-ta-mos.
Teu'-thra-ni-dēs.
Teu'-thrās.
Tha-lei'-a.
Thal'-pi-os.
Tha-ly'-si-a-dēs.
Tha'-my-ris.
Thau-ma'-ci-ē.
The-ā'-nō.
Thĕ'-bē.
The'-mis.
Ther'-si-lo-chos.
Ther-sī'-tēs.
Thes-pei'-a.
Thes'-sa-los.
Thes'-tōr.

The'-tis.
This'-bē.
Tho'-ās.
Tho'-ē.
Tho'-ōn.
Tho-ō'-tēs.
Thra'-si-os.
Thra-sy-mē'-dēs.
Thro'-ni-on.
Thry'-on.
Thy-es'-tēs.
Thym'-brē.
Thym-brai'-os.
Thy-moi'-tēs.
Tī'-ryns.
Tī'-ta-nos.
Ti-ta-rē'-si-on.
Tī-thŏ'-nos.
Tlē-po'-le-mos.
Tmō'-les.
Trē'-chīs.
Trē'-chos.
Tric'-cē.
Trī-to-ge-nei'-a.
Troi'-zēn.
Trōs.
Ty'-chi-os.
Tȳ-dei'-dēs.
Tȳ'-deus.
Tȳ'-phōs.

Ū'-ca-le-gōn.

Xan'-thos.

Za-cyn'-thos.
Ze-lei'-a.
Ze'-phy-ros.
Zeus.

THE MENTOR PHILOSOPHERS

The entire range of Western speculative thinking from the Middle Ages to modern times is presented in this series of six volumes. Each book contains the basic writings of the leading philosophers of each age, with introductions and interpretive commentary by noted authorities.

75¢ each

"A very important and interesting series."
—*Gilbert Highet*

THE AGE OF BELIEF: The Medieval Philosophers
edited by Anne Fremantle (#MT463)
"Highly commendable . . . provides an excellent beginning volume." —*The Classical Bulletin*

THE AGE OF ADVENTURE: The Renaissance Philosophers *edited by Giorgio de Santillana* (#MT437)
"The most exciting and varied in the series."
—*New York Times*

THE AGE OF REASON: The 17th Century Philosophers *edited by Stuart Hampshire* (#MT367)
"His (Hampshire's) book is a most satisfactory addition to an excellent series." —*Saturday Review*

THE AGE OF ENLIGHTENMENT: The 18th Century Philosophers *edited by Sir Isaiah Berlin* (#MT473)
"(Sir Isaiah) has one of the liveliest and most stimulating minds among contemporary philosophers." —*N. Y. Herald Tribune*

THE AGE OF IDEOLOGY: The 19th Century Philosophers *edited by Henry D. Aiken* (#MT421)
". . . perhaps the most distinct intellectual contribution made in the series." —*New York Times*

THE AGE OF ANALYSIS: 20th Century Philosophers *edited by Morton White* (#MT353)
"No other book remotely rivals this as the best available introduction to 20th century philosophy."
—*N. Y. Herald Tribune*

MENTOR Books on the Ancient World

THE SATYRICON *by Petronius*, translated
                           by William Arrowsmith
A classic re-creation of Nero's pleasure-loving Rome by
the cultured cynic, Petronius. In a brilliant new translation.   (#MP493—60¢)

THE ANVIL OF CIVILIZATION *by Leonard Cottrell*
This fascinating history of the ancient Mediterranean
civilizations reveals the long-buried secrets of the early
Egyptians, Hittites, Sumerians, Assyrians, Babyloni-
ans, Greeks and Jews, brought to light by archeologi-
cal discoveries.   (#MP413—60¢)

WAR COMMENTARIES OF CAESAR translated
                                 by Rex Warner
Julius Caesar's classic first-hand account of his military
campaigns in an outstanding translation by the author
of *The Young Caesar*.   (#MT333—75¢)

THE METAMORPHOSES *by Ovid*, translated
                           by Horace Gregory
Ovid's magnificent collection of legends and myths,
translated into vital modern poetry. (#MT291—75¢)

THE CIVILIZATION OF ROME *by Donald R. Dudley*
A cultural and social history of Rome from the earliest
times to the fall of the Empire.   (#MT472—75¢)

THE ANCIENT MYTHS *by Norma Lorre Goodrich*
A vivid retelling of the great myths of Greece, Egypt,
India, Persia, Crete, Sumer, and Rome.
                                           (#MP528—60¢)

GODS, HEROES, AND MEN OF ANCIENT GREECE
                               by W. H. D. Rouse
A retelling of the ancient Greek legends in a lively
narrative for readers of all ages.   (#KP385—60¢)
